Her Way

Mary-Ellen Siegel

Her Way

A Guide to
Biographies of Women
for
Young People
second edition

American Library Association
Chicago

Illustrations by
MARY PHELAN

Designed by Vladimir Reichl

Composed by Modern Typographers, Inc.
in Linotron 202 Primer

Printed on 50-pound Antique
Glatfelter, a pH-neutral stock,
by Malloy Lithographing, Inc.

Library of Congress Cataloging in Publication Data

Siegel, Mary-Ellen.
  Her way.

  Includes index.
  Summary: A two-part bibliography of over 1700 biographies of
more than 1100 notable women throughout history. Part one is
arranged alphabetically by subject and includes a short profile of
each woman cited; part two consists of collective biographies.
  1. Women—Biography—Juvenile literature.   2. Women—
Juvenile literature—Bio-bibliography.   [1. Biography.
2. Women—Bio-bibliography]   I. Title.
HQ1123.S56   1984   920.72   [920]   83-22375
ISBN 0-8389-0462-9 (pbk)

Printed in the United States of America.
First paperbound printing, September 1986

In memory of my parents
MIRIAM BAUM GREENBERGER
1904–1978
and
MONROE E. GREENBERGER, M.D.
1896–1982
for many reasons,
but mostly
because
I loved them and miss them.

Contents

Acknowledgments

Many people in the course of my work on HER WAY have encouraged me and offered suggestions.

I am particularly grateful to Betsy Baldwin, who as my editorial and research consultant not only judiciously used her blue pencil, but also was an enormous help in the conceptualization that went into the book.

Jaclyn Silverman's wisdom and assistance were extremely helpful in this edition.

Margery and Marc Epstein shared their expertise and graciously gave advice and assistance in the compilation of the appendixes and index.

A special thanks goes to Barbara Seaman for her initial encouragement and for introducing me to the feminist movement.

The librarians in the Children's Room at the Donnell Library of the New York Public Library and at the Hillcrest Branch of the Queens Borough Public Library were helpful in obtaining books. I am also grateful to the publishers who kindly made copies of biographies available for consideration.

My appreciation to my children, Betsy Baldwin, Peter Kulkin, and Vicki Kulkin, for their encouragement, suggestions, and valuable insights.

Thank you to my husband, Walter Siegel, who is always supportive, helpful, and understanding when I need it the most.

And to my friends and colleagues in the Departments of Social Work Services and Community Medicine of the Mount Sinai Medical Center—thank you for being there with your encouragement and support.

Introduction

For as long as I can remember, books have been an important part of my life. I loved realistic stories about girls who dared to defy societal expectations. If a heroine was a tomboy, showed reluctance to dress up, scorned her family's wealth and position, or refused to accept the limitations of her family's financially deprived status, I was enthralled. In the 1940s there were few juvenile biographies of women who were not members of royalty or presidents' wives, but I distinctly remember wonderful biographies of Elizabeth Blackwell and Katharine Cornell (which are described in this book).

Shortly after *Her Way* was published in 1976, my mother came across a picture of me taken in 1943, self-consciously posing as is the custom of eleven-year-olds. Smiling broadly, I am reading a book whose jacket clearly reads "Successful Women." Except for my teachers, the only real-life role models in my life were mothers or homemakers. It is clear that I was searching for some options beyond homemaking and child rearing.

In retrospect, I note that in most of what I read, a woman who achieved also sacrificed personal happiness and family life. In the 1940s and 1950s we were taught that a woman's natural destiny, regardless of education, talent, or inclination, was marriage and child rearing. Society generally gazed at women who chose otherwise with arched eyebrows or, even more insultingly, with pity. Careers were something to fit in between dishes and diapers—never the other way around, and never instead of homemaking. Women were educated and told to achieve, but encouraged to be dependent and to derive their status as well as satisfaction from the men in their lives.

After a brief and casual career as a television actress and newspaper columnist, I retired to raise a family. In 1970, when my youngest child was about to enter fourth grade, someone asked me what I thought I would be doing ten years from then. I panicked, realizing I wasn't even sure of what I would be doing that fall. Impulsively, I decided to begin college. I registered that fall for required freshman courses as well as a new course, Women in Literature. This course was, in part, consciousness raising, but it also exposed me to literature I had never heard of and introduced me to some fascinating women, both real and fictional.

Just as I began school, my youngest daughter, Vicki, was assigned to write a book report on a biography of someone from the Civil War or Reconstruction period. The teacher made several suggestions: Abraham Lincoln, Robert E. Lee, Ulysses S. Grant, Booker T. Washington, Clara Barton, and Mary Todd Lincoln. Vicki said she would like to read about a woman but since there were only a few books on Clara Barton and she wasn't much interested in a president's wife it didn't look like she would be able to find a book in time to get her report done. "Mom," she asked, "weren't there any other women from those days who did anything important enough to have a book written about them? Just Clara Barton and," she added with scorn, "a president's wife?"

"I don't know," I said sheepishly. "I never heard of anyone else."

"Well," she said indignantly, "there probably are, and *you* just haven't heard about them."

The next week, when I was assigned a term paper on any relevant subject for my Women in Literature course, I chose to explore biographies of women for children, figuring it would be a fairly short and easy subject and might prove useful in helping Vicki with her assignments. Beginning my research, I discovered a long list of biographies for youngsters about women, but some good ones were out of print and not readily available, and many current and popular ones were inadequate. Judging a biography or any work of literature for a youngster required application of a variety of criteria, and I could not simply rely on my own personal choices or experiences but needed to learn about children's literature, women in history, and a number of other topics to help me evaluate existing biographies. That term paper grew and grew until it eventually became the 1976 edition of *Her Way*.

An interesting thing happened to me on the way to publication of that book. As I became more and more interested in the ways children develop into multifaceted human beings with an array of personal and career choices available to them, I learned that it's never too early to start. And I learned that one must reach a child where he or she is, whether through real-life role models, toys, television, or books. I was pleased to see that there were all kinds of biographies available—some that are truly literary; others that are inspirational; there are those that are strictly factual, and even those that are fictionalized. All, as long as they meet certain criteria (see pages xiv–xvii) and have no distortions, have a place on the library shelf. I found good biographies in all styles and sizes and came to believe that elitism, like sexism and racism, has no place in the library or school.

The earlier edition of *Her Way* was a comprehensive guide and thus included books that were very poorly written, inaccurate, extremely racist, or sexist. Some were a combination of these and were described as unacceptable. All books were rated according to specific criteria. Six years later many of those unacceptable books had gone out of print, and although they may be still available on some library shelves, they appear to be gathering dust there. They have been omitted from this guide, as have some marginally adequate books which are either out of print and not readily available, or simply difficult to find, and not really worth the effort of the search.

In many instances, new, far better biographies of the same subject have been published, reflecting the response of publishers to the requests of teachers, librarians, parents, and young readers for more and better books about women. A great number of collective biographies have been published, and many are really splendid. They give the reader a chance to explore the lives of many people, and can act as a spur to reading and learning more about a particular person, lifestyle, or career.

In preparing the new edition of *Her Way*, I have examined biographies of women published through spring 1983. Most of these books are either in print or widely available at libraries. For a biography to be considered for this new, revised guide, it must either have been published for children in kindergarten through grade twelve or be an adult book that will be of interest to young readers. It must be available directly from the publisher or be on the shelves of many libraries. And, most important, it must meet the criteria for an acceptable biography. All of the biographies described in this edition of *Her Way* are acceptable; some are good, and many are excellent.

Many biographies, both individual and collective, have been published for older, less competent readers. These books are of principally inspirational value. Although they often focus on sports or entertainment celebrities, they frequently stress the values of perserverance and hard work and demonstrate ways to develop talents and interests. These books can encourage reluctant readers to enjoy reading.

Although this book serves chiefly as a guide to biographies published for children, I have included a number of books that publishers or librarians consider young adult titles. These books are often adult titles with special appeal to young people because of their subject matter. Young people will read a full-length, even scholarly adult biography of someone who is of special interest to them, but may shy away from a popular adult biography if the subject is someone whose life has no relevance to their own. "Young adult" titles have been so designated for various reasons, not necessarily because they were written for such an audience. For this reason, I have selected a number of these titles, choosing those that are especially worthwhile.

What makes a good biography? A good biography should be readable and accurate and give a sense of the person and the society in which he or she lived. It should show a person's strengths and weaknesses. A biography that is so laudatory or so burdened with moral lessons can have a discouraging effect upon a child who aspires to be like the subject and, therefore, creates for himself or herself an unrealistic and impossible task.

A biography should employ a style that is appropriate to the subject. A fast-moving journalistic style may be suitable in a biography of Billie Jean King or Nellie Bly, but it would be tasteless in a biography of Beatrix Potter or Phillis Wheatley.

While a biography for a child may not include the bibliography used by the author or a selection of recommended titles, evidence of research can be seen by the discerning critic. The adult considering a juvenile biography should ideally read some documented sources on the subject and should search for evidence that the author has not relied solely on secondary or tertiary sources. Occasionally, a juvenile biographer simply rewrites in simpler terms the subject's autobiography which may long be out of print or available only privately. Or a biography of a contemporary figure may be based on interviews with the subject, family, and friends. These biographies may be quite adequate, but be wary of the biography that appears to be a rewrite of a public relations firm's promotional material. These biographical profiles are not always well-rounded, unbiased accounts.

A good biography should be accurate and free of distortions, but it may at times omit some of the facts about a person because they seem to be inappropriate, incomprehensible, or irrelevant to the reader for whom the biography is intended. Recently there has been a trend to tell children the truth about all matters in terms they can understand. This seems to be a healthy and realistic approach, and writers who use it should be applauded.

A good biography can be a literary work, rather than just a collection of chronological facts put into a readable sequence. By judiciously selecting, organizing, and capturing an imagined essence of the subject, many biographies for young readers can hold their own next to a fine work of fiction. Whether or not the subject was a real person almost seems unimportant in such a book. That it combines biography and history is simply an extra dividend.

A good biography is nonsexist. Any biography that emphasizes and praises a traditional stereotyped role for men or women is sexist. A book that focuses on a woman's household and domestic achievements, physical attractiveness, charm, and gentle subservience to the exclusion of her contributions to society and her initiative, courage, and intelligence is sexist. Biographies that denigrate a man because he does not display independence, courage, and dominance or does not assume the financial support of women are also sexist. A book that presents a person as having nontraditional and nonstereotyped characteristics when he or she does not may not be sexist, but it is dishonest, a serious flaw in a biography.

A good biography should never take a patronizing, stereotyped, or negative view of any group or class of people. Prejudicial notions seriously detract from the worth of any book but are particularly deplorable in children's literature.

A biography should not only give a reader a sense of person, time, and place, it also must be careful to discuss such matters in terms of the subject's society. Achievements or lack of them should be judged not by today's values and lifestyles but in the context of the subject's own life. The author can, and should, remind young readers directly or subtly that times have changed (or have not changed, if such is the case), and that a subject's actions, while commonplace today, were extremely courageous or unusual then, or that a subject was not defaulting on her ambitions when she did not pursue a goal that she might have if she were living today.

Incidents of racism need to be explained in a similar fashion—many older books that dealt with blacks and Native Americans reflected the way society saw them. The young reader may have scant understanding of earlier times and often needs to be reminded of values and mores of the larger world in which a subject lived. Some books have been revised in the last several years, and incongruent aspects have been omitted.

Although any biography can be written interestingly and well, an author is working under a disadvantage when the subject is an appendage to someone else. I have tried to avoid evaluating the subject rather than the biography for inclusion in this guide, sometimes a difficult task. Some subjects are almost foolproof, for even a simply written, matter-of-fact account of the life of Harriet Tubman or Amelia Earhart is likely to be more than adequate. Similarly, biographies of some First Ladies or actresses, if written honestly and objectively, may not be inspirational or serve as positive role models for young readers.

Works of quality will satisfy literary or historical criteria, but those who match books to readers with diverse interests should not automatically reject those biographies that are easy to read, are for reluctant readers, or have as their subject people who are currently in the media; "superstars" are often of enormous interest to children. These books, too, must be written in appropriate style, accurately and objectively.

Anyone helping a child to choose a biography should remember that some children prefer books that may appear to be little more than a contrived curriculum aid. To such children, reading is a way of gathering information on a topic that interests them. Other children shy away from this straightforward textbook approach and are willing to read this kind of book only if they are required to do so. They want a good story. For these children, the fictionalized or anecdotal biography is a good choice. The introduction of conversation and private musing may give a biography an aura of fiction, but it is a widely accepted style. For the reader whose interest seems to be captured only by dialogue and "stories," biographies of this sort can be most enjoyable and profitable.

No discussion of biography as a literary form would be complete without mention of some existing series. Children do not usually sit down to read every title in a series such as the Bobbs-Merrill Childhood books. The third or fourth grader who sets upon such a task would not only have no time for the multiplication table or bike-riding and tree-climbing, but would probably get bored very soon. The children in the series, while sometimes dull and conventional, well-behaved and emotionally stable, show proclivity for their eventual accomplishments. More likely than not the readers will see little of themselves in the books. Librarians, teachers, and parents should try to steer children towards other biographies if these series are being read exclusively. In this edition I have included those titles which I feel are worthwhile.

Some subjects lend themselves to the childhood treatment format better than others do. The childhoods of Babe Didrikson Zaharias and Helen Keller, for example, provide absorbing and inspirational reading, for they were interesting children. On the other hand, many other women had rather uneventful childhoods, and some did little of interest or great consequence until midlife.

In a well-done biography children may find a direct reinforcement of their own ambitions and goals or they can sufficiently identify with the subject in such a way as to make their own goals seem possible.

Does reading biographies really help shape a young person's future goals? I have often believed so. James Haskins, the author of many excellent biographies of prominent contemporary men and women, interviews his subjects about their youth and frequently notes that even when they had no role models in their personal lives they found them in the library.

Many young people have told me that their life direction was closely related to the biographies they read as youngsters. Biographies, like other media and real people in youngsters' lives, can help with value clarification by providing models to emulate. My son, Peter, now a law student, reminded me about the summer after he finished second grade. Until then he had not been an enthusiastic reader, but that summer we discovered a beginning-to-read series of biographies of famous people, and he enthusiastically read them all: sports figures, scientists, and government leaders alike. Which of these first books does Peter remember most vividly? The ones about government leaders. These were the books which led him to read progressively more difficult books about government and history. By junior high school he was reading full-length adult biographies of world leaders. These people became his role models and significantly figured in his choice of a law career.

When my husband's oldest daughter began medical school, women composed only a small percentage of her first-year class (that percentage is now appraoching one-third). She says that even though no women in her family were physicians or even worked in the health field, she distinctly remembers reading Rachel Baker's biography of Elizabeth Blackwell when she was a youngster. Many of my female social work colleagues tell me they remember biographies of Lillian Ward and Jane Addams. Nurses who are women often state that they were inspired by tales of Florence Nightingale and Clara Barton. Perhaps some of those women might have considered other careers if there had been more role models, real or biographical, in their lives.

Today's young readers will not grow up, as I did, thinking that the only woman scientist was Marie Curie and that the highlight of Abigail Adams' life was when she hung the laundry in the East Room of the White House.

Boys need to recognize and expect that women will take their place alongside them in many careers. And they should learn that they themselves do not have to meet all the standards of traditional male behavior. As long as there are commonly shared beliefs regarding the appropriate characteristics and behavior of males and females, sex-role stereotyping will be reinforced, benefiting neither men nor women.

The number of books, both fiction and nonfiction, published in the last few years which show boys and girls, men and women of all ages assuming many roles, performing various tasks, and experiencing a wide array of emotions, all help to afford youngsters an opportunity to find their own way.

Biographies can help reinforce what is already relevant in a child's life or can widen horizons. My husband's young grandson was introduced to picturebooks which showed women as doctors, and he often visited his mother at the hospital during her residency. Later, if he reads biographies of early women physicians, he will be able to draw comparisons between those pioneers and his mother and to appreciate the changes.

In contrast, I remember back in 1965 the incredulous expression on the face of Laura, my daughter's four-year-old friend, when she learned her mother was a physician. Laura's mother had taken a one-year maternity leave when Laura's little brother was born, and when she carefully prepared her daughter for her return to work, Laura insisted, "No, Mommy, you can't be a doctor, you can be a nurse. Doctors are men." The pediatrician who cared for Laura and her brother was a man, as were all the doctors she saw in her picturebooks. In Laura's world, Mommies could work, but only at certain tasks.

How much luckier youngsters are today to find men and women engaged in many lifestyles and read about real people who have achieved their goals in fields which formerly excluded them.

Changes are occurring throughout society today at varying speeds and degrees. Authors, librarians, educators, publishers, and parents responsible for what children read all play an important part in creating this change. Those of us who have the opportunity to influence youngsters have an obligation to see that these changes continue and accelerate. Freedom of choice of lifestyle for everyone, boy, girl, man, and woman should be everyone's right. Such a belief on the part of all of us requires ongoing commitment and support. Helping children learn about lifestyles through biography is one important way to accomplish this.

How to Use This Book

Teachers and parents have told me they found the earlier edition of *Her Way* to be very helpful as a tool for preparing supplementary reading lists for a school subject. Youngsters with or without a helpful adult can choose books that meet interests or needs based on nationality, historical period, occupation, or a number of other criteria by consulting the appendixes. Librarians and booksellers will find the book helpful in choosing a biography for those "non-readers" who are interested only in tennis, dancing, or ice-skating, as well as for those engaged in serious research. A child who is guided to a biography of someone who holds special interest for him or her may be on the way to a lifetime of reading pleasure.

The book includes short profiles of women. Each profile is followed by a selected list of individual biographies which are intended for preschool through high school youngsters. The profiles are useful for both the youngster and the adult seeking to choose a biography. Children's librarians find that children like best the biographies of individuals with whom they are already familiar through television, textbooks, or teachers. Children do not spontaneously choose books about individuals unknown to them. Thus, these brief profiles can help one to become acquainted with the numerous women of whom one or more full-length biographies have been written.

Collective biographies fall into many categories. Usually the subjects are linked together by some common thread: occupation, ethnicity, or simply gender, for instance. These are suitable for those readers with a desire for less than full-length portraits, because of time or attention limits, because they want to learn about many similar people, or because they are searching for a subject about whom they wish to learn more. Some collectives are written in an informal, chatty style, and are very unlike the formal profiles found in reference books.

The Subject Index lists the approximately eleven hundred women included in individual and collective biographies. Three appendixes precede the indexes, Nationality Other Than American, Americans Classified by Ethnic Group, and Vocations and Avocations.

Each book has been considered and included on the basis of literary merit, historical and personal accuracy, freedom from racism and sexism, and interest and suitability for the age and grade level for which it is intended. The annotations point out the strengths and weaknesses in these biographies, and will guide the adult or youngster in choosing those that have the qualities they are seeking.

Individual Biographies

MANYA POLEVOI ABRAMSON
1896–1975

Pogrom survivor, Russian emigrant

Manya Polevoi Abramson, her husband, and their infant son, survived two vicious pogroms in the Russian Ukraine after the Russian Revolution, and came to the United States to be free and to live as Jews.

Their emigration in 1921 was made possible by HIAS, an organization formed during World War I to help Russian-Jewish refugees.

Like many women who had known hardship and were grateful to those who had helped them, Manya Abramson wanted to help pave the way to a better life for others. As her young family grew, she became active in volunteer work as a member of Hadassah Pioneer Women, in Zionist activities, and in building homes for orphans in Israel.

Before she died, she asked her youngest daughter, Bettyanne, to record her story.

Gray, Bettyanne Manya's Story Illus. with photographs. Lerner, 1978. (grades 7 and up)
Manya Polevoi Abramson's life story is written by her daughter. What emerges is a beautiful family story which is a tribute to the life and values of all Russian shtetl Jews. Some younger readers may find some scenes of the horrors of persecution overwhelming, but all readers will be moved by the heroism demonstrated during the Abramson's harrowing escape.

BELLA ABZUG
1920–

Congresswoman from New York, 1971–1977

Born and educated in New York, Bella Abzug planned at the age of eleven to become a lawyer to fight for social justice. She was a student activist at Hunter College. When Harvard Law School rejected her because she was a woman, she went to Columbia Law School where she graduated at the top of her class and was editor of the *Law Review.*

Despite her credentials, she continued to face sexual discrimination but determinedly continued her law practice and her work in civil liberties, civil rights, peace, and women's movements.

In 1970 Abzug ran for Congress as a representative from New York City's West Side. Her slogan, "This woman's place is in the House—the House of Representatives," and her impressive liberal platform and record won her the election. She served in Congress from 1971 through 1977, where she fought for equal rights for women, the end of the war in Vietnam, and open government against the seniority system.

Bella Abzug is a founder of the National Women's Political Caucus, Women Strike for Peace, and the New Democratic Coalition, and today she travels across the nation as a much sought-after public speaker. Her husband of over thirty-five years is one of her staunchest supporters. They have two grown daughters.

Faber, Doris BELLA ABZUG Illus. with photographs. Lothrop, 1976. (grade 5 and up)

Despite a tendency towards overfictionalization, this biography of Bella Abzug clearly shows her strengths, abilities, and impact on society. The book chronicles her political activism as a student leader at Hunter College, her legal career first defending those charged with un-American activities during the McCarthy era and later defending civil rights workers, and her role in the House of Representatives.

~~~~~~

ABIGAIL SMITH ADAMS
1744–1818

Feminist, First Lady, and mother of a President

One of America's earliest spokeswomen for women's rights, Abigail Adams wrote letters to her husband at the Continental Congress in Philadelphia, reminding him that the founding fathers should consider women in the new laws. She criticized proclamations of peace and good will to men, because they still insisted that men retain absolute power over their wives. She was ignored, even when she suggested that women might rebel if they were not represented in the new government and given an opportunity for equal education.

During the ten years John Adams was away serving the new nation, Abigail Adams took complete charge of their farm as well as their growing family. So outstanding an administrator was she, that later the farm supported the family with a regular income. Her husband, John Adams, was the second—and her son John Quincy Adams the sixth—president of the United States.

Akers, Charles W. ABIGAIL ADAMS: AN AMERICAN WOMAN Little, Brown, 1980. (grade 9 and up)
This very fine, serious biography is thoroughly researched and documented and gives a balanced, intelligent life history of this remarkable woman.

Kelly, Regina Z. ABIGAIL ADAMS Illus. Houghton Mifflin, 1962. (grades 4–6)
Somewhat bland biography conveys Abigail Adams's intelligence and intellect, but omits her interest in women's rights.

Peterson, Helen ABIGAIL ADAMS: DEAR PARTNER Illus. Garrard, 1967. (grades 2–5)
Brief and simply written biography depicting Abigail Adams's quick mind and amazing independence does not also convey her concern for women's rights.

~~~~~~

JANE ADAMS
1860–1935

Settlement house founder, social reformer, and winner of Nobel Peace Prize

Born to wealth and privilege, Jane Addams early showed concern for those who did not have her advantages. She spent her life seeking solutions to problems that beset society. Hull House, the settlement house she founded in Chicago in 1889, still stands. Her innovations to help improve the living conditions of slum-dwellers influenced the entire social work and welfare field.

By paving the way herself, she encouraged other women college graduates to enter professions relating to social problems. Her unusual administrative ability and magnetic personality attracted and inspired others, and together they worked to implement meaningful labor and social reforms.

She was a strong supporter of women's rights and suffrage and a founder of the American Civil Liberties Union. Addams's ceaseless efforts in behalf of peace were recognized when in 1931 she became the first American woman to win the Nobel Peace Prize.

Grant, Matthew G. JANE ADDAMS Illus. Creative Education/Children's Pr., 1973. (grades 2–4)

Very simple but comprehensive account of the life of Jane Addams is illustrated with colorful, vivid, eye-catching pictures. Despite its brevity, and the demands of a limited vocabulary and short sentences, the spirit of the woman and her accomplishments emerge.

Johnson, Ann Donegan THE VALUE OF FRIENDSHIP: THE STORY OF JANE ADDAMS Illus. Value Communications, 1978. (grades K–3)

A very good book for children in early grades who can either read it themselves or enjoy having it read to them. This is essentially a picture story, with an accurate and undistorted text. Marred only by one picture of children smiling as they worked in a candy factory, and a general minimizing of the impact of child labor.

Judson, Clara CITY NEIGHBORS: THE STORY OF JANE ADDAMS Illus. Scribner, 1951. (grades 4–9)

Convincingly fictionalized biography is limited mostly to Jane Addams's childhood and early days at Hull House. Based on extensive research as well as personal acquaintance, it is informative and inspiring without being eulogistic in tone.

Keller, Gail JANE ADDAMS Illus. Crowell, 1971. (grades 1–4)

Brief and easy enough for early readers to read alone, this outstanding biography is also good for reading aloud to young children. Even in this short book, the warmth and contributions of Jane Addams are made magnificently clear.

Meigs, Cornelia JANE ADDAMS: PIONEER FOR SOCIAL JUSTICE Illus. Little, 1970. (grade 7 and up)

Authoritative, carefully researched, and extremely well-written. Insightful and informative, it deals with many issues such as fair labor practices, child labor abuses, and Jane Addams's relationships with other pioneers in labor and social work. Valuable for older readers as well as mature junior high readers.

Peterson, Helen JANE ADDAMS: PIONEER OF HULL HOUSE Illus. Garrard, 1965. (grades 2–5)
Stirring, easy-to-read narrative, though brief, gives a full and interesting portrait of Jane Addams.

Wise, Winifred E. JANE ADDAMS OF HULL HOUSE Illus. Harcourt, 1935. (grade 7 and up)
Excellent, colorful, and well-researched biography makes clear Jane Addams's good fortune in growing up in a household where a woman's mind was treated as worthy of cultivation. Her many accomplishments are warmly detailed.

~~~~~~

LOUISA MAY ALCOTT
1832–1888

Author

Before the publication of *Little Women* made her famous and wealthy, Louisa May Alcott worked as a Civil War army nurse, seamstress, domestic servant, teacher, and governess. Her father, a prominent educator and philosopher, introduced her to many of the greatest thinkers of the day, and although he provided his family with much intellectual nourishment, he did not provide them with much of an income.

Alcott's childhood was happy in spite of poverty. Determined to lessen her mother's enormous burdens, she went to work early, and later, drawing upon her many experiences, wrote and sold short stories.

When *Little Women* was first published it became an immediate success, not only with the young people for whom it was intended, but with adults too. Semiautobiographical, it gave a vivid picture of the values and ideals of the nineteenth-century American middle-class family, and pioneered the portrayal of adolescence in fiction.

Though never drawn into an active role in the suffrage movement, Louisa May Alcott was eager for women to have opportunities to enter all the professions, and when Massachusetts allowed women to vote for certain local issues she was the first to register.

Colver, Anne Louisa May Alcott: author of little women Illus. Garrard, 1969. (grades 4–7)

In this excellent biography, Louisa May Alcott and her family emerge as warm, compassionate people and her spirit and achievements are dramatically described.

Fisher, Aileen, and Rabe, Oliver We Alcotts Illus. Atheneum, 1968. (grades 6–10)

This carefully researched and well-written book is not only a biography of Louisa May Alcott, it is also a family story being told by her mother. It offers valuable insights into the personalities of Louisa's parents. While this device limits somewhat the scope of the book, it adds warmth and personality.

Meigs, Cornelia Invincible Louisa Illus. Little, 1933. (grade 6 and up)

Fast-moving, exceptionally well-written with sensitivity and sympathy, this book gives an accurate portrait of Louisa May Alcott's early life and literary successes. The author gives background information on the social, intellectual, and historical period and carefully introduces Louisa May Alcott's family and their illustrious friends and associates.

Papashvily, Helen Louisa May Alcott Illus. Houghton Mifflin, 1965. (grades 4–7)

Alcott is portrayed as an independent child and her parents as rare human beings with warmth, compassion, and a genuine interest in their children's ideas and activities. Movingly told, the book cites her accomplishments and shows how she took over many of the financial problems that beset her family.

ALICIA ALONSO
1921–

Cuban ballet dancer

When Alicia Alonso was a little child in Havana, her mother noticed her inborn talent for dancing. When Alonso was nine years old, she began formal training. When she was twenty-one, her career was interrupted by a serious eye condition, which required three operations and a year in bed with her eyes bandaged, during which time she was not permitted to move. She overcame this obstacle to go on to artistic triumphs.

Alicia Alonso has performed ballet throughout the world but is best known as the director and prima ballerina of the Ballet Nacional de Cuba, a company she helped to found. A classicist, she has won special acclaim for her role of Giselle, which she danced throughout her early career in New York. When she danced Swan Lake with the American Ballet Theatre in 1975 at Lincoln Center in New York, she received a record-breaking eighteen-minute standing ovation.

She has performed with the greatest ballet companies in the world and has continued her outstanding performances at an age when most dancers have retired.

Alicia Alonso has been quoted as saying, "Art has no frontiers. Art belongs to the world, and the world is you and me."

Siegel, Beatrice Alicia Alonso Illus. with photographs. Frederick Warne, 1979. (grade 7 and up)
A very well-written biography gives a good picture of the Cuban dancer's childhood and professional life. Dance in both Cuba and the United States is depicted, adding to the well-balanced account.

~~~~~~

MARIAN ANDERSON
1902–

American concert singer

Marian Anderson began singing during childhood, performing first in churches in Philadelphia, later in schools and colleges, and eventually in concert halls all over the world. In 1939 she became a symbol of discrimination against black people when the Daughters of the American Revolution, owners of Constitutional Hall in Washington, D.C., refused her its use for a concert. This action so enraged First Lady Eleanor Roosevelt (page 201) that she resigned from the organization.

Marian Anderson gave a concert in Washington anyway. On Easter Sunday, 1939, the Lincoln Memorial became an outdoor integrated theater as seventy-five thousand blacks and whites stood together watching and listening to her, while millions more listened on their radios at home.

In 1955 Marian Anderson became the first black performer to appear with the Metropolitan Opera Company. She has taken an active role in promoting social understanding in the world by acting as a goodwill ambassador for the State Department and serving as a delegate to the United Nations. In 1980, she was chosen as a subject for the federal government's American Arts Gold Medallion, just one of many honors that have been bestowed upon her.

Anderson, Marian MY LORD, WHAT A MORNING Illus. Viking, 1956; Avon, 1964. (grade 7 and up)
Fine adult autobiography written simply enough for young readers. Warm and moving, it does not completely convey the extent of Anderson's accomplishments, for she is a modest reporter.

Newman, Shirlee MARIAN ANDERSON: LADY FROM PHILADELPHIA Illus. Westminster, 1966. (grades 5–11)
This biography does not place sufficient emphasis on the extent of racism that Marian Anderson has faced nor on her independence and amazing courage. However, it is warm, extremely readable, and faithful to the events of her life.

Tobias, Tobi MARIAN ANDERSON Illus. Crowell, 1972. (grades 1–5)
Superb biography in which Anderson emerges as a fine singer and human being who has faced many obstacles because she is black. Symeon Shimin's illustrations are especially effective in conveying the character and personality of Marian Anderson and those around her.

MAYA ANGELOU
1929–

Author, actress, dancer, director

Maya Angelou's childhood was spent in California and the South, most of it in the home of her grandparents. She was a very fine student, winning honors and scholarships. Her baby was born just after graduation from high school and she then took evening courses in dance and drama in college in California. She became a nightclub performer, singing and dancing throughout the world.

Her talents for writing, directing and producing were recognized and she moved her career in these directions. Her leadership qualities were also evident, and, at the request of the late Dr. Martin Luther King, she was the northern coordinator for the Southern Christian Leadership Conference.

She has been the recipient of numerous honors and awards and holds honorary degrees from several universities.

Maya Angelou's poetry, four books of her experiences as a black child and woman growing up in America, and her work in film and television have brought her wide acclaim. She has been appointed Reynolds Professor of American Studies at Wake Forest University in Winston-Salem, N. C.

Angelou, Maya I KNOW WHY THE CAGED BIRD SINGS   Random, 1970. (grade 9 and up)
————. GATHER TOGETHER IN MY NAME   Random, 1974. (grade 9 and up)
————. SINGIN' & SWINGIN' & GETTIN' MERRY LIKE CHRISTMAS Random, 1976. (grade 9 and up)
————. HEART OF A WOMAN   Random, 1981. (grade 9 and up)
Stirring series of autobiographical memories come alive on each page, and are remarkable for style as well as content. They are adult titles, but can easily be read by emotionally mature junior high and high school students.

~~~~~~

MARIE THERESE CHARLOTTE ANGOULEME
1778–1851

*Daughter of French King Louis XVI
and Queen Marie Antoinette*

Marie Therese was only one year old when the revolution broke out in France. She spent the second year of her life imprisoned with her family in the Tuileries Palace and after the execution of both her parents in 1793 became known as the "orphan of the temple," living in exile in various countries.

After the defeat of Napoleon and the restoration of the French monarchy in 1815, Marie Therese returned to her native country and served as a kind of "first lady"—first to her uncle, King Louis XVIII, and then to his successor, King Charles X.

Marie Therese's husband, Louis, the son of Charles X, never became king, for once again revolution spread throughout France and in 1830 Charles abdicated in favor of the liberal Duke Louis-Phillipe.

Prominent throughout her life, Marie Therese Charlotte Angouleme was both admired and despised for her connection to the Bourbon monarchs of France.

Desmond, Alice Curtis MARIE ANTOINETTE'S DAUGHTER Illus. with photographs, maps, and diagrams. Dodd, 1967. (grade 9 and up)
Very well researched and documented, convincingly fictionalized biography affords readers a thoughtful examination of Marie Therese's life and the society in which she lived. Well-written and interesting, it is a sympathetic though well-balanced portrait of the life of Marie Antoinette's daughter.

~~~~~~

MARY ANNING
1799–1847

Fossil collector

Mary Anning started her career as a fossil collector when as a youngster she helped her father collect petrified shells and mollusks near their home in the seashore town of Lyme Regis in England. Together they would climb the cliffs and hammer and chisel to remove the fossils they would then sell to tourists.

When Mary's father died she continued to collect and sell these natural curiosities to help support her family. She was only twelve when she discovered the huge creature that scientists named *Ichthyosaurus*, meaning fish-lizard. Later she found the first specimen of *Plesiosaurus*, meaning nearly-like-a-lizard, and the flying reptile, *Pterodactyl*, which means wing-finger.

Although she was not formally schooled in geology she devoted herself full-time to the study of fossils and her contributions to the field of geology were acknowledged by the most prominent people in the profession.

Museums all over the world have exhibited Mary Anning's fossil findings; many can be seen at the British Museum of Natural History in London.

Blair, Ruth Van Ness MARY'S MONSTER   Illus. Coward, 1975. (grades 3–7)

Fascinating, historically sound, though highly fictionalized account of Mary Anning's search for "curiosities" surrounding her seaside home which led to her discovery of important fossils. The persistence and seriousness of her pursuit are made clear, despite the correct indications that Mary Anning was not a geologist or a scientist in the true sense of the word. Life in the early nineteenth century is vividly depicted, and the black-and-white illustrations further enhance the text.

~~~~~~

SUSAN BROWNELL ANTHONY
1820–1906

American suffragist

Susan B. Anthony's Quaker upbringing taught her that women and men are equal under God, and she devoted most of her long life trying to realize this equality for American women. First as an abolitionist and a temperance leader, later as a participant in the movement to grant women rights over their children and property, she eventually put all of her extraordinary energies and abilities into the suffrage movement. With Elizabeth Cady Stanton (page 228) Anthony organized the movement, published a newspaper, and worked tirelessly to change women's restrictive role in society.

Susan Anthony was arrested for voting in the 1872 presidential election. She refused to pay the fine levied on her, hoping for imprisonment and the opportunity to take the case to the Supreme Court. However, her hopes were dashed when the charges against her were ignored.

Not until 1920, fourteen years after her death, were women able to vote in all elections in the United States. The Nineteenth Amendment to the Constitution, which granted this long overdue right, is sometimes called the "Susan B. Anthony Amendment," in honor of the woman whose long, tireless efforts helped women's suffrage become a reality.

Grant, Matthew G. SUSAN B. ANTHONY Illus. Creative Education/ Children's Pr., 1974. (grades 2–5)
Colorfully illustrated biography attempts to cover too many details in a brief narrative. Easy-to-read, and generally good, it may serve older reluctant readers better than younger elementary school children.

Noble, Iris SUSAN B. ANTHONY Messner, 1975. (grades 6–9)
Outstanding biography of Susan Anthony has a great deal of information packed into it about the entire women's movement, as well as much about Elizabeth Stanton, with whom Anthony was closely linked. Much of the history of the movement often omitted from biography is included here. The book ends by saying that perhaps the ghost of Anthony is now hovering over modern women, telling them the fight has not yet been won.

Peterson, Helen S. SUSAN B. ANTHONY: PIONEER IN WOMEN'S RIGHTS Illus. Garrard, 1971. (grades 3–6)
Nonfictionalized, straightforward, and accurate account of the life of Susan Anthony is occasionally stilted. Ms. Anthony emerges as a strong, courageous leader in this absorbing biography.

Salsini, Barbara SUSAN B. ANTHONY: A CRUSADER FOR WOMEN'S RIGHTS SamHar Pr., 1972. (grade 7 and up)
Excellent informative account of the life of Susan Anthony is brief (30 pages), but covers all the important events of her life and of the times. Ms. Anthony is revealed as a warm human being as well as an outstanding crusader.

~~~~~~

JACQUELINE AURIOL
1917–

French aviator

Flying was a hobby for Jacqueline Auriol until the day she crashed. Her entire face was crushed and she was almost killed, but her determination to become a professional pilot and her characteristic spirit and courage sustained her through her long ordeal. After more than fifteen operations, her face was restored and, despite sexual discrimination, she enrolled in a school for test pilots.

Jacqueline Auriol became the world's only officially qualified woman test pilot, and is a five-time winner of the women's world flying speed record.

Auriol, Jacqueline I LIVE TO FLY Illus. with photographs. Dutton, 1970. (grade 9 and up)
Fast-moving autobiography chronicles Auriol's flying career since her near-fatal accident. Informally written and greatly enhanced by photographs, this book reveals her determination and courage. Dramatic and inspiring for adults as well as young readers, the book describes what it is like to be a test pilot and to be a woman in the usually male field of aviation. Some aspects of her personal life are discussed, and the reader is introduced to her husband and her father-in-law, Vincent Auriol, one-time president of France.

~~~~~~

JANE AUSTEN
1775–1817

British novelist

Jane Austen's sheltered, quiet, and rather uneventful life in an English parsonage did not restrict her from becoming a great novelist. The youngest daughter of a clergyman, she spent her entire life in small, quiet English country towns, and her novels reflect these communities and the middle-class people who resided in them.

Although she is best known for her novel *Pride and Prejudice*, her other novels—*Sense and Sensibility, Mansfield Park*, and *Emma*—have also achieved lasting literary fame and popularity. Jane Austen's genius lay in her remarkable ability to observe and then imaginatively represent the lives of small provincial families, without relying on great passion, religious themes, or crimes.

Laski, Marghanti JANE AUSTEN AND HER WORLD Illus. Scribner, 1975. (grade 7 and up)
A well-written responsible biography, sometimes dry but lavishly illustrated, which helps to enliven it.

~~~~~~

TRACY AUSTIN
1962–

Tennis champion

At age fourteen, Tracy Austin became the youngest tennis player ever to enter the Wimbledon and U.S. Open tennis tournaments. In 1979 she became the youngest champion in the history of the U.S. Open, a tournament she won again in 1981.

She has been a finalist or semifinalist in singles and doubles at the U.S. Open and Wimbledon almost every year since then and has won the Italian Open and numerous other important tournaments including the Avon, Colgate and Family Circle.

Tracy Austin was the youngest tennis player to attain the U.S. top ten ranking and the first player to be ranked simultaneously in the U.S. adult top ten and in two junior classifications.

Her parents are avid tennis players, and her two older brothers and sisters were national junior champions. She began playing tennis when she was only three years old; at age four her picture was on the cover of a tennis magazine. By the time she was nine years old, she was a seasoned tournament player.

In 1983 Tracy Austin was ranked number four in the world.

Burchard, S. H. TRACY AUSTIN Illus. with photographs. Harcourt, 1982. (grades 2–5)
Lively, accurate biography of the tennis player is further enlivened by good photographs. Will appeal to older, less able readers as well as young tennis fans.

Hahn, James, and Hahn, Lynn TRACY AUSTIN Illus. with photographs. EMC, 1978. (grades 4–6)
Highly readable, spirited biography gives a good picture of Austin's family, early tennis practice and success, and the hard work needed to become a champion. For older, less able readers as well as younger ones with an interest in tennis.

Harler, Anne TRACY AUSTIN: TEENAGE CHAMPION Illus. with photographs. Childrens Pr., 1980. (grade 4 and up)
Easy-to-read, fast-moving biography of the youthful tennis star gives a good picture of the arduous road to becoming a tennis champion. Older, reluctant readers will find this book enjoyable.

Robison, Nancy TRACY AUSTIN: TEENAGE SUPERSTAR Illus. with photographs. Harvey, 1978. (grade 3 and up)

————. TRACY AUSTIN: TEEN TENNIS CHAMPION Illus. with photographs. Harvey, 1980. (grade 3 and up)

The latter book is the same as the earlier one, with two additional chapters added to make the book reflect Austin's current activities. Very good, easy-to-read biography is well balanced, giving information on Austin's early home life as well as her tennis career. Especially good for older readers who are not reading at grade level.

Rothaus, Jim TRACY AUSTIN Illus. with photographs. Creative Ed., 1980. (grade 4 and up)

Convincingly fictionalized, fast-moving, easy-to-read account of the tennis star's life captures her spirit, but offers only sparse information about her career.

Talbert, Peter TRACY AUSTIN: TENNIS WONDER Illus. with photographs. Putnam, 1979. (grade 7 and up)

Excellent book describes Tracy Austin's career in tennis and also gives a good picture of the world of tennis. Well written, it has style as well as content. Many excellent photographs enhance the text.

~~~~~~

PEARL BAILEY
1918–

Singer and actress

Pearl Bailey danced and sang in her minister father's revivalist church before she was even three years old. During World War II she toured the country as an entertainer with the USO. In 1946 she made her Broadway debut in *St. Louis Woman*, an all-black musical, and won an award as the season's best newcomer. Since then she has performed in other Broadway shows, movies, and nightclubs, and made recordings. The high point of her career came in 1967 when she headed an all-black cast in a new Broadway production of the musical comedy *Hello, Dolly!*, for which she received many awards.

She continues to delight audiences in personal appearances and on television.

Bailey, Pearl THE RAW PEARL   Harcourt, 1968. (grade 9 and up)

Adult autobiography is distinguished for its down-to-earth, highly read-able style which appeals to reluctant as well as more enthusiastic readers. This book is not ghostwritten as are so many personal narratives by celebrities; Bailey's own distinctive style and manner are captured on each page.

~~~~~~

EMILY DUNNING BARRINGER, M.D
1876–1961

First American woman ambulance surgeon

Her once well-to-do family was impoverished after Emily Dunning Barringer's father's death, but a family friend recognized young Emily's intelligence and convinced her mother to allow her to study medicine.

Emily Dunning Barringer graduated second in her class at medical school and won first place in competitions for positions at two leading New York hospitals, but was denied both appointments because of her sex. A year later she became the first woman intern in a city hospital. The men on the staff conspired to make her quit, but she refused to be intimidated. She raced to emergencies in a horse-drawn ambulance, attracting much attention and comment as the first and only woman ambulance surgeon.

During her long medical career she served as president of the American Medical Women's Association, and during World War II worked to see that women doctors got equal status with men doctors in the armed services.

Noble, Iris FIRST WOMAN AMBULANCE SURGEON Messner, 1962. (grades 6–10)

Exciting and inspiring biography discusses Dr. Barringer's childhood and years of study culminating in her exciting but difficult year of internship at New York's Bellevue Hospital. It also discusses her later years of accomplishment. The stereotypes of sex roles are also explored.

ETHEL BARRYMORE
1879–1959

American actress

Ethel Barrymore and her two brothers John and Lionel were known as "the American royal family of the theater." She was a star for over fifty years, appearing on the stage and in motion pictures.

Born to a family of actors, Ethel Barrymore was the third generation to appear on the stage. Given family responsibilities at an early age, as well as an opportunity to appear on the stage, she grew up quickly.

Acknowledged as the head of the family, she was, her brother Lionel said, "always on hand when the chips were down."

She was a pioneer in the organization of the actors' union, Actors Equity Association, and organized benefits and performances to raise funds during its first long strike.

Ms. Barrymore received many honors, including an Academy Award in 1944, and continued to perform until she was almost eighty years old.

Fox, Mary Virginia ETHEL BARRYMORE: A PORTRAIT Reilly & Lee, 1970. (grades 4–6)
Basically faithful to her life, this biography focuses on Barrymore's role as head of the family as well as on her professional career. However, the author fails to excite the reader in this slightly bland biography.

CLARA BARTON
1821–1912

Founder of the American Red Cross

Clara Barton, the founder of the American Red Cross, was a shy and lonely child who early showed an interest and talent for nursing. She began teaching school at eighteen, and founded one of New

Jersey's first public schools where she quickly noticed the salary and promotion inequities between men and women. Later she maintained a close association with leaders of the women's rights movement and made clear her strong support for suffrage and equal pay for equal work.

During the Civil War, Clara Barton distributed first aid supplies. She often went right into the lines of fire to aid the injured, earning herself the title "angel of the battlefields." She initiated the practice of preparing and distributing lists of those dead or missing in action.

After the war Barton was acclaimed as a great patriot, humanitarian, and war heroine. Later, in Europe, she became involved in war relief and the newly formed Red Cross. She worked indefatigably urging the United States to form an American Red Cross, and when this was finally accomplished, Clara Barton was chosen as the first president, a post she held for twenty-three years.

Her lifetime devotion to the service of humanity made her the best-known and most honored woman of her time.

Bains, Rae CLARA BARTON: ANGEL OF THE BATTLEFIELD Illus. Troll, 1982. (grades 2–5)
This childhood biography gives a good picture of the young Clara Barton and will be of interest to those young readers who are already familiar with her adult accomplishments.

Boylston, Helen CLARA BARTON: FOUNDER OF THE AMERICAN RED CROSS Illus. Random, 1955. (grades 4–6)
Excellent biography clearly states Barton's contributions to humanity. Focuses on her early work in nursing but also details her founding of the American Red Cross.

Grant, Matthew G. CLARA BARTON Illus. Creative Education/Children's Pr., 1974. (grades 3–6)
Generously illustrated, this biography gives a fine portrayal of Clara Barton's life and also describes the services of the Red Cross in peace as well as war. Easy to read, and quite brief, it has appeal to reluctant readers as well as young, enthusiastic ones.

Mann, Peggy CLARA BARTON: BATTLEFIELD NURSE Illus. Coward, 1969. (grades 3–5)
Well-rounded biography treats the fact that women were not given equal treatment with men during this period. Though easy to read, this biography has a high interest level which makes it suitable for older readers, too. Clara Barton's nursing contributions are made clear, and the

book also chronicles her efforts to establish the Red Cross in America and to extend its work to peacetime.

Nolan, Jeannette STORY OF CLARA BARTON OF THE RED CROSS Messner, 1941. (grade 6 and up)

Excellent biography gives an absorbing portrayal of Clara Barton and discusses the prejudices against women with which she had to contend throughout her life. Her contributions are made clear in this warm and moving biography.

Rose, Mary C. CLARA BARTON: SOLDIER OF MERCY Illus. Garrard, 1961. (grades 2–5)

In this nonfictionalized biography Clara Barton's achievements are movingly told with great sincerity. Her early shyness and the emotional support she gained from her family are stressed.

Stevenson, Augusta CLARA BARTON: GIRL NURSE Illus. Bobbs-Merrill, 1946. (grades 3–6)

Highly fictionalized but sugar-coated account of Clara Barton's childhood is based on true events and situations which Clara Barton revealed in her own writings. Her later achievements are presented well, but too briefly. Although this book is widely available (now in paperback), the other biographies listed above are far superior.

~~~~~~

DAISY BATES
1920–

Civil rights worker

Daisy Bates, perhaps more than anyone else, is responsible for the successful integration of Little Rock High School in 1957. Bates had been the state president of the National Association for the Advancement of Colored People (NAACP) when the United States Supreme Court ruled in 1954 that segregation in public schools was unconstitutional.

The governor of Arkansas refused to comply with the decision, but Daisy Bates with other leaders of the black community decided to fight back. Her life was in constant danger and the newspaper she and her husband owned was forced out of business. Daisy Bates stood firm, giving courage to the students and parents involved in the struggle, and today blacks and whites go to school together in Little Rock.

Bates, Daisy LONG SHADOW OF LITTLE ROCK McKay, 1962. (grade 8 and up)
Although Daisy Bates relates the story of the struggle for school integration in Little Rock, this is essentially a personal memoir, providing a dignified but moving account of Bates's own life.

~~~~~~

KATHERINE LEE BATES
1859–1929

American poet and professor

Katherine Lee Bates wrote the poem "America the Beautiful" on a trip across the country, inspired by the view from the top of Pikes Peak in Colorado.

She was the youngest in her family and for financial reasons the only one to attend college. After her graduation from Wellesley College she studied literature at Oxford University in England. Bates taught new approaches to the study of English literature, served as chairman of Wellesley's English department, and wrote critical reviews, articles, and poetry.

Myers, Elisabeth P. KATHERINE LEE BATES: GIRL POET Illus. Bobbs-Merrill, 1961. (grades 3–7)
Good biography focuses on the childhood of Katherine Lee Bates, giving a vivid picture of the times and of life in a family that valued education and independence. Bates's later achievements are stated briefly and accurately.

PATRICIA "PATTY" BERG
1918–

Golf champion

For almost forty years Patty Berg won numerous amateur and professional golf tournaments. She was one of the original golfers included in the World Golf Hall of Fame.

Always an athletic youngster, she became interested in golf at thirteen and within a few years was winning major tournaments and was Woman Athlete of the Year three different times. She served as an officer in the Marines during World War II. In 1948 she helped found the Ladies' Professional Golfers Association (LPGA) which helped raise the status of women in the sport. Patty Berg has written books on golf. Today Berg lives in Florida and gives clinics and exhibitions. She recovered from surgery for cancer and served as chairman of the Cancer Crusade for Florida. She continues to exercise, hitting golf balls, swimming, and bicycling.

Hahn, James, and Hahn, Lynn   PATTY!   Illus. with photographs. Crestwood, 1981. (grade 4 and up)
   Careful review of the golfer's career will interest golf fans, but this close attention to detail results in an occasionally dry biography. The book is enlivened by a great number of action photographs. Easy to read, it is especially recommended to older readers with limited reading skills.

SARAH BERNHARDT
1844–1923

French actress

"Divine Sarah," as she was known, was one of the world's most famous actresses, equally adept at classic tragedies and modern melodramas. Sarah Bernhardt toured England, the United States, and European countries where audiences clamored to see her, even when they could not understand her native French.

She had been a willful and difficult child, and her mother arranged for her to be educated in a convent. One of her mother's male admirers thought she would be a good actress and helped her to enter the Consevetoire, a French government sponsored school of acting. She remained there from the age of sixteen to eighteen, and then was accepted by the National Theatre Company.

Even though a leg amputation prevented her from walking or standing unaided, Bernhardt continued to perform, and during World War I she entertained the soldiers in the trenches.

The Legion of Honor was conferred upon her in 1914.

Skinner, Cornelia Otis Madame Sarah Illus. Houghton Mifflin, 1967. (grade 9 and up)

Full-length, adult biography gives an objective, elucidating account of the life of one of the world's most fascinating women. The author, an actress as well as writer, brings unusual insight into her examination of the life of Bernhardt.

~~~~~~

MARTHA BERRY
1866–1942

Educator, philanthropist, and founder
of Appalachian schools

Beginning with a Sunday school for a few neighboring mountain children in Georgia, Martha Berry eventually built an educational complex that today includes over one hundred buildings scattered over thousands of acres in Mount Berry, Georgia.

Her ideas of education were unusual for her time, for she believed that young people would benefit from practical and vocational learning as well as academic studies. Thus, Berry students not only learned and practiced the newest methods in agriculture and home-making, but also made the school almost self-supporting by their labor. Martha Berry also had a unique gift for raising funds, a quality which allowed Berry College to become established within twenty years.

Blackburn, Joyce MARTHA BERRY: A BIOGRAPHY Illus. Lippincott, 1968. (grades 7–9)

Outstanding, fast-moving, and faithful biography vividly recreates the life of this warm, compassionate woman who did so much for the people of Appalachia and for students from all over the world.

Kane, Harnett, and Henry, Inez MIRACLE IN THE MOUNTAINS: POR- TRAIT OF MARTHA BERRY Doubleday, 1956. (grade 9 and up)

Henry was a long-time associate of Martha Berry, and has given her readers an excellent, first-hand, well-balanced account of the life of the educator and philanthropist. Though an adult book. it is readable, fast-moving, and suitable for young readers.

Myers, Elisabeth P. ANGEL OF APPALACHIA: MARTHA BERRY Messner, 1968. (grades 6–10)

Fine portrayal of Martha Berry is highly fictionalized but accurate, providing a good, honest account of the life of the educator.

Phelan, Mary Kay MARTHA BERRY Illus. Crowell, 1972. (grades 1–4)

Excellent, brief, introductory biography conveys a good sense of Martha Berry's accomplishments, humanity, and personality.

~~~~~~

MARY McLEOD BETHUNE
1875–1955

Educator and advisor to presidents

Her parents and fourteen older brothers and sisters were born in slavery, but Mary McLeod Bethune, the first freeborn member of the family, was encouraged by her parents to go to school. Intend- ing to use her education to help other blacks, particularly young people, she founded a small school which through her persistent efforts eventually became Bethune-Cookman College.

Ms. Bethune won many honorary degrees, was a founder of the National Council of Negro Women, and was a leader in many political, religious, civic, and business organizations. She served

Presidents Coolidge, Harding, Roosevelt, and Truman in advisory positions on many matters relating to blacks, youth, and women.

Anderson, La Vere Mary McLeod Bethune Illus. Garrard, 1976. (grades 3–7)
  Excellent biography skillfully combines readable conversation and straightforward facts to provide a full survey of Bethune's life.

Burt, Olive Mary McLeod Bethune: girl devoted to her people Illus. Bobbs-Merrill, 1970. (grades 3–6)
  Good, moving biography focusses on the subject's youth, but is marred by comparisons between young Mary and other less gifted or ambitious black children. Insufficient information is given regarding her adult achievements, making this book less worthwhile than the other biographies listed here.

Carruth, Ella Kaiser She Wanted to Read: the story of mary mcleod bethune Illus. Abingdon, 1966. (grades 3–7)
  Dramatic and inspiring biography provides a good picture of a woman who achieved greatness despite numerous obstacles.

Greenfield, Eloise Mary McLeod Bethune Illus. Crowell, 1977. (grades 2–4)
  Highly readable examination of Bethune's life is a moving personal story from which emerges a believable portrait of her life and work.

Peare, Catherine Owens Mary McLeod Bethune Vanguard, 1951. (grades 7–10)
  Good biography is a moving and inspirational account of Bethune's achievements, but an implication that she was different and thus superior to other blacks detracts from its value.

Radford, Ruby L. Mary McLeod Bethune Illus. Putnam, 1973. (grades 2–4)
  Extremely good biography throws interesting light on Bethune's work in civil rights as well as in education. Easy to read, it is a stirring, dramatic portrait.

Sterne, Emma Gelders Mary McLeod Bethune Illus. Knopf, 1957. (grades 7–11)
  Fast-moving, interesting biography incorporates background of Bethune's African roots into the compelling narrative of a distinguished lifetime helping her people.

MARY ANN BICKERDYKE
1817–1901

Civil War hospital worker

While organizing the distribution of a relief fund to servicemen in the early stages of the Civil War, Mary Ann Bickerdyke was shocked to discover the terrible conditions at combat hospitals. She spontaneously began caring for the wounded, while also cooking, distributing supplies, and doing laundry.

"Mother" Bickerdyke, as she became known, was proficient at raising funds and demonstrated tremendous competence and energy in all her endeavors. Although she gained much love and respect from the soldiers, her impatience with military inefficiency and bureaucracy made many dislike and fear her.

After the war, she worked in a home for poor women and children, helped unemployed veterans settle on farms, raised funds for victims of a locust plague, worked for the Salvation Army, assisted veterans in obtaining their pensions, and helped in the organization of the Women's Relief Corps. In 1886, Mary Ann Bickerdyke's efforts were belatedly recognized by Congress when she was awarded a $25-a-month pension.

DeLeeuw, Adele CIVIL WAR NURSE: MARY ANN BICKERDYKE Messner, 1973. (grades 6–9)
The subject's fighting spirit is clearly evident in this excellent biography. The history of the time is incorporated into the text, and the reader is made privy to the bureaucracy and red tape that existed in the army even at that time. The author describes Bickerdyke's individualist style with humor, but never becomes patronizing.

ELIZABETH BLACKWELL, M.D.
1821–1910

First woman in America to receive a medical degree

Elizabeth Blackwell, determined and well-qualified to become a doctor, was turned down at many medical schools. She was finally accepted at the Geneva Medical School of New York where her admission had been left to the students by an indecisive administration. The male students thought it was a hoax, but no longer considered it such when, as the first woman to receive a medical degree, she graduated at the head of her class. She opened a private dispensary in New York which later became the New York Infirmary and College for Women.

Elizabeth Blackwell inspired and helped many other young women to become doctors, both in the United States and in England. During the Civil War she and her younger sister, Dr. Emily Blackwell, helped select and train nurses. As a pioneer in stressing preventive medicine, sanitation, and public health, Elizabeth Blackwell has left a legacy not only to all the women doctors who followed her, but to her entire profession.

Baker, Rachel FIRST WOMAN DOCTOR: STORY OF ELIZABETH BLACKWELL, M.D. Messner, 1944. (grade 6 and up)
Superb biography has become almost a classic. Bound to spark the imagination and inspire would-be doctors, it is a dramatic, well-written biography which pays tribute to the courage and persistence of Elizabeth Blackwell.

Clapp, Patricia DR. ELIZABETH: A BIOGRAPHY OF THE FIRST WOMAN DOCTOR Lothrop, 1974. (grades 6–9)
A good biography. However, the author has chosen to write Blackwell's story as a diary and in doing so has introduced a sense of artificiality into the text. Although generally nonsexist for the emphasis is on Blackwell as an independent, goal-oriented individual, the few "romantic" aspects of her life are somewhat stereotyped.

Grant, Matthew G. ELIZABETH BLACKWELL: PIONEER DOCTOR Illus. Creative Education/Childrens Pr., 1974. (grades 2–4)
Attractively and abundantly illustrated, the extremely easy-to-read, brief text attempts to cover all the salient aspects of Elizabeth Blackwell's life. This it does accurately and objectively. However, it lacks emotion and therefore she does not emerge in a warm, humanistic, and inspirational manner.

Heyn, Leah CHALLENGE TO BECOME A DOCTOR: THE STORY OF ELIZABETH BLACKWELL Illus. Feminist Pr., 1971. (grades 4–8)
Written from a feminist perspective, this biography carefully points out sexual inequities and discrimination. The writing is at times somewhat uneven and stilted, detracting from an otherwise fine biography.

Latham, Jean Lee ELIZABETH BLACKWELL: PIONEER WOMAN DOCTOR Illus. Garrard, 1975. (grades 3–5)

Lively, dramatic portrayal of Elizabeth Blackwell clearly conveys her determination to become a doctor and to open roads for other women. Her early nonsexist education and her later interest in preventive medicine are included in the easy-to-read text, and there is a welcome discussion that she did not always want to become a doctor. Many portrayals of Dr. Backwell indicate that it was an early ambition, which it was not.

Matthew, Scott THE FIRST WOMAN OF MEDICINE: THE STORY OF ELIZABETH BLACKWELL Illus. Contemporary Perspectives, 1978. (grades 2–5)

Easy-to-read biography, colorfully illustrated, is fictionalized but accurate. The focus is on Blackwell's struggle to become a doctor rather than on her later professional life. Although informationally sparse, it is an inspiring book for young elementary-school readers because it describes the rewards of hard work and perseverance.

Sabin, Francene ELIZABETH BLACKWELL: THE FIRST WOMAN DOCTOR Illus. Troll, 1982. (grade 3 and up)

This attractive book, highly fictionalized and not always accurate, does provide a good picture of the prevailing discrimination against women. The focus is on Blackwell's earliest years, but the tone of the book is warm and motivating.

Wilson, Dorothy Clarke LONE WOMAN: THE STORY OF ELIZABETH BLACKWELL Illus. Little, 1970. (grade 9 and up)

An adult, full-length biography gives a detailed portrait of Elizabeth Blackwell, recreating in depth her long and productive life. Written with authenticity it is, for young readers, a definitive biography of the first woman to receive a medical degree in the United States.

~~~~~~

JUDY BLUME
1938–

Children's author

New Jersey–born Judy Blume is one of those rare adults who really remembers how growing up feels. Her stories are based on familiar experiences and have sold over six million copies. Some of her most popular titles, including *Are You There God? It's Me, Margaret;*

Blubber; Starring J. Freedman as Herself; Forever; It's Not the End of the World; and *Superfudge;* have been translated into other languages. *Wifey,* an adult title, was also a huge success. Her readers send her thousands of letters each year, asking her questions they feel only she can answer, because she seems to understand young people so well.

A fine sensitive writer, Judy Blume is also an outspoken critic of book censorship, believing youngsters should be permitted to read books that reflect the "real world." Some libraries and schools have refused to place her honest and realistic books on their shelves or later removed them.

Judy Blume has homes in Santa Fe and New York. Her children, Larry and Randy, now young adults, were her earliest inspirations for books, and their enthusiasm and encouragement have been of great importance to her.

Lee, Betty JUDY BLUME'S STORY   Illus. with photographs. Dillon, 1981. (grade 5 and up)

An excellent, absorbing biography introduces the best-selling prolific children's author to her millions of fans. This book provides more than a glimpse into Judy Blume's life and the experiences that motivate her work.

~~~~~~

NELLIE BLY
(Elizabeth Cochrane Seaman)
1867–1922

Journalist and reformer

Elizabeth Cochrane Seaman, or "Nellie Bly" as she called herself, began her colorful newspaper career when she wrote an indignant letter to a newspaper editor who opposed the idea of suffrage and careers for women. The editor was so impressed with her ability that he hired her as a reporter, thus beginning Nellie Bly's sensational reporting of the need for reforms in factories, slums, and prisons.

Nellie Bly completed one of her best-known series of articles after feigning insanity and being committed to a psychiatric ward in a

New York hospital so that she could expose the brutal and neglectful treatment accorded the inmates. Her social reforms were somewhat overshadowed by her spectacular record-breaking trip around the world: daily reports of this trip were avidly followed by her readers. Nellie Bly, one of the best-known and most adventurous figures in the history of American journalism, was a pioneer in opening doors for women to enter the profession.

Baker, Nina NELLIE BLY, REPORTER Scholastic, 1972. (grades 4–6)
  Colorful biography moves quickly and reveals Nellie Bly's resourcefulness, independence, and journalistic ability.

Graves, Charles NELLIE BLY: REPORTER FOR THE WORLD Illus. Garrard, 1971. (grades 3–5)
  Very readable, this biography clearly indicates Nellie Bly's pioneer spirit as well as her skills as a reporter. Lively and exciting, it is a dramatic inspiring story.

Hahn, Emily AROUND THE WORLD WITH NELLIE BLY Illus. Houghton Mifflin, 1959. (grades 6–9)
  Remarkably good feminist biography reveals Nellie Bly's anger at discovering how many obstacles to achievement were placed before women. Her efforts to overcome much of this prejudice and to become a successful reporter are clearly demonstrated.

ROSA BONHEUR
1822–1899

*French painter, first woman to win Grand Cross
of the Legion of Honor*

Rosa Bonheur's artist father encouraged her talent, and even before she was out of her teens she had a painting exhibited at the Paris Salon, the most important yearly exhibition of the works of living French artists.
  Most of her subjects were animals, and she visited slaughterhouses and owned many animals so that she could study their muscular movements.

Bonheur's paintings were remarkable for their accuracy, drama, and power. Her most famous work, the huge lifelike *The Horse Fair*, has had special appeal to youngsters, and has been widely reproduced. It hangs now in the Metropolitan Museum of Art in New York City.

Price, Olive   ROSA BONHEUR: PAINTER OF ANIMALS   Illus. Garrard, 1972. (grades 4–6)
This good biography is somewhat stilted and lacks Bonheur's excitement and vitality. However, it does offer a good accurate study of the artist, and the accompanying illustrations and reproductions, though rather ordinary, add to the book's interest.

~~~~~~

DEBBY BOONE
1956–

Singer

Debby Boone began appearing with her father, Pat Boone, and her three sisters while she was in her teens. In 1977 the first song she ever recorded, "You Light Up My Life," made her an instant star. She has appeared on numerous television shows, including her own special program in 1980. In 1977 she won many important music awards, including the Grammy award for best new artist, the Country Music Award for best new country artist, the American Music Award, and gold and platinum records.

Boone was educated in parochial schools, and religion is an important part of her life.

Eldred, Patricia Mulrooney   DEBBY BOONE   Illus. with photographs. Creative Educ. Soc., 1979. (grade 5 and up)
A warm, readable biography discusses her personal life, her early conflicts with her father, her career, and her renewed religious faith, as well as her successful professional life.

EVANGELINE BOOTH
1865–1950

General of the Salvation Army

"Little Eva," as General Evangeline Booth was called, grew up in England in a family whose whole life centered around their evangelistic organization, the Salvation Army. While other children played house or played school, Evangeline and her brothers and sisters played at preaching and talked of saving the souls of sinners.

While still in her teens, Evangeline became an effective administrator and leader, earning the title "angel of the slums." She was a dramatic lecturer and later organized the Salvation Army's first all-women band. Her various posts took her to Canada and later the United States where she worked to create hospitals, clinics, community centers, nurseries, and lodgings for the homeless. Later, as General of the International Organization, Evangeline Booth travelled to eighty countries and colonies.

Lavine, Sigmund EVANGELINE BOOTH: DAUGHTER OF SALVATION Illus. Dodd, 1970. (grade 7 and up)

Outstanding portrait of Evangeline Booth combines biography with the story of the developing Salvation Army. General Booth is seen in a full-dimensional light, as a competent, compassionate, and successful woman.

MARGARET BOURKE-WHITE
1905–1971

*Photojournalist, first woman to become an
accredited war correspondent*

Photographer Margaret Bourke-White's first assignments were to photograph steel mills and other industries in the United States. Her interest in people and places took her all over the world where she photographed poor farmers, unemployed urban dwellers, the famous and the unknown. With her camera she reported wars,

33

social upheavals, and political revolutions for *Life* magazine, and her photographs filled several books.

During World War II, as the first woman to become an accredited war correspondent, she earned the rank of lieutenant colonel. During her lifetime, Bourke-White received many awards and honors for her depictions of the depression in the United States, the emerging industrialization of Russia, the growing munitions industry in Germany, poverty in India, racial discrimination in South Africa, World War II, and the horrors of the concentration camps.

A twenty-year heroic struggle with the crippling effects of Parkinson's disease ended with her death in 1971.

Bourke-White, Margaret PORTRAIT OF MYSELF Illus. with photographs. Simon & Schuster, 1963. (grade 9 and up)
Excellent autobiography intended for adults is also interesting and comprehensible to much younger readers. Written after illness forced her to stop photographing, the book reflects the independence and courage of this remarkable woman.

Callahan, Sean, ed. THE PHOTOGRAPHS OF MARGARET BOURKE-WHITE Illus. with photographs. New York Graphic Society, Ltd., 1972. (all ages) Introduction by Theodore M. Brown.
Large, handsome adult volume of Bourke-White's photographs includes a skillfully and interestingly written biographical introduction. Though clear and to the point it may prove difficult reading for some younger teens, but the photographs that constitute the major part of this book will be of interest to readers of any age. The volume would be a fine accompaniment to any full-lengh or shorter profile intended for young readers.

Iverson, Genie MARGARET BOURKE-WHITE Illus. with photographs. Creative Ed., 1980. (grade 4 and up)
Fine, short biography for younger or reluctant readers captures the essence of this daring and heroic woman. Both her personal and professional lives are simply but well recounted, and she emerges as a multifaceted talented woman.

Noble, Iris CAMERAS AND COURAGE: MARGARET BOURKE-WHITE Messner, 1973. (grade 8 and up)
In an unusually fine biography Bourke-White emerges as the courageous, talented, and fiercely independent woman she was. The author combines information about photography, the depression, Gandhi's non-violent movement in India, World War II, Parkinson's disease, and the process of rehabilitation with a good personal and professional portrayal of an indomitable woman.

Siegel, Beatrice AN EYE ON THE WORLD: MARGARET BOURKE-WHITE, PHOTOGRAPHER   Illus. with photographs. Warne, 1980. (grade 6 and up)
Enhanced by many photographs, this straightforward nonfictionalized narrative of Margaret Bourke-White's life is an excellent introduction to her life and work, suitable for all ages.

~~~~~~

BELLE BOYD
1844–1900

Confederate spy, actress, and lecturer

At the start of the Civil War, Virginia-born Belle Boyd worked to raise funds for the South. Later she used her fine equestrian skills and knowledge of the surrounding area as well as her intelligence to become a valuable spy for the Confederacy.

She was frequently caught, but after gaining release resumed her activities. Her exploits were reported in the newspapers and soon Belle Boyd became as notorious in the North as she was famous in the South.

After the war, Boyd wrote a book about her experiences, became an actress, and later was a popular lecturer in both the North and South.

Nolan, Jeannette BELLE BOYD: SECRET AGENT   Messner, 1967. (grade 6 and up)
Biography provides a picture of Belle Boyd that shows her to be heroic, assertive, and intelligent. Lacking in some of the vitality and excitement displayed by Boyd herself, the book is, nevertheless, a good account of her life.

~~~~~~

ANNE DUDLEY BRADSTREET
1612–1672

Early American poet

English-born Anne Bradstreet came to the New World with her husband and family when she was eighteen years old. Despite the hardships of colonial life and care of her eight children, she managed to find time for extensive reading and the writing of poetry.

Nature, history, or family were the usual themes of her poetry, and in one poem she comments on those "who say my hands a needle better fits," and continues, "If while I do prove well, it won't advance/They'll say it's stol'n, or else it was by chance."

She wrote primarily for her own satisfaction and the pleasure of her family, but a collection of her poetry which was published in England marked her as a first poet of the American colonies.

Dunham, Montrew ANNE BRADSTREET: YOUNG PURITAN POET Illus. Bobbs-Merrill, 1969. (grades 3–7)
Good biography highlights the childhood and youth of Anne Bradstreet, and despite fictionalization is a reasonably faithful account of her life. Young Anne emerges as highly intelligent, and her father is portrayed as willing and eager to encourage her education when he hires tutors for her in England.

~~~~~~

MARY BRECKINRIDGE
1877–1965

*Founder of the Frontier Nursing Service
in Kentucky*

After completing nurses' training, wealthy and socially prominent Mary Breckinridge took further degrees at Columbia University in New York and studied midwifery in the British Isles. After her return to the United States she used her skills and funds to establish the Frontier Nursing Service in Kentucky, where she spent the remainder of her life giving medical attention to the poor of that rural area.

Mary Breckinridge and her nurses rode horseback to bring their care to all who needed it, delivering babies and nursing infants, children, and adults in the primitive conditions of isolated areas.

Wilkie, Katherine, and Moseley, Elizabeth FRONTIER NURSE: MARY BRECKINRIDGE Messner, 1969. (grade 7 and up)
Smooth narrative dramatically and inspirationally traces the life of this capable, compassionate nurse who gave unselfishly of herself and inspired others to do the same.

LAURA BRIDGMAN
1829–1889

First educated blind deaf-mute

A serious illness completely destroyed Laura Bridgman's senses of hearing and sight, and to a great extent, taste and smell, when she was two years old. Her plight came to the attention of Dr. Samuel Gridley Howe of the famed Perkins Institution, a school for the blind in Boston. She enrolled there as a student, and he began the revolutionary experiment of educating a blind deaf-mute. Detailed reports of this success were later carefully studied by Anne Sullivan Macy (page 152) before she began to teach deaf and blind Helen Keller (page 126).

Laura Bridgman remained at Perkins all her life, performing simple duties, selling her handiwork, occasionally teaching sewing, maintaining an extensive correspondence, and communicating with the young students at Perkins, all of whom learned the manual alphabet.

Hunter, Edith Fisher Child of the Silent Night Illus. Houghton Mifflin, 1963. (grades 3–6)

Warm, sensitive biography reveals Laura Bridgman to be a persevering and intelligent young woman. Convincingly, but not overly fictionalized, the book closely follows her young life and relates the tireless efforts of those who helped her.

THE BRONTËS
Charlotte Brontë (pen name Currer Bell) 1816–1855
Emily Brontë (pen name Ellis Bell) 1818–1848
Anne Brontë (pen name Acton Bell) 1820–1849

Nineteenth-century British novelists

Life on the isolated bleak Yorkshire moor with their eccentric clergyman father was restrictive and lonely for the Brontë sisters.

With their brother Bramwell they wrote imaginative stories which furnished their lives with excitement and drama.

The young Brontë girls attended an oppressive, harsh boarding school which only increased their loneliness and misery, and this and their later experiences as governesses and teachers are reflected in their romantic novels.

Charlotte Brontë's *Jane Eyre* and Emily Brontë's *Wuthering Heights* are today's most widely read Brontë novels. Like the other Brontë works, these not only provided rare insights into the role of women in nineteenth-century England but also served as models for many other romantic and Gothic novels.

Kyle, Elisabeth GIRL WITH A PEN: CHARLOTTE BRONTË Holt, 1964. (grades 5–9)

Extremely well-written but highly fictionalized biography portrays the early life of Charlotte Brontë from her late teen years to the publication of *Jane Eyre*. Much information is provided about the close bond that existed between the young Brontës, and their lively imaginations are conveyed.

Vipont, Elfrida WEAVER OF DREAMS: THE GIRLHOOD OF CHARLOTTE BRONTË Illus. Walck, 1966. (grades 7–9)

In this splendid biography, Charlotte Brontë expresses resentment at the stereotyped notions of a girl's role. This book is beautifully written, focusing on the youth of the Brontës and detailing the imaginary world in which they lived.

~~~~~~

ELIZABETH BARRETT BROWNING
1809–1861

British poet

Elizabeth Barrett Browning could read Homer in the original Greek when she was only eight years old, and at age fourteen she had written an epic poem. An accident left her a semi-invalid, and she was completely dominated by her unreasonable, wealthy father. She was already a popular poet when she met Robert Browning. They fell in love and she escaped from her home to marry him. Her unforgiving father refused to see or hear from her again.

Elizabeth continued to write and publish poetry and corresponded with many other women writers. She never became active in the women's rights movement, but her long poem, *Aurora Leigh*, deals sympathetically with women's rights and unwed mothers. Her long work, *The Cry of the Children*, helped awaken England to the terrible conditions of child labor. However, it is for *Sonnets from the Portuguese* that Elizabeth Browning is best known today.

Burnett, Constance SILVER ANSWER: A ROMANTIC BIOGRAPHY OF ELIZABETH BARRETT BROWNING   Illus. Knopf, 1955. (grades 7–11)
Fine biography emphasizes the oppression to which young Elizabeth Barrett was subjected, as well as drawing a thoughtful portrait of her later life, her work, and her marriage.

Lupton, Mary Jane ELIZABETH BARRETT BROWNING   Feminist Pr., 1972. (grade 9 and up)
Written from a feminist perspective, this adult book is a critical treatment of Browning's work, as well as a personal biography. Substantially documented, it contains much information not found in most other popular sources. A discussion of *Aurora Leigh* is interesting and useful, and despite the scholarly treatment the biography is fairly brief and quite suitable for high school students.

Waite, Helen HOW DO I LOVE THEE?   Macrae, 1953. (grades 7–11)
Though stylistically uneven, this is a moving biography. The portrait of the poet lacks sufficient depth, but her work is discussed well and there are many quotations from her sonnets and letters.

~~~~~~

PEARL BUCK
1892–1973

Author

American-born Pearl Buck grew up in China where her missionary parents provided her with an education that combined the cultures of China and America. Throughout her long and active lifetime she worked to promote understanding between the East and West.

She began writing as a youngster and during her career published more than eighty major works. She wrote for children and for adults, often using the Orient as a setting. A frequent theme of her novels is women and their place in the world. Her nonfiction was on many subjects, and she published innumerable magazine articles.

Pearl Buck's most famous novel, *The Good Earth*, won her the Pulitzer Prize in 1931. In 1938 she won a Nobel Prize for literature and commented, "In my country it is important that this award has been given to a woman."

Herself a mother of a retarded child, Buck worked, through both her writing and organizations, to help retarded children. She also founded the Pearl S. Buck Foundation to help children of mixed heritage.

Block, Irvin THE LIVES OF PEARL BUCK: A TALE OF CHINA AND AMERICA Illus. with photographs. Crowell, 1973. (grades 7–10)

Beautifully written, warm, personal biography focusses on Pearl Buck as an independent, brilliant, compassionate woman. Interwoven into the biography are the plots of some of her best-known works, and her literary style is carefully commented upon. Buck emerges as the multidimensional woman she was, and her mother too is depicted as a remarkably courageous and independent woman.

Buck, Pearl S. MY SEVERAL WORLDS: A PERSONAL RECORD (abridged for young readers) Day, 1954. (grades 6–9)

Very fine book relates some of Buck's experiences in China and America. She acknowledges how grateful she is that her schooling was equal to that offered boys: "We were not corrupted by home economics or cookery or any such soft substitute for hard thinking . . . the theory was . . . that any educated woman can read a cookbook or follow a dress pattern."

Schoen, Celin V. PEARL BUCK: FAMED AMERICAN AUTHOR OF ORIENTAL STORIES SamHar Pr., 1972. (grade 7 and up)

Extremely brief (thirty pages) but excellent nonfictionalized biography deals with Pearl Buck's personal and professional life. Emphasis is on her experiences rather than on her works, and the book provides a thoughtful examination of one of America's most prolific writers.

Westervelt, Virginia PEARL BUCK: A BIOGRAPHICAL NOVEL Nelson, 1979. (grades 6–9)

Despite heavy fictionalization, this biography gives a richly detailed account of the life of Pearl Buck. Readers who enjoy this style of biography will find this book a most satisfactory study of her life.

ABBIE BURGESS
1839–1892

Lighthouse keeper

The Burgess family lived on a small island where young Abbie's father was the lighthouse keeper. The mother was ill so teenager Abbie took care of her sisters and ran the household. When her brother left the island she helped her father with his duties and, during a two-year period when violent storms kept her father on the mainland, she alone tended the whale oil lamps on the lighthouse towers. Her commitment to that difficult and often hazardous task helped save many passing ships.

After her own family left the island, she assisted the family who took over the job. She later married the new lighthouse keeper's son and the two left to take over another lighthouse.

Jones, Dorothy, and Sargent, Ruth S. ABBIE BURGESS: LIGHTHOUSE HEROINE Funk & Wagnalls, 1969. (grades 7–10)
The major events in this good biography are true, but much of the story is fictionalized. Abbie Burgess emerges as a young woman with unusual courage and a sense of responsibility to her family and to the duties of managing a lighthouse. The early chapters are particularly inspirational; the later ones are somewhat more romantic when young Burgess meets and marries the young son of the new lighthouse keeper.

CAROL BURNETT
1934–

Actress

Born in Texas and raised in Hollywood, Carol Burnett lived her early life with her grandmother in economic hardship. Her parents were alcoholics, and later she cared for her younger sister when they no longer could do so.

She was editor of the Hollywood High School newspaper. She discovered her interest and talent in performing while a college student at the University of California at Los Angeles. After college she went to New York. After playing on stage and bit parts on television, she became a regular performer on Garry Moore's television show. She also starred in a Broadway show. In 1967 "The Carol Burnett Show" began on television. A very popular entertainer, Burnett has won numerous awards and continues to appear on her own television specials as well as in movies.

Although usually thought of as a comic performer, she has won awards for her serious roles in movies and television.

She has established scholarships at many schools and made other substantial contributions to worthy causes. In 1982 the Variety Clubs dedicated the Carol Burnett Wing in the pediatrics department of UCLA Medical Center.

An open and honest person, Burnett has shared her family problems with the public to encourage others with problems to seek help for themselves.

Church, Carol B.   CAROL BURNETT: STAR OF COMEDY   Illus. with photographs. Crestwood, 1976. (grades 5 and up)
An excellent book that depicts Burnett as both performer and person. Older, slower readers as well as enthusiastic younger ones will be inspired by her struggle to succeed.

~~~~~~

FRANCES HODGSON BURNETT
1849–1924

Author

Living in poverty in the Tennessee mountains was a radical change for Frances Hodgson Burnett's once wealthy British family, but teenager Frances ambitiously tried to help by raising chickens, starting a school, and giving music lessons. However it was the short stories which she sold to magazines that started her on the road to literary and financial success.

Among her short stories and novels for children and adults was the enormously popular, now little-read *Little Lord Fauntleroy*. The novels *Sarah Crewe* and *The Secret Garden* continue to be read and loved by each new generation of readers.

Burnett, Constance B. HAPPILY EVER AFTER: A PORTRAIT OF FRANCES HODGSON BURNETT Vanguard, 1965. (grade 7 and up)
A good biography written by Frances Burnett's daughter-in-law is a thoughtful, documented, and honest examination of the personal life of the popular author. Lacking in the drama and excitement found in Burnett's own novels, the biography may have more appeal to adults interested in children's literature than to children themselves.

Thwaite, Anne WAITING FOR THE PARTY: THE LIFE OF FRANCES HODGSON BURNETT Scribner, 1974. (grade 9 and up)
Older readers and adults interested in learning more about the famous children's author will appreciate this fine book, which gives an excellent portrait of Burnett's life.

~~~~~~

ROBIN CAMPBELL
1959–

Olympic track competitor

Robin Campbell was only nine years old when she joined a track clinic at a Washington, D.C., playground and was invited by the coach, Brooks Johnson, to join the Sports International Club. After winning local races, she began competing in national, and eventually international, events. Her parents and four older brothers encouraged and supported her, and her two younger sisters also became runners.

Specializing in the eight-hundred-meter event, she has been ranked since 1977 when she was eighth in the United States. Each year her record improved, and she was third in the 1980 United States Olympic tryouts. (She would have been a serious contender for an Olympic medal, but the United States boycotted the 1980 Olympics for political reasons.)

For the 1984 Olympics Campbell will be training under Brooks Johnson, who has been chosen to be the women's Olympic coach.

Jacobs, Linda ROBIN CAMPBELL: JOY IN THE SKY Illus. with photographs. EMC, 1976. (grade 5 and up)
Good, lively biography also reveals the hard work demanded of track competitors, and the lifestyle of those who are serious about the sport.

~~~~~~

RACHEL CARSON
1907–1964

Marine biologist, conservationist, and author

Rachel Carson's rare gift for writing and her knowledge of marine biology led her to become the first woman scientist to write for the United States Bureau of Fisheries. Her books *Under the Sea Wind, The Sea around Us*, and *Edge of Sea* were well received, but when *Silent Spring* was published in 1962, her plea for biological control (instead of chemical control) of insects and pests enraged and threatened the huge chemical industry. The manufacturers of DDT and similar products tried to denounce her as an emotional, nonscientific crank, but she succeeded in alerting the public and the President's Science Advisory Committee to the poisonous nature of pesticides.

Ms. Carson received many honors and awards for her work. Unfortunately she died in 1964, before the present American environmental drive, which, to a large extent, is due to the principles and discoveries which were her life's work.

Brooks, Paul RACHEL CARSON AT WORK Illus. with photographs. Houghton Mifflin, 1972. (grade 9 and up)
Excellent, full-length, adult biography of Rachel Carson offers an account of her personal life, but focusses on her scientific work. A distinguished, competent treatment of great interest to those readers with knowledge of the sciences. Extensive quotations from her works add considerably to the value of this thoroughly researched, well-documented work.

Latham, Jean Lee RACHEL CARSON: WHO LOVED THE SEA Illus. Garrard, 1973. (grades 2–5)

Very fine biography reveals Rachel Carson's rare combination of writing and scientific background and shows her to be a crusader and pioneer in ecology awareness. The criticism of her work by the pesticide industry is not indicated here, but Carson's consciousness of herself as a pioneer woman in her particular scientific field is clearly shown. She emerges as a warm person, devoted to her family, energetic, and resourceful.

Sterling, Philip SEA AND EARTH: THE LIFE OF RACHEL CARSON Illus. Crowell, 1970. (grades 5–8)

Outstanding, thoroughly researched and documented biography offers a well-rounded portrait of the woman who combined her literary and scientific talents with a courageous desire to enlighten the public and who became one of the most influential people of our times. The author writes with clarity, revealing Carson's contributions but also depicting her as a warm human being.

~~~~~~

ROSALYNN SMITH CARTER
1927–

First Lady

Rosalynn Smith Carter, the eldest of four children, was born in Plains, Georgia. She met Jimmy Carter, also born in Plains, when she was attending college and he was a student at the United States Naval Academy in Annapolis. They were married after his graduation. After he completed his Navy tour of duty they took over the family peanuts and fertilizer business. She kept the books and tax records for the business as they raised three sons.

She worked in Jimmy Carter's successful campaigns for state senator and later for governor of Georgia. Amy, their daughter, was born during those years. During the 1976 presidential campaign Rosalynn Carter was an active participant and made speeches all over the country.

After becoming First Lady, Rosalynn Carter continued the work she had begun in Georgia toward improving mental health programs.

Warm, hospitable, and clearly intelligent, Rosalynn Carter has been considered by many to be one of the more influential First Ladies.

Rogers, Jan Falk First Lady: rosalynn carter Illus. with photographs. Childrens Press, 1978. (grades 1–5)

Very easy-to-read, enjoyable biography of Rosalynn Carter covers the main aspects of her life and depicts her as a hard-working, intelligent woman with a life of her own beyond her husband.

~~~~~~

ROSEMARY CASALS
1948–

*Tennis champion, advocate of equal rights
for women in tennis*

Professional tennis champion Rosemary Casals learned to play tennis on San Francisco's public courts. Her father began teaching her when she was eight, and by the time she was fifteen she had won almost every junior title in California. While she was a high school student she was invited to coach the girls' tennis team, and after graduation won almost every important title in women's tennis.

At five feet, two inches, Rosemary Casals is short for a tennis player, but she compensates for this with her fast running and scrambling. With her frequent doubles partner Billie Jean King, Casals organized the professional women's boycott of major tournaments to demand equal rights, prize money, and center court time. In 1973 she won the Family Circle Cup Crystal Trophy and $30,000, then the biggest prize in the history of women's tennis.

Since then she has been a winner or finalist in the U.S. Open doubles, Colgate Series doubles, and Avon Championships. She has been a member of the Wightman Cup team and the Federation Cup team. She headed Women in Tennis, an organization which works to bring players and businesspeople together for endorsements and sponsorship arrangements, and she remains a high-ranking player.

Jacobs, Linda Rosemary Casals: the rebel rosebud Illus. with photographs. EMC, 1974. (reading level, grades 4–6; interest level through high school)

The somewhat pedestrian approach and occasional apologies for the subject's caustic wit detract from an otherwise excellent biography. The author has traced Casal's life from the beginning of her interest in tennis, and goes into careful detail about the politics of women's tennis.

Thatcher, Alida RAISING A RACKET: ROSIE CASALS Illus. with photographs. Raintree, 1976. (grade 4 and up)
Lively biography captures the personality of the outspoken player and describes in detail her early days in tennis as well as her successful career. Good book for older, less able readers.

~~~~~~

MARY CASSATT
1845–1926

American painter

When American-born Mary Cassatt decided to become a serious artist, she defied the social convention that a woman use her talents just for decorative purposes. She studied first in Philadelphia, then in Paris, and became one of the greatest painters of children and women. The mothers in her paintings are frequently depicted as active individuals, not idle as usually painted by other artists.

Although not an Impressionist herself, Cassatt worked closely with them, and due to her efforts, many French Impressionist paintings were acquired by collectors in the United States.

Mary Cassatt received many awards for her work and was a highly successful artist in her lifetime. Today her works hang in museums throughout the world.

McKown, Robin THE WORLD OF MARY CASSATT Illus. Crowell, 1972. (grades 5–8)
Outstanding nonfictionalized biography of interest to the student of art as well as to the general reader. The book combines the development of the French Impressionists with the life story of the woman who worked with them and introduced their work to the United States.

Myers, Elizabeth MARY CASSATT: A PORTRAIT Illus. Reilly & Lee, 1971. (grades 4–7)
Absorbing biography gives a personal and professional account of the life of the artist. Written for a wide audience, the book will appeal to casual readers who have no special interest or knowledge of art, as well as to those with a background in that area.

Scheader, Catherine MARY CASSATT Illus. with photographs and art reproductions. Children's Pr., 1977. (grade 5 and up)

Fictionalized portrait of the artist is intended for older, reluctant readers but may be of greater interest to younger readers. Cassatt's life and career are recounted in a highly readable, enjoyable manner.

Wilson, Ellen AMERICAN PAINTER IN PARIS: A LIFE OF MARY CASSATT Illus. Farrar, 1971. (grade 5 and up)

Good biography gives straightforward account of the life of the American artist, but does not fully capture the spirit of her life or times. The author indicates that Cassatt in her later years regretted not marrying and having children.

~~~~~~

WILLA CATHER
1873–1947

American writer

The author of *O Pioneers!*, *My Antonia*, and other prairie novels grew up in Nebraska where she learned to love the outdoors, and became interested in science and literature. At college, Willa Cather's talent for writing became apparent, and after graduation she worked for newspapers and magazines. After her first novel was published, Ms. Cather decided to forgo her magazine job and to write fiction only. Her novels deal mainly with American experiences, and specifically with the American drive to achieve and express individuality.

Ms. Cather received many honorary degrees and awards, and though she directed that none of her novels be made into films or anthologized in textbooks, her works remain popular with young people as well as adults. Their appeal lies in her style, subject matter, and ability to recapture the not-so-distant past.

Bonham, Barbara WILLA CATHER Illus. Chilton, 1970. (grade 7 and up)

Outstanding biography thoughtfully discusses Willa Cather's life as well as the famous and talented people with whom she associated. Her works are briefly described, a device which succeeds in encouraging youngsters to read her novels or to reconsider them with new insights.

Brown, Marion, and Crone, Ruth   WILLA CATHER: THE WOMAN AND HER WORKS   Illus. Scribner, 1970. (grade 7 and up)
A good, mature biography gives a detailed, substantial account of the life of Willa Cather. Despite occasional slow-moving sections of the book, a good portrait of the writer emerges.

Franchere, Ruth   WILLA: THE STORY OF WILLA CATHER'S GROWING UP   Illus. Crowell, 1958. (grade 5 and up)
Sympathetic, well-paced biography of Willa Cather is for youngsters not yet ready to read her works. The emphasis is on her childhood and youth, but the author perceptively describes the young girl who will later become a fine writer. A moving and exciting book, it offers a good picture of the last years of frontier life and of a family who encouraged their daughter to express herself.

~~~~~~

CATHERINE OF ARAGON
1485–1536

Queen of England

Catherine of Aragon, daughter of Ferdinand and Isabella of Spain, was widowed at sixteen by the eldest son of England's King Henry VII. Several years later she married the king's younger son who by then had assumed the throne to become Henry VIII. Despite her opposition, Henry VIII later broke with the Roman Catholic church and annulled their union. She subsequently passed the rest of her life in seclusion and in religious devotions.

Catherine of Aragon was a well-educated, cultured woman who showed extraordinary courage under great misfortunes and difficulties.

Roll, Winifred   THE POMEGRANATE AND THE ROSE: THE STORY OF KATHERINE OF ARAGON   Prentice-Hall, 1970. (grade 7 and up)
Good nonfictionalized book combines biography with history. Fine historical treatment, giving a perceptive picture of a woman living in a very difficult situation.

49

CATHERINE THE GREAT
1729–1796

Empress of Russia

Catherine the Great was an obscure German princess who went to Russia to marry the Grand Duke Peter. When he became emperor of Russia, she led a revolt to remove him from the throne, and became empress of Russia. She ruled with absolute power for thirty-five years, during which time she extended the Russian borders, took away power from the church, and introduced some local government throughout the empire.

Catherine fostered the love of the French language and culture and was herself a good sculptor and painter. She wrote a history of Russia, memoirs, comedies, and stories in French and Russian. After her death her son succeeded her as emperor of Russia.

Kochan, Miriam CATHERINE THE GREAT Illus. St. Martin's, 1977. (grade 7 and up)
Honest, sympathetic biography brings Catherine alive in an objective vigorous manner.

Noble, Iris EMPRESS OF ALL RUSSIA: CATHERINE THE GREAT Messner, 1966. (grade 7 and up)
Extremely well-balanced, interesting account of the life of Catherine the Great. Convincingly fictionalized, the biography provides a thoughtful examination of the historical period as well as the personality of Catherine.

EDITH CAVELL
1865–1915

Nurse and World War I spy

English-born Edith Cavell trained as a nurse in London and later went to Belgium to head that country's first nursing school and national nursing program. When World War I broke out, the Germans occupied Belgium. Edith Cavell's hospital treated German and Allied soldiers, but as a member of the underground resistance movement, she aided the escape of hundreds of Allied soldiers. Her activities eventually became known by the Germans, who apprehended her and sentenced her to death by a firing squad. Edith Cavell was regarded as a martyr in England. After the war, services were held for her in Westminster Abbey and today a statue of her stands near Trafalgar Square in London.

DeLeeuw, Adele Louise EDITH CAVELL: NURSE, SPY, HEROINE Illus. Putnam, 1968. (grades 5–7)
Good biography focusses on Cavell's activities during World War I, and though fairly sensitive and lively, lacks some substance.

Elkon, Juliette EDITH CAVELL: HEROIC NURSE Messner, 1956. (grade 6 and up)
Dramatic, stirring account of the life of this heroic nurse skillfully conveys her dedication to human life and values.

Grey, Elizabeth FRIEND WITHIN THE GATES: THE STORY OF EDITH CAVELL Illus. Houghton Mifflin, 1961. (grades 5–9)
Excellent biography places emphasis on Cavell's earlier years as a nurse, but also vividly depicts her efforts on behalf of the Allies during World War I.

~~~~~~

LYDIA MARIA CHILD
1802–1880

Author and abolitionist

Lydia Maria Child sacrificed a career as a popular and financially successful author to devote herself to abolitionist writings. When her strong denunciation of slavery and racial inequalities entitled *An Appeal in Favor of That Class of Americans Called Africans* was published in 1833 and angered book dealers, they stopped carrying her other books. Child wrote pamphlets and other books against slavery and became the only American woman newspaper editor when she took over the publication of the *National Anti-Slavery Standard.*

Lydia Maria Child was a prolific writer and a woman of boundless energy. Besides fictional works, she wrote on such varied subjects as homemaking, child care, society, and history. She was also the editor of the first American periodical for children.

Meltzer, Milton TONGUE OF FLAME: THE LIFE OF LYDIA MARIA CHILD Crowell, 1965. (grade 7 and up)
Thoroughly and competently researched biography gives a vivid portrait of the era as well as a thought-provoking portrait of the woman who risked her career to attack slavery. An appendix lists not only works about Child, but also those by her, adding to the value of an already fine book.

~~~~~~

SHIRLEY CHISHOLM
1924–

Congresswoman from New York

Shirley Chisholm was the first black woman to serve in Congress. From the start of her first term she was the outspoken advocate of bills that criticize military spending, encourage day care, revise social security laws, and encourage equality between races, ethnic groups, and men and women.

A brilliant student in Jamaica where she spent some of her early childhood and in Brooklyn where she grew up, Chisholm has earned graduate degrees in education and served as a supervisor of day care centers in New York. As a member of the New York State Assembly she figured importantly in legislation which supported education.

As a congresswoman, Chisholm became well known throughout the nation and was a serious candidate in the 1972 presidential primary. Although she did not win a place on the November ballot, a large number of supporters had joined her on the "Chisholm Trail" and she earned the respect and admiration of the nation.

In 1982 she decided to leave Congress, stating "we have an administration that is not responsive to our constituency," and "many of us can't be effective at this time." She has been named a professor at Mount Holyoke College where she teaches courses on politics related to Congress, race, and women.

Brownmiller, Susan SHIRLEY CHISHOLM Illus. with photographs. Archway, 1970. (grades 4–8)

Outstanding feminist biography of the dynamic congresswoman has appeal for older reluctant readers as well as younger ones. Chisholm's childhood, youth, and adult accomplishments are well presented against the background of New York and the Caribbean where she spent her earliest years.

Chisholm, Shirley UNBOUGHT AND UNBOSSED Houghton Mifflin, 1970. (grade 7 and up)

Excellent autobiography was not written for youngsters but is clear, thought-provoking, and inspiring for them. The prose is not difficult to understand, and young competent readers will be engrossed in this intimate portrayal of the career of the first black congresswoman.

Haskins, James FIGHTING SHIRLEY CHISHOLM Illus. with photographs. Dial, 1975. (grade 6 and up)

Outstanding book—the epitome of a good biography. Dialogue is used effectively and there is clear evidence of the author's thorough research into the subject's life. The essential spirit of Shirley Chisholm emerges as the author traces her life from early childhood to her political career. The author is fully aware of his subject as a black and as a woman and uses these facts to underline her minority status clearly and often, but never self-consciously. An appendix to the book lists her legislative accomplishments, further enhancing the biography.

Hicks, Nancy THE HONORABLE SHIRLEY CHISHOLM: CONGRESSWOMAN FROM BROOKLYN Lion, 1971. (grades 5–9)

Excellent portrait of Chisholm is a straightforward narrative, employing good journalistic style. Young readers will find it easy to follow; older ones will also find it interesting.

~~~~~~

EUGENIE CLARK
1922–

Ichthyologist and oceanographer

Even as a child in New York City, Eugenie Clark was interested in fish. She visited the aquarium regularly and soon knew her life's work would be in science, with fish as a specialty. She majored in zoology at college, earned a master's and a doctorate degree, and won many fellowships and scholarships including a Fulbright.

As an ichthyologist and oceanographer, Clark undertook underwater research expeditions throughout the world and has developed a major marine laboratory in Florida. Internationally known, she has travelled extensively to explore, work, study, and lecture, and has written numerous articles for general readers as well as for scientists. Her scuba-diving expedition to the Red Sea was one of the highlights of her career.

Clark, Eugenie LADY AND THE SHARKS   Illus. with photographs. Harper, 1969. (grade 9 and up)

Adult, personal narrative is more oriented towards the scientific reader, but its fast-moving, readable style is not weighted down with complicated terminology or concepts. Provides a good biography for the general reader of a woman who has carved out an exciting life for herself in marine biology.

————. LADY WITH A SPEAR   Illus. with photographs. Harper, 1953; Ballantine, 1974. (grade 8 and up)

Interesting adult biography will have special appeal to those interested in various fields of marine biology. The author discusses her childhood and youth, and general readers will find this to be a fast-moving, immensely readable story of a woman's exciting life.

McGovern, Ann SHARK LADY: TRUE ADVENTURES OF EUGENIE CLARK   Illus. Four Winds, 1978. (grades 3–5)

Fictionalized but excellent fast-paced biography of Eugenie Clark emphasizes her work and earliest interests but also discusses her personal life.

~~~~~~

JACQUELINE COCHRAN
1910–1980

Aviator and businesswoman

After a childhood marked by physical and emotional hunger, almost no schooling, and work in the cotton mills, Jacqueline Cochran became a beauty shop operator.

In 1932 she decided to learn to fly, and within a few years was winning air races and setting records for speed, distance, and altitude. During World War II she served as director of the Women Auxiliary Service Pilots (WASP).

Although flying was one of her chief interests, she also founded a highly successful cosmetics business, took an active part in politics, worked as a correspondent for a leading national magazine, and served as an officer in several aeronautic associations.

As a pilot her achievements have seldom been surpassed. In 1953 she became the first woman to break the sound barrier, and set many jet speed records for both men and women. Among her numerous awards for aviation are the Air Force Association Award, the Distinguished Flying Cross, and the French Legion of Merit. In 1971 she became the only living woman to be included in the Aviation Hall of Fame. Her outstanding accomplishments in business have been widely acknowledged, and she twice was named "Woman of the Year in Business."

Fisher, Marquita O. JACQUELINE COCHRAN: FIRST LADY OF FLIGHT Illus. Garrard, 1973. (grades 3–5)

Fast-moving, anecdotal, and brisk narrative traces Cochran's life from her early impoverished childhood to her success as an aviator and businesswoman. Easy-to-read, this book is warm and dramatic, and includes most of the major accomplishments of Cochran's life.

~~~~~~

NATALIE COLE
1950–

Singer

Grammy-award winner Natalie Cole grew up knowing many famous singers and musicians. Her father was Nat "King" Cole, and her mother, a former singer, helped to raise their five children and was also her husband's business manager.

As a child Natalie Cole took piano lessons and occasionally appeared with her father, who died when she was fifteen. She majored in sociology at the University of Massachusetts where she gained a sense of black identity and began singing regularly at a lounge near school. Although many doors were opened to her because of her father she was determined to develop her own style and identity. Her Grammy award for best new artist was an important start in that direction.

Jacobs, Linda NATALIE COLE: STAR CHILD Illus. with photographs. EMC, 1977. (grade 4 and up)
   Good biography shows Natalie Cole's desire to achieve on her own ability by working hard and not relying on being Nat "King" Cole's daughter.

~~~~~~

NADIA COMANECI
1961–

Olympic gold medal–winning gymnast

Nadia Comaneci began training as a gymnast in Rumania when she was only six years old. She was the youngest contestant when she entered her first serious competition at seven, and she was only eight when she won the Rumanian Junior Championship title. When she reached the 1976 Olympics she became one of the most famous fourteen-year-olds in the world. Viewers were spellbound when she received seven perfect scores. She won three gold medals and one bronze medal.

   She was the first woman to do a double backward somersault on the floor, and her exercises in the air are spectacular. She has been named sportswoman of the year by United Press International and "absolute woman gymnast" of Rumania where she has been awarded the highest honors Rumania confers.

Burchard, S. H. NADIA COMANECI Illus. with photographs. Harcourt Brace, 1977. (grade 3 and up)
   Highly readable biography convincingly describes Nadia Comaneci's family life, and school training as well as the world of gymnastics.

McMillan, Constance Van Brunt NADIA COMANECI: ENCHANTED SPARROW Illus. with photographs. EMC, 1977. (grade 3 and up)
   Easy-to-read biography focuses on the gymnast's family, training, and achievements and also offers a glimpse into her personality. Of interest to older, less able readers as well as younger ones.

KATHARINE CORNELL
1898–

Actress and theater manager

Since 1925 Katharine Cornell has been a theatrical star and the recipient of many awards and honorary doctorate degrees. Cornell has played a wide variety of roles in her long career and has won wide critical acclaim for her performances in *Romeo and Juliet* and *Antony and Cleopatra* and as Elizabeth Barrett Browning in *The Barretts of Wimpole Street*. She has managed most of her own productions and often has been directed by her producer-husband, Guthrie McClintic.

During World War II she toured army bases, bringing live performances to servicemen who had never before seen professional theater. Katharine Cornell is among the few successful actresses who has spent much of her time performing on the road. For this dedication to her career and to her audiences, and for her extraordinary talent, Cornell has received the respect and devotion of theater lovers across the United States.

Malvern, Gladys CURTAIN GOING UP: THE STORY OF KATHARINE CORNELL   Messner, 1943. (grade 7 and up)

Outstanding biography of the great actress and manager Katharine Cornell clearly shows that the theater is not all glamour, but entails hard work, intellect, loyalty, and perseverance. Exciting to read as a novel, the biography is faithful to the life of Cornell, and has appeal for all readers, not only those interested in the theater.

ELLEN CRAFT
c.1826–c.1897

Fugitive slave, abolitionist

Light-skinned Ellen Craft and her husband escaped from slavery by travelling north in disguise. Ellen Craft dressed as a man and assumed the role of a deaf and ill white master, while her husband posed as a slave. They escaped detection and found refuge with Quaker abolitionists in Philadelphia. They settled first in Boston, where they became leading figures in the antislavery movement. They then moved to Great Britain to raise a family.

After the Civil War they returned to the United States and bought a large plantation in Georgia on which they established an industrial school for blacks. Ellen Craft and her husband played major roles in abolitionist and freedmen societies and were greatly admired by their contemporaries.

Freedman, Florence TWO TICKETS TO FREEDOM Illus. Simon & Schuster, 1971. (grades 4–7)
Unusually fine narrative is thoroughly researched, well-documented, and gives a vivid, realistic picture of the era. The escape of the Crafts from slavery reads almost like a suspense novel, but it is based on contemporary sources and is faithful to the truth. Illustrations by Ezra Keats add immeasurably to the book's value.

~~~~~~

PRUDENCE CRANDALL
1803–1889

Educator, abolitionist, and feminist

When Prudence Crandall accepted a black student in her Connecticut school, white parents and financiers withdrew their children and support. Like most Quakers, she opposed slavery and this incident strengthened her abolitionist convictions. Crandall consequently reopened her school to train middle-class and well-to-do northern black women to be teachers. The local citizens strenuously objected and, when she refused to close the school, they harassed her and arrested her on a trumped-up charge. When these measures failed, the townspeople broke windows, polluted the well, and attempted to set the school on fire. Mob action finally forced Prudence Crandall to close her school and to move west with her husband. There she taught and worked in the women's rights movement.

Fuller, Edmund PRUDENCE CRANDALL: AN INCIDENT OF RACISM IN NINETEENTH-CENTURY CONNECTICUT Illus. with photographs. Wesleyan Univ. Pr., 1971. (grade 8 and up)

Short scholarly book is a detailed, thoroughly researched and documented chronicle of the violent opposition in Connecticut to Prudence Crandall's school for black girls. Though it is her story, it is not as much a biography as it is a historical document.

Yates, Elizabeth PRUDENCE CRANDALL: WOMAN OF COURAGE Illus. Dutton, 1955. (grade 7 and up)

Touchingly written account of the life of an unusually heroic woman and of the episodes that precipitated her finally closing her school and leaving Connecticut. The issues of the day are clearly depicted, as is the faith Ms. Crandall's father had in her. Their truly unusual relationship is well described.

~~~~~~

MARIE CURIE
1867–1934

Discoverer of radium, first woman to win Nobel Prize in sciences, first person to win Nobel Prize twice

Despite a strong academic background in the sciences, Marie Curie was denied admission to the University of Warsaw because of her sex. After experiencing years of political and financial hardships in Czarist-ruled Poland, she went to Paris to study at the Sorbonne and graduated there with honors in physics and mathematics.

After her marriage to scientist Pierre Curie, Marie successfully integrated her scientific career with marriage and motherhood. The Curies won the 1903 Nobel Prize in physics for their work on radioactivity, and after her husband's tragic death, Marie Curie succeeded him as a professor at the University of Paris, becoming the first woman to hold such a position. In 1911, Marie Curie again won the Nobel Prize, the first person to win the award twice.

Marie Curie was honored throughout the world for her discovery of radium and its contribution to medicine. Ironically, it was long exposure to its penetrating rays that caused her death in 1934.

Bigland, Eileen MADAME CURIE Illus. S. G. Phillips, 1957. (grades 5–9)

Very fine inspiring narrative of Marie Curie's life clearly describes her contributions to science and does a competent job of explaining radium and scientific techniques to readers unfamiliar with such terms and principles.

Curie, Eve MADAME CURIE Illus. Doubleday, 1949. (grade 8 and up)

Outstanding biography written by Marie Curie's daughter is a thorough, analytical account, in which she emerges as a multidimensional woman—scientist, teacher, wife, and mother.

DeLeeuw, Adele MARIE CURIE: WOMAN OF GENIUS Illus. Garrard, 1970. (grades 4–7)

Outstanding narrative biography gives a good, clear portrait of the woman whose contributions to science have been recognized throughout the world.

Keller, Mollie MARIE CURIE Illus. with photographs. Watts, 1982. (grade 7 and up)

Warm but serious biography of the famed scientist gives a straightforward account of her childhood and career. Moves along smoothly in an interesting fashion.

Henriod, Lorraine MADAME CURIE Illus. Putnam, 1970. (grades 2–4)

Unusually fine biography gives a simple but inspiring account of Marie Curie's life. The limitations imposed on women are discussed, and her contributions to science are clearly described.

Henry, Joanne MARIE CURIE: DISCOVERER OF RADIUM Illus. Macmillan, 1966. (grades 4–6)

Nonfictionalized narrative gives account of Marie Curie's life, carefully explaining many scientific principles and focussing on her professional work. She emerges as thoroughly competent, although her accomplishments seem to have developed in partnership with her husband, rather than independently.

McKown, Robin MARIE CURIE Illus. Putnam, 1971. (grades 4–8)

Excellent short account of Marie Curie's life is warm and inspiring, succinctly depicting her many accomplishments.

Veglahn, Nancy THE MYSTERIOUS RAYS: MADAME CURIE'S WORLD Illus. Coward, 1977. (grades 3–5)

An outstanding book that concentrates on the search and discovery of radium, and captures the personality of the scientist. Although not a full-length biography, this book will be of special interest to readers interested in science, and is useful in conjunction with science studies.

~~~~~~

FRANCIS REED ELLIOT DAVIS
1882–1964

First black nurse in the American Red Cross

Francis Elliot Davis's father was the son of a former slave and an Indian, and her white unmarried mother the daughter of a minister. Her mother died when Francis was five and she went to live with various black foster families, some of whom were indifferent to her. Later, a white family, for whom she did domestic work, befriended her and helped her to gain an education and to become a nurse.

Highly skilled, intelligent, and dedicated, Francis Davis became the first black nurse to be officially enrolled in the American Red Cross. She worked in the Henry Street Settlement House, served tirelessly through the 1918 flu epidemic, and constantly fought prejudice in schools, hospitals, and the United States Army nurse corps.

Pitrone, Jean TRAILBLAZER: NEGRO NURSE IN THE AMERICAN RED CROSS Harcourt, 1969. (grade 6 and up)

Stirring, informal biography competently and completely details Davis's life. She emerges as a figure of rare determination and fortitude. The author also presents, in this extremely readable book, a good picture of prejudices against blacks.

~~~~~~

DOROTHY DAY
1897–1980

Social reformer, founder of The Catholic Worker

Until the end of her long life, Dorothy Day fought for social justice and social reform and for the poor.

61

Her father was a journalist, and she and her four brothers and sisters moved about the United States with her parents. At sixteen she enrolled in college where she joined the Socialist party and learned more about radical movements. She later wrote for Socialist papers in New York. She became increasingly aware of and sympathetic to the suffragist movement, and spent time in jail for demonstrating for women's right to vote. Continuing to write, she achieved some financial success and independence.

She had a daughter, Tamar, in 1927. After she decided to become a Catholic the relationship with Tamar's father, whom she never married, ended.

With a Peter Maurin she founded *The Catholic Worker* during the Depression. As its circulation and influence grew, Day began giving financial aid to the poor, and later started some farming communities. She worked for peace, and after World War II for an end to nuclear armaments, for civil rights, and for migrant workers and all oppressed and minority groups. Adhering to her Catholic faith, she was a remarkable woman with endless energy who believed that a good Catholic should always be actively concerned for human rights.

Church, Carol Bauer DOROTHY DAY: FRIEND OF THE POOR Illus. with photographs. Greenhaven, 1976. (grade 5 and up)

This biography captures much of the spirit of the woman and imparts information but, disappointingly, sometimes flows unevenly.

~~~~~~

GRAZIA DELEDDA
1875–1936

Italian author, winner of Nobel Prize for literature

By the time Nobel Prize–winner Grazia Deledda was ten years old her formal education had ended. Even though her father was the mayor of Nuoro, Sardinia, she received no more education than other girls of her town. Recognizing her intelligence, her father encouraged her to continue to read and learn on her own.

Her first story was published while she was a teenager and because it told of love and violence the townspeople greeted it and her with hostility. This did not deter Deledda, and by the time she was twenty she had a novel and many shorter works published. Her writing then and later was inspired by Sardinian peasants, traditions, and lifestyles. Despite numerous family tragedies, Grazia Deledda continued to write and publish as well as to correspond with leading authors, editors, critics, and journalists of the day.

After her marriage she moved to Rome, where in 1908 she opened the Congress of Italian Women and supported the suffragist movement. A very popular and highly acclaimed author, she wrote until the end of her life. She published 33 novels and 250 short stories. Grazia Deledda was nominated several times for a Nobel Prize, and in 1926 became the only Italian woman, and second of only six women, to win it for literature.

Balducci, Carolyn A SELF-MADE WOMAN: BIOGRAPHY OF NOBEL PRIZE WINNER GRAZIA DELEDDA Houghton Mifflin, 1975. (grade 9 and up)
Beautifully written prose captures the spirit of the gifted writer Grazia Deledda. Although the focus is on her own life, it is seen within the context of her large family and childhood in Sardinia, and the experiences of those close to her are given full attention. Her work itself is discussed briefly; this is not a critical biography but a personal one.

~~~~~~

AGNES De MILLE
1908–

Dancer, choreographer, director of Broadway musicals and ballets

Although Agnes De Mille was born into a distinguished theatrical family, she had to struggle to achieve success in the dance world. Her revolutionary use of American dance forms in her ballet *Rodeo* and her choreography of the musical *Oklahoma!* have directly influenced almost every musical produced since the 1940s. After those successes De Mille went on to choreograph *Bloomer Girl, Carousel, Brigadoon, Gentlemen Prefer Blondes*, and several other shows.

Agnes De Mille was the first woman to stage the book and dance of an entire Broadway musical. She has performed with her own dance company, choreographed films, given a series of dance lecture programs on television, and has worked to improve basic minimum salaries, and conditions for dancers.

Among the many honors bestowed on her are two Antoinette Perry (Tony) Awards and eleven honorary doctorate degrees. DeMille has also written eight books, some autobiographical and some textbooks for dancers.

De Mille, Agnes DANCE TO THE PIPER Illus. Little, 1952; Da Capo, 1980. (grade 9 and up)
————. AND PROMENADE HOME Illus. Little, 1956; Da Capo, 1980. (grade 9 and up)
Together these books form a good personal account of deMille's life and tell much about dancing as well as about other dancers. Of particular interest to those considering a career in the dance or theatre, they also have wide general appeal. These two books are also available in a single paper bound volume.

————. REPRIEVE: A MEMOIR Doubleday, 1981. (grade 9 and up)
Agnes De Mille has had a stroke in recent years; this absorbing, interesting book tells of her recovery.

~~~~~~

EMILY DICKINSON
1830–1886

American poet

Considered by many critics to be America's finest poet, Emily Dickinson spent most of her life in her parents' home in Amherst, Massachusetts. She attended Mt. Holyoke College for one year, but the strong evangelistic atmosphere proved too great an emotional strain for her.

Once thought rather social, she slowly withdrew from all contacts outside the family, and by the time she was in her thirties had become a veritable recluse. Few people knew she wrote poetry, and only a handful of her poems were published during her lifetime. She kept up extensive correspondence with some intellectuals who showed interest in her literary talents, but not until after her death and the discovery of 1,775 poems was the full extent of her poetic vision revealed. While her most recurrent themes are of death and faith, Dickinson can be appreciated by a wide audience for her concise, realistic style.

Barth, Edna I'M NOBODY! WHO ARE YOU? THE STORY OF EMILY DICKINSON   Illus. Seabury, 1971. (grades 3–7)
Very good, albeit brief, biography of Emily Dickinson includes thirty-five of her poems. Written for youngsters who may be too young to appreciate her poetry, the biography is quite readable and should act as a spur to understanding her work.

Longsworth, Polly   EMILY DICKINSON: HER LETTER TO THE WORLD Crowell, 1965. (grade 7 and up)
Outstanding biography is a sensitive, well-rounded portrayal of Emily Dickinson, and the people and places who helped influence her. Excerpts from her letters and poetry are judiciously combined with biography, resulting in a dramatic and moving narrative.

Wood, James Playsted   EMILY ELIZABETH DICKINSON: A PORTRAIT Nelson, 1972. (grade 7 and up)
Excellent biography is directed to serious, or more mature, students. Scholarly in its approach, it is also a warm personal portrait of the sensitive, brilliant poet.

~~~~~~

DOROTHEA LYNDE DIX
1802–1887

Reformer and crusader for the mentally ill,
superintendent of army nurses during the Civil War

Dorothea Dix's life-long crusade for better treatment of the mentally ill took her across the country and abroad investigating the cruelty and abuses to which the insane were subjected. Presenting powerful arguments and evidence of the shocking neglect she found, she convinced legislators and philanthropists to build humane hospitals where the insane would no longer be chained and confined to stalls and filth. She was directly responsible for the founding of thirty-two state mental hospitals, and she inspired countless others.

During the Civil War, Dorothea Dix was appointed superintendent of the United States Army nurses. After the war she resumed her work for the mentally ill.

Baker, Rachel ANGEL OF MERCY: STORY OF DOROTHEA LYNDE DIX
Messner, 1955. (grade 6 and up)

Outstanding, stirring, informal, fictionalized biography gives a warm, well-rounded portrait of the woman whose crusade for better treatment of the mentally ill had such a profound effect upon the world.

Malone, Mary DOROTHEA L. DIX: HOSPITAL FOUNDER Illus. Garrard, 1968. (grades 2–5)

Very good biography is readable, but lacks the spark displayed by the subject. Sympathetic and accurate, it is nevertheless somewhat dry.

~~~~~~

KATHERINE DUNHAM
1910–

Dancer, choreographer, and anthropologist

Katherine Dunham is generally considered the pioneer of black dance art for she combined dance, music, and anthropology to create an accurate and beautiful new dance form and has established highly acclaimed schools.

Despite financial and emotional hardships in her early years, she graduated from college and was awarded a fellowship for dance research in the Caribbean Islands. She employed anthropological methods to learn the island dances and songs, and also acquired some of the natives' unique musical instruments.

The influence of this study is seen in her dance form, and led to her great success as a performer and choreographer throughout the world.

Bienmiller, Ruth DANCE: THE STORY OF KATHERINE DUNHAM Illus. Doubleday, 1969. (grades 6–9)

Outstanding fast-moving, informal portrait will interest older readers as well as those for whom the reading level is intended.

Harnan, Terry   African Rhythm—American Dance: a biography of katherine dunham   Illus. Knopf, 1974. (grades 5–9)

Good, extremely objective, occasionally dry biography places great emphasis on Dunham's professional career, detailing her techniques and style as well as details of her personal life.

Haskins, James   Katherine Dunham   Illus. Putnam, 1982. (grade 6 and up)

Excellent, warm, and informative biography brings the subject to life.

~~~~~~

ABIGAIL SCOTT DUNIWAY
1834–1915

Suffragist and journalist

Seventeen-year-old Abigail Scott Duniway kept a daily journal of her family's trip west, a journey her mother feared. Her mother and her baby brother died on the trail. Duniway taught school, married, and had six children. Her life was harsh, and when her husband had a crippling accident, she opened a shop to support her family.

Encouraged by her husband, who favored women's suffrage, she started a newspaper, *The New Northwest*, which supported women's rights and suffrage. When Susan B. Anthony visited the area, Duniway joined her on a thousand-mile speaking tour. She later took the lecture stand herself for the next twenty-five years traveling the West to work for woman suffrage.

Finally, in 1912, Oregon, her own state, became the last to give women the vote. Duniway's efforts were recognized as she signed the proclamation jointly with the governor. She was the first woman in the state to register to vote.

Pathbreaking, her autobiography written in 1914, tells of some of her conflicts with the National Woman Suffrage Association, and her other experiences in forty-one years of working for the rights of western women.

Morrison, Dorothy Nafus   Ladies Were Not Expected: abigail scott duniway and women's rights   Illus. with photographs. Atheneum, 1977. (grades 4–8)

This excellent biography gives a very fine picture of women's role and lack of options in the West, as well as the life and work of this determined, dedicated leader.

~~~~~~

NATALIE DUNN
1956–

Roller-skating champion

Natalie Dunn was roller-skating from the time she could walk. When she was seven she entered her first competitive event. Her parents were skating teachers and gave her the opportunity to learn and excel, but it was her hard work and determination as well as talent and grace that earned her the top place in the women's world championship figure roller-skating event in 1976, 1977, and 1978.

Natalie Dunn was the National Tiny Tot Champion in 1964, and from then on there was no stopping her. Injuries forced her out of some events, but her own spirit and her family's devotion and enthusiasm kept her from giving up.

Although she no longer competes, Natalie Dunn is still very much involved with roller-skating. She teaches in Bakersville, California, and is now married.

Miklowitz, Gloria D. NATALIE DUNN: WORLD ROLLER SKATING CHAMPION   Illus. with photographs. Harcourt, 1979. (grade 4 and up)
   Very good nonadulatory biography will appeal to older readers as well, especially those who are interested in skating. Her success is seen as the result of hard work, motivation, and strong family support as well as talent.

~~~~~~

AMELIA EARHART
1898–1937

First woman to fly the Atlantic Ocean alone,
first person to fly solo between Hawaii and California

When pilot Amelia Earhart became the first woman to cross the Atlantic by air as a passenger and log-keeper, she became instantly famous. She continued to fly, and lectured and wrote about her experiences, always working towards her goals that women should have economic opportunities and independence.

Amelia Earhart became the first woman pilot to fly the Atlantic alone as well as the first person to fly solo between Hawaii and California and nonstop between Mexico City and Newark, New Jersey. For her achievements she was awarded the Distinguished Flying Cross, the Cross of the French Legion of Honor, the Harmon International Trophy, and other awards and cash prizes. Purdue University appointed her to their faculty to advise young women on careers in new fields.

In 1937 Amelia Earhart and her copilot set off on a flight around the world. The plane disappeared in the Pacific and neither the plane nor its occupants has ever been found. While many theories have been advanced to explain the disappearance, none has been proved. In a letter to her husband, opened after her disappearance, she wrote, ". . . women must try to do things as men have tried. When they fail, their failure must be but a challenge to others." Amelia Earhart's courage, independence, achievements, and personality did much to further interest in aviation and to liberate women from traditional roles.

Davis, Burke AMELIA EARHART Putnam, 1972. (grade 6 and up)
Very fine biography is a substantial account of the adult motives, goals, and achievements of the aviator. Moving and dramatic, it is an informative narrative.

Earhart, Amelia LAST FLIGHT ed. George Putnam. Harcourt, 1968 (reprint of 1937 edition). (grade 8 and up)
Fine personal narrative was edited and arranged by Amelia Earhart's husband from material she sent back or left by way of dispatches, letters, diaries, and charts. The writing reveals much of her personality and is of particular interest to those readers who are already acquainted with one of her biographies and now wish to read an account in the flier's own words.

Garst, Shannon AMELIA EARHART: HEROINE OF THE SKIES Messner, 1947. (grade 7 and up)
Absorbing, exciting, vivid biography of Amelia Earhart is told with plausible fictionalized dialogue. The subject is introduced as a warm, ambitious, and dynamic woman; her story is competently told.

Hazen, Barbara S. AMELIA'S FLYING MACHINE Illus. Doubleday, 1977. (grades 2–4)

Although based on real incidents in her life, this book is simply an easy-to-read "story" about Amelia Earhart. It reflects the personality of the aviator and can serve as a biography, but would be used best in conjunction with a more comprehensive biography.

Howe, Jane Moore AMELIA EARHART: KANSAS GIRL Illus. Bobbs-Merrill, 1950. (grades 3–7)
Despite its emphasis on her childhood, this excellent biography clearly reveals the freedom Amelia Earhart was allowed in defying the prevailing stereotyped sex roles and customs of the day. Only one chapter deals with her adult life, but her childhood is accurately and perceptively portrayed in an exciting, readable manner.

Mann, Peggy AMELIA EARHART: FIRST LADY OF FLIGHT Illus. Coward, 1970. (grades 5–8)
Exceptionally lively and exciting, immensely readable biography also has appeal for older readers than those for whom it is intended. Simply written, it is a stirring, colorful portrait of Amelia Earhart.

Morrissey, Muriel Earhart AMELIA EARHART Illus. Bellerophon, 1977. (grade 5 and up)
Abundantly illustrated book is excerpted from *Courage Is the Price*, a longer biography written by the pilot's younger sister. A straightforward account, it is sometimes stilted, but the facts are clearly stated, and Amelia Earhart's daring personality emerges.

Parlin, John AMELIA EARHART Dell, 1971. (grade 7 and up)
Vividly written, well-paced account of the life of the pioneer flier is dramatic, displaying clearly the color and excitement the subject showed in her life.

———. AMELIA EARHART: PIONEER IN THE SKY Illus. Garrard, 1962. (grades 2–5)
Excellent account of the life of the aviator is animatedly told, in depth yet with simplicity. Dramatic and inspiring, Earhart's efforts are shown to have challenged and helped other fliers, both men and women, to achieve greater successes.

Ziefau, Lilee AMELIA EARHART: LEADING LADY OF THE AIR AGE SamHar, 1972. (grades 7–10)
Brief, but very fine informative account of Amelia Earhart's life is told in a straightforward fashion, without resorting to fictionalization. Succinctly recreates all the known facts about her life in crisp, clear text.

GEORGE ELIOT
1819–1880

British novelist

Novelist George Eliot, who was recognized, even in her own time, as a writer of genius, chose a masculine pen name in order to be judged by tough literary standards rather than treated lightly as a woman writer.

Mary Ann Evans, as she was known in her personal life, was a brilliant student, whose facility with languages led to her great success as a translator. Although she was self-supporting and aided her widowed sister's six children, Evans's family considered her a failure for not marrying.

When she and George Henry Lewes, a philosopher and literary critic, met and fell in love they decided to live as husband and wife even though he was still married to a woman who had deserted him. With his encouragement, she began writing novels, and even those who criticized her way of life appreciated her enormous literary talent. *The Mill on the Floss*, one of her most famous novels, is based on her own life. Many of her other works, including *Adam Bede, Silas Marner,* and *Romola,* continue to be read and admired.

Vipont, Elfrida Towards a High Attic: the early life of george eliot Illus. Holt, 1971. (grade 7 and up)
  Very fine biography focuses on her earlier years but also discusses her novels and her life after she began writing them. A balanced, smoothly written biography, it gives an intimate and moving picture of the brilliant author.

QUEEN ELIZABETH I
1533–1603

Queen of England, 1558–1603

When Elizabeth Tudor ascended the British throne in 1558 she faced a nation with a dwindling treasury and a people torn by religious fears. Relying on her own intelligence and skillful leadership, as well as a wise selection of advisors, she used diplomacy rather than military might to keep England at peace and to maintain the European balance of power.

By founding the Church of England, Protestant Elizabeth I put an end to the age of persecutions of both Catholics and Protestants. She established colonies in America and other parts of the world, and built the British Navy to new and greater strengths. The defeat of the once mighty Spanish Armada during her reign clearly demonstrated the naval supremacy England had achieved.

Elizabeth's reign is further noted as a time of great contributions to the literary world. Among the English poets of the age, Ben Jonson, Christopher Marlowe, and of course William Shakespeare are outstanding.

Elizabeth chose never to marry, and during her forty-four–year reign remained popular with her subjects, making England a powerful and prosperous nation.

Bigland, Eileen QUEEN ELIZABETH I Criterion, 1965. (grade 7 and up)
Very good, well-balanced account of Elizabeth's life assumes a certain knowledge of British history. Without this background the reader may have difficulty in following the biography.

Hanff, Helene QUEEN OF ENGLAND: THE STORY OF ELIZABETH THE FIRST Illus. Doubleday, 1969. (grades 6–8)
Excellent biography is a good treatment for young or uninformed readers, for its clear, easy-to-understand narrative gives a good background on the Elizabethan era as well as portraying the queen as a strong, independent, and intelligent woman.

Jenkins, Elizabeth ELIZABETH THE GREAT Illus. Coward, 1959. (grade 9 and up)
An outstanding, soundly researched, well-documented biography of the queen which depicts her accurately with vigor and sensitivity. A fairly complete survey of her long life, this book is suitable for casual readers as well as serious students of history.

Kendall, Alan ELIZABETH I Illus. with photographs. St. Martin's, 1975. (grade 6 and up)
Invitingly arranged, this book provides useful background reading for history and reference for those with a special interest in Queen Elizabeth.

Peach, L. Du Garde THE FIRST QUEEN ELIZABETH Illus. Ladybird, 1958. (grades 4–8)

A small, colorfully illustrated informative and well-written biography of Queen Elizabeth gives a good, factual picture of the times and of her life.

Zamoyska, Betka   QUEEN ELIZABETH I   Illus. McGraw, 1981. (grades 4–8)

Attractive, very fine, straightforward account of the monarch and her times is readable and useful.

∿∿∿

CHRIS EVERT
1954–

Tennis champion

Chris Evert won her first tennis tournament when she was eight years old, and by the time she was twenty she was ranked first in the United States. Noted for her two-handed backhand, classic forehand, intense concentration, and great poise, she quickly became one of the biggest attractions in tennis.

When Chris Evert was only sixteen, she won forty-six consecutive matches against some of the leading players in the world and was a member of the United States Wightman Cup Team. That same year she reached the semifinals at Forest Hills and came in second for the Associated Press Female Athlete of the Year award. The following year, after she helped the United States win the Wightman Cup from Great Britain, the press covering the matches chose her the most valuable player.

Chris Evert turned professional on her eighteenth birthday. She was the first player in women's tennis to reach one million dollars in tournament earnings and is one of only three women to win the United States Open six times.

Since 1975 she has been ranked number one or two each year. In 1982 she won the U.S. Open and was a finalist at Wimbledon. In 1983 she was a finalist in the United States Open, losing the championship to Martina Navratilova.

In 1979 she married the British tennis player, John Lloyd, and although she is best known as Chris Evert, she uses her full name.

Burchard, S. H. CHRIS EVERT Illus. with photographs. Harcourt, 1976. (grades 3–6)

Easy-to-read, lively biography is further enchanced with many photographs of Evert in action and with her family.

Hahn, James, and Hahn, Lynn CHRIS! THE SPORTS CAREER OF CHRIS EVERT LLOYD Illus. with photographs. Crestwood, 1981. (grade 3 and up)

Easy-to-read biography will appeal to older reluctant readers as well as younger ones. Focus of the biography is on the specifics of her tennis career.

Haney, Lynn CHRIS EVERT: THE YOUNG CHAMPION Illus. with photographs. Putnam, 1976. (grades 5–9)

A good picture of Evert which also tells a great deal about other women tennis players. The sport itself is well described.

Phillips, Betty Lou CHRIS EVERT: FIRST LADY OF TENNIS Illus. with photographs. Messner, 1977. (grades 4–8)

Informal but not overly fictionalized biography employs conversation to reveal incidents in Evert's life. The author maintains a good balance between the private and public lives.

Sabin, Francene SET POINT: THE STORY OF CHRIS EVERT Illus. with photographs. Putnam, 1977. (grade 5 and up)

Informal biography is excellent. Her family and religious background and the focus on her training and career and her impact on tennis can serve as an inspiration and role model for other young women.

Schmitz, Dorothy Childers CHRIS EVERT: WOMEN'S TENNIS CHAMPION Illus. with photographs. Crestwood, 1977. (grade 3 and up)

This is an excellent read-aloud biography for younger children who enjoy watching tennis, for beginning-to-read youngsters, and for older readers with limited reading ability.

Smith, Jay H. CHRIS EVERT Illus. Creative Educ. Soc., 1975. (grades 3–7)

Attractive and colorfully illustrated with many action pictures, this text is a fast-paced, well-balanced portrait of the tennis star. Her techniques and personality are revealed and several of her important matches are excitingly described. Young tennis enthusiasts will find it interesting, and older, less able readers will find it easy to read, but unfortunately it is not current.

DOROTHY CANFIELD FISHER
1879–1958

Author

Dorothy Canfield Fisher's parents offered her every educational opportunity, and at a time when higher education for women was still a rarity, she earned a doctorate in literature. She was such a successful author of articles, short stories, and novels for children and adults that much of her work is still widely read. *Understood Betsy*, a novel for children, remains as popular today as when it was written.

She and her husband had a most unusual working partnership. He gave up his own writing ambitions to serve as her editor, critic, and business manager. He also made the children's clothes, tended the garden, and did much of the housework. Dorothy Fisher's prodigious writings are a testimonial not only to her talent and ambition but also to the fact that she was free to devote all her time to her work.

When the Book-of-the-Month Club was formed, Dorothy Canfield Fisher became one of the first judges, and was instrumental in introducing new and established authors to the general public.

Yates, Elizabeth LADY FROM VERMONT: DOROTHY CANFIELD FISHER'S LIFE AND WORLD (rev. ed. Original title, PEBBLE IN A POOL, now out of print but available.) Illus. Greene, 1971. (grade 8 and up)
    Vividly written biography of the prolific author gives a good picture of the life of an educated woman who was able to realize her potential. As well as being a colorful biography, it provides interesting glimpses of city and country life in the early part of the century.

~~~~~~

ALICE FITZGERALD
1874–1962

Nurse, teacher, and advisor in public health

Nursing was still not widely accepted as a respectable profession when Alice Fitzgerald announced to her wealthy, socialite family that she planned to become a nurse. She became an excellent student, a fine nurse, and an outstanding administrator and teacher. During World War I she travelled throughout Europe organizing hospitals, and served as chief nurse for the American Red Cross. Her work with the Public Health Nursing Service helped establish nursing schools in the Philippines and in the Far East.

She received honors, decorations, and medals from many countries, but with great humility announced that it was the nursing profession, more than herself, that had been so honored. When Alice Fitzgerald retired, at the age of seventy-four, she sent all the medals and decorations to her former school, Johns Hopkins School of Nursing.

Noble, Iris NURSE AROUND THE WORLD: ALICE FITZGERALD Messner, 1964. (grade 7 and up)
Dramatic, inspiring profile of Fitzgerald is also the story of the nursing profession in its early days. Judicious use of dialogue adds warmth and reality, making this an unusually absorbing biography.

~~~~~~

ROBERTA FLACK
1940–

Grammy Award–winning singer, musician, composer

Roberta Flack's intellectual abilities were recognized early by her teachers, and when she was only fifteen she won a scholarship to Howard University. She became a teacher, and although she had been schooled in classical music, decided, in 1967, to begin a career in popular music.

After some success in a nightclub, she began recording, and within a few years had several successful albums, best-selling single records, two Grammy Awards, and was immensely successful as a concert performer. In 1971 she was named by *Downbeat* magazine as Female Vocalist of the Year.

She often accompanies herself on the piano; two of her most popular recordings, "The First Time Ever I Saw Your Face" and

"Killing Me Softly with His Song," both won her several awards. She has had her own television specials, composed music for herself and others, and owns two music publishing firms.

Roberta Flack, who is black, does not consider herself a soul singer, stating "there is no color in music." Her taste in music is varied, for she sings pop, blues, jazz, rock, spirituals, and European as well as American folk songs.

Jacobs, Linda ROBERTA FLACK: SOUND OF VELVET MELTING Illus. EMC, 1975. (grade 4 and up)

Though occasionally gushy, a good portrait of the singer which clearly shows her intelligence and commitment to her work. An equal emphasis on her personal and professional life shows their interrelatedness. Will be of special interest to reluctant readers.

Morse, Charles, and Morse, Ann ROBERTA FLACK Illus. Creative Educ. Soc., 1975. (grades 4–8)

Colorfully illustrated, occasionally glib biography is written in the colloquium of musical journalism. Based on interviews she has given to major newspapers and magazines, it constitutes good reporting and moves along quickly. Fans of the star, as well as other readers, will find it interesting.

~~~~~~

PEGGY FLEMING
1948–

Olympic gold medal–winning skater

Peggy Fleming began ice skating when she was nine years old and at age twelve won her first major competition. In the next few years she won five consecutive United States National Championship titles, three consecutive International Figure Skating titles, and, in 1968, was the only American to win an Olympic gold medal.

Peggy Fleming's skating style has been frequently likened to the ballet, for she is not only a superb athlete but magnificently graceful. In her free skating routines she dazzled judges and audiences alike.

After turning professional in 1968, Fleming appeared on her own television special and has skated as a guest star with the Ice Follies.

In 1975 she was inducted into the Skating Hall of Fame, the youngest skater ever to be so honored. In 1970 she married a physician, and she is now a mother.

Morse, Charles, and Morse, Ann   PEGGY FLEMING   Illus. Creative Educ. Soc., 1974. (grades 4–8)

Fast-moving, attractively illustrated biography of the skating star also explains clearly and understandably the elements of skating that are considered in the competitive scoring. Fleming's talent and ambition are well portrayed in this account.

Van Steenwyck, Elizabeth   PEGGY FLEMING: CAMEO OF A CHAMPION   Illus. with photographs. McGraw, 1978. (grades 4–8)

Fast-moving biography is somewhat fictionalized, but the use of conversation is done judiciously, and this results in a very readable, enjoyable biography which will appeal to those not especially interested in skating, as well as those who are.

JANE FONDA
1937–

Actress, writer, social activist

Jane Fonda is one of the best known people in the United States today for her work in three areas: show business, social reform, and publishing.

She has starred in several films, including *They Shoot Horses Don't They?*, *Klute*, *Coming Home*, *The China Syndrome*, *On Golden Pond* and many others. She has won the Academy Award, The Golden Globe Award and the New York Film Critics Award. She is a tireless worker for peace and nuclear disarmament and other social causes. Her books on exercise and fitness are best sellers.

Jane Fonda and her brother Peter are the children of the late actor Henry Fonda and they both have described their unhappy childhoods despite economic advantages. Although her relationship with her father was strained for many years, they demonstrated devotion to each other in his last years and costarred in *On Golden Pond*.

Jane Fonda is married to Tom Hayden, and she has two children.

Fox, Mary Virginia, and Weston, Paul JANE FONDA: SOMETHING TO FIGHT FOR Illus. Dillon, 1980. (grades 3–7)

Written at a reading level of third grade, this is an excellent book for older, less able or slow readers. Some younger readers may find the numerous details of her life confusing but older readers will find it very interesting and inspiring. The book sensitively deals with her unhappy childhood, family relationships, and later political role.

~~~~~~

BETTY FORD
1918–

First Lady

Betty Ford (Elizabeth Bloomer Ford) consistently emerges as one of the most respected and best-liked first ladies of all time.

Before her marriage to Gerald Ford in Grand Rapids, Michigan, she was a dancer. They later lived near Washington, while Jerry Ford served in Congress for twenty-five years.

Long separations necessitated by her husband's career meant that Betty Ford had almost sole responsibility for raising their four children. Although she would have preferred that her husband not seek higher office, he was chosen to replace Spiro T. Agnew when Agnew resigned as vice-president. In 1974, President Richard Nixon resigned because of the Watergate scandals, and Gerald Ford succeeded him as president of the United States.

Betty Ford then became first lady and immediately made plans for the national programs and projects which she would lead. However, only two months after assuming this role, she was diagnosed as having breast cancer. Surgery, followed by chemotherapy, achieved excellent results. The immense pressure of her activities for mental health, cancer research, and the arts; her support of the Equal Rights Amendment; and, in 1976, a vigorous reelection campaign, combined with the effort of coping with arthritic pain and discomfort from cancer treatment, contributed to her abuse of drugs and alcohol.

With characteristic intelligence and candor, Betty Ford admitted her problems, sought help, and today remains active in many important, worthwhile programs. She feels strongly that physicians should be careful not to prescribe medication to solve people's emotional problems. She is a true first lady in the minds and hearts of those who have long admired her.

Ford, Betty, with Case, Chris THE TIMES OF MY LIFE Illus. with photographs. Harper, 1978. (grade 9 and up)
A serious but highly readable book written in a lively style. It traces her life from early days in Grand Rapids through marriage, White House days, campaigns, working for the Equal Rights Amendment, 1976 presidential loss, and her hospitalization at the Long Beach Hospital alcohol and drug rehabilitation program in California, where she went for treatment of her dependency on drugs and alcohol.

~~~~~~

CHARLOTTE FORTEN
1838–1904

Teacher, author, and abolitionist

Charlotte Forten's wealthy, free black Philadelphia family was active in the antislavery movement and encouraged and appreciated her intellectual abilities. Her appointment as a teacher in Salem, Massachusetts, made her the first black teacher of white children.

Her abolitionist and educational activities led her to volunteer during the Civil War as a teacher in an experimental school for freed slaves in Port Royal, on the Sea Islands off South Carolina. After the war Charlotte Forten did some teaching, published articles, translated a book from the French, and held a position in the federal Treasury Department. She married Francis Grimké, a prominent pastor who was the son of a South Carolina planter and a slave woman and the nephew of the influential abolitionists and feminists Angelina and Sarah Grimké (page 99).

Charlotte Forten's *Journal*, a record of her life and an important addition to the history of slavery and abolition, was published after her death.

Douty, Esther CHARLOTTE FORTEN: FREE BLACK TEACHER Garrard, 1971. (grades 4–7)

Very fine biography offers a dramatic, sensitive portrayal of Charlotte Forten as well as recreating the period. Especially useful for youngsters studying the Civil War period, this is an absorbing, moving narrative.

Longsworth, Polly   I, CHARLOTTE FORTEN, BLACK AND FREE   Crowell, 1970. (grades 5–9)

Excellent biography of the abolitionist, teacher, and author is based on her own *Journal*, and is written as though it were an autobiography. As biography it is unusually compelling, and its value is increased by the inclusion of much material on women's rights, other black leaders, and abolitionists. Limited to the years between 1854 and 1864, as was Forten's *Journal*, this book has an epilogue which succinctly summarizes events and experiences after those years and a good bibliography provides readers with information on how to learn more about the period and people discussed.

~~~~~~

ABIGAIL KELLEY FOSTER
1810–1887

Abolitionist, women's rights lecturer

Reared as a Quaker, Abigail Kelley Foster later rejected her religion because it did not support her strong antislavery beliefs.

She participated in the first women's antislavery convention, then gave up her job as a school teacher to devote herself completely to this cause. She travelled, often without proper "chaperones," and lectured before public audiences of both men *and* women and, as a result, was subjected to severe critical abuse.

Abigail Kelley organized antislave societies, rallies, and fairs, and influenced many other women such as Susan B. Anthony (page 13) and Lucy Stone (page 231) to become active feminists and abolitionists. Many women learned their debating techniques from her.

After her marriage to Stephen Symonds Foster, she often toured and lectured with him and at one time refused to pay taxes on their farm, on the grounds that she was being taxed without representation.

Bacon, Margaret Hope I SPEAK FOR MY SLAVE SISTER: THE LIFE OF ABBY KELLEY FOSTER Illus. Crowell, 1974. (grades 5–9)

Carefully researched and documented biography gives, with warmth and drama, an unvarnished picture of the abolitionist and feminist. Combining biography with a good picture of the period in which she lived, this is an intelligent, well-written portrait.

~~~~~~

ANNE FRANK
1929–1945

World War II heroine, author

During World War II, from the time she was thirteen until she was fifteen, Anne Frank, an intelligent, gifted young Jewish girl, and her family hid from the Nazis. Crowded into an attic in Holland, isolated from the outside world, young Anne courageously matured from childhood to adolescence. The family was eventually captured by the Germans, and Anne died in a concentration camp.

After the war her father returned to the attic that had sheltered them and discovered, in its hiding place, the diary Anne had secretly kept. He allowed it to be published; it was translated into many languages, and was turned into a successful play and movie. Anne Frank's name has been given to villages and schools in Europe, and through her moving diary, she has become a symbol of the suffering inflicted by the Nazis.

Frank, Anne ANNE FRANK: DIARY OF A YOUNG GIRL Doubleday, 1952, 1967. (grade 6 and up)

Touching, intimate view is offered in the now classic diary by young Anne Frank. It is a dramatic, emotional book that reveals the way a highly intelligent youngster gains courage and insights when placed in a most unusual situation.

Schnabel, Ernst ANNE FRANK: A PORTRAIT IN COURAGE Illus. Harcourt, 1967. (grade 9 and up)

Very good, somewhat interesting portrait of Anne Frank is less emotional and dramatic than her own diary. Based on interviews with many people who knew Anne, it provides a valuable supplement to the diary, revealing much additional information.

Steenmeijer, Anna G., ed. A Tribute to Anne Frank   Illus. Double-day, 1970. (grade 7 and up)

Truly magnificent volume makes use of color and black-and-white photographs, documents, and previously unpublished material about and by Anne Frank to reveal not only the many dimensions of the young Nazi victim but the effect she has had on the post–World War II world. The beautiful book is really an anthology composed of introductory material, historical background, excerpts from the *Diary*, discussions of it and of Anne Frank herself, and excerpts from the prefaces to English and foreign editions. Included too is poetry written by youngsters and adults in reaction to the *Diary*, and a discussion of its influence on German, Israeli, and American children today. There are many photographs of Anne Frank, of busts, medallions, and other works of art of her, as well as photographs from the plays and the film of the *Diary*. This is an outstanding tribute.

~~~~~~

ARETHA FRANKLIN
1942–

Grammy Award–winning gospel and soul singer

The "queen of soul" or "lady soul," as Aretha Franklin is often called, began singing at local churches when she was only eight years old.

She had a lonely childhood for her mother left her and later died, and her father, a well-known prosperous minister, was often busy and away. However, their home was a mecca for some of the best black blues, gospel, and jazz musicians, and when Aretha was only a young teenager she was travelling and singing in gospel concerts. It was on these tours that she became acutely aware of racial discrimination, for although they could have afforded choice hotels and restaurants, they were often barred from them.

Aretha Franklin was well known to soul and gospel fans for a long time before winning five gold records in 1968. She has been chosen female vocalist of the year by leading magazines, has won Grammy Awards, and has starred in her own television specials. She often accompanies herself on the piano.

In addition to performing commercially, Aretha Franklin gives many benefits, has her own talent company with a number of musical performers under contract, and with her sister started her own record company. She is considered by many critics to be one of the finest classic soul singers.

Olsen, James T. ARETHA FRANKLIN   Illus. Creative Educ. Soc., 1975. (grades 4–8)
  Vividly designed and illustrated biography of the successful singer shows her to be a sensitive, talented, and ambitious performer. Written in an easy-going and competent journalistic style, it is fast-moving with appeal for reluctant readers as well as all young fans of Aretha Franklin.

~~~~~~

ROSALIND FRANKLIN
1920–1958

Research scientist

Rosalind Franklin is recognized today as one of the four scientists whose work made possible the discovery of DNA.
  Born in Great Britain of an eminent Jewish family, she early demonstrated interest in science and earned a doctorate from Cambridge. In 1951 she became a researcher at Kings College, London. She worked with Maurice Wilkins on DNA, and her x-ray photographs of the molecular structure of DNA were the major clue in unravelling and understanding the double helix.
  In 1962 the Nobel Prize for Medicine was awarded to British scientists Francis Crick and Maurice Wilkins and to American scientist James Watson. Franklin's contribution was noted, but her death from cancer four years earlier made her ineligible for the award.
  Six years later James Watson's best-seller *The Double Helix* was published, and in it a vaguely disguised Rosalind Franklin was so negatively pictured as to completely minimize her contribution.
  Many scientists today feel that the male-dominated field resented Rosalind Franklin, a precise and careful researcher, and that she never received full acknowledgment for her work.

Sayre, Ann Rosalind Franklin and DNA Norton, 1975. (grade 9 and up)

Extremely well-written, interesting book is a fine biography of Rosalind Franklin as well as a thoughtful protest against the mistreatment of women in science and the discouraging attitudes of others towards young women contemplating such a career. This book reflects attitudes still prevalent, but now, fortunately, fading.

~~~~~~

JANE FREDERICK
1952–

Pentathlon champion

Jane Frederick's athletic family was not surprised when she was voted the most athletic girl in junior high school. When she was thirteen she was good at so many events her coach suggested she compete in the pentathlon (five different events consisting of hurdles, shot put, high jump, long jump, and two hundred–meter run).

She began competing in local AAU meets as a youngster and is now considered by many to be one of the finest all-around athletes in the world—nothing tests strength, speed, and endurance as much as the combination of running, jumping and throwing which is required of a pentathlon champion.

The winner of national and world medals, Jane Frederick would have been a competitor at the 1980 Olympics, but the U.S. boycotted those games. She hopes to compete in Los Angeles in 1984.

She is a woman of varied interests, and is talented in several areas of art. In college she had a special interest in comparative literature.

Emert, Phyllis Raybin Jane Frederick: pentathlon champion Illus. with photographs. Harvey, 1981. (grade 4 and up)

A good lively biography that interestingly describes the skills needed for the pentathlon and tells the very human story of Jane Frederick. Easy to read, the book will be especially suitable for older, less competent readers who are sports fans, but other readers will also enjoy this biography.

ELIZABETH "MUMBET" FREEMAN
1744–1829

First slave to win freedom in courts
of Massachusetts

"Mumbet" Freeman was born a slave and remained one until, at thirty-seven, she became the first slave to achieve freedom in the courts of the state of Massachusetts. She then worked for a judge and his family, taking over the duties of an ill mother.

Her courage and wit saved the household when, during Shays's Rebellion, they were threatened with attack. Although Mumbet never learned to read or write, her intelligence and resourcefulness contributed to the support and education of grandchildren and great-grandchildren.

Mumbet Freeman was known and loved throughout her community, and when she died, the youngest of the grown children she had cared for composed the words on her tombstone. Although she was mourned by the family who loved her, she was not buried with them, but instead in the section of the cemetery reserved for blacks.

Felton, Harold W. MUMBET: THE STORY OF ELIZABETH FREEMAN Illus. Dodd, 1970. (grades 3–7)

Compelling, fictionalized account of a little-known former slave provides an intimate, realistic glimpse into the life of a remarkable woman. Simply and briefly told, it is dramatic and exciting, and offers a good and accurate picture of the times. Despite a paucity of information available about Mumbet Freeman, the author has consulted all available sources, and cites them in the introduction.

ELIZABETH FRY
1780–1845

English prison reformer

Marriage and ten children didn't prevent Quaker-born Elizabeth Fry from becoming a preacher and visiting London's Newgate

Prison, where she was horrified at the dreadful conditions of the prisoners. She organized the Association for the Improvement of Female Prisoners, which recommended that some level of decency should be afforded prisoners, and that they should be separated according to sex and seriousness of crime, and she worked to establish education and employment programs. She began schools for the children of prisoners, and advocated improvement of the department procedures of prisoners to Australia.

Elizabeth Fry also visited institutions all over Britain and Europe, and through her efforts major reforms in prisons finally occurred.

Johnson, Spencer THE VALUE OF KINDNESS: THE STORY OF ELIZABETH FRY Illus. Value Communications, 1976. (grades K–3)

Highly fictionalized picture book conveys Elizabeth Fry's accomplishments but is at times overly admiring and occasionally gushy. The text is followed by a one-page factual profile suitable for older readers and adults.

Peach, L. Du Garde ELIZABETH FRY Illus. Ladybird, 1973. (grades 3–7)

Very good, well-balanced account of the life of the prison reformer and of the conditions that prevailed in the prisons and the attitudes of the time.

~~~~~~

MARGARET FULLER
1810–1850

Author, critic, feminist

Margaret Fuller's father, a prominent Massachusetts attorney, was disappointed that his firstborn was a girl, so he proceeded to educate her in the classical fashion usually reserved for boys. She was a brilliant student, and by the time she was seven she could read English and Latin better than most men. Her education proceeded in an orderly but severe and intellectually taxing manner. This "unnatural childhood," as she later described it, led to emotional and social deprivation and probably explained her temperament, but it certainly helped to produce one of the greatest minds, male or female, of the day.

For a time she took over the responsibility of educating the younger children in the family and supervising the household. She taught school, wrote critical essays and became editor of the transcendentalist journal *Dial*. She held "conversations," gatherings of women who wished to become better educated. Wives of famous men, as well as feminists like Elizabeth and Sophie Peabody and Elizabeth Cady Stanton, attended. In 1845 she wrote *Women in the Nineteenth Century*, which became a major influence on the Seneca Falls conference on women's rights in 1848.

Margaret Fuller associated closely with prominent intellectuals including Ralph Waldo Emerson. Horace Greeley sent her to Europe as a journalist for the New York *Tribune*. There she met with William Wordsworth, George Sand, Frederic Chopin, Robert and Elizabeth Barrett Browning and others, all of whom were already familiar with her writings.

In Italy she met a young nobleman, the Marchese d'Ossoli. They married and had a son. She participated in the Italian revolution and was working on a history of it when they decided to return to America. Just before reaching shore, the ship was caught in a storm. Margaret Fuller, her husband, and child drowned, and her manuscript was lost.

Chevigny, Bell Gale THE WOMAN AND THE MYTH: MARGARET FULLER'S LIFE AND WRITINGS Feminist Press, 1976. (grade 9 and up)

As the title indicates, this is both biography and excerpts from her works. It also includes material her contemporaries wrote to and about her. Scholarly and substantial, this adult book will be of use and interest to many high school students.

Slater, Abby IN SEARCH OF MARGARET FULLER Delacorte, 1978. (grade 9 and up)

A good biography in which Margaret Fuller emerges as an intellectual and important figure in the nineteenth century. It is sympathetically written, but her erratic personality is candidly revealed.

Wilson, Ellen MARGARET FULLER: BLUESTOCKING, ROMANTIC, REVOLUTIONARY Illus. Farrar, 1977. (grade 7 and up)

An accurate, well-documented and researched biography of the feminist is smoothly written and highly readable.

WANDA GÁG
1893–1946

Artist and author of children's books

Wanda Gág, author and illustrator best known for her much loved
picture books—*Millions of Cats, The Funny Thing, Snippy and
Snappy, The A B C Bunny, Gone Is Gone,* and *Nothing at All*—grew
up in Minnesota where her artistic talents were noticed early. Her
father died when she was fifteen and her mother was ill, so she
became the head of the family. She sold drawings to newspapers,
painted and sold greeting cards, and gave art lessons to children
while simultaneously attending high school, caring for her five
sisters and one brother, and running the household.

After high school she won numerous art scholarships in Minnesota and then went to New York to attend the Art Students League.
There she worked as a commercial artist but it was her drawings,
woodcuts, and lithographs which were featured in shows and won
her several awards.

Wanda Gág had been a popular storyteller to the children of her
many friends, and when she turned this talent into the writing and
illustrating of children's books she met with great success. Her
books have a folk-like simplicity that have endeared themselves to
generations of children and continue to be enormously popular.

Duin, Nancy E. WANDA GÁG: AUTHOR AND ILLUSTRATOR OF CHILDREN'S
BOOKS SamHar, 1972. (grade 7 and up)
Unusually fine, warm, straightforward biography of the artist-author-
illustrator is short but captures her personality and character as well as
detailing her professional career.

INDIRA GANDHI
1917–

Prime minister of India

Indira Gandhi, the prime minister of India, came from a wealthy family dedicated to achieving the independence of India. Her father, Jawaharal Nehru, became the first prime minister of India and her aunt was Vijaha Pandit (page 180), the diplomat and ambassador.

Though education for women was a rarity in India, Indira was educated both at Oxford and in India, and from her earliest youth her intellectual abilities were encouraged by her father. She always remained close to him and when he was prime minister they travelled together on official missions throughout the world. Her skills in dealing with political and economic situations were put to good use at home and on many trips of her own. She was the third member of the Nehru family to serve as president of the India National Congress, and also served as minister of information and broadcasting. She was elected prime minister in 1966.

One of only a few women elected as a head of state, she has worked long and hard to further modernize India, to increase foreign trade, to urge women to go into professions, and to play an important role in India's affairs.

Church, Carol Bauer   INDIRA GANDHI: ROSE OF INDIA   Illus. with photographs. Greenhaven, 1976. (grade 3 and up)
A very fine biography which maintains a good balance between her political and personal self, and gives a good picture of the time and place.

Garnett, Emmeline   MADAME PRIME MINISTER: THE STORY OF INDIRA GANDHI   Illus. Farrar, 1967. (grade 7 and up)
Very fine portrait of Indira Gandhi also provides a good account of the struggle for independence in India, as well as substantial information on the entire Nehru family. Nontheless, it is her story, and it is told with warmth, understanding, and admiration resulting in good biography as well as history, past and current.

Wilcoxen, Harriet   FIRST LADY OF INDIA: THE STORY OF INDIRA GANDHI   Illus. Doubleday, 1969. (grades 4–7)
Very clear, easy-to-understand biography of Indira Gandhi also discusses India's independence. Concise, but fairly comprehensive, the biography is an inspiring narrative for young or less competent readers who are unacquainted with India's story.

~~~~~~

ALTHEA GIBSON
1927–

Championship tennis player, professional golfer

Being born in South Carolina to poor black sharecroppers and growing up in the slums of New York's Harlem helped make Althea Gibson a tough fighter. Determined to find a way out of the misery that surrounded her, she started to play paddle tennis on a local street. At age twelve she won the New York paddle tennis championship. Seeing her potential as a tennis player, a wealthy southern black doctor offered her free tennis lessons and sponsored her general education.

After winning all the black tennis championships, Althea Gibson faced a difficult struggle to become the first black tennis player to break the color line and to play at Forest Hills. She then toured for the State Department, played in numerous biracial tournaments, and became a top-ranking international player.

In 1957 and again in 1958 Althea Gibson won the Wimbledon and United States nationals. After retiring from competitive amateur tennis, Gibson became a nightclub singer, and then a professional golfer.

She has served as New Jersey state athletic commissioner and has also been active in government.

Gibson, Althea I ALWAYS WANTED TO BE SOMEBODY   Harper, 1958. (grade 9 and up)

Despite a warm reception at its publication, this does not meet good literary standards. Furthermore, since it was written before the civil rights movement and heightened black consciousness, much of the biography is out of tune with today's sentiments and probably no longer reflects Gibson's own beliefs. However, it does provide a good picture of the tennis star's rise to fame, and clearly shows her struggles.

Gibson, Althea, and Curtis, Richard So MUCH TO LIVE FOR   Putnam, 1968. (grade 7 and up)

Intimate story of Althea Gibson's career is directed not only to the athletically oriented reader but to anyone interested in warm, dramatic biography. Well-written, it is immensely readable, colorful, and dramatic.

~~~~~~

EMMA GOLDMAN
1869–1940

Anarchist, lecturer, feminist, and
early advocate of birth control

Emma Goldman, cruelly oppressed by her family and school, also suffered the intense anti-Semitism of czarist Russia. In Saint Petersburg, university students introduced her to radical ideas and she emigrated to the United States. Here she was disillusioned to note the exploitation of factory workers and was drawn to the anarchist movement. She embraced some of the violence the theorists espoused, but later rejected it as a necessary accompaniment to reform. Emma Goldman directed her public speaking and writing talents in support of birth control, antidraft measures, peace, and freedom of lifestyles for women. For many years she was an editor of the radical magazine *Mother Earth*.

During the "red scare" of 1917, her advocacy of civil rights and liberties was seen by the United States government as dangerously subversive and "Red Emma," as she was called, was deprived of citizenship and deported to Russia.

Disillusioned by the totalitarianism of postrevolutionary Russia, Emma Goldman left to write, lecture, and travel in Sweden, Germany, England, and Canada. She published her autobiography, *Living My Life*, and actively supported the Spanish Civil War.

Shulman, Alix To the Barricades: the anarchist life of emma goldman   Crowell, 1971. (grades 6–10)
Superb feminist portrayal skillfully incorporates a good introduction to radicalism and anarchism. Few finer biographies of women exist for this age group, for it is sympathetic, yet objective and thoroughly researched but without scholarly pretensions. The author also relates Emma Goldman's life and work to the contemporary scene, increasing the value of the book for casual readers as well as students of history.

~~~~~~

JANE GOODALL
1934–

English ethnologist (animal behaviorist)

From early childhood, English-born Jane Goodall was interested in observing animals in their natural surroundings. When she was twenty-three she travelled to Kenya, Africa where she obtained a job as secretary to the famed anthropologists Louis and Mary Leakey. They encouraged her to travel to the Gombe Stream Reserve in Tanzania where she studied the daily life of chimpanzees, actually living with them. She was the first person to undertake a long-term study of chimpanzees and she was able to demonstrate that, contrary to previous beliefs, they are able to communicate with each other through gestures, sounds, and facial expressions and to actively hunt meat and use tools. Her work has implications for anthropologists as well as students of primate behavior.

Although Jane Goodall never went to college, she was admitted to Cambridge University where she earned her doctorate in ethnology. Her son, "Grub," born in 1967, spent much of his childhood on safari with her. In 1970 she wrote *In the Shadow of Man* with Baron Hugo van Lawwick, her husband, which helped bring her work to the attention of the general public. Today she is one of the best-known scientists in the world.

Coerr, Eleanor B. JANE GOODALL Illus. Putnam, 1976. (grades K–4)

An excellent read-aloud or early reading book which moves quickly and captures her work and shows her strong commitment and motivation.

Fox, Mary Virginia. JANE GOODALL: LIVING CHIMP STYLE Illus. Dillon, 1981. (grade 3 and up)

An excellent biography which will be enjoyed by older, less able readers as well as younger ones. Nonfictionalized narrative moves quickly and conveys the details of Goodall's life and work.

EVONNE GOOLAGONG
1951–

Australian tennis champion

Often described as the best mover in women's tennis, Wimbledon champion Evonne Goolagong seems to float on the court. A gifted, graceful athlete, she has been playing tennis since she was six years old.

Evonne Goolagong's family are aborigines, that is, descendants of the original, native Australians, and thus subjected to the same kind of discrimination and prejudices that American Indians and blacks face. Although her family is accepted in their own town, she has frequently been made uncomfortable because of her origins.

Her great aptitude for tennis was noticed early by Vic Edwards, one of Australia's best-known tennis coaches. He began coaching her when she was ten years old, and later became her legal guardian. By the time she was sixteen she had won all the junior titles in Australia and between 1968 and 1970 won forty-four tournaments and thirty-eight doubles.

In 1971 she became the fifth youngest Wimbledon singles champion. She has won over ninety singles titles, and was ranked among the world's top four each year between 1971 and 1976.

In 1975 she married English businessman Roger Cawley, who was once a tournament player and who practices with her often. They have two children, born in 1977 and 1981.

Jacobs, Linda Evonne Goolagong: smiles and smashes   Illus. EMC, 1975. (grade 4 and up)
Readable, interesting, accurate biography is somewhat adulatory and old-fashioned in its gushy approach to the tennis champion. Many photographs of her in action contribute a great deal to the book. Directed towards reluctant readers.

Heida, D.J. Free Spirit: evonne goolagong   Illus. with photographs. Raintree, 1976. (grade 4 and up)
Nonfictionalized, straightforward account of the tennis player's life and career will appeal to readers who prefer this approach.

May, Julian   Evonne Goolagong: smasher from australia   Illus. with photographs. Crestwood, 1975. (grade 4 and up)

An accurate and interesting biography gives a good picture of the tennis player's training and highlights of her career.

Morse, Charles, and Morse, Ann   Evonne Goolagong   Illus. Creative Educ. Soc./Children's Pr., 1974. (grades 3–8)

Absorbing, exciting, and fast-moving like its subject, this biography is colorfully illustrated and appealing both to younger elementary school age children who are interested in tennis, and older reluctant readers. Although not completely up-to-date (always a problem with a contemporary sports figure), the book covers her career well, highlighting most of the important events.

~~~~~~

SHANE GOULD
1956–

Australian Olympic gold medal–winning swimmer

When, in 1972, fifteen-year-old swimmer Shane Gould won three gold, one silver, and one bronze medal at the Olympics, she became the youngest Australian athlete ever to win an Olympic gold medal.

The champion began swimming when she was only three, at the advice of a physician, to help heal her skin after being burned in an accident. By the time she was nine years old she was swimming in school meets and starting to break records for her age group.

An outstanding student and avid reader, she still found time to swim three to four miles every day before and after school. At fourteen Shane set her first world record in the 400-meter freestyle and went on to break the 200- and the 100-meter freestyle records. Before her magnificent victory at Munich in 1972, she had won every freestyle record, and was the pride of Australia. After her great success in the Olympics she was named Australian of the Year.

Shane Gould continued winning meets, but lost much of her enthusiasm for competition and, in 1973, announced her retirement from competitive swimming.

Jacobs, Linda   Shane Gould: olympic swimmer   Illus. with photographs. EMC, 1974. (grade 4 and up)

Excellent, exciting biography of the young Australian swimmer discusses both her family life and her training and achievements in swimming. Many photographs of her, some with family and friends but most in action, contribute greatly to this easy-to-read biography. Less able or reluctant readers in junior high and high school will find this book interesting as will younger readers.

~~~~~~

MARTHA GRAHAM
1894–

Dancer and choreographer

In her long career as a dancer and choreographer, Martha Graham has increasingly influenced the world of dance and theater and has accumulated numerous honors attesting to her ability.

As a youngster she studied under the famed dancer Ruth Saint Denis and later taught at Denishawn, the school Saint Denis and Ted Shawn founded. Graham also taught at Rochester's Eastman School, established the School of Modern Dance at Bennington College, and started her own school, the Martha Graham School of Contemporary Dance. Her company performs regularly to enthusiastic audiences all over the world.

Martha Graham's choreography, unique and often experimental, draws its subjects from many human experiences such as history, the Bible, literature, and other cultures. Among the almost two hundred dances she has created are *Frontier, Letter to the World* (based on the life of Emily Dickinson), *Appalachian Spring, Clytemnestra, Phaedra,* and *Triumph of Saint Joan.* For many of these and other works, outstanding composers have written the music.

Her honors have been many. In 1932 she became the first dancer to win a Guggenheim Fellowship; her film *A Dancer's World* won awards at film festivals, and many of her world tours have been under the auspices of the State Department.

Petite, dynamic, and seemingly ageless, Graham in her eighth decade of life is still active as a producer, teacher, and lecturer.

Terry, Walter Frontiers of Dance: the life of martha graham   Illus. Crowell, 1975. (grade 6 and up)

Splendidly told, nonadulatory biography of Martha Graham by the dance critic who has known her for a long time focuses on her career as a dancer and choreographer, although her personal life is also discussed. The author captures not only the personality and character of the subject, but also imparts, in an interesting manner, much material about modern dance and some of the other pioneers in the field. Of interest not only to those with knowledge of the dance, but to others as well.

~~~~~~

ANNE MacVICAR GRANT
1755–1838

Author

Scottish-born Anne MacVicar Grant went to the New World with her mother to join her army officer father who was already there. She was taught to read by her mother who approved only of Bible reading, but through the interest of a neighbor, the distinguished Madame Schuyler, young Anne became acquainted with other academic and cultural pursuits. Anne MacVicar Grant later wrote a popular biography of her teacher, *Memoirs of an American Lady*.

During the American Revolution the young Scottish-American woman was torn between her friends who supported the Revolution and her own loyalty to the king. She returned to Scotland, where she spent the remainder of her long life. When her husband, a clergyman, died, she supported herself and her children with her writings.

Bobbe, Dorothie The New World Journey of Anne Mac-Vicar   Putnam, 1971. (grades 7–9)

Very fine account of the life of young Anne MacVicar from the time she left Scotland until she returned as a young woman. Her intellectual and emotional development is traced in an engaging, fast-moving narrative which also offers a good, intimate view of the era in which she lived. The author, though not condoning slavery or some of the white-Indian relationships, explains them well in terms of the prevailing customs and beliefs. An appended bibliography includes Grant's own works as well as those about other people discussed in the biography.

ROSE O'NEAL GREENHOW
1817–1864

Confederate spy

Prominent, popular, and influential Washington hostess Rose
O'Neal Greenhow was a Southern sympathizer and spy who oper-
ated quite openly from her home during the Civil War. Even the
Union's famed detective Alan Pinkerton could not put an end to her
espionage activities. Placed under arrest she continued to transmit
messages, to confuse her guards, to wave a Confederate flag out of
the window, and—with her young daughter—to create general
confusion.

When Greenhow was offered parole on the condition that she
cease her activities, she refused and was ordered south. Received
there as a heroine, she published her memoirs and acted as an
unofficial agent of the Confederacy in Europe. She was returning to
discuss her trip with Jefferson Davis when her ship was beset by
storms. Fearful of capture, she attempted to get ashore in a small
boat. The heavy gold coins she was carrying so weighted her down
that when the boat overturned, she sank and drowned. She was
buried, with the honor befitting a heroine on a wartime mission, in a
military funeral.

Faber, Doris ROSE GREENHOW: SPY FOR THE CONFEDERACY Illus. Putnam, 1968. (grades 5–7)
   Good portrait of the Confederate spy gives an objective view of the Civil
War, and depicts Greenhow as clever, manipulative, and competent, but
lacks some excitement in the telling.

LADY JANE GREY
1537–1554

Queen of England for nine days

Lady Jane Grey, the unwilling queen of England for only nine days,
was something of a child prodigy. Though unhappy in her rela-

tionships with her parents, she found comfort in academic pursuits and became proficient in Greek and Latin, learned Hebrew, Arabic, French, and Italian, and studied philosophy, science, and the arts.

Her father-in-law, John Dudley, the duke of Northumberland, a power-hungry man eager to get the throne in his family, persuaded King Edward VI to leave the crown to Lady Jane Grey's male heirs. He then changed the edict to read Lady Grey *and* her male heirs. After the king's death, when Lady Jane was only sixteen, she reluctantly permitted herself to be crowned queen.

Ten days later the legitimate heir Mary Tudor forced her from the throne. Though Mary was aware of Lady Jane's innocence, she was convicted of high treason and, with her husband, was beheaded in the Tower of London.

Malvern, Gladys THE WORLD OF LADY JANE GREY Illus. Vanguard, 1964. (grade 9 and up)
Very well-written, romantic biography is smoothly fictionalized, placing the young queen in proper perspective in her historical setting. Those readers unacquainted with the period may not find this book sufficiently comprehensible.

~~~~~~

GRIMKÉ SISTERS
Sarah M. Grimké 1792–1873
Angelina Grimké Weld 1805–1879

Southern abolitionists and feminists

Sarah and Angelina Grimké, reared on a typical southern slave-operated plantation, grew not only to despise the entire system but to work diligently to change it. They went north and became Quakers and then active abolitionists and feminists. They were prolific writers and embarked on successful lecture tours of New England to be among the first women to speak before mixed audiences of men and women.

Their powerfully written antislavery and feminist pamphlets were often banned and burned in the South. They attracted considerable attention, not only for their pioneering, well-articulated demands, but because they represented a small and unusual group—southern white women abolitionists.

When it was discovered that two young black men who bore the Grimké name were the sons of their brother and a slave woman, the sisters treated them as nephews and extended their hospitality and encouraged them in their academic pursuits. Both men achieved national prominence in their chosen vocations, the only male members of the large, otherwise white Grimké family to do so.

Lerner, Gerda Grimké Sisters from South Carolina: pioneers for women's rights and abolition Houghton Mifflin, 1967; pap. ed., Schocken, 1971. (grade 9 and up) (Original title: Grimké Sisters from South Carolina: rebels against slavery)

Adult biography is thoroughly researched and documented, offering a substantial, illuminating account of the Grimké sisters. Despite its scholarly approach, it is immensely readable, offering a colorful and elucidating account for older high school students.

Willimon, William, and Willimon, Patricia Turning the World Upside Down Illus. Sandlapper Pr., 1972. (grade 6 and up)

Despite some minor literary flaws, a very fine, moving biography of two remarkable women. Providing an intimate and dramatic picture, it comprehensively and thoughtfully covers their lives in a fast-moving, easy-to-read style.

~~~~~~

CONNIE GUION, M.D.
1882–1971

Physician and professor of clinical medicine

Connie Guion deferred attending medical school in order to teach chemistry to women at Vassar College and to earn money for the education of her younger sisters. At the age of thirty-five she graduated from Cornell Medical School at the top of her class and began the career that led her to accumulate many honors and "firsts" as a woman physician.

She helped organize a clinic at New York Hospital, was later its chief, became the first woman member and first woman honorary member of the hospital's medical board, maintained a private practice, served on the board of numerous civic organizations, taught at Cornell Medical School, and, in 1946, became the first woman in the country to be appointed a full professor of clinical medicine. In 1961 New York Hospital's Doctor Connie Guion Building was opened to patients, making her the first living woman doctor to have a building named after her.

Although Guion is regarded as the modern dean of women doctors, her warmth and personality, her lifetime involvements in behalf of humanity, her many outdoor interests, and her long-time hobby of stamp collecting make her more than just a physician with an impressive list of honors, degrees, and appointments.

Campion, Nardi, and Stanton, Rosamond W. LOOK TO THIS DAY: THE LIVELY EDUCATION OF A GREAT WOMAN DOCTOR, CONNIE GUION M.D. Illus. Little, 1965. (grade 7 and up)

Outstanding, warm, personal biography, based on firsthand interviews with the subject, gives a vivid, informal, and comprehensive portrait of the woman whose career was marked by many "firsts" for women.

~~~~~~

JANET GUTHRIE
1938–

Race-car driver

Thousands of spectators watched in 1976 when Janet Guthrie became the first woman ever to compete in the Indy 500. Two years later she placed ninth despite a broken wrist.

Janet Guthrie was accustomed to adventure. Her father was a pilot and she learned to fly when she was a young teenager. At seventeen, she had a pilot's license. At college she majored in physics and became an engineer with Republic Aviation Company. She was one of four women to qualify for the scientist-astronaut program but her lack of a doctorate later disqualified her.

In 1963 she began racing her Jaguar XK140 and won several races, and within a few years achieved a fine record in auto racing. She competed in sports cars, championship Indy racers, and stock cars, and gave up her regular job to become a freelance technical editor to have more time for racing.

Despite the opposition of male drivers who feared she would slow races, she built her reputation on skill and coordination to become an outstanding racecar driver.

Dolan, Edward F., Jr., and Lyttle, Richard B. JANET GUTHRIE: FIRST WOMAN DRIVER AT INDIANAPOLIS Illus. with photographs. Doubleday, 1978. (grade 6 and up)

Excellent book captures the spirit of sportscar racing as well as the woman who made history. Easy-to-read book will be of special interest to teens who are not highly skilled readers.

Fox, Mary Virginia JANET GUTHRIE: FOOT TO THE FLOOR Illus. Dillon, 1981. (grade 4 and up)

Good, objective, straightforward account of Janet Guthrie will be of interest to older readers whose reading skills are not well developed.

Hahn, James, and Hahn, Lynn JANET GUTHRIE: CHAMPION RACER Illus. with photographs. EMC, 1979. (grade 4 and up)

Easy-to-read, lively biography of the racecar driver gives a well-balanced picture of her, demonstrating the discrimination she faced in a "man's sport" and how her family was instrumental in her development as a risk taker. Book of special interest to followers of the sport, including teens who are reluctant readers.

Olney, Ross P. JANET GUTHRIE: FIRST WOMAN AT INDY Illus. Harvey, 1978. (grades 4–9)

An excellent book gives a good picture of Janet Guthrie as well as sports-car racing. Guthrie is clearly depicted as a pioneer in the field.

Robison, Nancy JANET GUTHRIE: RACE CAR DRIVER Illus. Childrens Press, 1979. (grade 4 and up)

Easy-to-read biography appealingly highlights the career of Janet Guthrie as she strives to become a racecar driver and to enter the Indy 500. Older, less competent readers as well as younger ones will find the book of interest.

~~~~~~

SARAH HALE
1788–1879

Editor and author

Sarah Hale was educated at home, guided by her brother whose college syllabus she followed. When widowhood necessitated supporting herself and five young children she turned to writing. Among her first efforts was a book of nursery verse which included the well-known "Mary Had a Little Lamb."

As the first editor of the immensely popular magazine *Godey's Lady's Book*, Hale was influential in instituting reforms in women's education, health, dress, and career opportunities. Despite her tireless efforts on behalf of education for women, Sarah Hale did not embrace most of the demands of the feminist movement, nor did she advocate women's suffrage.

An editor for forty years, she was responsible for the increased circulation of *Godey's Lady's Book*, and the many outstanding authors and poets represented on its pages. Sarah Hale was instrumental in the establishment of Thanksgiving Day as a national holiday and Mount Vernon as a national shrine. She authored and edited over fifty books.

Burt, Olive FIRST WOMAN EDITOR: SARAH J. HALE Messner, 1960. (grade 6 and up)

Enjoyably detailed portrayal of the famed editor concentrates on her achievements and, despite undistinguished writing, offers an engrossing and inspiring account.

Fryatt, Norma R. SARAH JOSEPHA HALE: THE LIFE AND TIMES OF A NINETEENTH CENTURY CAREER WOMAN Hawthorn, 1975. (grade 9 and up)

Nonfictionalized, straightforward account of this unusual woman is thoroughly researched and documented. Well-written, it is sometimes formal in tone, but still moves along at a fast pace.

FANNIE LOU HAMER
1917–1977

Civil rights worker

Even as a child, Fannie Lou Hamer worked hard picking cotton. The twentieth child of poor black sharecroppers in Mississippi, she noticed, as a youngster, that the dishonesty of white landowners kept her family in a constant state of poverty.

An early civil rights worker, Hamer was arrested and beaten during the 1962 Mississippi voter-registration drive. Although her husband lost his job and they lost their home, she still had hopes for a better future for the poor and hungry.

Fannie Lou Hamer lectured and travelled all over the country to raise funds for the Freedom Farm Collective, a 640-acre cooperative farm where people could work and benefit together.

Jordan, June FANNIE LOU HAMER Illus. Crowell, 1972. (grades 1–4)
Moving, emotional, and unusual treatment of the life of a woman whose earliest childhood was marked by great indignities, but who demonstrated courage and dignity throughout her life. Informal grammar and idiom of southern blacks is used successfully and adds authenticity to this easy-to-read biography. Written for early readers, it will be greatly appreciated by older children regardless of reading level, and by adults seeking material to read aloud to young children.

DOROTHY HAMILL
1956–

Olympic gold medal–winning skater

Like many other eight-year-old girls, Dorothy Hamill fell in love with ice skating, and she was willing to devote the time and hard work necessary to become a champion.

Dorothy Hamill entered her first competition when she was only ten, and then began to win championships. In 1971 when she was only fourteen she placed fifth in the nationals as a Senior Lady, and soon after took third place in her first international competition.

Her family supported her decision at fourteen to move from her home in Connecticut to live in Denver where she could study with Carlo Fassi, the world-famous skating coach, and there she gained the training which helped her to win an Olympic gold medal.

Dorothy Hamill won the nationals, came in second in the world competition, and then in 1976 she took home the Olympic gold medal.

Television coverage of the Olympics had brought her into living rooms throughout the world, and people love her skating, charm, and style. She had offers from advertisers for magazine ads and commercials, and opportunities to do television specials and to skate in the Ice Capades. She accepted many of these offers, and continues to delight audiences everywhere.

Dorothy Hamill also does many benefit performances, and gains much satisfaction when she gives skating clinics for handicapped youngsters.

Burchard, S. H. DOROTHY HAMILL   Illus. with photographs. Harcourt, Brace, 1978. (grade 4 and up)
Excellent, easy-to-read biography clearly portrays Dorothy Hamill as a dedicated hardworking skater who was encouraged and supported by her family.

Dolan, Edward F., Jr., and Lyttle, Richard DOROTHY HAMILL: OLYMPIC SKATING CHAMPION   Illus. with photographs. Doubleday, 1979. (grade 4 and up)
Highly readable lively biography reflects the spirit and determination of the skater. Her family is depicted as an important part of her life.

Hamill, Dorothy with Elva Clairmont ON AND OFF THE ICE   Illus. with photographs. Knopf, 1983. (grade 7 and up)
An extremely readable book that relates the exciting career of the skater, and also reveals her close family relationships to parents, grandparents, and brother and sister. It will be of interest to nonskating enthusiasts as well as ardent fans.

Phillips, Betty Lou THE PICTURE STORY OF DOROTHY HAMILL   Illus. with photographs. Messner, 1978. (grades 4–6)

In this excellent, easy-to-read, well-balanced biography the skater and her family come alive.

Schmitz, Dorothy Childers   DOROTHY HAMILL: SKATE TO VICTORY   Illus. with photographs. Crestwood, 1977. (grade 3 and up)
This very easy-to-read, lively biography is enhanced by photographs and will have appeal to those older readers with limited reading ability.

Smith, Miranda   DOROTHY HAMILL   Illus. with photographs. Creative Ed., 1977. (grade 3 and up)
Straightforward narrative is a satisfactory account of the skater, but lacks the excitement and spirit of the subject.

〰〰〰〰〰〰〰〰〰〰〰〰〰〰〰〰〰〰〰〰〰〰〰〰〰〰〰〰〰

ALICE HAMILTON, M.D.
1869–1970

*Pathologist, first woman appointed to
Harvard University faculty*

Alice Hamilton, whose family stressed education and supported her intellectual interests, spent her professional career after graduating medical school investigating diseases that developed as a result of a person's occupation. Not merely content to discover their causes, she also worked to change the conditions that led to these diseases in the first place. The results of her long, careful studies clearly showed the dangers of carbon monoxide, lead, and mercury.

Dr. Hamilton was the first woman ever appointed to the Harvard University faculty. She was professor of industrial medicine there, and wrote the first authoritative text on industrial poisons.

Alice Hamilton spent much time as a Hull House resident. Her lifelong association with Jane Addams (page 5) and her activities on behalf of peace indicate the wide scope of her interests. Her sister, Edith, was a well-known author (see below).

Grant, Madeline   ALICE HAMILTON: PIONEER DOCTOR IN INDUSTRIAL MEDICINE   Illus. Abelard-Schuman, 1967. (grade 7 and up)
Unusually fine and thorough examination of the life of the woman who combined medicine with social reform. Hamilton's early family influences are presented, but the focus is on her long professional career. The author

makes clear the outstanding contributions of Alice Hamilton in a fluent, readable style which is not overburdened with details.

~~~~~~

EDITH HAMILTON
1867–1963

Classicist, author, and authority on ancient Greeks

Edith Hamilton's parents encouraged her to learn modern and classical languages and to pursue any intellectual activities. Even as a child she was inspired and fascinated by tales of ancient Greece.

As the headmistress of Bryn Mawr School, the first strictly college preparatory school for girls in the United States, Edith Hamilton demanded of her students a deep dedication to academic excellence. Not until retiring from that position did she begin writing the books that brought her great fame. Her *The Greek Way*, published first in 1930 and still considered the standard work on ancient Greece, was followed by *The Roman Way, Mythology*, and several other acclaimed books on classical life.

Edith Hamilton, a modest woman despite her numerous honors and degrees, was honored just before her ninetieth birthday by the Greek government who declared her a citizen of Athens. She wrote two books after this, made a film for television, and was at work on another book when, at the age of ninety-six, she died. Her sister, Alice, was a famous pathologist (see above).

Reid, Doris Fielding EDITH HAMILTON: AN INTIMATE PORTRAIT Illus. Norton, 1967. (grade 9 and up)
Outstanding, warm, and personal view of a remarkable woman written by a close associate. Of particular interest to those who are familiar with Edith Hamilton's works, it also can spark the imagination and act as a spur to those who have not yet read any of her books. Hamilton emerges as the strong, hearty, and independent personality she was; her life, as well as this book, is a remarkable example of what a woman of any age can accomplish.

LORRAINE HANSBERRY
1930–1965

Playwright

Lorraine Hansberry's educated middle-class black family chose to live in non-black neighborhoods despite the hostility directed at them. Her father's legal fights resulted in a Supreme Court decision which allowed them to do so legally, if not always amicably.

She attended college, then moved to New York where she worked on a newspaper, was active in civil rights and peace movements, and married Robert Nemiroff, who shared her same ideals and interests.

Her first play, *Raisin in the Sun*, opened in New York in 1959. It was the first play by a black woman ever to appear on Broadway. It was a huge success and was made into a movie. She became the youngest American, the fifth woman and the first black playwright to win the New York Drama Critics Circle award for best play of the year. A 1975 musical version of the play, *Raisin*, won the Tony award.

In 1964 her second Broadway play, *The Sign in Sidney Brustein's Window*, opened. At the time she was in the hospital, terminally ill with cancer.

Robert Nemiroff, whom she named the executor of her literary estate although they had been divorced, edited some of her published and unpublished works.

Hansberry, Lorraine, adapted by Robert Nemiroff TO BE YOUNG, GIFTED AND BLACK: AN INFORMAL BIOGRAPHY OF LORRAINE HANSBERRY Prentice-Hall, 1970. New American Library, 1970.

An introduction by James Baldwin is followed by carefully edited adaptations of the playwright's own words to form a biography of her. Although this is not biography in the true sense, it serves well as one in that it captures her style and her essence.

Scheader, Catherine LORRAINE HANSBERRY Illus. Children's Press, 1978. (grades 6–9)

Excellent biography traces the life, work, and surroundings of the brilliant young black writer who died at thirty-four of cancer.

ESTHER HAUTZIG
1930–

Author, World War II exile

In 1941, ten-year-old Esther Hautzig and her family were taken by
the Russians from their wealthy home in Vilma, Poland, and sent on
cattle-trains to a forced labor camp in Siberia where they coped with
extreme poverty, freezing winters, and insufficient food. At the end
of World War II, the family was reunited in Poland and young
Esther then went to the United States where she completed her
education. Hautzig wrote, at the urging of those who knew her
story, a memoir of her years in exile. She is the author of fifteen
books. She is married, has two young adult children, and lives in
New York.

Hautzig, Esther   THE ENDLESS STEPPE: GROWING UP IN SIBERIA   Crowell, 1968. (grade 6 and up)
   Outstanding, restrained but dramatic personal narrative of childhood
years spent in exile. Esther, her mother, and her grandmother emerge as
figures of great courage who, despite having enjoyed the comforts of a
wealthy life in Poland, coped with the extreme hardships in Siberia. Other
women, including a strong, kindly, Russian doctor and many Polish depor-
tees, are also depicted as possessing unusual strength and fortitude. This
personal memoir contains the elements of a classic and is actually for
readers of all ages.

SOPHIE PEABODY HAWTHORNE
1809–1871

Artist and author

Sophie Peabody Hawthorne displayed both artistic and literary talent as a youngster, and achieved some success in the arts before her
marriage to Nathaniel Hawthorne. Her bust of Laura Bridgman
(see page 37) was later reproduced in plaster and widely distributed.

After she married the man who later became known for *The Scarlet Letter* and *The House of Seven Gables*, she actively participated in his work by illustrating and editing it, and helped to shape some of his characters.

She also did some independent writing, and after her husband's death she edited his notebooks. The Hawthornes had three children, one of whom, Rose, later became a lay nun who founded the first hospital for the care of advanced cancer patients. Two of Sophie Peabody's sisters also were prominent in nineteenth-century America. One, Elizabeth Palmer Peabody, was a social and education reformer, and Mary Peabody Mann, the other, was an educator like her husband, Horace Mann.

Sophie Peabody Hawthorne, although she never became as famous as her husband, made important literary and artistic contributions at a time when women's opportunities were very limited.

Gaedhert, Lou Ann A NEW ENGLAND LOVE STORY: NATHANIEL HAWTHORNE AND SOPHIE PEABODY Illus. Dial, 1980. (grade 7 and up)

Well-researched and documented dual biography of Hawthorne and Peabody makes liberal use of excerpts from letters, interwoven into narrative. The complex personalities of the two subjects emerge with some clarity, but the intelligently written book is sometimes dry and moves slowly.

~~~~~~

CAROL HEISS
1940–

Olympic gold medal–winning ice skater

Carol Heiss's Olympic gold medal for ice-skating was the culmination of fourteen years of working six days a week, four-and-a-half hours a day. At ten, the New York–born skater became the youngest girl ever to win the National Junior Championship. By the time she was twelve she had won every other junior title and at thirteen finished fourth in the World Figure Skating Championship.

An accident causing a cut calf tendon resulted in a short setback, but she recovered to become the youngest female member of the 1956 United States Olympic skating team, and to win the world championship three times. She turned down many tempting offers to turn professional in order to remain eligible for her goal of winning an Olympic gold medal. Carol Heiss accomplished this in 1960, and soon after retired from competitive skating.

Parker, Robert CAROL HEISS: OLYMPIC QUEEN   Illus. Doubleday, 1961. (grades 7–9)

Good and enjoyable biography of the Olympic ice skater might be particularly attractive to would-be skaters, but is equally interesting to other readers. Simply written, light in tone, it appears to be directed to either younger readers or less able junior high readers.

~~~~~~

BILLIE HOLIDAY
1915–1959

Blues singer

Billie Holiday's childhood in Baltimore was bleak and impoverished. By the time she was ten, she was working as a maid in a neighborhood brothel to supplement her mother's meager earnings. There she heard jazz and blues recordings which greatly influenced and shaped the future course of her life.

She later joined her mother, who had moved to New York, and while still in her teens she began to work in Harlem nightclubs, first as a dancer and then as a singer.

Her combination of jazz and blues resulted in a unique style, and it was not long before Billie Holiday attracted the public's attention. She began to make recordings and to tour with major bands. As her fame increased in the United States and abroad, she was in big demand as a performer. Racial discrimination, exploitive management, and her own inner turmoil led to a growing dependence on drugs and alcohol. Between hospitalizations and imprisonments, she continued to record and to perform worldwide, but eventually drugs and alcohol killed her.

During her career, Billie Holiday recorded songs that continue to keep "Lady Day," as she was called, alive, even to those who never saw her perform.

111

Her interpretations of songs such as "Night and Day," "The Man I Love," "Strange Fruit," and "God Bless the Child" reflect both her outstanding style and her own tragic life.

A movie based on her life, *Lady Sings the Blues*, starred Diana Ross (page 205) and brought Billie Holiday's story and talent to a new generation.

De Veaux, Alexis DON'T EXPLAIN: A SONG OF BILLIE HOLIDAY Illus. Harper and Row, 1980. (grade 7 and up)
   In rhythmic prose, this excellent book conveys the mood of the time and also traces the life of "Lady Day."

Holiday, Billie, and Duffy, William LADY SINGS THE BLUES Double-day, 1956; Avon (paper), 1976. (grade 9 and up)
   The raw details of Billie Holiday's own vivid story make a moving, dramatic, and honest self-portrait.

~~~~~~

HANYA HOLM
1893–

Dancer, teacher, choreographer

German-born Hanya Holm has lived in the United State over forty years and has made numerous contributions to the world of dance and musical comedy.

Her early piano study and training, which stressed the integration of music and body movement, led Hanya Holm to believe that dancers ought to freely develop individual creative ability. She initiated the prestigious summer dance festivals at the University of Colorado where she has taught, performed, choreographed, and directed concerts, dances, and operas.

Hanya Holm's choreography of the Broadway musicals *My Fair Lady, Kiss Me Kate, Where's Charley?* and *Camelot* as well as her work in ballet, films, and television have brought her many honors and awards. She has won the New York Drama Critics Award, a Tony nomination, and an honorary doctorate from the City College of New York.

112

Sorell, Walter HANYA HOLM: THE BIOGRAPHY OF AN ARTIST Wesleyan Univ. Pr., 1969. (grade 9 and up)

Absorbing biography, written by an expert in the field, follows the development of the artist in terms that may be understood by those not familiar with the world of the dance. However, it is particularly recommended for those readers with an interest in dance, either as spectators or participants.

~~~~~~

ANNE HUTCHINSON
1591–1643

Colonial religious dissenter who attacked
Puritan orthodoxy

Anne Hutchinson is best remembered as an early American religious dissenter who argued that neither men nor women ought to subordinate themselves to the doctrines and authority of the Puritan church and who was the first woman to preach to women. Her beliefs that salvation was possible despite earthly failings and that the spirit of God was in everyone challenged the rigid beliefs of Puritanism, but attracted many followers, some of whom were prominent and influential men.

Her opponents saw her as an anarchist who placed an individual's conscience above all conventional authority, and she was brought to trial by both civil and ecclesiastical courts. Despite her sixteenth pregnancy, she was made to stand throughout the trial, and was declared guilty of heresy.

Excommunicated and banished from the colony, the Hutchinsons, with thirty-five other families, moved to Rhode Island where people seemed more tolerant. They later settled in New York where Hutchinson was killcd in an Indian raid.

Faber, Doris COLONY LEADER: ANNE HUTCHINSON Illus. Garrard, 1970. (grades 3–6)

Outstanding, simply told profile of Anne Hutchinson skillfully conveys her beliefs, activities, and the mood of the colonies. Hutchinson emerges as a strong, independent, and energetic woman in this sympathetic, warm biography.

Heidish, Marcy WITNESSES: ANNE HUTCHINSON AND HER TRIALS Houghton, 1980. (grade 5 and up)
This book is described by publisher and author as a novel, but it is so well-researched that it is worth including here. It moves quickly and gives a good picture of Anne Hutchinson and the times. A historical afterword adds to the usefulness of the book as an adjunct to more factual biography and history of Anne Hutchinson. It will interest competent young readers and older readers.

Williams, Selma R. DIVINE REBEL: THE LIFE OF ANNE MARBURY HUTCHINSON Holt, 1981. (grade 9 and up)
Well-documented, scholarly biography will be of special interest to serious students of American, women's, or religious history.

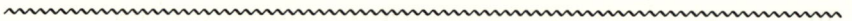

~~~~~~

TRINA SCHART HYMAN
1939–

Children's artist and illustrator

Artist and illustrator Trina Schart Hyman has illustrated more than ninety books, and for the last ten years has been art director of *Cricket*, the critically acclaimed magazine for young people.
She was a shy and timid youngster who was happiest in the world of make-believe. She later was a serious art student. She likes illustrating books for children because, she says, "I love to draw, love stories and I love kids."
She and her daughter live on a farm with their dogs, cats, sheep, and chickens, and that is where she maintains her studio.

Hyman, Trina Schart SELF PORTRAIT: TRINA SCHART HYMAN Illus. Addison-Wesley, 1981. (grade 4 and up)
Biography traces the artist's life and her feelings of being different until she became totally enmeshed in art. Those readers already familiar with her work will be particularly interested in this very fine book, but others will also enjoy it and be interested in seeing more of her work.

QUEEN ISABELLA
1451–1504

Queen of Spain

Queen Isabella of Spain, known best to Americans as the financier of Columbus's expeditions to the New World, ruled jointly with her husband, Ferdinand II. Isabella became queen of Castille in 1474. In 1479, the union of Aragon and Castile brought about a strong central government despite the two states' differences in language, customs, and laws.

Queen Isabella's determination to unite Spain under Catholicism led to excesses of intolerance such as the Spanish Inquisition and the proscription of the Jews.

Highly intelligent, intensely patriotic, and in some ways extremely moral, she managed to raise the level of the court from its low moral stance to one of greater repute. Needless to say, her sponsorship of Columbus's voyage affected the course of history and changed the map of the world.

Noble, Iris SPAIN'S GOLDEN QUEEN ISABELLA Messner, 1969. (grade 7 and up)

Well-written, satisfactory biography of Queen Isabella gives a good picture of her intelligence and determination and provides a good background for further study of the period. Interesting and well-paced, it employs much dialogue without overfictionalization.

~~~~~~

ANNE JACKSON
1926–

Actress

Born in Pittsburgh to an Irish mother and a Croatian father, young Anne Jackson became a New Yorker when they moved there during the Depression. Encouraged by teachers, she began to enjoy performing before audiences, and soon became stagestruck. Her teenage years were marked with great heartache for her mother suffered an emotional breakdown, resulting in hospitalization, and later death. She and her sister remained close to their father.

After graduating from high school Anne began seriously studying acting with some of the best teachers in New York. She won first prize in a major talent audition, and from then on worked steadily, achieving her first success in *The Cherry Orchard* in 1945.

She has co-starred in several productions with her husband, actor Eli Wallach. They appeared on Broadway with two of their daughters in *The Diary of Anne Frank*.

Anne Jackson is a serious actress who continues to appear in films, television, and theater and who has the good fortune and ability to combine a significant career with home and family. They reside in New York City.

Jackson, Anne EARLY STAGES   Little, Brown, 1979. (grade 9 and up)
Excellent biography portrays the actress as a multidimensional person. The focus is on her adolescence and her strong family ties. Her early theater beginnings also vividly emerge.

~~~~~~

MADELINE MANNING JACKSON
1948–

Olympic gold medal–winner for track

Frail and delicate from birth, constantly ill with everything from colds to spinal meningitis, Madeline Manning Jackson was, nonetheless, a fun-loving, sports-minded youngster who also enjoyed playing piano and singing in the church choir. Her mother was devoutly religious, and Madeline too had a strong commitment to her faith.

The coach of the Cleveland Track Club saw her run when she was in high school and invited her to join. She travelled throughout the United States and Europe, winning gold medals in prestigious meets and games everywhere.

She won a track scholarship to Tennessee State University, training there under one of the best track coaches in the world. Her hard work and talent were demonstrated when she became a gold medal winner in the 1968 Olympics. She competed in the 1972 and 1976 Olympics, and if the United States had not boycotted the 1980 Olympics, she would have been a member of the team.

Madeline Manning Jackson, mother of a teenager, John Jackson, Jr., retired from racing in 1981 after making the American World Cup Team.

Jacobs, Linda MADELINE MANNING JACKSON: RUNNING ON FAITH Illus. with photographs. EMC, 1976. (grade 4 and up)

A good biography which focusses on her determination, religious faith and musical talent, as well as her track achievements. Of interest even to those without a special interest in running.

~~~~~~

MAHALIA JACKSON
1911–1972

Gospel singer and civil rights worker

Mahalia Jackson brought traditional Gospel singing from black churches to the entire world through personal appearances in concert halls, recordings, and performances on radio and television.

A woman devotedly faithful to God, Jackson refused to sing anywhere that liquor was served, and although she could easily have become a great blues performer, she preferred to sing "the glory of God."

She wholeheartedly embraced the civil rights movement and was one of its symbols. She performed at benefits for bus boycotts, sit-ins, and Martin Luther King's Southern Christian Leadership Conferences. One of her most memorable appearances was before 200,000 people at the Lincoln Memorial during the civil rights march on Washington in 1963. Jackson also performed at President Kennedy's inauguration in 1961, at the Newport Jazz Festival, and in benefit performances throughout the world. Among her best known and loved songs are "He's Got the Whole World in His Hands," "I Can Put My Trust in Jesus," "I Believe," and "We Shall Overcome."

Cornell, Jean Gay MAHALIA JACKSON: QUEEN OF GOSPEL SONG Illus. Garrard, 1974. (grades 3–5)

Warm, tender biography moves quickly as it gives not only a good personal and professional account of the life of Mahalia Jackson, but also describes the meaning of Gospel music and discusses the civil rights movement.

Dunham, Montrew MAHALIA JACKSON: YOUNG GOSPEL SINGER Bobbs-Merrill, 1974. (grades 3–6)

Although highly fictionalized, this is an absorbing, sympathetic, and accurate picture of Mahalia Jackson's early life. There is emphasis on civil rights, religion, and family life. Although little of the book deals with her later success, it gives a vivid picture which captures the essence of her life.

Jackson, Jesse MAKE A JOYFUL NOISE UNTO THE LORD: THE LIFE OF MAHALIA JACKSON, QUEEN OF GOSPEL SINGERS Illus. with photographs. Crowell, 1974. (grades 5–9)

Exceedingly good, dramatic, and compassionate biography of the Gospel singer also gives a substantial picture of Gospel music, and a perceptive, thoughtful portrait of segregation and the civil rights movement.

McDearmon, Kay MAHALIA: GOSPEL SINGER Illus. Dodd, 1976. (grades 2–5)

Easy-to-read, beautifully illustrated book brings Mahalia Jackson to life. She is seen as a religious, unselfish woman as well as a talented artist.

~~~~~~

ANDREA JAEGER
1965–

Tennis champion

Coached by her father, Andrea Jaeger was only fourteen when she became the second youngest player ever to win a professional tennis tournament.

She had begun playing tennis when she was only eight, hitting balls with her father in front of the house. At 12 was rated number one in her age group, and at fourteen she won thirteen consecutive matches to claim the title at the Avon Futures and tied the circuit record for most consecutive matches won.

118

The holder of many national titles, Andrea Jaeger became the youngest player ever to be seeded at Wimbledon, and in 1980 she was a quarterfinalist there, the same year she was a semifinalist in the U.S. Open.

Despite a heavy schedule of practice and play, she maintained a "straight A" average when she was a high school student in Prairie View, Illinois.

Now ranked number three in the world, she was a semifinalist in the 1982 U.S. Open. In 1983 she was a finalist at Wimbledon and reached the quarter finals in the U.S. Open.

Fogel, Julianna A. ANDREA JAEGER, TENNIS CHAMPION Illus. with photographs. Harper & Row, 1980. (grades 3–7)

More a personal story than a traditional biography, told in the first person, this book will be of special interest to youngsters who want to play tennis. Realistic, not overly romanticized, it holds the reader's interest.

Sons, Ray ANDREA JAEGER: PRO IN PONYTAILS Illus. with photographs. Childrens Pr., 1981. (grade 2 and up)

Very easy-to-read biography gives a good picture of the player and will be of interest to even those readers who aren't familiar with the process of competition.

~~~~~~

MARY JEMISON
1743–1833

Indian captive

Fourteen-year-old Mary Jemison, who was born on a ship enroute from Ireland to America, was captured by Indians and adopted by a Seneca family. She so thoroughly learned to consider herself an Indian that when given a chance to return to her own people she refused. She married first a Delaware Indian and, after his death, a Seneca warrior.

Mary Jemison became independently wealthy as a land and cattle owner and was known throughout the community for her hospitality and generosity to both Indians and whites. She became a legend in her own time when her life story, as she related it, was published.

Gardner, Jeanne MARY JEMISON: SENECA CAPTIVE Illus. Harcourt, 1966. (grades 5–7)

Good account of Mary Jemison's entire life describes her changing attitudes as she assimilated into the Seneca community.

Lenski, Lois INDIAN CAPTIVE: THE STORY OF MARY JEMISON Illus. by the author. Lippincott, 1941. (grades 7–9)

Excellent biography focusses on only a short period of Jemison's life but is based on careful and thorough research. Convincingly fictionalized and effectively illustrated, the book gives a good picture of the Seneca Indians as well as the story of Mary Jemison. Maps add to the understanding and value of the book.

~~~~~~

JOAN OF ARC
1412–1431

French heroine

According to legend, Joan of Arc was born at Domremy of a comfortable peasant family. At the age of thirteen, she heard "voices"—first advising her to lead a holy life, later directing her to rally the French army behind her.

She led the army against the British and Burgundian forces, and was captured when she was only eighteen. The British turned her over to a French ecclesiastic court which accused her of heresy and witchcraft. Among the sins listed during her long, disgraceful, and unfair trial was one that she dressed like a boy.

Convicted and condemned to death, she was burned at the stake at the marketplace in Rouen. Her innocence was proclaimed in 1455, and Joan, known also as the Maid of Orleans, was beatified in 1909 and canonized in 1920.

Churchill, Winston JOAN OF ARC (Her life as told by Winston Churchill in A HISTORY OF THE ENGLISH-SPEAKING PEOPLES) Illus. Dodd, 1969. (grade 3 and up)

Beautiful illustrations by Larren Ford complement this dramatic story of Joan of Arc. Told with direct simplicity, this brief book is suitable for all ages.

Fisher, Aileen JEANNE D'ARC Illus. Crowell, 1970. (grades 3–6)
Excellent account of the life of the fifteenth-century heroine is enhanced by outstanding illustrations by Ati Forberg. Stirringly told, but lacking in some authenticity, this will also serve well as a read-aloud book for younger children.

Gies, Frances JOAN OF ARC Harper & Row, 1981. (grade 9 and up)
An adult, full-length, scholarly biography for serious students of history. Well-written, thoroughly researched and documented.

Paine, Albert Bigelow GIRL IN WHITE ARMOR Illus. Macmillan, 1967. (grade 7 and up)
Abridged from author's full-length adult biography, *Joan of Arc: Maid of France*, this is a faithfully told, nonsexist account of the French heroine which gives a proper perspective in a historical setting. Maps, chronology, and a cast of characters and drawings contribute to make a truly distinctive biography.

Peach, L. Du Garde JOAN OF ARC Illus. Ladybird, 1971. (grade 5 and up)
Numerous colorful illustrations add to the value of this straightforward, rather objective biography which also gives a good historical background.

Ross, Nancy JOAN OF ARC Illus. Random, 1953. (grades 6–9)
Worthwhile biography offers the dramatic story of Joan of Arc in a fast-paced, readable style. The subject moves realistically and historical background is skillfully woven into story.

Williams, Jay, and Lightbody, Charles W. JOAN OF ARC Illus. American Heritage, 1963. (grade 6 and up)
Outstanding story of Joan of Arc traces her heroic deeds in a scholarly fashion, yet retains appealing and sympathetic style. Illustrations, maps, paintings, and illuminations do not overshadow but aid in the flow of the text. Although directed to young readers, it is certainly of value to adults as well.

~~~~~~

AMY JOHNSON
1903–1941

Pioneer British aviator

Amy Johnson's parents, despite some misgivings, encouraged her desire to become a pilot. At a time when women were barely accepted in the field of aviation, she met many obstacles but went on to set records and to win honors and awards.

She was the first woman to fly solo from London to Australia, the first woman to fly the Atlantic east to west, and she set a London to Cape Town record. Johnson was also a capable mechanic and became the first woman in the world to pass the test for the British Ground Engineers License.

Amy Johnson's achievements brought her much fame and she was in demand as a lecturer and newspaper writer. When World War II broke out, she volunteered as a pilot and drowned when bad weather forced her to land in the Thames estuary.

Grey, Elizabeth WINGED VICTORY Illus. Houghton Mifflin, 1966. (grades 7–10)
Vivid profile of the English aviator is moving and dramatic. Amy Johnson is depicted as the pioneering, brave, ambitious woman she was in this sometimes too admiring, but very well-written and engrossing biography.

PAULINE JOHNSON
1861–1913

Native American poet and entertainer

Poet and entertainer Pauline Johnson, the daughter of a Mohawk chief and a woman of English descent, became a spokeswoman for Canadian Native Americans in her extremely well-attended appearances throughout her country.

Her poem "The Song My Paddle Sings" is well known to Canadians, but during her lifetime she was better known as an entertainer. She travelled back and forth throughout Canada for seventeen years in a tour called the concert circuit, reading her verses.

When a Canadian stamp honored her, it was the first time any Canadian Indian and any woman not of the royal family had been so recognized. She was often called the voice of Canada, but enthusiasm for her poetry had lapsed until in 1961 interest was revived. Her poetry, remarkable for blending the Native American heritage with western style, was widely acclaimed by those who heard her read it aloud.

Hailey, Lucie PAULINE JOHNSON Illus. with photographs. Dillon, 1978. (grades 5–8)

An excellent biography which depicts the life of the poet and also gives a good portrait of the time and of Native North American life.

~~~~~~

IRENE JOLIOT-CURIE
1897–1956

French scientist, winner of Nobel Prize in chemistry

Like her famous parents, Marie and Pierre Curie, Irene Joliot-Curie became a scientist. During World War I, she and her mother established and supervised x-ray stations where the wounded could be immediately diagnosed and treated.

After the war, she worked with her mother at the Institute of Radium, and there she met Frédéric Joliot, another scientist. Their subsequent marriage was a complete partnership, and together they discovered artificial radioactivity. For this tremendous contribution to medicine and biochemistry they won the 1935 Nobel Prize in chemistry. Irene Joliot-Curie thus became the only woman besides her mother to achieve that award. Like her mother, too, she successfully integrated the roles of scientist, wife, and mother.

McKown, Robin SHE LIVED FOR SCIENCE: IRENE JOLIOT-CURIE Messner, 1961. (grade 7 and up)

Outstanding biography is sometimes quite technical, thus limiting its appeal to those readers interested in science. Despite some complicated material, the book moves along quickly and covers aspects of Joliot-Curie's personal and professional life.

~~~~~~

MARY HARRIS "MOTHER" JONES
1830–1930

Labor agitator and leader

Mary Harris Jones helped organize and publicize every major labor struggle in this country for over fifty years. The Irish-born labor agitator first became involved in union activities after her husband and four small children died of yellow fever. "Mother" Jones, as she was known, was dubbed the "patron saint of the picket lines" for her work against low wages, long hours, and dangerous conditions. She inspired striking workers to remain loyal despite imprisonment and starvation, and when mine owners hired strike-breakers she led the workers' wives to disperse the scabs with mops and brooms.

Her life was in constant danger—she was beaten and jailed—but she courageously persisted in helping to organize the United Mine Workers and to participate in most major coal, rail, textile, copper, steel, garment, and transit strikes throughout the nation. She worked to end child labor, demonstrating its evils by leading a "children's crusade" of little Pennsylvania mill workers to the home of President Theodore Roosevelt in New York.

Mother Jones actively involved herself in class and labor struggles past her ninetieth birthday and, at age ninety-four, sat down long enough to dictate her autobiography.

Atkinson, Linda MOTHER JONES: THE MOST DANGEROUS WOMAN IN AMERICA Illus. with photographs, prints. Crown, 1978. (grade 7 and up)
This biography includes Mother Jones's historical background in an interesting, readable and informal manner without sacrificing accuracy.

Bethell, Jean THREE CHEERS FOR MOTHER JONES Illus. Holt, 1980. (grades 2–5)
Despite fictionalization, this is a very fine book that introduces even very young children to the concept of social inequities and the need to struggle against them.

Jones, Mary AUTOBIOGRAPHY OF MOTHER JONES Charles Kerr, 1925; reprint 1972 with a new introduction and bibliography. Original foreword by Clarence Darrow. (grade 8 and up)
Fast-moving autobiography is written in a clear, compelling style with dry humor, warmth, and drama. Although not written for young readers, it is immensely readable and fairly accurate.

Werstein, Irving LABOR'S DEFIANT LADY: THE STORY OF MOTHER JONES Crowell, 1969. (grades 5–9)
Superior biography of the dynamic labor leader is distinguished by its brisk narrative, balanced portrayal, and vivid picture of the subject and the issues in which she was involved. Thoroughly researched, it offers a good, thoughtful summary of her long life.

BARBARA JORDAN
1936–

Congresswoman from Texas

Now the popular host of "Crisis to Crisis," a nationally acclaimed television show which examines important issues, Barbara Jordan has had a substantial, significant career in public service.

Barbara Jordan was a fine student who decided quite young to become a lawyer, and at Texas Southern University, an all-black college, she led the debating team to a series of championships. She earned a law degree at Boston University and then returned to Houston to practice law, with the family's dining room serving as her desk and office.

When she was elected to Congress in 1972 she became the first black woman to represent the Deep South. Before that, when she was a member of the Texas State Senate, President Johnson described her as "the epitome of the new politics."

She served in Congress until 1978 and was praised by government officials, news media, and her constituents alike for her keen mind and integrity. She held the distinction in Congress of being one of only a handful of representatives with a one hundred percent voting record, and she worked tirelessly for social issues to benefit the poor and minorities.

After deciding to leave Congress, she was appointed Lyndon Baines Johnson Public Services Professor at the University of Texas, and she continues to have an impact on American political life.

Haskins, James S. BARBARA JORDAN   Illus. with photographs. Dial, 1977. (grade 7 and up)

An unusually fine book which gives a good picture of Houston and black life in the 1930s, the influences of Jordan's father who believed in "brain power," and her later accomplishments.

Jacobs, Linda BARBARA JORDAN: KEEPING FAITH   Illus. with photographs. EMC, 1978. (grades 3–5)

A good, inspirational overview of her life and achievements chronicles the difficulties a black woman faces in the field of government. Her belief in herself and her nation that she would be able to achieve is demonstrated. This easy-to-read book is fine for older readers as well.

Jordan, Barbara, and Hearon, Shelby BARBARA JORDAN Doubleday, 1979. (grade 7 and up)
Good biography describes her childhood and youth as well as adult achievements. Barbara Jordan emerges as a warm, caring person as well as a woman of rare intelligence, energy, and purpose.

~~~~~~

HELEN KELLER
1880–1968

Author and humanitarian

Helen Keller, deaf and blind from infancy, was at age seven an overindulged, unkept, and unmanageable youngster who seemed headed for oblivion. Then the gifted, perseverant, young teacher Anne Sullivan Macy (page 152) came into the household and eventually she and Helen were spelling words into each other's hands. Helen learned to read raised print with her fingers, to type, and to be self-reliant. Later she learned braille and oral communication.

Keller's unusually high intelligence and unending hard work led to her acceptance and graduation with honors from Radcliffe College and to the publication and enormous success of her autobiography, *Story of My Life.* With Macy and later Polly Thomson as her "eyes and ears," Helen Keller wrote, lectured, and travelled on behalf of the handicapped, the women's suffrage movement, and the peace movement, and gained the admiration of the entire world.

Helen Keller was a major influence in obtaining opportunities for the training and employment of the blind, and her life has inspired millions of other handicapped people to live creative and productive lives of their own.

Bigland, Eileen HELEN KELLER Illus. S. G. Phillips, 1967. (grades 7–10)
Sensitive, dramatic biography gives a well-rounded portrait of Helen Keller. Anne Sullivan Macy's patience and skills are acknowledged, and Keller is seen from earliest childhood to her last years.

Brown, Marion, and Crone, Ruth SILENT STORM Illus. Abingdon, 1963. (grades 6–8)
See Anne Sullivan Macy.

Davidson, Margaret HELEN KELLER Illus. Hastings, 1970; Scholastic Book Service, 1973. (grades 3–5)
Stirring biography is clear, easy-to-read narrative prose, making use of fictionalization, but still remaining faithful to the truth. Vivid and intimate, it is colorful and absorbing.

Gibson, William THE MIRACLE WORKER Knopf, 1957. (grade 7 and up)
See Anne Sullivan Macy.

Graff, Stewart, and Graff, Polly HELEN KELLER Illus. Dell, 1965. (grades 2–7)
Very fine, moving profile of Helen Keller is quietly compelling, highlighting the important events and experiences in her life.

————. HELEN KELLER: TOWARDS THE LIGHT Garrard, 1965. (grades 2–5)
Excellent, simple profile of Helen Keller is a touching account of her life, showing her limitations, progress, and achievements.

Hickok, Lorena A. THE STORY OF HELEN KELLER Illus. Grosset, 1958. (grades 4–6)
Despite excessive fictionalization, this is a good biography which captures the mood of Keller's life, and shows clearly the way in which she learned to communicate.

Johnson, Ann Donegan THE VALUE OF DETERMINATION: THE STORY OF HELEN KELLER Illus. Value Communications, 1976. (grades K–3)
Fictionalized, charming account of Helen Keller focuses on her childhood. The value of determination is conveyed as demonstrated by Helen Keller. Although Anne Sullivan's determination was just as great, this is not indicated. A straightforward account of Keller's life follows the text in a one-page profile suitable for older readers or adults.

Keller, Helen STORY OF MY LIFE Doubleday, 1954. (grade 7 and up)
Warm and dramatic autobiography was written by Keller when she was a student at Radcliffe. It is dignified, appealing, and inspiring and because it was written early in her life, it just tells her story up to that point. An appended account of her education incorporates letters and reports.

Lash, Joseph HELEN AND TEACHER Illus. with photographs. Delacorte, 1980. (grade 9 and up)

This full-length, thoroughly documented and researched adult book is a distinguished biography of both Helen Keller and Anne Sullivan Macy. It will be of interest to competent high school readers. There are many photographs which add enormously to the work.

Peare, Catherine O. THE HELEN KELLER STORY Crowell, 1959. (grade 7 and up)
Very well-written, perceptive profile provides a thoughtful examination of Helen Keller's life, paying full tribute to the efforts of her teacher, as well as her own achievements.

Richards, N. HELEN KELLER Illus. Childrens Pr., 1968. (grade 6 and up)
Warm, dramatic biography is lavishly illustrated with drawings and photographs, adding to the interest and value of the book.

Sabin, Francene THE COURAGE OF HELEN KELLER Illus. Troll, 1982. (grades 2–5)
A very good biography of Helen Keller which focusses on her childhood and the amazing progress she made with Anne Sullivan Macy. May well motivate readers to read fuller biographies of both women.

Tibble, J. W., and Tibble, Anne HELEN KELLER Illus. Putnam, 1958. (grades 5–9)
Excellent, dramatic biography gives a vivid picture of the progress and achievements of Helen Keller.

Waite, Helen E. VALIANT COMPANIONS Macrae, 1959. (grade 7 and up)
See Anne Sullivan Macy.

~~~~~~

FRANCES "FANNY" KEMBLE
1809–1893

Actress, abolitionist, author

On tour in America, British actress Fanny Kemble met and married a wealthy Philadelphian, Pierce Butler, who she later discovered was a slave-owner. A stay at his Georgia plantation reinforced her abolitionist beliefs and filled her with disgust and horror, especially when her humane recommendations were rejected by her husband.

She kept a detailed record of her life there: "Journal of a Residence on a Georgian Plantation" provides a unique contribution to the history of slavery.

Fanny Kemble's views of slavery, her independence, and her refusal to act the role of a dutiful, subjugated wife antagonized her husband who subsequently treated her as a prisoner in her own home. He deprived her of any jurisdiction over their two daughters and allowed her to see them only at prescribed hours. Finding this unbearable, she left him and eventually found personal and artistic satisfaction and success giving readings of Shakespeare in England and America, and writing poems, plays, criticism, and journals.

Kerr, Laura FOOTLIGHTS TO FAME: THE LIFE OF FANNY KEMBLE Illus. Funk & Wagnalls, 1962. (grades 7–11)
Fictionalized biography of Fanny Kemble is overly romantic and bland in the early chapters about her childhood and theatrical career. As the book and her life progress, Kemble's oppressive marriage is described and she emerges as an independent woman.

Rushmore, Robert FANNY KEMBLE Macmillan, 1970. (grade 7 and up)
Excellent biography is analytical and well-researched. Lucidly and stirringly shows how an intelligent, well-educated nineteenth-century woman was cruelly oppressed.

Scott, John Anthony FANNY KEMBLE'S AMERICA Crowell, 1973. (grade 7 and up)
Superb biography gives a clear honest portrayal of Fanny Kemble's life in America and also gives an unusually fine picture of the period, revealing many facts of history which are not generally known to young readers. Intelligently written, this book evokes great emotion and shows the concepts of male/female and black/white equality as being closely related.

Wise, Winifred E. FANNY KEMBLE: ACTRESS, AUTHOR, ABOLITIONIST Illus. Putnam, 1966. (grades 7–10)
Excellent, competently researched biography describes Kemble's early professional career and her later conflicts concerning her marriage to a slave-owner. Vivid descriptions of slave life as described in Fanny Kemble's own journals are included.

Wright, Constance FANNY KEMBLE AND THE LOVELY LAND Illus. Dodd, 1972. (grade 9 and up)
This good adult biography is suitable for high school students. Well-documented with notes, comments, and a lengthy bibliography, the book

depicts Fanny Kemble as intelligent and courageous. Although slow-moving at times, there is extensive use of extracts from letters and journals into the narrative and into conversations.

~~~~~~

ROSE FITZGERALD KENNEDY
1890–

Civic leader, philanthropist, political campaigner, and mother of President John F. Kennedy

Rose Kennedy, a hard-working political campaigner, active philanthropist, and physical fitness enthusiast, had the unique ability to bring up sons and daughters who contributed much to their country. This ability and her dignity, unswerving religious faith, energy, and self-discipline even in the face of great tragedy combine to make her one of the most remarkable women of our time.

She purposefully and directly encouraged her children to be independent, competent, confident, competitive, and aware of current affairs. When her husband served as ambassador to Great Britain she assumed her role as hostess to world leaders with considerable success.

Her life has been marked by many tragic events. Her oldest son was killed during World War II, a daughter died in a plane crash, and another daughter is mentally retarded.

Her son John F. Kennedy, who became the thirty-fifth president of the United States, was assassinated in 1963, and only five years later his brother Senator Robert Kennedy was also assassinated.

Despite these great misfortunes she has managed to continue her activities in behalf of the Catholic church and mental retardation and takes great pride in her remaining son, Senator Edward Kennedy, and in her daughters and numerous grandchildren.

Church, Carol Bauer ROSE KENNEDY: NO TIME FOR TEARS Illus. with photographs. Greenhaven, 1976. (grades 3–8)
Good straightforward account gives a good picture of this remarkable woman, but at times lacks the luster of Kennedy herself.

BILLIE JEAN KING
1943–

*Tennis champion, advocate of equal rights
for women in tennis*

Tennis champion Billie Jean King won her first tournament at age thirteen. At seventeen, she won the women's doubles at Wimbledon and at eighteen was ranked fourth among Americans. In 1968, after three consecutive Wimbledon victories and wins in the United States Indoor, Easter Grass, and United States National, King was ranked first in the world.

During this time, Billie Jean King became infuriated by the fact that men's prize money so exceeded women's. In order to help women gain equal rights and equal prize money, she organized a boycott of women players against the official United States Lawn Tennis Association (USLTA) tournaments. King also helped to establish the first independent women's tennis tour and a new magazine, called *womanSport*.

On September 20, 1973, Billie Jean King beat the colorful male tennis star Bobby Riggs in a spectacular match watched by millions on television. She showed that women's tennis is as exciting as men's, and added another triumph to an already long list.

Since then she has won or been a finalist in numerous single and doubles tournaments and has helped found the Women's Sports Foundation, to increase opportunities for women to participate in sports. Despite numerous knee injuries and considerably younger competitors, in 1982 and 1983 she reached the Wimbledon semi-finals in singles and in 1983 won the mixed doubles there.

Her impact on women's tennis has been considerable, and the popularity and financial returns that professional women tennis players are able to enjoy today are due to her dedication and hard work.

Baker, Jim BILLIE JEAN KING Illus. with photographs. Grosset, 1974. (grade 4 and up)

Excellent, fast-moving biography of Billie Jean King is a balanced treatment, giving equal emphasis to her tennis playing and her involvement in the promotion of women's tennis and World Team Tennis. Many photographs of her on and off court enhance this biography which will be appealing to all her fans, but which is especially suitable for reluctant or less capable older readers. It is extremely easy to read, but also discusses issues that junior high and high school students will find of interest.

Burchard, Marshall, and Burchard, Sue SPORTS HERO: BILLIE JEAN KING Illus. Putnam, 1975. (grades 2–4)
Outstanding, dynamic portrait of the tennis champion explains the game as well as discussing her career. The role King played in promoting women's tennis is interestingly covered from a feminist perspective, and her famed match with Riggs is vividly and objectively described.

Church, Carol Bauer BILLIE JEAN KING: QUEEN OF THE COURTS Illus. with photographs. Greenhaven, 1976. (grades 3–7)
Good lively biography, enhanced by many photographs, is not current. Nonetheless, it is absorbing and will appeal to youngsters with an interest in tennis.

Hahn, James, and Hahn, Lynn KING! THE SPORTS CAREER OF BILLIE JEAN KING Illus. with photographs. Crestwood, 1981. (grades 3–6)
Billie Jean King comes to life in this clear and easy-to-read profile which will appeal to young tennis fans and older reluctant readers.

Olsen, James T. BILLIE JEAN KING, LADY OF THE COURT Illus. Creative Educ. Soc./Children's Pr., 1974. (grades 4–7)
Illustrated with many colorful action drawings, this biography, though not quite up-to-date, is packed with information about the subject and shows her to be a talented, ambitious tennis player. However, it is stylistically uneven, and in an attempt to be journalistically informal it sometimes awkwardly misses its mark.

CORETTA SCOTT KING
1927–

Civil rights leader, peace advocate, singer

Although best known as the wife and then widow of civil rights leader Martin Luther King, Jr., Coretta King is very much a dynamic, talented person in her own right.

At both Antioch College and the New England Conservatory of Music where she was awarded scholarships, Coretta King received a thorough foundation in academic work and in singing. She put aside her immediate career goals when she married, deciding instead to work with her husband to try to achieve better relations between the races.

Despite increasing family responsibilities she took an active part in the Southern Christian Leadership Conference, frequently filling speaking engagements and giving benefit concerts. She also taught voice in a college music department in Atlanta, and was a Women's Strike for Peace delegate at the International Disarmament Conference in Geneva in 1962.

When her husband was assassinated in 1968, Coretta King earned the respect of the world for her show of dignity and strength. She assumed many of his unfulfilled obligations in addition to her own and became the first woman to speak from the pulpit of Saint Paul's Cathedral in London.

Now president of the Martin Luther King, Jr. Center for Social Change in Atlanta, Georgia, she also holds important positions in many other organizations and has written a popular book about her life with her husband, and continues to work for civil rights.

Patterson, Lillie CORETTA SCOTT KING Illus. Garrard, 1977. (grades 3–6)

Excellent biography shows Coretta King as an individual with talent, intellect, and courage as well as in her role as the wife and widow of Martin Luther King, Jr.

Taylor, Paula CORETTA SCOTT KING Illus. Creative Educ. Soc., 1975. (grades 3–7)

Very fine, readable biography examines Coretta King's commitment to the civil rights movement, and also shows her to be an intelligent, talented woman who did not really subordinate herself to her hsuband, but merely shifted her goals from a musical career to one dedicated to helping humanity. This profile illustrates how she used her own training and background appropriately towards this direction.

JILL KINMONT
1938–

Championship skier, educator

Jill Kinmont was trying out for the 1956 United States Olympic Ski team when she fell, broke her neck, and severed her spinal cord. Permanently paralyzed from the shoulders down, she was determined to make herself physically and financially independent. After years of unrelenting efforts she learned to write again, and after many rejections was accepted in a teachers's training program at college.

For many summers she worked on a Piute reservation teaching youngsters and training tutors, and since 1965 she has been teaching regularly, specializing in working with reading disabled youngsters.

Jill Kinmont is married, has been the subject of two movies and a television special, and is in much demand as a lecturer.

Valens, E. G. LONG WAY UP: THE STORY OF JILL KINMONT Illus. Harper, 1966 (grade 9 and up)

Deeply moving, dramatic account of a young woman who suffered a tragic accident. Of interest to all readers, it may hold a particular attraction for either skiing enthusiasts or as an inspiration for those with handicaps of their own. Jill Kinmont is shown to be courageous and optimistic in this intimate and well-rounded biography.

ILSE KOEHN
1929–

Author and artist

Ilse Koehn, Berlin-born, was caught up in World War II and even drifted into Hitler's Youth despite her family's strong anti-Nazi sentiments.

Because her father had one Jewish parent, her parents separated during the war to help her and her mother survive. Both of Ilse's grandparents, vastly and dramatically different from each other, were alike in their desire to give Ilse a normal life during those times.

After the war she studied graphic design and illustration and later worked as a freelance writer and illustrator for various magazines. She came to the United States in 1958, where she has made her home and has had exhibitions of her paintings.

Ilse Koehn has written *Tilla*, a novel of the Holocaust for young people.

Koehn, Ilse MISCHLING, SECOND DEGREE: MY CHILDHOOD IN NAZI GERMANY Greenwillow, 1977. (grade 7 and up)
An important addition to the real life stories of the Holocaust, this is an absorbing tribute to the spirit of adolescence. Despite being only part Jewish (*Mischling*), Ilse was in constant danger of being discovered. The suspense that results is one of the unique qualities of the book.

〰〰〰〰〰〰〰〰〰〰〰〰〰〰〰〰〰〰〰〰〰〰〰〰〰〰〰〰〰〰〰〰〰

KÄTHE KOLLWITZ
1867–1945

German graphic artist

Social injustices, peace, and brotherhood were themes running through the work of German graphic artist Käthe Kollwitz. Her works attempt to demonstrate the happiness and tragedies of the mother-child relationship and to portray the emotions attached to death. Her drawings, woodcuts, etchings, and sculpture were widely praised and she became the first woman member of the Prussian Academy of Art.

One of her two sons was killed in World War I, and though she loved her German homeland, she used her art as a protest against the rise of detested Nazism. She was forbidden to teach or exhibit her work because its social theme was considered "degenerate." Much of it was burned by the Nazis.

During the years following the war and just after her death, her work gradually reappeared and has again found enormous popularity both for its artistic merits and its relevance to contemporary social issues.

Kearns, Martha KÄTHE KOLLWITZ: WOMAN AND ARTIST Feminist Pr., 1976. (grade 9 and up)

A very fine, well-documented biography of the artist is intended for adults, but will be read and appreciated by competent high school readers with an interest in art. It moves along smoothly, focussing on her work and personal life, and has a clear feminist perspective.

Klein, Mina C., and Klein, H. Arthur KÄTHE KOLLWITZ: LIFE IN ART Illus. Holt, 1972. (grade 9 and up)

Beautiful, touching, and sensitive book is a personal as well as artistic biography. Including more than one hundred reproductions of her drawings, woodcuts, etchings, and sculpture, this book is a delight to look at as well as read. The authors' distinguished writing, as well as Kollwitz's own work, clearly expresses the love she had for her work, husband, children, grandchildren, and her country, despite its actions.

~~~~~~

OLGA KORBUT
1956–

Soviet Olympic gold medal–winning gymnast

When four-foot, eleven-inch, eighty-four-pound Olga Korbut competed in the 1972 Olympics in Munich the sixteen-year-old gymnast not only won three gold medals but also stole the show for television viewers all over the world.

Under the Russian government's school sports system, she received training in gymnastics, and by her early teens was winning national and international awards. When she competed in the 1972 Olympics, she demonstrated the backward somersault on the uneven parallel bars and became the first person, male or female, to do so in competition.

It was not only her disciplined gymnastic ability and her apparent fearlessness but her natural, often emotional personality that endeared her to audiences. When she toured the United States the following year she was greeted by enthusiastic capacity crowds. She received ABC's "Wide World of Sports" athlete of the year award and the Associated Press's Babe Didrikson Zaharias Trophy for

Female Athlete of the Year, and was a favorite in the 1976 Olympics.

Now married to Leonid Bortkevich, a Russian singer, she has retired from gymnastic competition.

Evans, Given EASTERN SUPERSTAR: OLGA KORBUT Illus. with photographs. Raintree, 1976. (grades 3–8)

Good, nonadulatory biography discusses Olga Korbut's life as a gymnastic star, describing the interaction between the sport and politics.

Jacobs, Linda OLGA KORBUT: GIRL OF TEARS AND TRIUMPH Illus. EMC, 1974. (grade 4 and up)

Well-balanced account of the gymnast's life focusses on her athletic career, but also discusses her personality and private life. Numerous photographs of her in action greatly enhance the easy-to-read text making the biography particularly appealing to older reluctant readers as well as younger children.

Smith, Jay H. OLGA KORBUT Illus. Creative Educ. Soc., 1974. (grades 4–8)

Colorfully illustrated, this nonadulatory biography depicts the popular young gymnast as a fearless, determined competitor who shows her emotions to her fans. The emphasis is on her athletic career, but her early life is also described.

~~~~~~

SUSAN LA FLESCHE, M.D.
1865–1915

Native American physician

The youngest child of an Omaha chief, Susan La Flesche followed in the path of her older sister Susette (see below) and attended first a missionary school and then an Eastern girls' seminary.

Encouraged by the Women's National Indian Association, she enrolled in the Women's Medical College of Pennsylvania and graduated first in her class. After some additional training she returned to her tribe as a physician, often travelling long distances by horseback to treat the ill and to teach them health and hygiene.

After her marriage to Henry Picotte, of French-Sioux descent, she continued her medical practice and brought up their two sons. A leader in her community, she was active in church affairs, an organizer of the County Medical Society, and chairperson of the local board of health. In 1913 she established a hospital which was later named after her.

It was said that she had treated every member of the Omaha tribe during the years of her medical practice and managed, always, to combine the two cultures of her birth and her education.

Brown, Marion Marsh HOMEWARD THE ARROW'S FLIGHT Illus. Abingdon, 1980. (grade 7 and up)

Excellent biography traces Susan La Flesche's life from an Eastern school to college and medical school and the beginning of her practice on the reservation. It reveals her as a hardworking, intelligent, curious woman, dedicated to her people and desirous of combining professional activities with family commitments.

~~~~~~

SUSETTE LA FLESCHE
1854–1903

*Spokeswoman for Indian rights, author,
lecturer, and artist*

Susette La Flesche, an Omaha Indian, was the older sister of physician Susan La Flesche. She grew up on a reservation in Nebraska and attended a mission school, becoming fluent in French and English as well as her native language. Her quick mind and great thirst for knowledge came to the attention of her teacher, who arranged for her to attend an Eastern girls' seminary. Later she became a teacher on the Omaha reservation.

La Flesche, or Bright Eyes as she was also known, was imbued by her tribal leader father with a sense of responsibility to her people. She participated in many Indian reform movements, wrote articles for newspapers pleading their causes, and embarked on a lecture tour of the East with Thomas Tibbles, a white newspaperman; Standing Bear, an Indian Chief; and her brother. They were successful in making Americans aware of the grave injustices done to

Indians and through their efforts an act was passed which allotted reservation land and citizenship rights to individual Indians.

After her marriage to Thomas Tibbles she continued to lecture in the United States and England, contributed additional articles and stories to magazines and newspapers, and illustrated a historical book about the origin of the Omahas.

Crary, Margaret SUSETTE LA FLESCHE: VOICE OF THE OMAHA INDIANS   Illus. Hawthorn, 1973. (grades 7–10)
Very fine biography of the Indian spokeswoman also gives a good picture of the Omaha Indians and their fight for citizenship rights. La Flesche is depicted as an unusually intelligent, warm human being whose belief that Indians should be seen as people in the eyes of the law was a motivating force for her efforts to enlighten the public.

~~~~~~

MARY ELIZABETH LEASE
1853–1933

Populist party speaker and agitator

Life as a Kansas farmer's wife and mother of four had been too confining for former teacher Mary Elizabeth Lease, so when her husband returned to his practice of pharmacy, she engaged herself in civic and social affairs and formed the Hypatia Society, a women's group for discussion of current issues.

As her interests widened she became actively involved in politics and her stirring, resonant voice and charismatic quality made her a successful public speaker on behalf of local groups. Lease also edited the *Union Labor Press*, founded a labor paper, and was elected president of a chapter of the Knights of Labor. She made a major contribution to the local and national scene as a speaker and agitator for the Farmer's Alliance and the Populist party, explaining to farmers in Kansas, Missouri, the Far West, and the South how they were exploited by Eastern monopolies. Lease studied law and passed the Kansas bar examination; wrote for the New York *World*; published a book entitled *The Problem of Civilization Solved*; and was a continuous supporter of women's suffrage, prohibition, and birth control. She served as president of the National Society for Birth Control, and is remembered best as one of the first important women politicians in the nation.

Stiller, Richard QUEEN OF THE POPULISTS: THE STORY OF MARY ELIZABETH LEASE   Illus. Crowell, 1970. (grades 6–9)
Outstanding, completely written biography traces the Populist movement as well as giving a dramatic, perceptive portrait of the first important woman politician in America. The colorful personality of Lease emerges, and her important contributions are carefully noted in a vividly written book.

~~~~~~

ANN LEE
1736–1784

Founder of the religious group the Shakers

Nothing in Ann Lee's early life in England would have predicted that she would later be the founder of a religious group, the United Society of Believers in Christ's Second Appearing, known as the Shakers.

She reluctantly agreed to a marriage she didn't desire and had four children, all of whom died in infancy. She then suffered an emotional and physical breakdown. Convinced that sexual relations, even in marriage, were a sin against God, she carried her message in streets and churches. The singing, dancing and shouting that she and her followers indulged in earned them the name Shakers. In 1774 she came to American where she made many converts. The group made beautiful, simple, utilitarian, handcrafted furniture. Since Shakers could not marry or have children, their number slowly dwindled from six thousand men and women to only a handful in the 1950s.

Mother Ann Lee, as she was called, is best remembered today as the founder of the Shakers. Her advocacy of equal rights and responsibilities for men and women, dignity of labor, and true obedience to Christian beliefs and her charismatic personality made her a unique religious figure.

Campion, Nardi Reeder ANN THE WORD: THE LIFE OF MOTHER ANN LEE, FOUNDER OF THE SHAKERS Little, 1976. (grades 5–8)

A very fine, well-balanced, documented, and researched biography of the religious leader provides insight into her personality, and is written with dignity and respect.

~~~~~~

ISABELLA LEITNER
1929–

World War II concentration camp survivor

Isabella Leitner, a young Hungarian Jewish woman, was rounded up with her family and other Jews in 1944 and deported to Auschwitz, a death camp. Their father, who had escaped to the United States, was working to obtain their passage but received permission too late. Her mother and one sister were immediately selected for the gas chambers by the Nazis, but she, her other three sisters, and her brother managed to survive the concentration camps. One sister died after liberation.

Despite typhoid, chronic illness, starvation, and torture, they gave each other strength in the camps. After liberation they came to the United States, where Isabella later met her husband, Irving Leitner, author and editor. They have two sons.

Leitner, Isabella FRAGMENTS OF ISABELLA: A MEMOIR OF AUSCHWITZ Crowell, 1978. (grade 9 and up)

A personal memoir of the Holocaust, and Auschwitz in particular, as viewed by a teenager who lost her mother and sister to the gas chamber and formed a bond with her remaining siblings. An emotionally painful book to read, it is a tribute to all those who shared her experience, and to the physical and emotional strength of women who endure torture. The bitterness the author felt towards her captors as well as the Germans who "looked the other way" remains with her.

LOIS LENSKI
1893–

Author and illustrator of children's books

Popular author and illustrator of children's books, Lois Lenski began her professional career by illustrating books for other authors. The pictures she drew for her own son when he was young grew into the now classic picture books of the Mr. Small and Davy series. A thorough and exacting craftswoman, Lenski extensively researched lives and periods for *Indian Captive*, her biography of Mary Jemison (page 119), and for her historical novels *Blueberry Corners* and *Puritan Adventure*. For her regional books *Blue Ridge Billy, Prairie School, Strawberry Girl, Judy's Journey*, and *Cotton in My Sack*, Lenski did not rely only on scholarly library research but went directly to the locations and gathered her background material firsthand.

Lois Lenski has won many of the major book awards for her work, much of which remains enormously popular with youngsters. Educators find Lenski's books to be good supplements to classroom assignments in social studies.

Lenski, Lois JOURNEY INTO CHILDHOOD: THE AUTOBIOGRAPHY OF LOIS LENSKI Illus. Lippincott, 1972. (grade 9 and up)
Fine autobiography considers Lenski's childhood, youth, and adulthood in informal, enjoyable detail. However, because this book is far less engaging than her books for young readers, it may be of greater interest to adults or those older readers with fond recollections of Lois Lenski's juvenile books.

NANCY LIEBERMAN
1958–

Basketball player

New York–born Nancy Lieberman became the most widely publicized high school player in the history of women's basketball.

Nearly one hundred colleges and universities recruited her, and later when she became a professional she became the highest paid woman player in basketball.

In 1976 Nancy Lieberman won a silver medal in the Olympics, and would have been a member of the 1980 team if not for the American boycott of the Moscow games. A two-time winner of the Wade Trophy (women's basketball equivalent of football's Heisman Trophy), named a three-time Kodak All-American, she was also a gold medal winner at the Pan American games.

Her mother initially opposed her career choice, but soon became a staunch supporter. Nancy Lieberman, a firm believer in the important role that sports can play in a woman's life, and of women's important role in the world of sports, is a frequent speaker at youth and athletic groups.

Jones, Betty Millsaps NANCY LIEBERMAN: BASKETBALL'S MAGIC LADY Illus. with photographs. Harvey, 1980. (grade 4 and up)

An excellent biography reads quickly and well. Lieberman emerges multidimensional, and the book should interest general readers as well as sports fans.

~~~~~~

BETTY JEAN LIFTON
1926–

Author, adoptee rights advocate

Betty Jean Lifton, a journalist, playwright, and author of many books for young readers, was adopted. Eager to learn more of her biological origins, she searched out her mother who had given her up for adoption and became reunited with her. Since then she has advocated for open adoptions and the rights of the adopted to learn more about their beginnings.

Lifton is married to a psychiatrist and they spent seven years in the Far East; much of her writing reflects her interest in that culture and politics.

143

Lifton, Betty Jean Twice Born: memoirs of an adopted daughter McGraw, 1975. (grade 8 and up)

Absorbing story of the author's search for her biological mother and of her relationship with her, as well as with all the members of her family.

~~~~~~

JENNY LIND
1820–1887

Swedish opera star

Sometimes referred to as the "Swedish nightingale," Jenny Lind was born in Sweden where she early began her studies of drama and music. At sixteen she made her opera debut and quickly climbed to stardom, becoming a favorite in her native Sweden as well as in Europe. A two-year tour of the United States under the auspices of P. T. Barnum brought her even greater prominence. She married while in the United States, and upon her return to England continued her successful appearances in oratorios and concerts. Always interested in helping other musicians to learn and attain excellence, she encouraged them in their musical studies and became a professor of singing at the Royal College of Music.

Jenny Lind's great success derived from her magnificent voice, her fine musicianship, and her great acting ability. Generous and philanthropic, she gave much of her earned fortunes to causes in which she believed.

Cavanah, Frances Jenny Lind and Her Listening Cat Illus. Vanguard, 1961. (grades 3–6)

Animated, fictionalized account of the childhood of Jenny Lind offers a delightful and tender portrait of the young girl whose talents were early nurtured.

~~~~~~

BELVA ANN LOCKWOOD
1830–1917

Attorney, advocate of women's rights, peace worker

Belva Ann Lockwood was solely responsible for getting Congress to allow women to practice law before the United States Supreme Court. Until she was in her eighties, she was active in civil rights for women and minorities, and in efforts towards world peace.

She left school at fifteen, but later as a young widow with a child to support became a teacher and continued her own education. She then decided to go to law school, but was rejected at several law schools in Washington, D.C. When she finally gained acceptance she was later refused her diploma until President Grant met her "demand" and ordered that it be given to her.

The Supreme Court refused to allow any woman to plead cases before it, but through Lockwood's lobbying efforts, Congress finally passed a bill that eliminated this barrier, and she became the first woman to practice before the nation's highest court.

A tireless worker for women's legal rights, she also represented the Eastern Cherokee Indians in their case against the United States and won for them an award of five million dollars. She also sponsored the first southern black man to practice before the Supreme Court.

Throughout her active professional life, Belva Ann Lockwood gave not only inspiration but also concrete help to many aspiring women attorneys.

Dunnahoo, Terry BEFORE THE SUPREME COURT: THE STORY OF BELVA ANN LOCKWOOD Houghton Mifflin, 1974. (grade 6 and up)
Outstanding biography gives a strong impression of the subject's personality and accomplishments as well as describing the women's movement and the era with perception and inspiration. Discussions of law and politics are incorporated into this extremely readable biography.

Fox, Mary Virginia LADY FOR THE DEFENSE Harcourt, 1975. (grades 6–9)
Good, objective, and accurate biography is stylistically inconsistent. At times the author employs much conversation, other times the narrative

becomes quite formal. The accomplishments of the subject are clearly depicted, but the book lacks the excitement and inspiration that the subject herself displayed.

~~~~~~

NANCY LOPEZ
1957–

Championship golfer

Mexican-American Nancy Lopez began playing golf when she was only eight years old, and by the time she was twelve she had won New Mexico's women's amateur title, beating players considerably older than herself. At sixteen, Nancy Lopez was the top-ranked amateur golfer in the world, having won numerous championships.

She was allowed to play on the all-male golf team at high school, but only after bringing legal pressure on the local board of education. Nancy Lopez then helped her team win the state championship.

Discrimination was not new to her, since her Mexican-American heritage often stood in her way of receiving recognition and invitations to play on private golf courses. Her father was her coach, and her parents' personal sacrifices gave her much of the support she needed to maintain her determination to achieve.

In 1977 Nancy Lopez became a professional, and within a year won more money than any other rookie golfer, man or woman, had ever won. She attracted the biggest galleries in the history of the Ladies Professional Golf Association, attesting to her warm personality and charm as well as talent.

Nancy Lopez continues to draw record crowds as she competes and wins major tournaments.

Hahn, James, and Hahn, Lynn NANCY LOPEZ: GOLFING PIONEER Illus. with photographs. EMC, 1979. (grade 4 and up)
Very good biography focusses on Nancy Lopez's golfing career, and reveals the obstacles she overcame; racism, sexism, and financial limitations. She emerges as hardworking, determined, and appreciative of her family's emotional and financial support.

146

Phillips, Betty L. THE PICTURE STORY OF NANCY LOPEZ Illus. with photographs. Messner, 1980. (grades 4–7)
The golfer's strong family ties, her ambitions, and her hard work are completely identified in this warm, insightful biography.

Robison, Nancy NANCY LOPEZ: WONDER WOMAN OF GOLF Illus. with photographs. Childrens Pr., 1979. (grades 3–8)
Very easy-to-read, lively biography of the golf professional depicts her as a youngster encouraged by her father, as a hard-working committed athlete, and as someone who also enjoys herself off the course. For young readers and for older reluctant ones.

Schumacher, Craig NANCY LOPEZ Illus. with photographs. Creative Ed., 1979. (grades 3–8)
Very good, inspirational personal and professional biography is easy to read, but will be of interest to older, less able readers.

~~~~~~

ESTHER POHL LOVEJOY, M.D.
1870–1967

Physician, director and organizer of
American Women's Hospital Service

Esther Pohl Lovejoy, one of the first women graduates of the University of Oregon medical school, became the first woman in America to hold the position of chairperson of the Board of Health in a major city. Lovejoy was an early advocate of community medicine and better sanitary conditions, the founder of a hospital in Alaska, and an active supporter of women's suffrage. She achieved recognition during World War I for her work with the Red Cross and as director and organizer of the American Women's Hospital Service. Her help in developing orphanages, clinics, hospitals, and medical assistance to disaster victims and refugees in Europe and Asia won her many honorary degrees, decorations, and tributes from heads of state all over the world.

During World War II, Dr. Lovejoy helped the displaced and interned Japanese-Americans in this country, and aided in the selection of women doctors to serve in the Armed Forces. She worked tirelessly to achieve their equal status with male doctors in the services.

Esther Pohl Lovejoy did much to gain recognition for women in medicine. She wrote books about her own experiences and a history of women in medicine and served as the president of the American Medical Women's National Association.

Burt, Olive W. PHYSICIAN TO THE WORLD: ESTHER POHL LOVEJOY Messner, 1973. (grade 7 and up)
Lacking in distinctive literary style, this is nonetheless a dramatic, vivid account of a woman whose single-mindedness, persistence, boundless energy, and intelligence were determining factors in her great achievements.

~~~~~~

JULIETTE GORDON LOW
1860–1927

Founder of the Girl Scouts of America

Juliette "Daisy" Gordon Low was, until the time she founded the Girl Scouts of America, a woman with few interests and ambitions. Known for her charm and good sense of humor, she had many artistic and creative talents but lived rather aimlessly as did many women of her high social position. At age fifty-one she met General Sir Robert Baden-Powell, founder of the Boy Scouts, and became interested in the Girl Guides, a similar organization for girls.

Low formed groups in Scotland and London and then returned to her native Savannah, Georgia, to organize units there. The first troop she organized in 1912 generated so much interest throughout the country that by 1915 Juliette Low had organized the Girl Scouts of America and was serving as their first president. During this early period she paid all the expenses herself and travelled throughout the country convincing, and sometimes coercing, prominent women to become leaders and organizers.

Girl scouting continued to grow during World War I. Low retired as president in 1920 but continued her active involvement as the founder. Despite a somewhat romantic, impractical nature, Juliette

Low was a superb, intelligent organizer whose commitment to worldwide girl scouting was realized during her lifetime.

Radford, Ruby L. JULIETTE LOW: GIRL SCOUT FOUNDER   Garrard, 1965. (grades 2–5)
Very good, immensely readable profile of Juliette Low may be particularly attractive to young Brownies and Girl Scouts, but is of sufficient general interest to be enjoyed by others.

~~~~~~

JANET LYNN
1953–

Olympic figure-skating champion

From the time Janet Lynn first put on a pair of ice skates at two-and-a-half, she showed the grace and superb balance that would later make her the first ranked amateur figure skater in the United States.

She reached the Nationals in 1963, the youngest skater ever to qualify, and at twelve she won the Junior Figure Skating Nationals. In 1968 she became the youngest skater ever to make the United States Olympic team and in 1969 she won her first Nationals Championship.

Free skating and jumping are her strong points; the mechanical exactness required for the compulsory school figures constitutes her weak area. Nevertheless, in 1971, Janet Lynn was ranked first in the United States and fourth in the world and won a bronze medal in the 1972 Olympics.

In 1973 after her fifth straight win in the Nationals, she decided to turn professional. She signed a contract with the Ice Follies for a great sum of money, much of which she has given to charity. In 1974 she won the first Professional Figure Skating Championship. In 1975, respiratory problems caused her to retire from skating. The allergies that she later found were the cause are now under control.

Janet Lynn, now married and the mother of three little boys, has begun to skate again and has appeared in exhibitions and on television.

Jacobs, Linda   JANET LYNN: SUNSHINE ON ICE   Illus. with photographs.
EMC, 1974. (grade 4 and up)

Good, fast-moving, highly readable portrait of skater Janet Lynn describes her years of training and achievements, as well as her religious
faith and commitment. At times overly laudatory, the author tends to
depict her as an almost storybook perfect individual. Many photographs of
her on and off the ice are good contributions to the biography. Suitable for
older reluctant readers as well as younger ones.

~~~~~~

LORETTA LYNN
1935–

Country and western singer and
songwriter

Loretta Lynn was the first woman in country music to earn a gold
album, and the first woman to win the Country Music Association
award for entertainer of the year.

The poor, coalminer's daughter from Butcher Hollow, Kentucky,
was married at fourteen and had four children by the time she was
eighteen. Between having babies and caring for them, she and her
husband struggled to launch her career, travelling constantly.

She became a regular favorite at the Grand Ole Opry, and toured
throughout the country. Her live performances, recordings, and
television appearances made her enormously successful. She
writes many of her own songs, most of which are based on her own
or country neighbors' real life experiences.

Devoted to her family, and deeply religious, she is admired even
by those who do not usually enjoy country music. A film based on
her autobiography *Coal Miner's Daughter* was well received and
increased her popularity still more.

Krishef, Robert K.   LORETTA LYNN   Illus. with photographs. Lerner,
1978. (grades 4–9)

Good, fast-moving biography depicts Loretta Lynn as devoted to family
and traditional values, but also as ambitious and highly dedicated to her
work.

Lynn, Loretta with George Vecsey LORETTA LYNN: COAL MINER'S DAUGHTER Illus. with photographs. Warner, Regnery, 1976. (grade 7 and up)

Informal autobiography captures the spirit of Loretta Lynn and her music, revealing her as a religious woman, dedicated to family and work.

~~~~~~

MARY LYON
1797–1849

Founder of Mount Holyoke College

Mary Lyon, the founder of Mount Holyoke College and a member of America's Hall of Fame, may be credited with opening the doors for women's higher education in the United States. Before opening Mount Holyoke, the first nonprofit, endowed institution of higher education for women, Lyon had already established a fine reputation launching schools and academies for young women. The college was conceived as an institution with academic standards equal to those at the finest men's colleges, and dedicated to Christian principles. Lyon placed all financial matters in the hands of trustees, to assure the college's continuity after her retirement.

In 1837 Mount Holyoke opened in South Hadley, Massachusetts, with eighty students. Under Mary Lyon's capable administration, the enrollment rose, curriculum grew, and new methods of teaching were successfully introduced. The first principals of the later-established Vassar and Wellesley colleges had been her students, as were the staffs of some of the finest schools throughout the nation. Many of Mount Holyoke's graduates, imbued with Lyon's evangelistic zeal, went into missionary work and community service. Today, Mount Holyoke is one of America's leading women's colleges.

Banning, Evelyn I. MARY LYON OF PUTNAM'S HILL Vanguard, 1965. (grades 5–8)

Excellent, warm picture of the founder of Mount Holyoke College traces Lyon's life from early childhood to her last years of great accomplishments. Written in an intelligent, but highly readable style, it may be of interest to readers older than those suggested by the publisher.

ANNE SULLIVAN MACY
1866–1936

Teacher to Helen Keller

Anne Sullivan Macy's tragic childhood was marked by near blindness, the death of her mother, desertion by her father, life in a public almshouse, and then the death of her beloved little brother. Surgery later restored much of her sight, and after her graduation from the Perkins Institute for the Blind she was offered a job teaching seven-year-old blind and deaf Helen Keller (page 126). Anne Sullivan Macy arrived at the Keller home to find an untutored, undisciplined but curious child. With determination, innovation, and insightful talent she soon had young Helen spelling words into her hands and behaving in a civilized manner.

When Helen Keller was later admitted to Radcliffe College, Macy attended classes with her, patiently spelling out the lectures and reading the course assignments to her. There she met young literary critic John Macy. They married, but eventually separated.

Anne Sullivan continued to live and travel with Helen Keller, lecturing, demonstrating their teaching methods, and raising money for philanthropic causes. Not until her last few years did Macy receive the recognition she so richly deserved; most people were unaware of the skill and years of unselfish dedication that preceded Helen Keller's great achievements. In 1955, Helen Keller wrote *Teacher*, a memoir and tribute to the remarkable woman who, though lacking social confidence and patience with her own handicaps, had taught those qualities to her student and brought her out of her darkness.

Brown, Marion, and Crone, Ruth THE SILENT STORM Illus. Abingdon, 1963. (grades 6–8)
Extremely moving and dramatic account of Anne Sullivan Macy's life depicts her miserable childhood, her difficult youth, and her long-time relationship with Helen Keller.

Davidson, Mickie HELEN KELLER'S TEACHER Illus. Four Winds, 1965. (grades 3–7)
Warm, intimate biography of Anne Sullivan **Macy** shows her grim

childhood as well as her later achievements as teacher to young Helen Keller. Very readable, this book has enormous appeal.

Gibson, William THE MIRACLE WORKER Knopf, 1957. (grade 7 and up)
   Outstanding dramatic play about Anne Sullivan Macy and Helen Keller which was presented on Broadway and then made into a motion picture is compelling and stirring both to read and to see.

Malone, Mary ANNIE SULLIVAN Illus. Putnam, 1971. (grades 2–4)
   Simplistic, but tender and perceptive biography is enhanced by Lydia Rosier's illustrations.

Waite, Helen E. VALIANT COMPANIONS Macrae, 1959. (grade 7 and up)
   Extremely fine, substantial narrative examines the remarkable relationship between Helen Keller and Anne Sullivan Macy. Dramatic and emotional, it is written more from the perspective of Macy's life, but is both their stories.

~~~~~~

DOLLEY MADISON
1768–1849

Washington hostess, First Lady

Popular, vibrant young widow Dolley Payne was living in Washington, D.C., when she met and married the brilliant congressional leader James Madison. A fine conversationalist with the rare gift of placing everyone at ease in all social situations, Dolley Madison soon became a prominent and successful Washington hostess. When James Madison served as Thomas Jefferson's secretary of state, Dolley was frequently called upon to act as unofficial First Lady.

During the War of 1812, when James Madison was President, the British burned the White House and Dolley Madison disregarded personal safety to salvage many important documents, including the famed Stuart portrait of George Washington.

After President Madison's retirement, they returned to their home in Virginia, Montpelier, where they continued their famed hospitality, receiving the public as well as dignitaries. When Dolley Madison returned to Washington as a widow, she retained her leading role in society. Her son's mismanagement of family funds placed her in a near state of poverty, but she was afforded some financial comfort when Congress, after years of deliberation, bought her husband's presidential papers from her.

In a recent poll, she emerged as one of the most respected first ladies of all time.

Desmond, Alice Curtis GLAMOUROUS DOLLEY MADISON Illus. Dodd, 1946. (grade 9 and up)
Extremely well-written and absorbing biography of Dolley Madison draws a well-rounded picture of her and offers a worthwhile view of the time in which she lived.

Grant, Matthew G. DOLLEY MADISON Illus. Creative Educ. Soc./Childrens Pr., 1974. (grades 2–4)
Lovely, abundant illustrations add to a warm, responsible biography of Dolley Madison. She is depicted as an intelligent, capable woman. Brief and easy to read, the biography also gives a good picture of the period.

Melick, Arden Davis DOLLEY MADISON, FIRST LADY Putnam, 1970. (grades 4–6)
Somewhat uneven biography is a good portrayal of Madison. However, the format (short sentences, large print) indicates this is for very young readers, despite occasional difficult vocabulary.

Nolan, Jeannette DOLLEY MADISON Messner, 1959. (grades 6–9)
Enjoyable biography of Dolley Madison introduces the subject as an intelligent, colorful woman in this convincingly fictionalized portrait.

Thane, Elswyth DOLLEY MADISON: HER LIFE AND TIMES Macmillan, 1970. (grade 7 and up)
Substantial narrative is a somewhat detailed, scholarly account which combines history and biography with the life of Dolley Madison.

~~~~~~

MARIA MARTÍNEZ
1881–1980

Indian potter

By rediscovering pottery techniques which had been lost for centuries, Maria Martínez transformed the poor farming village of San

Ildefonso into a prosperous place filled with successful artisans. She and her husband worked together, demonstrating and selling their finished and decorated pottery at fairs before gaining national recognition. They perfected an award-winning firing technique which resulted in black-on-black pottery. Maria's distinctively original work is done freehand, without the aid of a potter's wheel or closed kiln.

Maria Martínez later worked with her son, artist Povov-Da, who decorated her pottery, and then with her grandchildren and great-grandchildren. An extremely clever businesswoman herself, she encouraged other Pueblo women to learn, thus giving them some of the economic security she enjoyed.

Nelson, Mary Carroll MARIA MARTÍNEZ Dillon, 1972. (grades 5–9)

Outstanding portrait incorporates cultural aspects of the Pueblos with the life story of Maria Martínez, resulting in a fine combination of anthropology and biography.

~~~~~~

MARY I
1516–1558

Queen of England

As the oldest living offspring of King Henry VIII, Mary I (also known as Mary Tudor), was heir to the throne of England. However, her father had his marriage to her mother, Catherine of Aragon, annulled in order to marry Anne Boleyn (the future mother of Queen Elizabeth I) which put Mary's legitimacy and her succession in doubt.

She became queen of England in 1553, but the years of uncertainty over her status made Mary Tudor a bitter and suspicious woman. King Henry had defied the Pope and made England a Protestant country. Mary was a devout Catholic with ties to Spain through her mother and her marriage to Philip II. The people accepted her as Henry's daughter, but her religious fanaticism led to cruel persecutions of England's Protestants in her attempt to restore the old religion to England. Her ties to Spain brought political and military disasters to England.

Her marriage was childless, despite her yearnings for a son. Mary's childhood had been a time of confusion and passionate conflicts. Her father's attention had been erratic, his love uncertain, and her husband's feelings for her were equally in doubt. She inherited not only a throne but also the religious and political tensions of a tumultuous time. It was not only the problems of her own personality, but also the legacy of the past and the play of forces in history that made for her brief and bitter five-year reign.

Roll, Winifred MARY I Prentice-Hall, 1980. (grade 9 and up)
A well-rounded, nonfictionalized biography of the queen is a scholarly, thoroughly researched study which is highly readable. Readers interested in British history and royalty will find it useful; less serious readers may find it of minor interest.

~~~~~~

MARY, QUEEN OF SCOTS
1542–1587

Queen of France and Scotland

Mary, Queen of Scots, assumed the throne of Scotland when she was only a few days old. Raised in France by her mother, she became, by marriage, queen of France, but after the king's death went to live in Scotland.

Her royal position was difficult because she was a Roman Catholic, and Scotland, like England, was Protestant. Marriage to Lord Darnley afforded her little happiness and when he was murdered by the earl of Bothwell, whom she subsequently married, her subjects believed she was an accomplice. Forced to abdicate, she escaped to England only to be kept imprisoned for nineteen years by her cousin, Queen Elizabeth I.

Mary was constantly accused of conspiring to kill Elizabeth and to place herself on the throne. Seriously implicated in one such plot, she was tried and found guilty. Mary accepted the death sentence with great dignity and courage, and to the end declared her innocence.

Hahn, Emily Mary, Queen of Scots Illus. Random, 1953. (grades 7–9)

Good biography recreates the society in which Mary, Queen of Scots, lived in a well-balanced account of her life.

Plaidy, Jean Young Mary Queen of Scots Illus. Roy, 1962. (grades 6–10)

Well-written and sympathetic, this book emphasizes Mary's childhood and early years. A good picture of the times is drawn and the politics are carefully woven into the biography. A short concluding chapter discusses the queen's later years.

~~~~~~

MARGARET MEAD
1901–1978

Anthropologist, author

For almost fifty years Margaret Mead was a leading anthropologist. She was one of the first professionals to engage in field work, actually living among primitive cultures and learning their languages. Mead lectured, taught at major universities, and wrote on subjects as varied as tribes in New Guinea, American Indians, world population, peace, family relationships, racial tensions, and careers for women. For many years a member of the department of anthropology at the American Museum of Natural History, and curator of ethnology there, Margaret Mead directed the new and outstanding permanent exhibit, Peoples of the Pacific.

During World War II when her visits to the Pacific were curtailed, Mead lectured, wrote, and directed studies for the Office of War Information and took care of her young daughter. Her books *Coming of Age in Samoa, Growing Up in New Guinea, Male and Female*, and *Sex and Temperament* have the dual distinction of being best-sellers and of having gained scholarly regard, for when they were written they met all of anthropology's standards for scientific research.

Church, Carol Bauer Margaret Mead, Student of the Global

157

VILLAGE Illus. with photographs. Greenhaven Pr., 1976. (grade 5 and up)

Excellent, accurate profile of Margaret Mead is fast-moving, and will appeal to older, slower readers as well as younger ones.

Epstein, Sam, and Epstein, Beryl SHE NEVER LOOKED BACK: MARGARET MEAD IN SAMOA Illus. Garrard, 1980. (grades 4–6)

Excellent book focusses on Margaret Mead's first field trip as a young anthropologist and gives a good picture of her long-term goals, and of her hard-working dedication. A final chapter deals with her later accomplishments. The author makes anthropology sound fascinating, but realistically depicts it as arduous.

Frevert, Patricia MARGARET MEAD: HERSELF Illus. with photographs. Creative Ed., 1981. (grades 3–7)

Excellent biography of Margaret Mead reveals the strong influences her parents and grandparents had on her as a child and the belief and support they offered her, helping to lead to her remarkable achievements.

Ludle, Jacqueline MARGARET MEAD Illus. with photographs. Watts, 1983. (grades 7 and up)

Very good biography of Margaret Mead is a straightforward, serious account of her childhood, youth, and mature career. Gives a good picture of anthropology as well as her life.

Mead, Margaret BLACKBERRY WINTER: MY EARLIER YEARS Illus. Morrow, 1972. (grade 9 and up)

Outstanding autobiography by Mead introduces the subject as youngster, student, mother, and grandmother as well as leading anthropologist. Fascinating and inspiring, it will motivate readers to learn more about her work, and perhaps to read her own writings based on field work.

Morse, Ann, and Morse, Charles MARGARET MEAD Illus. Creative Educ. Soc., 1975. (grades 4–8)

Unusually fine biography of Margaret Mead explains the entire concept of anthropology in terms elementary school children can understand. At the same time the authors give a well-balanced, fairly full account of her personal life as well as her work in the field, her writings, lectures, and philosophy.

Rice, Edward MARGARET MEAD: A PORTRAIT Illus. with photographs. Harper and Row, 1979. (grade 7 and up)

An excellent nonfictionalized, fast-paced, rich narrative biography of Margaret Mead is well researched and makes use of liberal quotes from her own writings.

MARY E. MEBANE
1933–

Author, educator

Mary E. Mebane was born in Dunham, North Carolina, when segregation was still the law of the land. Realizing her future was limited to factory or domestic work because she was black, she aimed for college, although her family could see no reason for it. An aunt who believed in her made a small provision for her to go to college, but died before Mary ever got there.

Determined to obtain an education, she received her bachelor's degree from North Carolina College and a master's and doctorate from the University of North Carolina. She has written for many publications and now teaches at the University of Wisconsin.

Mebane, Mary E. MARY Viking, 1981. (grade 8 and up)
    Excellent book traces Mebane's life until graduation from college. Author gives a vivid picture of the segregated South and of a talented, highly intelligent young woman and her determination to have a good life. Moving at a lively pace, it is at the same time sad, amusing, and filled with honest insights and reality.

GOLDA MEIR
1898–1978

Prime minister of Israel

Golda Meir's family left anti-Semitic Kiev to go to the United States when she was eight years old. Her great desire for higher education was discouraged by her traditional family who saw no need of it for women. Golda Meir was an independent, ambitious young woman whose Zionist beliefs were so strong that after she finally completed her education and married, she and her husband embarked in 1921 for Palestine. There they lived in a kibbutz and later in cities where their financial hardships were so great that at one time she washed clothing to help pay for their children's education.

Always active in civic and political work, Golda Meir became a member of the Israeli Knesset (Parliament) and during World War II served on the War Economy Advisory Council. She was instrumental in arranging many Jewish immigrations to Palestine and was one of the thirty-seven signers of Israel's declaration of independence. Meir became Israel's first ambassador to the Soviet Union, minister of labor, and foreign minister. As head of the Labor party she was chosen prime minister in 1969, thus becoming one of only three women so far elected as heads of state. She died in 1978 after a long, courageous battle with cancer.

Davidson, Margaret   THE GOLDA MEIR STORY   Scribner, 1976; new revised edition, 1981. (grades 5–7)

The author gives a good picture of her life and times, but reliance on fictionalized dialogue detracts from the overall quality of the book.

Dobrin, Arnold   A LIFE FOR ISRAEL: THE STORY OF GOLDA MEIR   Illus. Dial, 1974. (grades 3–6)

Outstanding biography gives a full picture of the life of Golda Meir and the growth of Israel. Without a textbook quality, the history of Israel is interestingly explained to young readers who may have no prior knowledge of it. The salient points of Meir's career are well told, with warmth, drama, and excitement.

Keller, Mollie   GOLDA MEIR   Illus. with photographs. Watts, 1983 (grade 7 and up)

Straightforward biography gives a good portrait of the woman, her work, and her important contributions to Israel and the world.

Mann, Peggy   GOLDA: THE STORY OF ISRAEL'S PRIME MINISTER   Illus. Coward, 1971. (grade 9 and up)

Outstanding profile of Golda Meir is an immensely readable and substantial in-depth study of Israel's prime minister. Her life story is related against the background of the independence and growth of Israel.

Meir, Golda   MY LIFE   Illus. with photographs. Putnam, 1975. (grade 7 and up)

A lengthy, in-depth autobiography traces her life from early childhood through the Yom Kippur War. For enthusiastic readers who want to know about her life in her own words.

Morris, Terry SHALOM, GOLDA Illus. Hawthorn, 1971. (grades 7–9)
   Very fine, clear, and colorful biography gives an intimate personal view of Meir, at the same time drawing a good portrait of Israel.

Noble, Iris ISRAEL'S GOLDA MEIR: PIONEER TO PRIME MINIS-TER Messner, 1972; rev. ed. 1974. (grade 6 and up)
   Excellent lively portrait of Golda Meir is clearly Israel's story as well. Informal, dramatic, and inspiring, it moves along quickly, bringing its subject to life. The revised edition is brought up to date with Meir's resignation.

Syrkin, Marie, ed. A LAND OF OUR OWN: AN ORAL AUTOBIOGRAPHY BY GOLDA MEIR Putnam, 1973. (grade 9 and up)
   Very well-organized and intelligently selected interviews and material from published and unpublished statements by Meir comprise a warm, moving, and highly readable picture of the woman and her contributions to Israel and all of humanity.

———. GOLDA MEIR, ISRAEL'S LEADER Putnam, 1969. (grade 9 and up)
   Superb, authoritative biography of Golda Meir is a vividly written, absorbing, and comprehensive examination of her life and her contributions to Israel.

~~~~~~

LISE MEITNER
1878–1968

*Nuclear physicist, winner of Atomic Energy
Commission Award*

Lise Meitner, the Austrian-born physicist, and her long-time scientific partner, Nobel Prize–winner Dr. Otto Hahn, lay much of the groundwork for the atomic bomb. Meitner was persistent in pointing out that she had nothing to do with the use made of their studies and felt that it was unfortunate that their discoveries had occurred during the war.

   Her interest in atomic physics was initially fostered when, as a student, she read newspaper accounts of the Curies' work and, despite the lack of opportunities for women in science, chose this as her career.

161

In 1938 rising anti-Semitism forced this Jewish scientist to leave Austria for Sweden where she spent the next twenty years. Her departure from Dr. Hahn's lab was, she said, one of the great tragedies of her life.

With her nephew, Otto Frisch, she reported on the fission of uranium and thorium, and in 1966 she shared the Atomic Energy Commission's Enrico Fermi Award with Otto Hahn and Fritz Strassman. A proponent of greater participation of women in the professions and of the peaceful use of atomic energy, she lived long enough to see the beginnings of both.

Crawford, Deborah LISE MEITNER, ATOMIC PIONEER Crown, 1969. (grade 7 and up)

Very fine, somewhat technical biography is suitable more for the student of science than the casual reader. However, it is also a warm, dramatic profile of the brilliant and sensitive scientist, and combines not only science and biography but also recreates the climate and society in which Meitner lived and worked.

~~~~~~

EDNA ST. VINCENT MILLAY
1892–1950

Pulitzer Prize–winning poet

Edna St. Vincent Millay began writing verse as a youngster and at age fourteen had her first poem published in *Saint Nicholas* magazine. After graduation from high school she entered her poem "Renascence" into a national contest, won fourth prize, and garnered much critical attention and praise which in turn led to the award of a scholarship from Vassar College.

After graduation she moved to New York and took some minor writing jobs to help support herself. In 1923, *The Ballad of the Harp-Weaver and Other Books* won Millay the Pulitzer Prize, making her the first woman poet to be so honored. She won further acclaim for the libretto to Deems Taylor's opera *The King's Henchman*.

Millay's early work dealt with personal feelings, frequently employing themes of freedom and liberation of women. Her later work dealt with social problems and expressed her antiwar, anti-isolationist attitudes. For many young people she symbolized the emancipation of the age in her famed lines: "My candle burns at both ends/It will not last the night;/But ah, my foes, and oh, my friends/It gives a lovely light!"

Gurko, Miriam RESTLESS SPIRIT: THE LIFE OF EDNA ST. VINCENT MILLAY Crowell, 1962. (grade 7 and up)
Outstanding, well-written biography of the poet discusses her personal life and work, clearly indicating her independence in both areas. Carefully researched and faithfully told, it is of interest to both those who know her poetry and those not yet well acquainted with it.

Shafter, Toby EDNA ST. VINCENT MILLAY: AMERICA'S BEST LOVED POET Messner, 1957. (grade 7 and up)
Very fine portrait of Millay covers aspects of both her personal life and her poetry, introducing her as a dynamic, multidimensional woman.

~~~~~~

MARIA MITCHELL
1818–1889

Astronomer, discoverer of a comet

Maria Mitchell combined a distinctly Nantucket-woman self-reliance and an insatiable intellectual curiosity with her father's tutelage to become a skilled astronomer. She spent the time spared from her librarian duties reading scientific, classical, philosophical, and feminist works and gazing at the skies from the observatory her father had built for them.

In 1847 she discovered a new comet which was named for her. The king of Denmark awarded her a gold medal, she became the first woman elected to the American Academy of Arts and Sciences (an honor not bestowed upon another woman until 1943), was invited to join other prestigious organizations, and received wide acclaim both in Europe and the United States. She was later elected to the American Hall of Fame.

A member of Vassar's original faculty, she remained there for twenty-three years as one of the college's finest and best-known teachers. Instituting and insisting upon many unconventional

163

teaching methods, she ignored the usual rote method and grading system and encouraged student participation in her own research. Maria Mitchell inspired many women students to follow in her footsteps and exerted great efforts to show that the sciences should include women on an equal basis with men.

Baker, Rachel, and Merlen, Joanna B. AMERICA'S FIRST WOMAN ASTRONOMER: MARIA MITCHELL   Illus. Messner, 1960. (grade 6 and up)
Excellent, convincingly fictionalized biography of the astronomer shows the development of her scientific interests and traces her long and successful career. A warm, informal portrait avoids technical jargon and is thus of interest to casual readers as well as students of science.

Melin, Grace H. MARIA MITCHELL: GIRL ASTRONOMER   Illus. Bobbs-Merrill, 1964. (grades 3–7)
Good, highly fictionalized but accurate biography focusses on the childhood of Maria Mitchell. Because Mitchell's scientific and astronomic interests developed early, her childhood is a significant part of her life and worthy of discussion. The author offers good explanations of the elements of astronomy, comprehensible to very young readers, and devotes a small portion of the book to Mitchell's later achievements.

Morgan, Helen L. MARIA MITCHELL: FIRST LADY OF AMERICAN ASTRONOMY   Westminster, 1977. (grades 5–8)
Good, fictionalized biography, sometimes self-conscious in style, gives a good picture of Maria Mitchell's life and times.

Wilkie, Katherine E. MARIA MITCHELL: STARGAZER   Illus. Garrard, 1966. (grades 2–5)
Despite its brevity and simplicity, this is a biography of unusual substance. The fast-paced narrative describes Mitchell's Nantucket childhood, interest in astronomy, and then her career as a professor at Vassar College.

~~~~~~

MARIA MONTESSORI, M.D.
1870–1952

Physician and educator

The prejudices of her time and place did not prevent Maria Montessori from achieving her goals. In 1896 she became the first woman doctor in Italy. Later she revolutionized traditional teaching methods. Utilizing the natural curiosity of children, presenting them with learning materials and challenges, she found that children can teach themselves and enjoy doing it. The well-known Montessori method began when her medical practice involved her in teaching retarded children. Their unexpected progress encouraged her to try the same methods on children of normal learning potential. Children at a young age learned to read and write more quickly than had ever been thought possible. Educators from all over the world came to visit her school and learn her methods, and then began their own Montessori schools.

During World War II Montessori schools in Italy and Germany were closed, because the nations' leaders did not want children trained to think for themselves and develop independent personalities.

Maria Montessori gave up her medical practice to concentrate on educating children, for she believed this was the most important mission she could perform. She lived and worked until she was eighty-two years old, earning the honors and appreciation of the world.

Leone, Bruno MARIA MONTESSORI, KNIGHT OF THE CHILD   Illus. with photographs. Greenhaven, 1978. (grade 5 and up)

This biography of the educator may be of special interest to children in Montessori schools but can be enjoyed by all readers. Older, less competent readers will find it of interest also.

~~~~~~

ANNE MOODY
1940–

Civil rights worker

Anne Moody's parents were poor black sharecroppers in Mississippi. They never had enough to wear or to eat, and even before Anne entered her teens she worked as a domestic for white families. With great determination, despite great odds, she graduated from high school and attended college where she became active in the civil rights movement, participating in demonstrations and working in voter registration drives in Mississippi. Like those of other members of the Congress of Racial Equality (CORE), Moody's life was often in danger, but she persisted, and after graduation from college continued her work in the movement. She has also served as coordinator of the civil rights training project of the School of Industrial and Labor Relations at Cornell University.

Moody, Anne COMING OF AGE IN MISSISSIPPI Dial, 1968. (grade 9 and up)
Absorbing, tender, and dramatic personal narrative for mature readers covers the early years of Moody's life and traces her development until she begins her higher education. A good picture is presented of her own life as well as life in the South for poor blacks before and at the beginning of the civil rights movement.

~~~~~~

ANNE CARROLL MOORE
1871–1961

Pioneer in children's library work

The library profession was largely dominated by men when Anne Carroll Moore began her long career as a children's librarian. Moore truly loved children and books, and with her imagination and determinism, made children's literature an important part of the library system. She single-handedly shaped the present practices and philosophies of the New York Public Library children's rooms.

For ten years she was in charge of the children's room in the Pratt Free Library in Brooklyn, and for thirty-five years she administered the children's department of the New York Public Library. During this period her ideas and practices were widely emulated by libraries throughout the world. Even after her retirement she continued to lecture, write, and serve as a consultant to the world of children's books.

Sayers, Frances Clark ANNE CARROLL MOORE: A BIOGRAPHY Illus. with photographs. Atheneum, 1972. (grade 9 and up)
Fascinating, skillfully written biography incorporates excerpts from Anne Carroll Moore's writings and letters, offering a warm, informative

view of her life. Young adults considering library work as a career or those attracted to children's literature will find this adult biography particularly interesting for it chronicles the history of children's libraries as well as telling the story of Moore's life—a wise approach, for it is impossible to separate the two.

~~~~~~

ANNA MARY ROBERTSON MOSES
1860–1961

Landscape artist

If anyone could be considered a legend in her time, it would be "Grandma" Moses, one of the world's greatest landscape artists. As a child she drew pictures and maps, and later, as a young hired girl and mother and grandmother, she "painted" with needles and threads, making samplers and worsted pictures and occasionally little gifts and cards. Not until she was 75 did she cease using house paint and brushes to work with artists' oils and brushes.

A few of her paintings which were exhibited in a local drugstore came to the attention of a New York art collector. He encouraged her and she won wide acceptance with exhibits all over the world. When she was 89 years old she was invited to the White House to receive an award from President Truman, and later she and President Eisenhower corresponded and exchanged painted Christmas cards. She continued to paint almost to her death, at 101 years of age.

Grandma Moses's work, the result of exacting craftsmanship, has a simplicity and country quality about it that appeals to children, city and country dwellers, and sophisticated art critics. Her painting *July 4* hangs in the White House and is reprinted on a United States postage stamp.

Armstrong, William BAREFOOT IN THE GRASS: THE STORY OF GRANDMA MOSES Illus. Doubleday, 1970. (grade 5 and up)
Beautiful color reproductions of her work accompany a very good, though occasionally dry biography. Thoughtful and accurate, it gives a good, well-balanced account of the famed artist.

Graves, Charles GRANDMA MOSES: FAVORITE PAINTER Illus. Garrard, 1969. (grades 3–5)
Necessarily simplified, but nonetheless superb biography of the artist includes many good black-and-white reproductions of her work, photographs of her family, and other illustrations. A warm, intelligent, and fast-moving biography depicts Grandma Moses as the highly independent, talented, and fascinating woman she was.

Laing, Martha GRANDMA MOSES: THE GRAND OLD LADY OF AMERICAN ART SamHar, 1972. (grade 7 and up)
Very fine, interesting, soundly researched, and well-documented account of the life of Grandma Moses is very brief (twenty-seven pages) but a substantial, straightforward narrative.

LUCRETIA MOTT
1793–1880

Abolitionist, Quaker minister and preacher,
feminist leader

Since Nantucket men were away months at a time on whaling ships, Nantucket women, like Lucretia Mott, were self-reliant and believed that women had the same abilities and rights as men. When Lucretia became a teacher and discovered salary discrepancies between men and women, her feminist consciousness was raised to even greater heights.

She and her husband were dedicated abolitionists who refused to use any product of slave labor and played leading roles in the movement. Mott, the mother of six children, was an outstanding Quaker minister and preacher who was chosen as a delegate to the World's Anti-Slavery Convention in London in 1840. Indignant that women were refused any part in the proceedings, she and Elizabeth Cady Stanton (page 228) planned a women's rights convention. Held in the summer of 1848 in Seneca Falls, New York, this historic meeting really began the American feminist and suffrage movement. Its participants issued a "Declaration of Sentiments" which, modelled after the Declaration of Independence, focussed on the issues that kept women subordinate to men.

For over fifty years Lucretia Mott, supported by her husband in her beliefs and causes, was a firm, determined, and highly respected leader in the many organizations dedicated to equality and freedom for blacks and for women.

Bacon, Margaret Hope VALIANT FRIEND: LIFE OF LUCRETIA MOTT Walker, 1980. (grade 9 and up)

This adult title combines well-developed biography and history and will be of interest to competent high school readers. Well-researched and documented, it is interesting and highly readable.

Faber, Doris LUCRETIA MOTT: FOE OF SLAVERY Illus. Garrard, 1971. (grades 2–4)

Excellent biography of Lucretia Mott is simple, straightforward, and interesting. Despite its simplicity, it clearly shows the independence, accomplishments, and lifestyle of the abolitionist and feminist.

Kurland, Gerald LUCRETIA MOTT: EARLY LEADER OF THE WOMEN'S LIBERATION MOVEMENT SamHar, 1972. (grade 7 and up)

Excellent short biography of Mott gives an intelligent, straightforward account of her life. Her many accomplishments are interestingly detailed. Extremely well researched and documented.

~~~~~~

DAISY HOOEE NAMPEYO
1910–

Native American potter

Daisy Hooee Nampeyo has fused her training, talent, and artistic traditions to bring to vibrant new life a native American art form. Born on an Indian reservation in Arizona, she took up the pottery-making she learned as a child after studying painting and sculpture in Europe. She proved her talents as a sculptor and could have attained popular success as a modern artist, but decided instead to devote her efforts to developing and preserving the ancient pottery forms of the Pueblo people. Her pottery is based on the Hopi and Zuñi styles. She has created beautiful objects and gained renown while developing the themes of the Pueblo Indians.

New generations of Indian children will learn the pottery skills

Daisy Nampeyo was taught by her grandmother. And they will enjoy the new respect which the talent of Daisy Hooee Nampeyo has brought to an ancient tribal skill.

Fowler, Carol DAISY HOOEE NAMPEYO Illus. with photographs. Dillon, 1977. (grades 5–9)
   Biography gives good picture of Hopi life in early twentieth century and the changes that have occurred. The manner in which Nampeyo bridged the ancient and modern cultures is shown clearly.

~~~~~~

CARRY NATION
1846–1911

Prohibition advocate

Born in Kentucky, Carry Nation spent most of her childhood travelling with her family. Her mother suffered from a chronic progressive mental disorder, and other members of the family were also afflicted. Her father and their slave families offered the youngster the only emotional stability she knew, but the verbal and physical abuse afflicted on her by her mother and the guilt-evoking religious extremes she was exposed to kept her from having any inner peace.

   Her first husband suffered from severe alcoholism, and her second marriage did not offer her either financial or emotional security. Her adult life was filled with incredible hard work and constant moving. Gradually she became known as a self-appointed guardian of morals, and although also known as helpful and kind to those less fortunate, her severe mood swings made her appear peculiar.

   When she went on the crusade against liquor her methods were open to ridicule as well as criticism. She literally smashed bars with her hatchet. Although she had followers, she had many more detractors. Carry Nation became an object of humor and to this day is depicted as a figure at which to poke fun. She was subject to beatings and fines, and although seldom taken seriously, she did have an effect on making people realize alcoholism destroys families as well as individuals. Her tactics, foolish as they appeared, did contribute to the prohibition against alcohol.

Madison, Arnold CARRY NATION Nelson, 1977. (grades 5–8)
Excellent, well-researched, lively book is very readable and can be enjoyed by older readers as well as those for whom it is intended. Author gives an unbiased view of Carry Nation, depicting her sympathetically and in the context of times, and showing much psychological insight into her feelings and behavior.

~~~~~~

MARTINA NAVRATILOVA
1956–

Tennis champion

Martina Navratilova is a tennis player by training, aptitude, talent, inclination, and family tradition. She won the Czechoslovak National Championship at sixteen, and travelled all over the world, including the United States, in a series of tournaments. She joined the Virginia Slims Tour in 1974, was voted Player of the Year in 1978 by the Women's Tennis Association and won awards wherever tennis players meet in competition, including Wimbledon and the United States Open.

She is a natural sportsperson who skied at three, played tennis at five, and enjoyed playing ice hockey, soccer, and golf. Her many trips to the United States "Americanized" her, to the dismay of her government, which did not allow her to join the Cleveland Nets. Finally she decided to defect to the United States in 1975 to broaden the opportunities for her professional career.

She delights in speaking about her life as an American, and is proud of her United States citizenship, which she gained in 1981. In 1983, Martina Navratilova won her fourth Wimbledon title and her first United States Open championship. She is ranked number one in the world.

Dolan, Edward F., Jr., and Lyttle, Richard B. MARTINA NAVRATILOVA Illus. with photographs. Doubleday, 1977. (grades 5–9)
An easy-to-read, lively biography depicts the tennis player as fun-loving, ambitious and hard working.

Jacobs, Linda MARTINA NAVRATILOVA: TENNIS FURY Illus. EMC, 1976. (grades 4–7)

This good biography traces Martina Navratilova's early life and tennis career and concludes when she asked for political asylum in the United States.

~~~~~~

CINDY NELSON
1955–

Championship skier

America's favorite woman skier, Cindy Nelson, was skiing by the time she was two years old. Her parents owned a ski resort in Minnesota, and she was entering and winning local races while she was still in kindergarten. Her talent and spirit were displayed early, and at eleven she competed in the Junior Nationals at Stowe, Vermont.

A World Cup winner, she won the 1980 woman's downhill in the U.S. National Alpine Championships, and continues to offer stiff competition to skiers from all over the world although she is the oldest woman on the U.S. ski team.

Jacobs, Linda CINDY NELSON: NORTH COUNTRY SKIER Illus. with photographs. EMC, 1976. (grades 4–8)
An enjoyable biography of the championship skier which will appeal to older, less able readers as well as younger ones with an interest in the sport.

~~~~~~

OLIVIA NEWTON-JOHN
1948–

Popular singer

British-born, Australian-reared Olivia Newton-John grew up in an academic atmosphere. However, her interests were in show business, and while a student she organized a singing group. She won a singing contest in Australia, and her prize, a trip to London, launched her on a successful career. She was a recording star in the United States even before her arrival there.

Olivia Newton-John's first record, "Let Me Be There," was a top country-western hit in the United States and won her a Grammy Award. Her second hit, "If You Love Me Let Me Know," was an even bigger success and "I Honestly Love You" won her another Grammy.

She starred in the film *Grease* and on several television specials. A devoted animal lover, she once cancelled a tour of Japan in protest of slaughter of dolphins by fishermen there. The winner of many Grammy awards as well as numerous other awards, she now lives in California.

Jacobs, Linda OLIVIA NEWTON-JOHN: SUNSHINE SUPERGIRL Illus. with photographs. EMC, 1975. (grade 4–6)
Interesting biography traces Newton-John's life from her early days in England and Australia and her career beginnings to her huge American success. The focus is evenly divided between her personal and professional life, and is at times too laudatory, but will appeal to older, reluctant readers.

~~~~~~

FLORENCE NIGHTINGALE
1820–1910

Reformer, organizer, and founder of the nursing profession

Florence Nightingale's wealthy, British, social family did not object to her attempts to alleviate suffering in family members, animals, or even close neighbors, but were horrified when she talked of making nursing her life's work. Hospitals were usually filthy and nurses were recruited from the lowest and most disreputable classes, but intelligent, well-educated Nightingale decided to obtain whatever training she could. She then took an unpaid position as supervisor of a nursing home where she immediately made efficient changes.

During the Crimean War, the secretary of war called upon her to organize and supervise nurses at the front. This was the first time a woman was asked to fill an official military mission and she was given full authority. Her radical changes reduced the death rate from 430 to 22 per 1,000.

She founded the Nightingale Training School for nurses, which soon served as a model for schools all over the world. Though mainly an administrator, Florence Nightingale was keenly aware of the importance of bedside nursing. Her philosophy, practices, and dedication have given the profession of nursing the highly respected position it holds today.

Colver, Anne FLORENCE NIGHTINGALE: WAR NURSE Garrard, 1961. (grades 2–5)
Extremely moving, very simple, readable biography of Florence Nightingale succinctly summarizes her personal and professional life, skillfully conveying her motives as well as accomplishments.

Harmelink, Barbara FLORENCE NIGHTINGALE: FOUNDER OF MODERN NURSING Illus. Watts, 1969. (grade 7 and up)
Outstanding, well-balanced, straightforward account of Florence Nightingale's life clearly indicates that despite her own opposition to women's suffrage she was a strong supporter of the rights of nurses, and was single-handedly responsible for the elevation of nursing to professional status.

Hume, Ruth F. FLORENCE NIGHTINGALE Illus. Random, 1960. (grades 6–10)
Very fine, inspiring portrait of Nightingale also thoughtfully examines the society in which she lived.

Nolan, Jeannette FLORENCE NIGHTINGALE Illus. Messner, 1947. (grade 6 and up)
Dramatic picture of the pioneer nurse is convincingly fictionalized, affording an interesting and accurate picture of Nightingale, her work, and the times.

Peach, L. Du Garde FLORENCE NIGHTINGALE Illus. Ladybird, 1959. (grades 4–7)
Small, attractively illustrated book gives a straightforward account, focusing on the work Florence Nightingale did during the Crimean War.

~~~~~~

DIANA NYAD
1950–

Marathon swimmer

New York–born, Florida-raised, Diana Nyad was swimming at six months, and seriously swimming at eleven years. In junior high school she won the state championship in 100- and 200-meter backstroke, and in 1970 she began long distance racing, setting a record.

A fine student, she graduated from college with membership in Phi Beta Kappa, and then entered a doctoral program at New York University.

Accomplished in many fields, she speaks several languages, is a competent musician, has written widely, and has been a swimming coach at Barnard College in New York.

Her 1976 swim around Manhattan Island in seven hours, fifty-seven minutes attracted much attention, and in 1978 she attempted to swim from Cuba to the tip of Florida. Although she swam for nearly forty-two straight hours, she finally agreed to stop when her trainer convinced her it couldn't be done. She is now a respected sportscaster, lively and well informed.

McLenighan, Valjean   DIANA: ALONE AGAINST THE SEA   Illus. Raintree, 1980. (grades 4–8)
Exciting, readable biography focuses on Diana Nyad's attempted swim from Cuba to Florida.

Nyad, Diana   OTHER SHORES   Random, 1978. (grade 7 and up)
Exciting, fast-moving story of and by the woman who, at the time of writing, had achieved fame for her record-setting swim around Manhattan Island.

ANNIE OAKLEY
1860–1926

Markswoman

The star of Buffalo Bill's Wild West show, Annie Oakley, known as the "girl of the Western plains," learned sharpshooting as a child in the Ohio woods. There her earnings from the birds she shot helped support her family and paid off the mortgage on their farm. At sixteen she married Frank Butler, an expert marksman from whom she had won a match, and they toured vaudeville, eventually joining Buffalo Bill's Wild West show.

Small in stature, Annie Oakley could outshoot anyone, male or female, and developed an uncanny showmanship which made her a favorite with audiences. She was also popular with the cowboys and Indians in the show, and Sioux Chief Sitting Bull made her an adopted daughter, naming her "Little Sure Shot."

She made successful tours of the United States and Europe; was presented to Queen Victoria; performed for the Kaiser; and amassed numerous trophies, medals, honors and decorations. During World War I, though retired as a performer, Oakley toured army camps demonstrating marksmanship.

Alderman, Clifford Lindsey ANNIE OAKLEY AND THE WORLD OF HER TIME Illus. Macmillan, 1979. (grades 5–9)
Excellent biography is conversational in tone, describing her childhood, career, and final days. Not overly fictionalized or romanticized, it moves at a good pace, holding the interest of readers.

Graves, C. P. ANNIE OAKLEY: THE SHOOTING STAR Garrard, 1961. (grades 2–5)
Anecdotal, engaging narrative traces her life in a log cabin in Ohio to stardom in Buffalo Bill's Wild West show to give a well-rounded though brief portrait of a fascinating woman.

Wilson, Ellen ANNIE OAKLEY: LITTLE SURE SHOT Illus. Bobbs-Merrill, 1958. (grades 3–7)
Excellent biography of Annie Oakley emphasizes her childhood, and despite heavy fictionalization is quite faithful to her life. Oakley's child-

hood was an independent, achievement-oriented one, and thus concentration on that period does not lessen the value or interest of the biography.

~~~~~~

SANDRA DAY O'CONNOR
1930–

Justice of the United States Supreme Court

Sandra Day O'Connor is the first woman appointed to the United States Supreme Court. A daughter of the frontier tradition, she grew up on a ranch on the Arizona–New Mexico border. Encouraged by her parents to develop her abilities and pursue goals, she graduated third in her class from Stanford University Law School in 1952.

She met the resistance of a legal profession determined not to hire a woman lawyer. After turning down an offer of a job as a secretary to a law firm, she opened her own law office. She became an assistant attorney general, competently combined marriage and childrearing with her career, and was active in community affairs and politics. She was elected to the Arizona State Senate, became Superior Court Judge for Maricopa County, and later was appointed judge for the Arizona Court of Appeals. In 1981 she was named by President Reagan to the Supreme Court of the United States.

She has three grown sons, a family home in Arizona and a permanent place on the most important bench in America and in the ranks of America women who have proven their ability, as well as their right, to a full partnership in our society.

Greene, Carol SANDRA DAY O'CONNOR: FIRST WOMAN ON THE SUPREME COURT Illus. with photographs. Children's Pr., 1982. (grades 3–7)
Excellent, very easy-to-read and understand biography clearly but simply explains the importance of O'Connor's appointment, the work the Supreme Court does, and the personal and professional life which led her to her appointment. Neither adulatory nor sugarcoated, this book could inspire any youngster.

KITTY O'NEILL
1948–

Stuntperson

Her record as a woman athlete would be impressive even if Kitty O'Neill had not been deaf since babyhood. She is a world-class record-breaking sportswoman and stuntperson, the first woman ever admitted to Stunts Unlimited. Her accomplishments are in many fields. She has been AAU Junior Olympic diving champion, a sky diver, champion water skier, car and dune buggy racer, record holder in long distance falls for women, winner of all-time free fall (men and women) record, world-class diver, and motorcycle racer. She achieved fame as the double for the star of the "Wonder Woman" television show.

Kitty O'Neill's mother, a full-blooded Cherokee, was determined that her daughter would overcome the problems of deafness. After Kitty's father died, her mother and Kitty moved near the University of Texas so that her mother could learn how to best help Kitty. Kitty learned to swim when she was a baby. Later she learned to speak and became an expert lip reader. Today she does much public lecturing, telling her audience that deafness need not be a handicap but a challenge to conquer.

Kitty O'Neill has proved that many obstacles can be overcome.

Ireland, Karen KITTY O'NEILL: DAREDEVIL WOMAN Illus. with photographs. Harvey, 1980. (grades 4–8)
A very good biography which not only tells the life story of this unusual woman but also provides inspiration.

Thacher, Alida FASTEST WOMAN ON EARTH Illus. with photographs. Raintree, 1980. (grades 3–7)
Easy-to-read, fast-moving, motivating story for anyone who has odds to overcome. The author describes O'Neill's work, but concentrates on her spirit.

ALICE FREEMAN PALMER
1855–1902

President of Wellesley College, pioneer educator

Though Alice Freeman Palmer's family respected and encouraged education, they wanted to use their limited funds to pay for her brother's college education. By promising to help educate him and her sisters she was able to persuade them to allow her to enroll in the University of Michigan, where she alternated work and study and earned undergraduate and graduate degrees in history.

Appointed first as head of the history department at the all-women's Wellesley College, Alice Freeman Palmer at the age of twenty-seven became president of the college. During her administration, scholastic standards were implemented and outstanding preparatory schools for Wellesley were initiated.

After her marriage she retired to concentrate her talent and energies on church and mission work, and to serve as a leader of numerous state and national committees for the education of women. She became a member of Wellesley's board of trustees, temporarily served as a dean at the University of Chicago, and helped Radcliffe achieve status as a college. A supporter of women's suffrage, Alice believed she best contributed to the cause by academically preparing women for citizenship and voting.

Fleming, Alice ALICE FREEMAN PALMER: PIONEER COLLEGE PRESIDENT Prentice-Hall, 1970. (grades 5–8)

Very good biography of the woman who became one of the first presidents of Wellesley College is dramatic and warm, but lacks some of the spirit displayed by Palmer. Written for younger readers rather than those who might be interested in learning about a college president, it is necessarily less than comprehensive and complete.

179

VIJAYA LAKSHMI PANDIT
1900–

*Ambassador, diplomat, and United Nations delegate
from India*

Vijaya Lakshmi Pandit, the first woman to address the United
Nations General Assembly, was one of the pioneers in India's struggle for independence. Wealthy and cosmopolitan, her family supported Gandhi's nonviolent movement and her brother Nehru later
became India's first prime minister. Like her politically active
mother and sisters, Pandit was often arrested and spent her first
prison term in 1932 when the youngest of her three children was
only three years old. Her niece, Indira Gandhi (page 89) became
prime minister of India.

During World War II she lectured in the United States on the
Indian independence movement, and in 1945 she was an observer
at the United Nations. After India achieved independence in 1947
she held many diplomatic positions. Pandit was a member of Parliament, minister of health, and ambassador to Russia and to England.
Later, as the ambassador to both the United States and Mexico, she
was the first woman to carry simultaneously two diplomatic posts.

As an author and recipient of many honorary awards and degrees,
Pandit is one of the United Nations' most respected leaders. She
received her widest recognition when she served as the president of
the eighth General Assembly.

Guthrie, Anne MADAME AMBASSADOR: THE LIFE OF VIJAYA LAKSHMI
PANDIT Illus. with photographs. Harcourt, 1962. (grade 9 and up)

Very fine, dramatic account of the life of Vijaya Pandit is told by a close
friend, affording the reader an intimate though somewhat admiring view
of the subject. The author tells not only the story of Vijaya Pandit, but also
the story of India and its independence in restrained but moving prose.

~~~~~~

THE PANKHURSTS
Emmeline Pankhurst 1858–1928
Christabel Pankhurst 1880–1958
Sylvia Pankhurst 1882–1960
Adele Pankhurst 1885–

Militant suffragists and feminists

Emmeline Pankhurst was the founder of the Women's Political and Social Union, an organization in England whose initial function was to present petitions and quietly to try to influence Parliament to grant women the vote. As those methods proved futile, Emmeline and her group turned to mass demonstrations, arson, and actual fights with the police. When jailed, she went on hunger strikes, was brutally treated, and finally force-fed.

With her daughters, the widowed Emmeline Pankhurst organized the militant British feminist movement and played an influential role in the final American struggle. Christabel, an attorney and the most intellectual of the daughters, saw suffrage as a major goal of the women's rights movement, while Adele and Sylvia concerned themselves with bringing the movement to the working-class woman. Sylvia was also involved in the pacifist movement.

In 1918 Emmeline Pankhurst saw the first results of her long years of struggle when women over thirty years of age were given the vote. Not until 1928, though, the year of her death, did younger British women gain enfranchisement.

Noble, Iris EMMELINE AND HER DAUGHTERS: THE PANKHURST SUFFRAGISTS Messner, 1971. (grade 7 and up)
Outstanding account of the life of feminist Emmeline Pankhurst and her daughters is written with feeling, drama, and vitality. Traces the entire suffragist movement in England, discussing the difficulties and concentrating on the courage, strength, and abilities of Emmeline Pankhurst.

ROSA PARKS
1913–

*Civil rights worker, organizer of the Montgomery
bus boycott*

Rosa Parks, known as the "mother of the civil rights movement," had always suffered the humilities of black southerners. A quiet woman, she directed her resentments and energies into organizations like the National Association for the Advancement of Colored People, and into voter registration and education drives.

It was commonplace for a black person to be told by a bus driver in Montgomery, Alabama, to get up to give a white person a seat. On December 1, 1955, Rosa Parks, tired from a hard day of work, decided this time she would not relinquish her seat to a white man. Arrested and jailed, she was freed on bail and met with the black leaders of the city, including Martin Luther King, Jr. Together they organized the historic bus boycott of that city, during which no black person rode on a bus. The blacks of Montgomery walked miles to and from work, and though they were harassed and threatened, they held fast to their decision. Rosa Parks, the victim of many personal threats, took her case to the United States Supreme Court, which handed down the decision that the bus company could no longer discriminate. The Montgomery bus company changed its rules and one year after Rosa Parks refused to give up her seat, no other black could be asked to do this.

In 1980 she became the first woman to receive the Martin Luther King Junior Award.

Greenfield, Eloise ROSA PARKS Illus. Crowell, 1973. (grades 1–4)
   Outstanding book describes Rosa Parks's early experiences and feelings towards racial segregation, and clearly depicts her quiet heroism in defying the rules of her city. Her role in the Montgomery bus boycott is well described.

Meriwether, Louise DON'T RIDE THE BUS ON MONDAY: THE ROSA PARKS STORY Illus. Prentice-Hall, 1973. (grades 3–5)

Faithful to Rosa Parks's life, this book also clearly describes the Montgomery bus boycott. However, the writing is somewhat dry, lacking spark and emotion. Although this is a picture book, it is really too difficult for very young readers to read or comprehend, but too immature in appearance for older readers.

~~~~~~

DOLLY PARTON
1946–

Country and western singer and songwriter

Dolly Parton achieved fame as a country and western singer and songwriter, but is one of a small group of performers who have become crossover artists, becoming as popular for popular music as they did for country and western.

She was the fourth of twelve children of a poor dirt farmer and a preacher's daughter and they lived in mountain shacks and small farms in Tennessee. Her family loved music, and as a toddler she created songs, and soon learned to play the mandolin and guitar. After graduating from high school she took a bus to Nashville, the country and western capital, determined to achieve success, which she did within a few years.

Dolly Parton, whose versatile singing talent has won her numerous best female vocalist awards for her enormously successful records, is also a prominent songwriter whose songs have been recorded by other leading performers. She has made guest appearances on national television shows, where fans delight in her flamboyance and had her own syndicated shows. She maintains a heavy schedule, spending more than half of each year on the road.

When not travelling, she lives with her husband in a mansion near Nashville. Most of her close relatives live nearby.

Krishef, Robert DOLLY PARTON   Illus. with photographs. Lerner, 1980. (grades 5–9)
   Very good biography focuses on Parton's early life and professional career, but also provides a sense of her personal life.

~~~~~~

ALICE PAUL
1885–1977

Suffragist, feminist, and social worker

Prior to receiving her doctorate in social work, American-born Alice Paul was studying slum conditions in London when she was drawn into the British women's struggle for suffrage. She learned the militant techniques of her British sisters, and on her return to the United States assumed the chairpersonship of the congressional committee of the national American Woman Suffrage Association. She organized a lobby to convince the president and Congress to pass the amendment giving women the vote. The suffrage parade she planned just before Woodrow Wilson's inauguration created a riot and led to her imprisonment. Harshly treated in the workhouse prison, she and other prominent women went on a hunger strike and were force-fed. Their cause attracted much attention and sympathy and the courts later refused to uphold the arrests.
   Alice Paul founded the Congressional Union which later became the National Woman's Party whose single goal was the passage of the woman suffrage amendment. Their nonviolent but militant tactics served mostly to embarrass the president and other officials.
   The work of Alice Paul and other early twentieth-century feminists and suffragists was a significant force in the final passage of the Nineteenth Amendment.

Bratfisch, Virginia THE NON-VIOLENT ALICE PAUL   Illus. Women's Heritage Series, 1971. (grade 9 and up)
   Brief but excellent profile of Alice Paul is devoted mostly to her life in the suffragist movement. Provides a good background to the history of the movement, incorporating lengthy quotations of Paul.

JANE PAULEY
1950–

Television newscaster and host

Jane Pauley, the popular co-anchor of NBC's "Today" show, has always enjoyed public speaking. While still in high school in Indiana she joined the speech club and won many trophies at competitions and meets for impromptu speaking.

At Indiana University she was a political science major and worked in political campaigns. During the 1972 campaign she became a reporter at a local television station. When a position as co-anchor at a Chicago station became available, she won that job.

Less than a year later, she was invited to try out for the opening as co-anchor of the "Today" show in New York. After many auditions and tryouts, Jane Pauley was awarded the job.

On "Today," Jane Pauley interviews ordinary people as well as the famous. Her wide knowledge of contemporary issues and her ability to ask important questions and listen carefully to answers are clear to viewers.

She is married to Garry Trudeau, political cartoonist of "Doonesbury" fame, and is the mother of twins.

Jacobs, Linda and Simpson, Janice JANE PAULEY: A HEARTLAND STYLE   Illus. with photographs. EMC, 1978. (grades 3–7)
Very good biography is a fine recounting of Jane Pauley's life, explaining the training and talent that go into making a good television anchor. The book emphasizes that much more than good looks and a pleasant voice are needed to become successful.

ANNA PAVLOVA
1881–1931

Russian prima ballerina

When the world-famous Russian ballerina Anna Pavlova was eight years old she attended a performance of the ballet *Sleeping Beauty* and decided to become a dancer. At ten she was admitted to the Imperial Ballet School in Saint Petersburg, where she underwent the most rigorous training available to young dancers. At seventeen, she made her debut, not as a member of the corps de ballet, as is the usual custom, but in a role. Within three years Pavlova had risen to the rank of prima ballerina of the Imperial Ballet, and although her position was secure there, she chose to form her own company to bring Russian ballet to the rest of the world.

Michel Fokine, the famed choreographer, created Pavlova's most famous role—the "swan" in *Swan Lake*. However, the dancer also scored great triumphs in *Les Papillons*, *Les Sylphides*, and *The Magic Flute*. Between her extensive tours throughout Europe and the United States, she made her home in England with her husband who served as her advisor and manager.

The phenomenal success of Pavlova was due to her great talent as well as her intensive discipline and devotion to her art. She refused to stop dancing, even when ill, and died while on tour.

Malvern, Gladys DANCING STAR: THE STORY OF ANNA PAVLOVA Illus. Messner, 1942. (grade 6 and up)

Wonderfully moving, dramatic biography of the great Pavlova details her childhood, training, and sensational career providing a vivid picture of life in Russia and in ballet throughout the world. Not by any means limited to career-oriented readers, its appeal is much wider and is of interest to readers who are uninformed about ballet.

~~~~~~

FRANCES PERKINS
1882–1965

Secretary of Labor, first woman cabinet member

At a time when few women received a higher education, Frances Perkins attended Mount Holyoke College, where she became involved in crusades for social justice. Despite her father's conservative attitudes, she was determined to make social and labor reform her life's work, rather than teaching which her family considered more suitable.

Like many other young, idealistic college graduates of the day, she became closely allied with social reformer Jane Addams (page 5). She was a frequent resident at Hull House in Chicago, and then worked in Philadelphia and New York. In New York, Perkins entered government service as an aide to Alfred Smith and later to Franklin D. Roosevelt. When Roosevelt became president in 1932 he chose her to be his secretary of labor, the first woman to serve in a presidential cabinet. She remained throughout his terms and served also under President Harry Truman. Upon her resignation she wrote a book, *The Roosevelt I Knew*, contributed articles to magazines, and then returned to public life when President Truman appointed her as United States Civil Service Commissioner. Teaching, lecturing, and continued writing occupied her later years, and she was working on a book about Alfred Smith when, at eighty-four, she died.

Myers, Elisabeth P. MADAME SECRETARY: FRANCES PERKINS Messner, 1972. (grade 7 and up)
   Absorbing account of the life of the first woman cabinet member is smoothly written, gives a good picture of the early and mid-1900s in the United States, and makes clear Perkins's contributions and achievements in government.

Severn, Bill FRANCES PERKINS: A MEMBER OF THE CABINET Hawthorn, 1976. (grade 6 and up)
   Nonfictionalized, very complete account of Frances Perkins's life. Her impact on social policy in the United States is clearly demonstrated and provides good history as well as biography.

~~~~~~

ELIZA LUCAS PINCKNEY
c. 1722–1793

Plantation manager

When her father, a colonel in the British Army, had to return to the West Indies, seventeen-year-old Eliza Lucas Pinckney took over complete management of her father's three plantations in South Carolina.

South Carolina's main crop at the time was rice, but she decided to experiment with other crops, and painstakingly developed indigo, a seed used for making a blue dye. This crop became a major export of the Carolinas and had a profound effect upon the economic life of the Carolinas in the nineteenth century.

Eliza Pinckney had been educated in England and she was an accomplished musician and had a familiarity with the classics. She, in turn, educated her younger sister and the black children on the plantation. She also kept a journal and wrote numerous letters, one of the largest collections left by a colonial woman.

Eliza Pinckney married a successful attorney, and two of their sons became leaders in the early government of the United States and also brought new methods to their own plantations.

Lee, Susan, and Lee, John   ELIZA PINCKNEY   Illus. Childrens Pr., 1977. (grades 4–9)

Excellent biography depicts Eliza Pinckney as a woman who married the man of her choice, supported the American Revolution, ran a plantation, and brought indigo to the colonies. This portrait counteracts the stereotyped passive image of southern women, and stresses that other southern women also worked hard.

~~~~~~

POCAHONTAS
c. 1595–1617

Legendary Indian heroine

Princess Pocahontas, daughter of the great chief Powhattan, intervened for the Jamestown colony leader Captain John Smith when her father was about to kill him. Though the story has been frequently wrapped in legend, Smith himself documented the incident as occurring when Pocahontas was only twelve or thirteen years old.

Her abilities as an emissary were acknowledged when she negotiated the release of Indian prisoners in Jamestown and generally fostered goodwill between Indians and settlers.

Her marriage to John Rolfe, a colonist, led to Pocahontas's acceptance of Christianity and the birth of a son, Thomas. With her husband and child she went to England where she was presented to King James I and Queen Anne. Unaccustomed to the dampness and cold of England, Pocahontas took ill and died before her return. Over the years many romantic stories have grown around her and she has appeared, somewhat fictionalized, in the works of leading poets, playwrights, and novelists.

Bulla, Clyde Robert POCAHONTAS AND THE STRANGERS Illus. Crowell, 1971. (grades 4–7)
Distinguished writing and beautiful illustrations by Peter Burchard combine to create an outstanding, though somewhat fictionalized account of the legend of Pocahontas. Her conflicting loyalties are indicated, and she emerges as the real human being she was.

D'Aulaire, Ingri, and Parin, Edgar POCAHONTAS Illus. Doubleday, 1949. (picture book, reading level, grades 3–5)
Outstanding color illustrations and fine writing distinguish this picture book and early reader. Though fictionalized, it is faithful to the story of Pocahontas as it is known.

Jassem, Kate POCAHONTAS, GIRL OF JAMESTOWN Illus. Troll, 1979. (grades 4–8)
Despite fictionalization, this is a good biography of Pocahontas. It moves quickly and gives a good picture of the era.

Martin, Patricia POCAHONTAS Illus. Putnam, 1964. (grades K–4)
Satisfactory biography of Pocahontas is simple and suitable for reading aloud, but lacks vigor and color.

Phillips, Leon FIRST LADY OF AMERICA Westover, 1973. (grade 7 and up)
A serious biography of the legendary heroine gives a good picture of the events of the times and her role in them. The author researched the subject and era well, resulting in a biography that will appeal to high school readers or young, competent ones.

Richards, Dorothy. POCAHONTAS, CHILD PRINCESS Illus. Childrens Pr., 1978. (grades 1–5)
Highly fictionalized book focuses on her intervention to save Captain John Smith. A sense of Indian life and times is conveyed, and pleasant illustrations make this book satisfactory for very young readers or as a read-aloud book for younger children.

Wilkie, Katherine Pocahontas: indian princess Illus. Garrard, 1969. (grades 2–5)
Good account of Pocahontas is written with direct simplicity in a somewhat lively, narrative style.

~~~~~~

BEATRIX POTTER
1866–1943

Author and illustrator of children's books

Peter Rabbit, the best-known of Beatrix Potter's many books, is still loved by generations of children and parents. Throughout her lonely though not unhappy childhood, she only had servants and animal pets as her friends, and drawing and nature were her greatest interests. Later Beatrix Potter wrote a series of letters to a young friend which developed into the little, pale-colored, illustrated books which are familiar to children throughout the world.

No commercial publisher was willing to publish her first book, *Peter Rabbit*, so she published it herself. Later it, like all her successive stories about animals, was published by Frederick Warne & Co., Inc., New York.

She and her husband lived on a farm in England where she wrote, became an active member of the neighboring community, and bought additional property with the intention of protecting areas of natural beauty.

Aldis, Dorothy Nothing Is Impossible: the story of beatrix potter Illus. Atheneum, 1969. (grades 3–7)
Outstanding biography of Beatrix Potter discusses her lonely childhood, many interests and hobbies, and the development of her career. Warm and dramatic, it shows clearly her tremendous talents, success, and lifestyle. Of particular interest to devotees of her books, this biography has even wider attraction as a perceptive and inspiring study of an independent, imaginative woman.

Frevert, Patricia Dendtler Beatrix Potter: children's storyteller Illus. with photographs. Creative Ed., 1981. (grades 4–9)
Good lively biography will appeal to youngsters who enjoyed the Beatrix Potter books as well as to some older, reluctant readers.

Lane, Margaret THE MAGIC YEARS OF BEATRIX POTTER Illus. Warne, 1978. (grade 7 and up)

Very attractive, beautifully illustrated nonadulatory volume focusses on her first fifty years, when she was engaged in creative work. Of special interest to those readers who love the books of Beatrix Potter.

Lane Margaret THE TALE OF BEATRIX POTTER: A BIOGRAPHY (2nd ed.) Illus. Warne, 1968. (grade 9 and up)

Full-length, adult biography is formally written, but is nevertheless a very fine, substantial evaluation of Potter's life and work. For mature readers particularly interested in an in-depth study.

Potter, Beatrix LETTERS TO CHILDREN Harvard Univ. Pr., 1967. (grades 3–6)

Not really a biography, but a collection of reproductions of her letters to children in her own handwriting, as well as set in print for clarity. Complements other biographical studies of her life as well as the reading of her books.

～～～～～～～～～～～～～～～～～～～～～～～～～～～～～～～～～～～～～～～

ANNEMARIE PROELL
1953–

Olympic ski champion

Annemarie Proell, skier, is a six-time World Cup winner and a Olympic silver and gold medal winner. She is considered by many to be the greatest woman downhill racer of all time. She has won more events than any skier in the world, man or woman.

When she was only fifteen she was the youngest of eighteen women to belong to the Austrian National Ski Team and won her first World Cup in 1971.

A highly competitive, hard-working skier, Annemarie Proell-Moser is demanding of herself and never satisfied unless she is number one. She retired and then resumed skiing, but now married and the mother of a little girl, she says she has quit racing permanently.

Jacobs, Linda ANNEMARIE PROELL: QUEEN OF THE MOUNTAIN Illus. EMC, 1975. (reading level, grades 4–6; interest level through high school)

191

Well-balanced account of the life of the top skier is objective and non-adulatory. Emphasis is on her skiing career with a good deal of information about her personal life and personality. Further enhanced by numerous action photographs, the book gives the reader a good picture of the life of a champion skier.

~~~~~~

JEANETTE RANKIN
1880–1973

Suffragist, congresswoman, pacifist

In 1917, Jeanette Rankin became the first woman to be elected to the House of Representatives and the only member of Congress to vote against the United States entry into both World Wars. This determined pacifist stand against World War I cost her reelection after that war (she was elected again later), but she continued to fight for social legislation that would aid women and children. She lobbied for improved working conditions, health care, and education.

Her activities as a suffrage leader were combined with a lifetime of pacifist activities. She was in the forefront of many world peace organizations, and despite personal and philosophical conflicts with many of the suffragist leaders, continued her efforts for women's suffrage until the vote was won. She protested the foreign policy involvements of the United States. Many suffrage groups did not join the pacifist movement, but Jeanette Rankin believed that both causes were part of the fight for a better world.

She was elected to Congress again for one term, when she cast the only vote against the United States entry into World War II after Pearl Harbor.

Again, her political career did not survive this unpopular stand, and after leaving Congress she travelled widely, making a number of trips to India, studying Gandhi's methods and achievements.

During the Vietnam era she had popular support for her views and was actively involved in the antiwar demonstrations of the

1960s, and was a keynote speaker at a National Organization for Women convention after she was ninety.

Jeanette Rankin was a woman of determination and a fighter for causes, and valued her principles more than popularity. She has the added distinction of election to the House of Representatives from her state of Montana even before women had the vote in all of the other states.

Block, Judy R. THE FIRST WOMAN IN CONGRESS: JEANETTE RANKIN Illus. with photographs. Contemporary Perspectives, 1978. (grades 3–6)
Excellent, easy-to-read biography of the courageous congresswoman. Accurate depiction of her work for women's rights and for peace.

White, Florence M. FIRST WOMAN IN CONGRESS: JEANETTE RANKIN Illus. with photographs. Messner, 1980. (grades 5–9)
Very fine biography places Rankin into historical context as she worked for peace, women's suffrage, and the contemporary feminist movement.

~~~~~~

VINNIE REAM
1847–1914

Sculptor

Vinnie Ream and her parents were living in Washington, D.C., when she happened to visit a prominent sculptor's studio. Only sixteen years old at the time, she decided to sculpt and her result so impressed the artist that he took her on as a pupil. She was soon making busts of congressmen, and did one of President Lincoln. After he was assassinated, Congress contracted with the eighteen-year-old artist to do a full-scale marble statue to stand in the Capitol.

With her parents, she went to Rome to turn the work into marble and in 1871 it was unveiled at the Capitol. Other commissions followed but when, at the age of thirty, Ream married an army engineer, she gave up her professional art career and instead devoted herself to various charities. Many years later, though quite ill, she returned briefly to sculpture and just before her death completed a commission of the Cherokee Indian, Sequoya.

Hall, Gordon VINNIE REAM: THE STORY OF THE GIRL WHO SCULPTURED LINCOLN Holt, 1963. (grades 7–9)

Extremely well-researched and documented biography gives a good picture of the life of Vinnie Ream, depicting her as a highly talented, clever young woman.

~~~~~~

JOHANNA de LEEUW REISS
1932–

Author

When the Germans invaded Holland in 1940 many Jews thought they would be safe. Johanna de Leeuw Reiss's family thought so too, but two years later it was evident that this was not the case. Ten-year-old "Annie" and her sister left their parents to hide in an upstairs room of a farmhouse owned by sympathetic non-Jewish people. Until the war was over they stayed there, safe from the Germans but cut off from the rest of the world.

After the war she completed her education in Holland and became a teacher. After going to the United States she became an editor and then decided to write *The Upstairs Room* to answer her daughters' questions about her childhood. The book won several important American awards, and has been translated and published throughout Europe and in Japan. She was also awarded the Buxtehuder Bulle, one of western Europe's most prestigious book prizes, given to authors of children's books which promote peace. Reiss is the first American to win the prize and upon accepting it said, "I am glad that *The Upstairs Room*, which I wrote for my daughters, has been read by many more children. I hope they got from it that without hate, without bitterness, perhaps we can reach out to each other, just as we have done here today. That makes me have faith that there will never be a need again to write another 'Upstairs Room'."

Reiss, Johanna THE UPSTAIRS ROOM Crowell, 1972. (grade 5 and up)

Beautifully written, personal narrative is tender, moving, and dramatic.

Young "Annie" and her sister emerge as strong and courageous as the couple who sheltered them.

————. THE JOURNEY BACK   Crowell, 1976. (grade 4 and up)
In this excellent sequel to *The Upstairs Room*, the author describes her life after the war, and her adjustment to new surroundings.

~~~~~~

JOAN MOORE RICE
1954–

Olympic gymnast

Joan Moore Rice is a gymnast whose combined dancing and athletic ability result in beautiful ballet-like gymnastic routines.

She was an active and fearless youngster who began gymnastics when she was only six. Good training and coaching, as well as hard work and innate ability, enabled her to begin international competition by the time she was sixteen.

In 1971 and 1972 Joan Moore Rice tied for first place in the Elite Nationals. In the 1972 Olympics she tallied up a score high enough to rank twenty-first in the world. In both 1973 and 1974 she alone won the Elite Nationals, thus becoming the best amateur gymnast in the country.

In 1974 Rice retired from amateur gymnastics. Although this meant she would not be able to compete in the 1976 Olympics, it still enabled her to continue the work she enjoys. She and her husband, who is also a gymnast, opened a gymnastic school in Minneapolis. Here she has the opportunity to teach students the skills she has so beautifully mastered.

Jacobs, Linda   JOAN MOORE RICE: THE OLYMPIC DREAM   Illus. EMC. 1975. (reading level, grades 4–6; interest level through high school)
Well-rounded, interesting account of the subject's life also gives a good picture of the life of a gymnast and the training needed to achieve success. The author includes an interesting informative discussion of the sport of gymnastics.

ELLEN SWALLOW RICHARDS
1842–1911

Chemist, pioneer in home economics

At twenty-five, Ellen Richards entered Vassar College where, influenced by Maria Mitchell (page 163), the astronomer, she decided to make science her life's work. She was accepted as a chemistry student at the Massachusetts Institute of Technology (MIT). Later she discovered that the reason she had not been charged any tuition was so that the school would not have a woman officially recorded as a student. She became the first woman to graduate with a degree in chemistry and was hired by MIT as an instructor and acting director of the first chemistry laboratory to study sanitation.

Richards was the first woman elected to the American Institute of Mining and Metallurgical Engineers, organized the science department of a large correspondence school, was a founder of the group that came to be called the American Association of University Women, and worked for the improvement of physical education in colleges.

An expert in food and nutrition, she served as a consultant to schools, hospitals, institutions, and the federal department of agriculture and almost single-handedly made home economics a profession. Her numerous articles, books, and lectures on home economics and other subjects, as well as her inexhaustible efforts to increase women's participation in the scientific professions, are just a few of Ellen Richards's many accomplishments.

Douty, Esther AMERICA'S FIRST WOMAN CHEMIST: ELLEN RICHARDS Messner, 1961. (grade 7 and up)
  Outstanding biography is a warm, personal account of Ellen Richards's life. Nontechnical, it has appeal for all readers, but may be particularly attractive to those interested in science and home economics. Richards is introduced as a sensitive, diversified, and ambitious human being.

~~~~~~

LINDA RICHARDS
1841–1930

Nursing educator who received first American nursing diploma

Linda Richards's interest in nursing was encouraged by a local Vermont doctor who relied on her assistance. When the first American school of nursing opened, she enrolled and became the first nurse to receive a diploma in the United States.

After graduation Richards helped develop educational programs in nursing and journeyed to England where she conferred with Florence Nightingale (page 173) and studied her methods of training nurses. Upon her return she worked despite the opposition of doctors who were satisfied with the poor care given by untrained nurses.

Linda Richards opened the first nursing school in Japan where she also engaged in evangelical work. After returning to the United States, she became a pioneer in the training of visiting nurses and worked to raise the standard of nursing care in mental hospitals.

Scholarships and awards are named in her honor, and in the New England Hospital for Women and Children there is a room dedicated to her containing mementos of her life.

Baker, Rachel AMERICA'S FIRST TRAINED NURSE: LINDA RICHARDS Messner, 1962. (grade 7 and up)

Unusually fine narrative biography of Linda Richards also covers the history of nursing in the late nineteenth and early twentieth century, as well as the development of new practices and methods. Directed to all readers, not just those interested in the career of nursing, it is a warm, dramatic, and stirring portrait of a dedicated woman of many accomplishments.

Collins, David R. LINDA RICHARDS: FIRST AMERICAN TRAINED NURSE Illus. Garrard, 1975. (grades 2–4)

Written with direct simplicity, a warm, inspiring, and lively account of the pioneer nurse draws a good picture of her life, the early days of nursing, and the historical period in which she lived.

~~~~~~

SALLY RIDE
1951–

Astrophysicist, astronaut, first American woman in space

When Sally Ride was growing up in California she loved sports, and science was her favorite subject. At college she played on the tennis team, was a ranked player and yet still found time to graduate with two majors: one in science and the other in English. She earned her doctorate in physics at Stanford University, and then, in 1978 applied to National Aeronautics Space Administration for admission to the astronaut program. More than 9000 other people applied at that time, including over 1500 women. Thirty-five people were accepted, six of whom were women.

In the summer of 1983, when Sally Ride lifted off on the space shuttle *Challenger*, she became America's youngest and first woman astronaut to go up in space. Her wide scientific knowledge, training, and physical fitness were vital in the work she and her crew mates needed to do.

Sally Ride's parents always encouraged their children to accept challenges and to excel in any endeavors they chose, even if it involved an unconventional route. Her sister is a Presbyterian minister, and the family remains close.

Sally Ride hopes women will soon be so well represented in the astronaut program that they will no longer be singled out for the kind of attention focused on her before and after her flight.

She is married to another astronaut, Steven Hawley, who is also a physicist.

O'Connor, Karen SALLY RIDE AND THE NEW ASTRONAUTS: SCIENTISTS IN SPACE Illus. with photographs. Watts, 1983. (grade 5 and up)

A truly fine book that discusses Sally Ride's motivations, education, and training that led to her being the first American woman in space. The other women in the program are also discussed: Shannon Lucid, chemist; Judith Resnik, electrical engineer; Anna Fisher, physician; Rhea Seddon, surgeon; Kathryn Sullivan, marine geophysicist; Mary Cleaves, engineer; and Bonnie Dunbar, scientist. There is a good emphasis on the scientific aspects of the astronaut program and the need for all candidates to have a strong background in the sciences. The book will be of interest to the non-science oriented reader as well as those who may be interested in someday applying for the program.

~~~~~~

CATHY RIGBY
1952–

Olympic gymnast

At four feet, ten-and-a-half inches, eighty-nine pounds, Cathy Rigby was the smallest American on the 1968 Olympic gymnast team. Although she did not win any medals, her all-around scoring was the highest ever for an American gymnast.

Cathy Rigby, a premature baby, remained sickly for several years, but as she got older became an extremely active and physically daring child. At eleven she began intensive gymnastic training, and by the time she was fourteen, she was ready to compete in her first international meet.

In the 1970 World Games she took the silver medal for the balance beam competition, becoming the first American to win a medal in international gymnastics. The following year she became the first non-Russian to win a gold medal in competition held in the Soviet Union.

Outdoing all other Americans at the 1972 Olympics, she did not take any medals because the competition with the Russian and European gymnasts was too great.

Exhausted from years of hard work, the pressure of continuing the imposed "cute little girl" image, and the controlling influence of her coach, she decided to retire from gymnastic competition.

In 1974 she played the title role in a stage production of *Peter Pan*, and she continues occasionally to give exhibitions. Her success helped bring wide attention to gymnastics and has influenced many other young women to consider the sport for themselves.

She now lives in California with her husband and young son. She appears in advertisements and in commercials on television and has founded a gymnastic school.

Jacobs, Linda CATHY RIGBY: ON THE BEAM   Illus. with photographs. EMC, 1975. (grade 4 and up)

Interesting and readable but too laudatory in tone, the biography depicts Rigby and everyone else in her life as almost too good to be true. However, the photographs of her in action add considerably to the biography and the book will be of interest to older reluctant readers as well as younger ones.

~~~~~~

FELISA RINCÓN
1897–

Mayor of San Juan, Puerto Rico

Felisa Rincón was reared in a conservative middle-class Puerto Rican home. When her mother died, she was forced to quit high school to keep house and to care for her younger sisters and brothers. Not until 1932 did she take an active role outside the home. That year Puerto Rican women were first permitted to vote and, despite her father's initial objection, she went to the polls. Appalled to discover few other women had done so, she immediately became involved in Puerto Rican politics and set about urging women to exercise their right.

When appointed mayor of San Juan in 1946 to fill an unexpired term, Doña Felisa, as she was known to her constituents, became the first and only woman mayor of San Juan. Her reforms were immediate and she was reelected every four years, serving a total of twenty years.

Felisa Rincón's popularity rested not only on the close personal relationships and ready availability she maintained with the mostly impoverished residents of San Juan, but also on the improvements in housing, sanitation, health, and education she instituted. The development of a child care center was another one of her important contributions to San Juan.

A skilled politician, she worked closely with business and government officials on the mainland, bringing industry and other benefits to the island.

Gruber, Ruth FELISA RINCÓN DE GAUTIER: MAYOR OF SAN JUAN   Illus. Crowell, 1972. (grades 5–8)

Superb, warm portrait of Felisa Rincón not only shows the development of her as a political figure, but also discusses the culture of Puerto Rico and male and female relationships as they exist there.

~~~~~~

ELEANOR ROOSEVELT
1884–1962

Humanitarian, author, First Lady

Eleanor Roosevelt was a lonely youngster who overcame shyness and self-consciousness to become a woman of great influence in national and international affairs. As the wife of the thirty-second president of the United States, Franklin Delano Roosevelt, she chose not to be a social figure, but instead attended to more official business. She wrote newspaper and magazine columns and several books, lectured and toured the country, and during World War II visited army posts here and abroad. The press conferences for women reporters which she instituted comprised just one of her efforts to increase the participation of women at all levels of government and private industry. Placing particular emphasis on civil rights, she was a champion of all minority groups and resigned from the Daughters of the American Revolution when they refused the use of their concert hall to black singer Marian Anderson (page 9).

After her husband's death she was appointed a delegate to the first session of the United Nations, became the first chairperson of the United Nations' Human Rights Commission, and figured importantly in the Declaration of Human Rights. Her years of devotion to her own country and to all humanity earned her the title "First Lady of the world." Her death in 1962 was universally mourned.

Blassingame, Wyatt Eleanor Roosevelt Illus. Putnam, 1964. (grades 2–4)

Crisp, clear, easy-to-read text is a faithful and warm but not sentimental account of the life of the great humanitarian. It captures the essence of Roosevelt and serves well as an introduction to her life for young readers.

Davidson, Margaret Story of Eleanor Roosevelt Illus. with photographs. Four Winds, 1969. (grades 4–6)

Outstanding biography is accurate and well-written though very informal. The author brings Roosevelt to life, clearly stating her many accomplishments and capturing her personality.

Gilbert, Miriam Shy Girl: the story of eleanor roosevelt Doubleday, 1965. (grades 5–9)

A very readable, sympathetic account of Eleanor Roosevelt's unhappy childhood. Written at a very easy reading level, it should appeal to older less able readers, and may well spark their imagination to read a more complete biography of her.

Goodsell, Jane Eleanor Roosevelt Illus. Crowell, 1970. (grades 1–3)

Simple, but worthwhile biography is a stirring, thoughtful examination of Eleanor Roosevelt as youngster, wife, mother, and great humanitarian.

Graves, Charles Eleanor Roosevelt: first lady of the land Illus. Garrard, 1965. (grades 2–5)

Good account of Eleanor Roosevelt is immensely readable but does not place sufficient emphasis on her role as an individual, although it does cite her accomplishments.

Johnson, Ann Donegan The Value of Caring: the story of eleanor roosevelt Illus. Value Communications, 1977. (grades K–3)

Overly fictionalized, excessively adulatory biography does convey Eleanor Roosevelt's accomplishments and humanitarian values. While it may be appealing to preschool youngsters, it seems a little too gushy. A full-page factual biographical profile follows the colorful picture-book story, and this is a well-balanced account. This portion of the book will be of interest to older readers and adults.

Richards, Kenneth Eleanor Roosevelt Illus. Childrens Pr., 1968. (grade 6 and up)

Very fine black-and-white pohotographs and illustrations compose the major part of this study of Eleanor Roosevelt. The text is also substantial, warm, dramatic, and informative.

Roosevelt, Eleanor The Autobiography of Eleanor Roosevelt Harper, 1961. (grade 9 and up)

One-volume personal narrative consists of material selected from three volumes of memoirs of Eleanor Roosevelt. A final chapter which she added for this book tells of her activities through the 1960 elections. An outstanding book, it provides many warm, intimate glimpses of Roosevelt's life.

Whitney, Sharon ELEANOR ROOSEVELT Illus. with photographs. Watts, 1982. (grade 7 and up)
   Intelligently written, serious, well-rounded biography of Eleanor Roosevelt is a personal as well as historical biography.

~~~~~~

ERNESTINE ROSE
1810–1892

Feminist, reformer

As the daughter of a rabbi, Ernestine Rose received more education and freedom than is usually afforded young girls in Russian Poland, but her rebellious spirit railed against the subordination and inferiority of women taught in Jewish law. At age fourteen she completely disassociated herself from Judaism. Two years later, in objection to her widowed father's contractual agreement to marry her to an older man and to give her mother's inheritance to him as a dowry, she went to court and won back her rightful funds.

   Ernestine Rose left Poland for England where she became acquainted with, and influenced by, social reformers, including Robert Owen. She married, and moved to New York, becoming active in the women's rights and free-thought movements. An immensely dramatic and strikingly attractive woman, she soon became known as the "queen of the platform" when she lectured on a wide range of subjects that included temperance, abolition, peace, the rights of women, and free thought. Her progressive ideas made her a controversial figure, even among supporters of women's rights, but she remained in close alliance with Susan B. Anthony (page 13) and Elizabeth Cady Stanton (page 227) and, due to her dynamic personality and superior intelligence, influenced the reformers of her day.

Suhl, Yuri ELOQUENT CRUSADER: ERNESTINE ROSE Messner, 1970. (grade 7 and up)

Superior, well-written feminist biography is an outstanding, soundly researched examination of Rose's life as well as a good exploration of the reform movements of the day. The author is careful to paint an unvarnished, well-balanced account of the subject that is dramatic and colorful. As the only biography available of Ernestine Rose, it is recommended for older readers as well as the junior high and early high school ones for whom it was intended.

~~~~~~

BETSY ROSS
1752–1836

Legendary maker of the first American flag

Quaker-born Betsy Ross ran an upholstery business with her husband, and after his death continued her skilled needlework, making flags for Pennsylvanians and acquiring some property around the Philadelphia area. According to the well-known legend, George Washington, with a secret committee, visited her in her shop and commissioned her to design a flag for the new nation. She supposedly suggested a five-pointed star which could be cut with one scissor stroke. Some legends even say she was given an exclusive contract to manufacture the flags.

Her grandson first told the story of Betsy Ross and the first American flag at a historical meeting in 1870. The story, probably told to him by his mother, appealed to American patriotism and, despite lack of any documentation, was soon included in school textbooks.

A Betsy Ross Memorial Association was organized, funds were raised to make a national shrine of the house in which she supposedly made the flag, and her legend has been immortalized in stories and paintings.

Mayer, Jane   Betsy Ross and the Flag   Random, 1952. (grades 4–6)
   Despite fictionalization and much invention of facts, this is a very good historical treatment, with Betsy Ross emerging as an independent, intelligent, and inspiring individual.

~~~~~~

DIANA ROSS
1944–

Singer, actress

Diana Ross has won just about every award that a recording star can win, and she even won a Golden Globe award for her film portrayal of Billie Holiday in *Lady Sings the Blues* (see page 112)
   She grew up in a life of poverty in Detroit, sang in the church choirs, and maintained good grades in school. She and two friends formed a singing group called the Primettes. Renamed the Supremes they achieved huge popularity on the Motown record label.
   The electrifying, slick sounds and appearances of the Supremes propelled them to superstardom, and in 1970 Diana Ross left the group to perform on her own. Recordings, television, and concert appearances followed, and in *Lady Sings the Blues* her acting was as highly acclaimed as her singing, which incorporated her own style with that of Billie Holiday.
   Diana Ross continues to command huge salaries, travelling through the world giving concerts. She left Motown in 1981 and now has her own corporation, Diana Ross Enterprises. She lives in Hollywood with her two children and enjoys a lifestyle very different from the one she remembers in the ghetto of Detroit.
   During the summer of 1983 a free concert she gave in New York's Central Park attracted more than a half-million people.

Haskins, James   I'm Gonna Make You Love Me   Illus. with photographs. Dial, 1980. (grade 6 and up)
   Excellent, well-balanced, nonadulatory biography vividly describes Ross's life in the Detroit ghetto in the late 1940s, as well as her later professional and personal life.

HELENA RUBINSTEIN
c. 1870–1965

Founder of international beauty and cosmetic business

Helena Rubinstein, one of the wealthiest self-made women in the world, was, at fifteen, a bookkeeper for her father's small business in Poland. She then entered medical school, but decided not to complete the training, and went instead to Australia, where she opened a small shop in which she dispensed beauty advice along with cosmetics and creams she had brought from Europe. Immensely successful, she repeated this success in London and Paris, and at the start of World War I came to New York. Within a few years she had established salons across the country.

All her energies, thoughts, and time were concentrated on business and although she was a difficult taskmaster she was able to surround herself with competent, loyal people, many of whom were relatives. However, the success of her business was due almost in its entirety to the dedication, authority, and control which she exercised.

During World War II Helena Rubinstein helped innumerable Polish refugees find a welcome in the United States, and she did much to aid the war effort. The many foundations she created have given millions of dollars to charities, museums, and universities. Her private collection of paintings and jewelry contributed to the legend of beauty and opulence that surrounded her.

Fabe, Maxene BEAUTY MILLIONAIRE: THE LIFE OF HELENA RUBINSTEIN Illus. with photographs. Crowell, 1973. (grades 5–9)
Outstanding biography of the woman who made her fortune in the cosmetic business is a well-balanced, absorbing account clearly showing her abilities and energies and her commitment to business. Some of her personal failures are also dealt with.

WILMA RUDOLPH
1940–

Olympic track and field winner

That Wilma Rudolph ever learned to walk is something of a miracle. That she later became the first American woman to win three Olympic gold medals for track and field is not so much a miracle as it is the result of years of determination and hard work.

Illness had left Wilma, one of the youngest of nineteen children, badly crippled. The family worked together to follow medical rehabilitation instructions and by the time she was six years old she could walk.

From then on, nothing stopped her. In high school she played basketball and went out for track. At the age of sixteen, she became a member of the United States Olympic team, helping the women's team win a bronze medal. In 1960 she broke the Olympic record in the 200-meter dash, and along with her team mates set a 400-meter world record.

In 1961 Wilma Rudolph became the third woman ever to win the Sullivan Memorial Trophy for outstanding performance by an amateur athlete. She also was invited to race in the usually all-man Millrose Games held annually in New York's Madison Square Garden.

Wilma Rudolph has been busy since her days of competition, first as a junior high school teacher, now as director of the Youth Foundation in Chicago and coach of the women's track team. She is married and has four children, two of whom are track stars. She hosts television specials, speaks before various groups, and has taught at the University of California at Los Angeles.

In 1974 Wilma Rudolph was inducted into the new Black Athletes Hall of Fame. She was one of only three women included.

Jacobs, Linda WILMA RUDOLPH: RUN FOR GLORY Illus. with photographs. EMC, 1975. (grade 4 and up)

Inspiring, fast-moving biography of Wilma Rudolph traces her private life and career from sickly infancy through her Olympic achievements and her adult role as a coach, civic leader, television personality, and mother. Numerous photographs of her in action and with friends and family greatly enhance the easy-to-read text, as suitable for older reluctant readers as it is for elementary school youngsters.

~~~~~~

FLORENCE SABIN, M.D.
1871–1953

Physician, scientist, researcher

Florence Sabin, who has been described as one of the foremost scientists of all times, specialized in the investigation of the lymphatic system, blood vessels, and the origin of red blood cells. Before receiving her medical degree from Johns Hopkins medical school, Florence Sabin made a three-dimensional model of the brain which led to a clearer understanding of its structure. Copies of it continue to be used in medical schools today and the textbook which she later published to accompany the model was long considered the finest one on the subject.

She was primarily a researcher and teacher. Her discoveries and many publications altered medical thinking, and brought her honors and awards. Yet even though she was next in line to be named head of the department of anatomy at Hopkins, a man was appointed in her stead. She did, however, become the first female full professor there, and later at the Rockefeller Institute set up the department of cellular studies and pioneered in the study of tuberculosis.

The first woman elected to life membership of the National Academy of Science and first woman president of the American Association of Anatomists, she retired at age seventy-three to move back to her home in Colorado. There she led an energetic crusade for health and sanitation improvements.

Phelan, Mary Kay PROBING THE UNKNOWN: THE STORY OF DR. FLORENCE SABIN Crowell, 1969. (grades 5–8)
Outstanding biography of the famed scientist is warm, dramatic, inspiring, and of particular interest to students of science, for some of it is slightly technical. The author writes with clarity, and explains scientific

concepts and terms well, allowing uninformed readers to follow the text with ease.

~~~~~~

SACAJAWEA
1787–1812

Indian interpreter for Lewis and Clark

Sacajawea, the captured and enslaved Indian wife of French-Canadian Toussaint Charbonneau, played a significant role in the famous Lewis and Clark expedition.

When Charbonneau was hired as an interpreter for Lewis and Clark, Sacajawea and their infant went along: their presence served as a signal that the expedition was not a warring party. Sacajawea's knowledge of several Indian languages and ability to speak with many tribes through a chain of interpreters contributed greatly to the expedition's progress. She helped cook, introduced the men to edible substances, saved valuable instruments and records from loss, and was instrumental in obtaining guidance and services from Indian tribes.

According to legend, she regularly served as a guide; though this information is undocumented, it is certain that she provided some vital direction on their return trip. Throughout the West, statues, monuments, streams, and mountain peaks are named for the young Indian woman whose important role in American history had largely gone unrecognized in textbooks until recently.

Blassingame, Wyatt SACAGAWEA: INDIAN GUIDE Garrard, 1965. (grades 2–5)
Simplistic but very fine story of Sacajawea gives a good picture of Indian life and culture while at the same time showing Sacajawea to be an unusually wise and independent young woman.

Burt, Olive SACAJAWEA Illus. Watts, 1978. (grades 5–7)
Extremely well-written, nonfictionalized, documented biography of Sacajawea. Many of the events associated with her following the expedition are from unconfirmed sources, and the author presents then in this way.

Farnsworth, Frances WINGED MOCCASINS: THE STORY OF SACA-
JAWEA Illus. Messner, 1954. (grade 6 and up)
Excellent biography of the Indian interpreter and guide moves with
reality and warmth, emphasizing her intelligence, skills, and loyalty. Interesting and fast-moving, it also recreates the Lewis and Clark expedition
well.

Jessem, Kate SACAJAWEA, WILDERNESS GUIDE Illus. Troll, 1979.
(grades 3–6)
A very pleasant profile of Sacajawea gives a good picture of Indian life.

Johnson, Ann Donegan THE VALUE OF ADVENTURE: THE STORY OF
SACAGAWEA Illus. Value Communications, 1980. (grades K–3)
Highly fictionalized story book moves quickly, lavishly illustrated in full
color which will appeal to the youngest reader. The "value of adventure,"
as it can lead to worthwhile accomplishments, is conveyed. Following the
text, a full page offers a more straightforward account of her life, which is
useful for older children or adults who are reading the story aloud to
nonreaders.

Skold, Betty Westrom SACAGAWEA Illus. Dillon, 1977. (grades 4–7)
A fine book which gives a very good picture of life among the Shoshoni.
Author's spelling of the name, differing from the usual, is a reflection of
more recent studies.

Voight, Virginia SACAJAWEA Illus. Putnam, 1967. (grades K–4)
Good, but not outstanding biography of the young Indian woman. Not
especially dramatic, it is nonetheless an interesting tale, simply told.

~~~~~~

DEBORAH SAMPSON
1760–1827

Revolutionary soldier

Many women took over men's jobs during the American Revolution, but Deborah Sampson was one of only a few who actually
served in the Continental Army. She disguised herself as a man
and, using the name of Robert Shirtliff, enlisted with a Massachusetts regiment. She participated in several battles and when
wounded, hid. Only when she was hospitalized with typhoid was
her sex discovered, at which time she was discharged.

Deborah Sampson later married, had three children, and lectured on her experiences. She was eventually awarded a pension from the government for her services.

Felton, Harvey DEBORAH SAMPSON: SOLDIER OF THE REVOLUTION Illus. Dodd, 1976. (grades 5–7)
Highly fictionalized, but not obtrusively so, this biography gives a good picture of colonial life as experienced by a young, poor, fatherless girl.

McGovern, Ann DEBORAH SAMPSON GANNETT Four Winds, 1975. (grades 2–4)
Good, easy-to-read biography clearly states the limited options for women during the period in which Deborah lived. However, it does not fully capture the adventuresome spirit of the young revolutionary soldier.

~~~~~~

GEORGE SAND
1804–1876

French author

In nineteenth-century France the pen name George Sand was convenient for Amadine-Aurore Lucie Dupin, who wrote her many romantic novels in a time when women's roles and lives were narrowly confined by the conventions of the day.

She was the daughter of an aristocratic father and a mother of common stock. When her father died during her early childhood, her life was marred by the conflict between her strict paternal grandmother and her mother. She was brought up in her grandmother's country home, spent some years in a convent, was married, and had two children.

After several years, she made new friendships and began her career as a writer. She divorced her husband and went to Paris. From that time on George Sand lived as she chose, believing that a woman was as free as a man to create her own life, and expressed her independence by wearing men's trousers.

George Sand wrote unceasingly, and her many plays and novels drew on her rustic background. The most constant theme of her work is that of romantic attachments overcoming obstacles of convention and class. In her work she often rewarded the poor and innocent, for whom she felt compassion, with happy endings. Her works include *Indiana, Lelia, La mare au diable*, and, in her later years, *Histoire de ma vie. Contes d'une grand-mère* are the stories she wrote for her grandchildren.

She filled her own life with many deep friendships. The most famous of her emotional involvements was with the composer Chopin, a relationship which lasted eight years.

Hovey, Tamara A MIND OF HER OWN: A LIFE OF THE WRITER GEORGE SAND Illus. with photographs. Harper, 1977. (grade 7 and up)
Excellent, serious biography offers a well-balanced perspective as it traces the life of the famous novelist from childhood through marriage and on her own in Paris, as she achieved fame and success.

~~~~~~

MARIA SANFORD
1836–1920

Educator

Maria Sanford's mother instilled in her an appreciation of literature and biographical history and gave her the opportunity to receive a good education, although they were poor, hard-working New England country people.

Before she was even twenty, young Maria Sanford was a teacher, and as she gained confidence and acquired more education through self-study, she developed new and then unusual teaching methods. Her emphasis on interesting students in the subject, rather than strict rote learning, attracted much attention and she began lecturing and training other teachers.

She became a professor at Swarthmore College, and then at the University of Minnesota. Admired by most of her students, she was also subject to criticism because of some of her unusual methods, styles, and feminist ideas.

Her mother had also imbued her with a strong sense of integrity and commitment to family. When some poor investments left her in heavy debt she repaid every penny, although it took her almost twenty years. She never married but helped to educate many younger family members. After her retirement from teaching she gave poetry readings and lectures on art, public affairs, and women's suffrage.

The first women's dormitory at the Univesity of Minnesota was named after her and a statue of her as a resident of Minnesota stands in the national Capitol in Washington. She was remembered by generations of students as a teacher who gave them an appreciation of the arts while at the same time stressing the value of hard work.

Hartley, Lucie MARIA SANFORD: PIONEER PROFESSOR Illus. Dillon, 1977. (grades 5–9)
Lacking some animation, this biography does give a good picture of the hard-working, dynamic teacher who played an important role in the education of midwestern farm students.

~~~~~~

MARGARET SANGER
1883–1966

Feminist, reformer, and advocate of birth control

Margaret Sanger was well convinced of the health risk associated with pregnancy. Her own mother had died young, worn out from successive childbearing and, as a nurse, Margaret Sanger saw firsthand the relationship of large families, poverty, illness, and misery and the often tragic results of self-induced abortions. She believed contraception was the cure. She studied European methods and, despite laws which prohibited the dissemination of such information, published a magazine, *The Woman Rebel;* wrote pamphlets and articles; and found printers willing to risk printing what were then defined as "obscene materials." She set up a clinic for dispensing contraceptive materials and coined the phrase "birth control." Constantly arrested and jailed, she refused to plead guilty, claiming "the law was wrong, not I." She fought a lonely crusade when even doctors were unwilling to support her and most feminists preferred to place priorities on women's suffrage.

Sanger lived to see her ideas gain respectability and to be hailed a heroine. She was a consultant for population control and family planning organizations throughout the world.

Lader, Lawrence, and Meltzer, Milton MARGARET SANGER: PIONEER OF BIRTH CONTROL Illus. Crowell, 1969. (grades 5–9)
Outstanding biography of the reformer shows her selflessness, conflicts about her own family, and determination to achieve her goals. Questions of sex and contraception are dealt with sensitively and tastefully in this extremely well-written, moving, and stirring account.

Sanger, Margaret MARGARET SANGER: AN AUTOBIOGRAPHY Norton, 1938; reprinted by Dover, 1971. (grade 9 and up)
The reformer's own autobiography, written for adults, is an exciting, dramatic, and readable account of her life, clearly showing the forces that combined to propel her to the course she chose.

~~~~~~

SADAKO SASAKI
1943–1955

World War II victim

Sadako Sasaki was a toddler, living in Hiroshima when the United States Air Force dropped the atom bomb. A fun-loving school girl, she began running in school races when she was eleven, hoping to gain a place on her junior high school's racing team. She sometimes felt dizzy, and one day she collapsed. She was rushed to the emergency room of a nearby hospital. It was not long before she was diagnosed as having leukemia, a result of radiation exposure years before.

Her friends, remembering an old folk tale, brought her a paper crane explaining that if a sick person folds one thousand paper cranes, he or she will recover. Sadako, with great determination and courage, continued to fold cranes. As her disease progressed, she became weaker and finally, in 1955, she died.

Today, in Hiroshima Place Park, a statue stands in memory of Sadako and her attempt to fold the cranes, and Japanese children are familiar with the story.

Coerr, Eleanor B. SADAKO AND THE THOUSAND PAPER CRANES   Illus. Putnam, 1977. (grades 3–5)

Stirring, sad, and beautiful story is a tribute to the human spirit and a plea for peace and the horrors of nuclear exposure. Sadako died bravely, knowing her diagnosis and prognosis. A book that may be especially meaningful for those in need of courage for themselves or in understanding others' need.

~~~~~~

CLARA WIECK SCHUMANN
1819–1896

Concert pianist

German-born Clara Wieck was a child prodigy who learned piano from her father, a demanding but skilled teacher. Before she had even entered her teens she gave recitals and concert tours and became acquainted with Robert Schumann, the composer who was a student of her father's. The two later fell in love, but her father strenuously objected to the marriage fearing that he would lose his selfish hold on her and that she would sacrifice her brilliant career.

Torn between love for them both, young Clara decided to defy her father and to marry Robert. She then combined marriage and motherhood with her career as a concert pianist, performing both classical works and helping to popularize her husband's work. Schumann, whose emotions had long been unstable, later became mentally ill and died in an asylum twelve years after their marriage. Clara Schumann continued to perform, but later, when the strain of touring became too difficult for her, limited herself to teaching others.

Kyle, Elisabeth DUET: THE STORY OF CLARA AND ROBERT SCHUMANN   Holt, 1968. (grades 5–9)

Excellent, romantic story of Clara Schumann and her career, her love for her husband, and her relationships with her family. In this well-told and moving story, Clara is seen as a warm, sometimes ambivalent human being with a brilliant concert career of her own.

~~~~~~

HANNAH SENESH
1921–1944

World War II heroine

A national heroine in Israel, Hannah Senesh was born and raised in Hungary, but her interest in the Zionist movement grew and she decided in 1939 to emigrate to Palestine. Life there was difficult, and Hannah Senesh, despite her intellectualism, did the hard manual work expected of settlers.

During World War II she volunteered to join the parachute corps and, in 1944 when millions of Jews in Hungary and elsewhere were slated for certain death at the hands of the Nazis, she served in a relief mission to Hungary which attempted to thwart those plans. Hannah Senesh and five young men were the only Palestinians who parachuted down behind enemy lines in Hungary. It was a suicidal mission, she knew, and she was captured and executed by the Nazis.

Hannah Senesh had kept a diary since she was thirteen, and through these memoirs, letters, her poetry which is read and learned by Israeli children today, and the recollections of those who knew her, she has become and remained a legend.

Masters, Anthony THE SUMMER THAT BLED: THE BIOGRAPHY OF HANNAH SENESH Illus. Washington Square Pr., 1972. (grade 9 and up)

Primarily a biography of Hannah Senesh, this is also the story of prewar Hungary and Palestine and the attempt to rescue Hungarian Jews during World War II. The author recreates the events suspensefully, clearly, and dramatically to provide readers with a moving, warm account of the subject and of the times.

Senesh, Hanna HANNAH SENESH: HER LIFE AND DIARY Schocken, 1972. (grade 9 and up)

Stirring, dramatic account of the life of Hannah Senesh is composed of her diary, memories of her childhood as told by her mother, letters, personal recollections of coparachutists, and translations of her poetry. The diary shows, in a warm and poignant style, her development from a young, almost carefree girl to a mature, committed young woman.

MARY BRUCE SHARON
1878–1961

American primitive painter

Mary Bruce Sharon did not begin to paint until she was seventy years old, but almost immediately her work was treated seriously by critics. Her paintings are based on her childhood memories, and have been exhibited all over Europe and in major museums in the United States.

In her younger years, she often made drawings in pen and ink, and it was her son-in-law, an artist, who suggested she try painting. Her work met with immediate acceptance, and she continued to paint until her death at the age of eighty-three.

Sharon, Mary Bruce SCENES FROM CHILDHOOD Illus. with photographs of paintings. Dutton, 1978. (grades 6–9)
A beautiful book, full of color reproductions of her native paintings. The accompanying text is biographical, but this book is not a biography in the true sense. Her daughter hasn interesting introduction.

MARY WOLLSTONECRAFT GODWIN SHELLEY
1797–1851

Author

Mary Shelley's mother, the famed feminist author Mary Wollstonecraft (page 267), died in childbirth, leaving Mary to be brought up by her philosopher father, William Godwin.

She was only fifteen when she first met the twenty-year-old poet Percy Bysshe Shelley, and although he was already married the two began to live as husband and wife and later married. They were constantly moving and hounded by debts; two of their children died and then Shelley himself was drowned at twenty-nine.

Despite these trials, shy, intelligent Mary Shelley produced many lasting works of literature. She wrote six novels, several plays, short stories, two novellas, and several travel books. She completed her best-known work, *Frankenstein, or the Modern Prometheus*, before she was even twenty years old.

After her husband's death she published his *Posthumous Poems*, and edited and added notes to his *Poetical Works*. Her *Journal*, in addition to its own merit, forms the basis for all biographies of the poet.

Harris, Janet THE WOMAN WHO CREATED FRANKENSTEIN: PORTRAIT OF MARY SHELLEY Harper, 1979. (grade 7 and up)
Very fine, well-rounded biography also gives a good picture of the social and historical period in which Shelley lived. There is also quite a bit of biographical information about her mother, Mary Wollstonecraft (page 267). Her life is traced through childhood, young motherhood, widowhood and into midlife.

~~~~~~

SARAH KEMBLE SIDDONS
1755–1831

Actress

Sarah Kemble Siddons, raised in the theater, made her debut on the stage as a small child, and soon outshone the other members of her family. Her greatest success was in the Shakespearian role of Lady Macbeth, but her portrayals of Desdemona, Rosalind, Ophelia, and Queen Catherine were also memorable.

Her marriage was not a happy one, but she was a devoted mother, somehow managing to find time for career and family. A quiet, somewhat introspective, private individual, she nevertheless moved in a circle with prominent artists, writers, and government officials. Public opinion of her was mixed—she was loved by many, hated by others.

Celebrated in paintings by Gainsborough, Reynolds, and others, she had a dignity and warmth which was seldom equalled by other actresses.

Jonson, Marion A TROUBLED GRANDEUR: THE STORY OF ENGLAND'S GREAT ACTRESS, SARAH SIDDONS   Illus. Little, 1972. (grade 7 and up)

Extremely well-written biography of the famed British actress depicts her as a talented woman with great inner strengths, devoted to her family and able to support them emotionally and financially, and yet constantly developing as a performer.

∿∿

ARANKA SIEGAL
1930–

World War II survivor

Aranka Siegal was only a child when Hitler's persecution of the Jews began. She lived in Hungary with her warm and close family, and her mother tried to keep them together and help their Jewish neighbors, despite the slow but continual destruction of the Jewish community. She and her remaining family were first placed in a ghetto, and then sent to Auschwitz.

Aranka, known as Piri, and her older sister never again saw the rest of the family, but they survived Auschwitz and the march to Bergen-Belsen, and in April of 1945 were rescued by the British First Army. From there, they went to Sweden, and in 1948 came to the United States.

Siegal has a degree in social anthropology, and for a year hosted a radio show in which she recounted her experiences in Hungary and other cultures in which she has lived. She now lives in New York.

Siegal, Aranka UPON THE HEAD OF THE GOAT: A CHILDHOOD IN HUNGARY 1939–1944   Farrar, Straus, 1981. (grade 7 and up)

Excellent autobiography is the story of Aranka and her mother, a resourceful, spirited woman who not only kept her family together but helped others to hold on to hope. This is one of those all-too-rare books that combine contemporary history with personal biography and is suitable for all ages. Moving as a personal story, it is also an important addition to the literature of the Holocaust.

BEVERLY SILLS
1929–

Opera singer and director

Beverly Sills is the all-American opera star. A sparkling woman with a beautiful coloratura soprano voice, she grew up in Brooklyn, New York, where she was known as Beverly Silverman. She was a radio child star, spent ten years singing operetta roles all over the United States, and made her debut in grand opera in Philadelphia. She toured the United States with small opera companies for several years before she was admitted to the New York City Opera Company for what was to be a long and magnificent career.

When she discovered that one of her children was deaf and the other mentally retarded, her heartache made her consider halting her career, but with the encouragement of her husband and others, she continued. She went on to even greater professional heights, winning acclaim for her dramatic interpretations of many of the great opera roles.

Established as an American opera star, she received international acclaim when she sang in the great opera houses of Europe, but preferred to concentrate on the United States. Beverly Sills has always believed strongly in the interpretive role of the opera singer, and studied all material that she could to develop her characters. She has received many awards and honorary doctorates, has taken leadership positions in many charities, and has performed many times at the White House.

She has now chosen to cease performing on the opera stage while still at her peak, and has assumed the directorship of the New York Opera Company, where she spent so many of her years as a singer. In her new career, her verve, knowledge, enthusiasm, and innovative spirit promise to bring new and greater achievements to this company.

Sills, Beverly BUBBLES: A SELF PORTRAIT Grosset, 1976. (grades 7 and up)

220

————. Bubbles: an encore   Illus. with photographs. Grosset, 1981. (grades 7 and up)

Sills's autobiography takes the opera singer from early childhood to the present. The second book is an updated, expanded edition with new photographs and some new chapters. Written in a friendly, chatty tone, with innumerable photographs of her at home and on the opera stage, it carefully captures the personality and style of the popular opera star.

~~~~~~

CARLY SIMON
1943–

Singer, composer, Grammy award winner

Carly Simon discovered early that being the daughter of a famous, wealthy publisher was no guarantee of success and happiness. Although music was always an important part of her family life she did not start singing folk music seriously until college. At first she and her sister Lucy appeared together. Later Carly Simon decided to try going ahead on her own and began composing much of her own music and lyrics. Her own past and present experiences provide material for her songs, which give her a chance to express her thoughts and feelings.

In 1971 her first single, "That's the Way I've Always Heard It Should Be," won her a Grammy as the best new artist. Since then she has had several successful singles and albums and has performed in many concerts. Today she lives in New York with her two children and appears occasionally in concert. She is divorced from singer-songwriter James Taylor.

Morse, Charles, and Morse, Ann   Carly Simon   Illus. Creative Educ. Soc., 1975. (grades 4-8)

Colorfully and abundantly designed and illustrated, this good, well-paced biography of the singer-composer discusses both her private life and her musical career. At times it touches on complicated personal issues, and because of the brevity and superficiality of the treatment, may leave the reader a bit confused.

221

MARY SLESSOR
1848–1915

Missionary to Nigeria

Like many Scotch working-class girls of her day, Mary Slessor went to work in a factory at the age of eleven. She later became a missionary in Nigeria where, for thirty-nine years, she focused on bringing industrial skills to the natives and building schools and churches. She moved beyond the scope of religious conversions and worked particularly hard in raising the status of African women.

Slessor established a home for girls where they learned such skills as basket, bamboo, and cane weaving which enabled them to become somewhat economically independent. She personally cared for many homeless children and for sick men, women, and children, and through her teachings and work helped improve vast areas of West Africa.

Syme, Ronald NIGERIAN PIONEER: THE STORY OF MARY SLESSOR Illus. Morrow, 1964. (grades 5–9)
  Very fine story of Mary Slessor shows her to be not only a missionary but also a woman of rare fortitude and administrative ability as well as of warmth, tenderness, and foresight.

MAUDE SLYE
1879–1954

Scientist

Maude Slye was one of the first scientists to develop the theory that a tendency towards cancer was inherited. She was born in Minneapolis to parents with literary inclinations, but pursued her own intense interest in the natural sciences. After completing her education she began research with mice in the biology department of the University of Chicago. Before her long career was over she had recorded the genealogies of over 150,000 mice.

Her work convinced her that there existed one or more genes for cancer that were passed on and then activated by some factor in the environment. This theory was considered very controversial, and despite the skepticism of colleagues, she kept meticulous records and published many papers, and recommended the establishment of a central record bureau for human cancer statistics.

As a woman scientist in the early 1900s Maude Slye had to combat derision and prejudice. Her concentration on her work excluded marriage and children from her life but she did find time to publish two volumes of poetry. As a determined pioneer, her devotion to her mouse laboratory paved the way for many later studies which refined and developed her theories while proving her basic concept.

McCoy, J. J. THE CANCER LADY: MAUDE SLYE AND HER HEREDITY STUDIES   Nelson, 1977. (grade 9 and up)
Very good biography focusses on Maude Slye's laboratory work, and also offers excerpts from her poetry. A fine book for readers interested in biology, cancer research, and heredity, but a firm scientific background is not necessary for appreciation of the book.

〰〰〰〰〰〰〰〰〰〰〰〰〰〰〰〰〰〰〰〰〰〰〰〰〰〰

AGNES SMEDLEY
1892–1950

Journalist

Agnes Smedley, a successful newspaper and magazine correspondent in the Far East for many years, was the only American to march with the Red Army and the first to tell the story of the Chinese revolution from the Chinese point of view.

In 1949 she was accused by General Douglas MacArthur of carrying out espionage for the Soviet Army, but this accusation was later withdrawn by the Army in Washington.

Agnes Smedley had spent most of her life fighting injustice, poverty, and suppression in China, and her activities often brought her into conflict with the authorities of various governments. She had been charged with espionage in 1918 by the United States, but that charge too was never proved.

Her books *China's Red Army Marches* and *China Fights Back* recounted her experiences with the Chinese struggle and brought it to the attention of the Western world. Her autobiography *Daughter of the Earth*, written in 1920 is still widely read, but even now, as in her lifetime, she is better known in China than in her own country.

Milton, Joyce A FRIEND OF CHINA Illus. Hastings, 1980. (grade 6 and up)
A good, unbiased account of the adventuresome, controversial, and colorful woman who was frequently a target of conservatism.

~~~~~~

BESSIE SMITH
1898–1937

Singer and songwriter

Bessie Smith, known as the "empress of the blues," was orphaned at age nine, won a prize in an amateur talent contest, and came under the wing of Ma Rainey, the outstanding blues singer of the time. By the time she was thirteen, Bessie Smith had become a seasoned professional and was on her way to becoming America's best-loved blues singer. After World War I she went north, performed in clubs, and wrote and recorded blues music. She was popular and successful with both white and black audiences.

Smith's career and economic situation began to deteriorate during the depression. American interest in blues declined somewhat and she mismanaged her money and drank heavily. Just as life was beginning to look upward she was seriously injured in a car accident in Mississippi. Taken to the nearest hospital, she was refused admittance because she was black. By the time she reached a hospital that would accept her, the loss of blood was so great that she died.

Moore, Carmen SOMEBODY'S ANGEL CHILD: THE STORY OF BESSIE SMITH Illus. Crowell, 1970. (grades 5–8)

Beautiful, dramatic, and sad account of the life of the blues singer. Well-balanced and stirring, it traces her life from childhood to her untimely death.

~~~~~~

MARGARET CHASE SMITH
1897–

Republican senator from Maine

Margaret Chase Smith had worked closely with her late husband, a congressman from Maine, when in 1940 she was elected to fill his unexpired term. Not satisfied just to serve in his stead, she worked hard, campaigned tirelessly, and in the next regular election polled three times the vote her husband had previously received.

The first woman to serve in both houses, Margaret Chase Smith was elected to four House of Representatives terms and four Senate terms, and held one of the best attendance records in Congress. She was the first senator openly to critize McCarthyism, worked to raise the status of women in the armed forces, served on major congressional committees, and, as the 1967 chairman of the Conference of All Republican Senators, was the first woman elected to such a leadership post.

In 1964 Senator Smith became the first woman to be nominated for the presidency of the United States at the national convention of a major political party, and made an impressively good showing. She is the recipient of fifty-two honorary degrees and numerous awards. Her global tours, national syndicated columns, and legislative efforts have made her known and respected throughout the world.

Fleming, Alice SENATOR FROM MAINE: MARGARET CHASE SMITH Crowell, 1969. (grades 5–8)
Very fine, fast-moving account of the life of the senator covers her childhood in Maine through her remarkable career in Congress. One sees her as a young woman learning to be financially independent, and then as

a senator's wife learning the ways of politics. The author gives a good picture of Smith's life set against the politics and government of the last few decades.

~~~~~~

ROBYN SMITH
1944–

Jockey

Once an aspiring actress, Robyn Smith always loved athletics and sports and was fascinated with racing. Only in 1968, after Kathy Kusner won the legal right to ride, did she see the possibility of becoming a jockey.

In 1969 Robyn Smith became the first woman jockey in a major stakes race, and in 1973 won her first major stakes race at Aqueduct in New York. By her fourth season there, she was the fourth-ranked American jockey.

Despite difficulties in getting mounts and other instances of prejudice against women in the formerly all-male world of racing, she persevered, and helped to pave the way for other women to become jockeys. Today, Robyn Smith still rides, and is married to performer Fred Astaire.

Brown, Fern G. RACING AGAINST THE ODDS: ROBYN C. SMITH Illus. Raintree, 1976. (grades 3–7)
  Fast-moving biography depicts Smith as a dedicated professional whose achievements are well deserved. The book gives a good picture of racing as a sport, as well as the difficulties facing a woman in a man's traditional field.

Jacobs, Linda ROBYN SMITH: IN SILKS Illus. with photographs. EMC, 1976. (grades 3–7)
  Easy-to-read biography captures her personality, focussing more on the subject than on racing itself. A lively, fast-moving book, it will have appeal to older, less able readers as well as to younger ones.

MONICA SONE
1919–

Author

During World War II, President Franklin Roosevelt signed Executive Order 9066 which led to the evacuation and internship of more
than 110,000 Japanese-American citizens and aliens living on the
West Coast of the United States. Their property had to be sold or
stored, for they could only bring what they could carry themselves.
Monica Sone and her family were among these Japanese-
Americans forced to move from their home to the relocation center.
Monica had been born in Seattle, and her parents who had emigrated there from Japan brought her up to appreciate the cultures of
both her own native land and theirs. She attended Japanese school
as well as the local public schools, and even before the war began
had known prejudice and discrimination.

Like many other American-born citizens of Japanese origin, she
was released from the center so that she could attend college.

Sone, Monica NISEI DAUGHTER Little, 1953. (grade 8 and up)
Lively account is humorous and warm. Despite the great injustices
imposed on Japanese-Americans during World War II when they were
relocated in detention camps, Sone writes without bitterness, although
she is critical of the government she had grown to love. She discusses her
childhood in Seattle, a visit to Japan, and the hopes she had for carving out
her future in America.

~~~~~~

ELIZABETH CADY STANTON
1815–1902

Women's rights leader, author, lecturer

Elizabeth Cady Stanton, the daughter of a New York judge, learned
early that laws prevented women from having any rights over their
children and property. Despite the strain of running a household

and raising seven children, she worked for the abolitionist movement, and then, with Lucretia Mott (page 168), organized the Seneca Falls Convention of 1848 from which the women's rights movement was born.

For over fifty years Stanton closely collaborated with Susan B. Anthony (page 13) to organize the movement, to publish a newspaper, and to lecture throughout the nation. She endorsed divorce, held liberal viewpoints on child rearing, wrote prolifically and eloquently on many subjects, but concentrated most of her efforts on suffrage and women's rights. With Anthony she wrote three volumes of *History of Woman Suffrage,* and in her *The Woman's Bible* she interpreted the Bible from a nonsexist point of view.

Though the name of Susan B. Anthony is the more famous, Elizabeth Cady Stanton's contributions to women's rights were even more diverse. Believing that suffrage, though a major goal, was only one way to free women from their narrow spheres, Stanton suggested other means for female liberation.

Clarke, Mary Stetson BLOOMERS AND BALLOTS: ELIZABETH CADY STANTON AND WOMEN'S RIGHTS   Viking, 1972. (grade 6 and up)
Despite the somewhat frivolous title, this is a really superb, well-written, well-researched, accurate biography of Elizabeth Cady Stanton. The feminist movement is explained well, and Stanton's role in it clearly credited and defined.

Csida, June Bundy THE 19TH CENTURY RENAISSANCE WOMAN: ELIZABETH CADY STANTON   Illus. Women's Heritage Series, 1971. (grade 9 and up)
Excellent though very brief booklet is an account of the role Elizabeth Cady Stanton played in the women's rights movement. Not by any means an in-depth picture of her personal life, it is nonetheless a very fine treatment of her work.

Faber, Doris OH, LIZZIE! THE LIFE OF ELIZABETH CADY STANTON   Illus. Lothrop, 1972. (grades 5–9)
Good, lively biography treats Stanton with too much levity at times, not giving enough serious attention to her achievements and disappointments.

Oakley, Mary Ann B. ELIZABETH CADY STANTON   Feminist Pr., 1972. (grade 9 and up)

Exceptionally fine, feminist biography of the great women's rights leader is an in-depth, well-researched, documented, and dramatic study of a brilliant, courageous, and determined woman. We see Elizabeth Cady Stanton as a human being blessed with unusual gifts and the willingness to use them, competently combining motherhood with her reform work.

Salsini, Barbara ELIZABETH STANTON: A LEADER OF THE WOMAN'S SUFFRAGE MOVEMENT SamHar, 1973. (grade 7 and up)
Brief but straightforward account of the life of Elizabeth Cady Stanton is accurate, interesting, and clearly states her motives and talents as well as her achievements.

Stanton, Elizabeth Cady EIGHTY YEARS AND MORE Illus. Schocken, 1971. (reprint of 1898 edition) (grade 9 and up)
Elizabeth Cady Stanton's own autobiography, written when she was past eighty, is extremely readable and serves as the source for many of the other biographies and profiles written by others about her. This new edition has an excellent introduction which provides additional perspective on the life of the great reformer.

~~~~~~

GERTRUDE STEIN
1874–1946

Author and patron of the arts

Wealthy, American-born, Harvard-educated Gertrude Stein and her brother Leo moved to Paris in 1903 where they encouraged new modern artists. There they began their famed collection which included the works of Matisse, Cezanne, Picasso, and others. Stein, who later achieved prominence as an author, was the outstanding champion and popularizer of abstract paintings.

Her early writings, dominated by the theory of "stream of consciousness," were difficult to understand and not well received by critics or the public. Success as an author finally came to her upon the publication of *The Autobiography of Alice B. Toklas*, in which she discussed life in Paris as shared with Toklas, her friend, confidante, and critic.

When Gertrude Stein made a trip back to the United States in 1934 she was treated as a major celebrity. The apartment in Paris in which she lived most of her life attracted artists, critics, writers, and musicians from Europe and the United States. A huge, imposing woman, Stein dominated not only the room in which she presided, but the entire world of the arts as well.

Greenfeld, Howard GERTRUDE STEIN: A BIOGRAPHY Illus. with photographs. Crown, 1973. (grade 8 and up)

Excellent, nonfictionalized biography of Gertrude Stein is enhanced by photographs and captures the spirit of the woman. For readers unacquainted with the work or life of Gertrude Stein, this is a fine introduction, not only to her but also to the many talented and brilliant people with whom she associated. Her relationship with Alice Toklas is described well, with warmth and good taste.

Rogers, W. G. GERTRUDE STEIN IS GERTRUDE STEIN IS GERTRUDE STEIN: HER LIFE AND WORK Illus. with photographs. Crowell, 1973. (grade 9 and up)

Outstanding biography of Gertrude Stein combines a study of both her personal life and her literary work. Of special interest to those who are acquainted with her work, it can also inspire others to read some of it. The talented and famous people who were so closely associated with Stein are described in the book, and her long-time companion Alice B. Toklas is prominently featured. Enhanced by many photographs and prints of her art collection as well as a good bibliography by and about her, this is a truly fine book.

Wilson, Ellen THEY NAMED ME GERTRUDE STEIN Illus. Farrar, 1973. (grade 9 and up)

Very readable and extremely warm account of the life of Gertrude Stein is more a personal biography than one that describes her work. It deals most honestly with her personal life-style and is well researched, containing a fine bibliography of books about and by her.

NOTE: These three biographies do not duplicate each other as do most juvenile biographies about the same subject. For a reader with a particular interest in Gertrude Stein, therefore, all three should be considered for their different information, anecdotes, and perspectives.

~~~~~~

LUCY STONE
1818–1893

Feminist, abolitionist, suffragist

Lucy Stone, a leading abolitionist and suffragist, would not subordinate herself to a man, and so even after her marriage to abolitionist and feminist Henry Blackwell, she retained her maiden
name.

As a young child Lucy Stone was disturbed at the hours of
drudgery imposed on her mother, rejected the biblical stand that
men should rule over women, and was determined to go to college.

At sixteen she began teaching and by twenty-five had saved
enough money to enroll in coeducational Oberlin College, a school
with a strong antislavery philosophy. The first Massachusetts
woman to earn a college degree, Lucy Stone soon was hired as a
lecturer for abolition and also became an effective crusader for the
women's movement.

With Julia Ward Howe she organized and led the American
Woman Suffrage Association and after the Civil War worked for
both black and female suffrage. With her husband she founded and
largely financed a weekly newspaper, *Woman's Journal*, which she
later edited. Considered the major voice of the feminist movement,
the paper constituted an important chapter in the long history of
women's rights.

Blackwell, Alice Stone LUCY STONE: PIONEER OF WOMAN'S RIGHTS
Little, 1930. (Now out of print, but reproduced by both Krauss Reproductions and Gale, 1972.) (grade 9 and up)

Outstanding, definitive biography of Lucy Stone written by her daughter. Immensely readable, it is full of warm details and anecdotes and offers
a good picture of the women's movement.

Stapelton, Jean VANGUARD SUFFRAGIST: LUCY STONE Illus. Women's
Heritage Series, 1971. (grade 7 and up)

A lovely biography of Lucy Stone is extremely brief, but vividly written,
dramatic, and informative.

HARRIET BEECHER STOWE
1811–1896
Author

Harriet Beecher Stowe firmly believed that the evil of slavery lay in the system and that the North was as guilty as the South. Stowe saw herself as an instrument of God and her great antislavery novel, *Uncle Tom's Cabin*, more as a religious work than a novel. Its enormous success made her wealthy and famous for it was translated into thirty languages, dramatized, and became a universal best seller. The moving story personalized slavery and stirred many people to action who had, until then, remained neutral.

Before the book's publication, Stowe cared for her large family and helped support them by writing for magazines and newspapers. Despite the enormous responsibility and interruptions of home and children, she became a very prolific writer. She published more than thirty books and numerous essays and children's stories, many of which won critical acclaim.

Hooker, Gloria I SHALL NOT LIVE IN VAIN   Illus. Concordia, 1978. (grades 5–8)
Written from a religious perspective, this biography moves smoothly, depicting Harriet Beecher Stowe as a woman with faith and a belief that she was an instrument of God in describing slavery. The book achieves its purpose in showing Stowe as a woman whose accomplishments were a result of faith as well as talent.

Johnson, Johanna HARRIET AND THE RUNAWAY BOOK: THE STORY OF HARRIET BEECHER STOWE AND UNCLE TOM'S CABIN   Illus. Harper, 1977. (grades 2–6)
A truly outstanding, easy-to-read or read-aloud book which depicts Harriet Beecher Stowe as a woman fired with ambition to make a significant impact upon the world. It also depicts her as a woman who lived in a time when women had few options. The events leading up to the writing of *Uncle Tom's Cabin* and the story of the book itself are succinctly, poetically recounted.

Rouverol, Jean HARRIET BEECHER STOWE: WOMAN CRUSADER   Illus. Putnam, 1968. (grades 3–6)

Excellent account of the life of the great author is extremely simple, but clear in its explanations of her life and her achievements. Although readers of this book could not yet comprehend *Uncle Tom's Cabin*, the author has managed to make Stowe a meaningful subject.

Scott, John Anthony   WOMAN AGAINST SLAVERY: THE STORY OF HARRIET BEECHER STOWE   Illus. with photographs. Crowell, 1978. (grades 6–9)

Well-balanced account of Harriet Beecher Stowe describes her circumscribed life and her driving mission to truthfully depict slavery.

~~~~~~

DONNA SUMMER
1948–

Singer and songwriter

Donna Summer is a true superstar, the first to come out of disco music. She makes use of electronic recording devices which are so closely associated with disco, but considers herself a "singer who does disco songs," rather than just a product of the recording studio.

The winner of a Grammy award and gold and platinum records, she is one of seven children. Her father worked at many different skilled jobs to support the large family in their ethnically mixed neighborhood in Boston. There she began singing in local churches. Against the wishes of her father, she left high school before she graduated to join the German touring company of the rock musical *Hair*. She remained in Europe for seven years, singing in many productions.

In 1975 she recorded a song she wrote, "Love to Love You, Baby," in a European studio. The song and the album in which it is included became a huge success. When she arrived back in the United States she was surprised to learn it was number one on the charts.

She continues to record her own songs and those by other composers and attracts high crowds whenever she tours. Donna Summer is more than a soul singer or a disco artist; she's a pop singer who can sing a variety of songs.

Haskins, James DONNA SUMMER; AN UNAUTHORIZED BIOGRAPHY
Illus. with photographs. Little, 1983. (grade 6 and up)
  Lively, informal well-written biography gives a good picture of the
best-selling popular recording star, capturing both her personal life and
her work.

~~~~~~

BERTHA VON SUTTNER
1843–1914

Austrian peace advocate, winner of Nobel Peace Prize

Baroness Bertha von Suttner, Austrian lecturer, organizer, and
writer on peace, was a close friend of Alfred Nobel, the inventor of
dynamite. She strengthened his interest in peace and is believed to
have influenced him to establish the Nobel Peace Prize.

  Her novel, *Die Waffen Nieder* (*Lay Down Your Arms*), was a
powerful plea for peace, and it met with great success. It was
translated into more than a dozen languages and became known as
one of the most important "novels of purpose" of all time.

  As Bertha von Suttner's interest and involvement in the peace
movement grew she wrote for peace magazines, founded the Austrian Peace Society, and worked tirelessly for the cause of peace.
She was the only woman among ninety-six delegates from twenty-
six countries at the 1899 Peace Conference at The Hague, and
although the results of this conference were considerable, they did
not go far enough to satisfy the firm believer in peace.

  To further her beliefs that governments should employ arbitra-
tion before rather than after the use of force and should put an end
to all fighting, she wrote and lectured extensively. In 1905 her
efforts were rewarded when she was awarded the Nobel Peace
Prize. She continued her work almost until her death, travelling
throughout the world to lecture, reaping honors from other peace
lovers and abuse from the militaristic.

Lengyel, Emil AND ALL HER PATHS WERE PEACE: THE LIFE OF BERTHA
VON SUTTNER Nelson, n.d. (grade 8 and up)

Extremely well-written, nonfictionalized biography of the highly gifted and influential Nobel Peace Prize winner is both interesting and inspirational. The author places equal emphasis on von Suttner's personal life and her work, achieving a fine balance.

~~~~~~

HENRIETTA SZOLD
1860–1945

Founder of Hadassah, Zionist leader, educator

Henrietta Szold, the founder of Hadassah, a women's Zionist organization, was born in Baltimore, Maryland. The first of eight daughters of a rabbi, she received the education usually reserved for a Jewish firstborn son, and she became fluent in German, French, and Hebrew. She taught high school and religious school, and organized the first night school in the United States where adult immigrants could learn America's history, customs, and language. Henrietta Szold also contributed articles to Jewish periodicals, translated and edited Jewish literature into English, and was editor of the American Jewish Year Book.

A visit to Palestine in 1910 strengthened her growing interest in Zionism, a cause to which she devoted the remainder of her life. She founded Hadassah and became the first director of Youth Aliyah, which began bringing Jewish youngsters from Germany into Palestine during the 1930s.

The recipient of many honors, she was the first woman to receive the honorary degree of Doctor of Hebrew Letters, conferred on her by the Jewish Institute of Religion, and was known as the "Mother of the Yishuv," the Jewish settlement in Palestine.

Dash, Joan SUMMONED TO JERUSALEM: THE LIFE OF HENRIETTA SZOLD Illus. with photographs. Harper, 1979. (grade 9 and up)

A very fine, thoroughly researched and documented adult biography is a revealing study of her personality as well as her many achievements. Although written for adults, it will be appreciated by serious high school readers, particularly those with an interest in the history of modern Judaism and Jewish education.

SHIZUYE TAKASHIMA
1928–

Artist and author

Like many Americans of Japanese descent, Canadian-born Shizuye Takashima was interned during World War II. She looks back at the four years she spent in a prison camp for Japanese-Canadians with sadness rather than bitterness and hatred.

After the war she studied at the Ontario College of Art and has since become a successful painter. Her work has been exhibited in galleries in the United States and Canada, and she has won several honors and awards.

Her personal memoirs, *A Child in Prison Camp,* won her the award for the best illustrated book in Canada. It has been translated into Japanese, and both film and radio adaptations are planned.

Takashima, Shizuye A CHILD IN PRISON CAMP Illus. Morrow, 1974. (grade 5 and up)

In a touching personal memoir, the Japanese-Canadian artist describes her life as a child in an internment camp during World War II. Simply written in the present tense, it has a dignified, distinguished style that extends its appeal to older readers as well as young ones. The beautiful full-color illustrations by the artist are an important component to the book.

MARIA TALLCHIEF
1925–

Prima ballerina

Maria Tallchief began studying ballet at age four and at eighteen made her New York debut in a leading role. She worked under the brilliant, famed choreographer George Balanchine, who created several ballets for her. One of her most notable roles was the sugar plum fairy in *The Nutcracker.*

Her father was an Osage Indian, and her mother Scotch-Irish-Dutch; although she and her sister Marjorie, also a dancer, grew up without any particular Indian consciousness or culture, they are proud of their heritage, and both women have been honored by the Osage Tribal Council.

Maria Tallchief is now the artistic director of the Chicago City Ballet, a company she helped to found in 1980.

Gridley, Marion E. MARIA TALLCHIEF: THE STORY OF AN AMERICAN INDIAN. Dillon, 1973. (grades 5–9)
Especially fine biography of the prima ballerina chronicles her childhood, youth, career, and activities since retirement in a warm, fast-moving text. The author shares her wide knowledge of Indian life with the reader by first telling the history of the Osages, and then moving on to the life of Maria Tallchief.

Tobias, Tobi MARIA TALLCHIEF Illus. Crowell, 1970. (grades 2–5)
Although lively and colorful, and generally liked by children and critics alike, the book implies that career and homemaking are incompatible.

~~~~~~

IDA TARBELL
1857–1944

Journalist, historian, muckraker, and lecturer

Ida Tarbell's early interest in the women's rights movement led her to see education as a means to achieve freedom. After graduating from college she went to Paris to study the role of women in the French Revolution, and while there began her career as a journalist and historian, contributing to prominent American periodicals.

In 1904, after two years of extensive research, Ida Tarbell published *The History of the Standard Oil Company*, which revealed the unscrupulous methods the Rockefeller-owned company used to force smaller rival companies out of business. Her exposé resulted in lawsuits, new antitrust laws, and the landmark United States Supreme Court decision that forced Standard Oil to break up into smaller, separate companies. For this pioneer muckraking work, she won national acclaim and the nickname "terror of the trusts."

Throughout her long career, Ida Tarbell published and edited a national magazine, researched and wrote extensively on Lincoln, wrote biographies of business leaders, lectured, served on advisory committees to the government, taught at many colleges, and, at eighty-two, published her autobiography.

Conn, Frances G. IDA TARBELL, MUCKRAKER Nelson, 1972. (grades 4–7)
Good biography of Tarbell clearly indicates her ability, intelligence, and accomplishments, but lacks excitement and color.

Fleming, Alice IDA TARBELL: FIRST OF THE MUCKRAKERS Crowell, 1971. (grades 5–8)
Very fine, intelligent biography of Ida Tarbell discusses her personal life as well as her crusading efforts and exposé of the trusts. Warm, dramatic, and vigorous, this book captures the many dimensions of Tarbell.

~~~~~~

SUSIE KING TAYLOR
1848–1912

Teacher, nurse

Her grandmother taught her to read, even though it was illegal, and when she was only fourteen, slave Susie King Taylor escaped to freedom. She married a liberated slave, and when he joined the Union's First South Carolina Volunteers she became the regimental laundress. She also served as nurse and teacher to these first black soldiers and, after the war, taught at a freedmen's school in Savannah. Later, when she moved north, she became a founder of the Boston branch of the Women's Relief Auxiliary of the GAR (Grand Army of the Republic) and served as the president of the group that aided veterans of the war and their dependents.

Booker, Simeon SUSIE KING TAYLOR, CIVIL WAR NURSE McGraw, 1969. (grades 4–9)
Based on her own diary, this biography gives a fine picture of the intrepid young woman who was laundress, teacher, and nurse to a group of black Union soldiers. Simply written, it is directed to older reluctant readers as well as enthusiastic younger ones. The author does a good job of combining history and biography.

~~~~~~

MOTHER TERESA
1910–

Roman Catholic nun

From behind the high walls of the secluded convent school in Calcutta, India, Mother Teresa looked out at the horrors of the hungry, the helpless and the uncared-for. With the hard-won permission of the church authorities, she discarded her habit, left the convent and went out to live and work among the poor. She taught the children, took the dying from the streets, and opened a home for children. She founded workshops for men and clinics for lepers. Young women from all over India and the world came to work with her. They formed the Missionaries of Charity. Mother Teresa turned religious zeal into love and service to others, helping Christians and Hindus alike.

Her fame spread as her good works increased. The pope invited her to open a center for her sisters in Rome, and from the original twelve nuns in 1950, Mother Teresa's followers grew to over 100,000 nuns and lay people helping in their own communities.

Mother Teresa has received many honors and is the most famous Catholic nun in the world. She was awarded the Nobel Peace Prize in 1979 when she was sixty-nine years old. She accepted the award with these words—"For all those people who feel unwanted and unloved . . . I accept the award."

Doig, Desmond MOTHER TERESA Illus. with photographs. Harper & Row, (grade 9 and up)
   This beautifully written book is the story of India's poor as well as the life of Mother Teresa for they are intertwined.

Greene, Carol MOTHER TERESA: FRIEND OF THE FRIENDLESS Illus. with photographs. Childrens Pr. (grades 2–6)
   Very easy-to-read, honest biography of Mother Teresa clearly depicts her work and earliest motivations. Will be useful for older elementary school children with minimal reading skills, as well as for younger ones who are reading at grade level.

Lee, Betsy CARING FOR ALL GOD'S CHILDREN: MOTHER TERESA Illus. with photographs. Dillon, 1981. (grades 3–9)

An excellent book for youngsters of all denominations. Mother Teresa is shown to be truly a woman of God. The book straightforwardly details her accomplishments, and will be of interest to older less competent readers as well as the younger ones for whom it is intended.

~~~~~~

VALENTINA TERESHKOVA
1937–

Soviet cosmonaut, first woman in space

History was made on June 16, 1963, when a former Soviet amateur parachutist, Valentina Tereshkova, became the first woman in space. Her spaceship, Vostok V1, returned to earth after 48 orbits and 1.2 million miles in 70 hours, 50 minutes.

After Soviet Cosmonaut Yuri Gagarin became the first man to orbit the earth, Tereshkova, an active member of Jomsomol (Young Communist League), wrote to the authorities volunteering herself as a cosmonaut. She was accepted, but only after proving that her physical endurance and stamina matched that of the male cosmonauts. In preparation for her historic flight she underwent arduous technical and physical training.

After her return to earth Premier Khrushchev commented upon the West's "bourgeois" notion that woman is the weaker sex, reminding the world that Tereshkova was in flight longer than all four American astronauts combined.

Valentina Tereshkova received her country's greatest honor when she was named a hero of the Soviet Union. She has also received the Order of Lenin and the Gold Star Medal, as well as honors and tributes from other nations.

She continued her training and now is an aerospace engineer in the Soviet space program. She is married to a fellow cosmonaut and they have a family.

Sharpe, Mitchell "IT IS I, SEA GULL": VALENTINA TERESHKOVA, FIRST WOMAN IN SPACE Illus. with photographs. Crowell, 1974. (grade 7 and up)

A good account of the life of the Soviet cosmonaut is mostly scientific, space-oriented in its focus, but occasionally shifts to the romantic. Sometimes self-conscious in its feminist perspective, it suceeds best when it is a straightforward narrative, emphasizing the scientific aspects of her work. Although it may appeal to the general reader, it will probably be of special interest to those eager to learn more about space.

~~~~~~

ELLEN TERRY
1848–1928

British actress

At age nine Ellen Terry, the child of successful British touring actors, made her theatrical debut. She became one of England's greatest performers, and continued to perform almost until her death. She was married a few times, but was greatly devoted to two children she had with a man to whom she was not married.

Both a comic and tragic performer, Ellen Terry scored one of her greatest triumphs as Portia in Shakespeare's *Twelfth Night*. She also appeared in plays of George Bernard Shaw, with whom she maintained a lengthy correspondence. For twenty-five years she was a leading lady to the famed Sir Henry Irving, touring with their successful company in England, the United States, and Canada.

In her later years Terry lectured and gave readings in England, the United States, and Australia on the works of Shakespeare. In 1925 she received the Grand Cross of the Order of the British Empire.

Fecher, Constance BRIGHT STAR: A PORTRAIT OF ELLEN TERRY Illus. Farrar, 1970. (grade 7 and up)

Extremely well-written story of the actress discusses her personal life as well as the roles she played. The great actor Sir Henry Irving plays a prominent role in the book, as he did in her professional life, affording the reader an interesting perspective on nineteenth-century British theater.

241

TITUBA
c.1692–?

Slave, suspected witch

Tituba grew up as a slave in the West Indies where the practices of herbal medicine, card reading, and spells and magic were common. She was forced to come as a slave to the cold bleak New England village of Salem during a period in which its citizens were accusing women of witchcraft. Tituba's native customs naturally made her an early suspect.

When brought to trial she pleaded guilty, for this was her only chance to avoid death by hanging, drowning, or burning. Her tales of the witchcraft she and others "practiced" surpassed even the wildest imaginations of the citizens of Salem.

Eventually Tituba was released, but still she remained a slave. She was sold for her jail fees to a weaver who then purchased her husband. Tituba lived long enough to see the hysteria surrounding the Salem witch trials come to an end.

Petry, Ann TITUBA OF SALEM VILLAGE Crowell, 1964. (grade 5 and up)
Beautifully written, dramatic, and highly fictionalized story of Tituba is based on thorough research, but reads more like a story than a biography. The character of Tituba—independent, bright, and resourceful—emerges distinctly and colorfully, and the reader is swept along by events. This is a book that lends itself beautifully to reading aloud to family or classroom—the author has employed outstanding literary skill. *Tituba* is as suitable for adults as it is for elementary school children.

ALEXANDRA TOLSTOY
1884–1979

Founder of the Tolstoy Foundation to Help Refugees

Alexandra "Sasha" Tolstoy, the youngest daughter of famous writer and Russian folk hero Leo Tolstoy, lived a privileged life as a child, surrounded by wealth. As she began to understand her father's beliefs in nonviolence and humanism she became one of his most dedicated follower.

During World War I she joined the Red Cross and served as a nurse on the war front. The leaders of the Russian Revolution later imprisoned her because of her connections with the landowners. Finally released, she worked at organizing schools, starting an orphanage, and setting up hospitals for the peasants. Then, under Stalin's government, she was no longer permitted to work. She escaped to Japan in 1929, and two years later came to the United States, arriving penniless.

She struggled to survive the depression and in 1939 founded the Tolstoy Foundation, which has resettled over 100,000 refugees from oppressive nations.

When "Sasha" Tolstoy died at ninety-five, she had not been back to Russia for fifty years.

Sadler, Catherine   SASHA: THE LIFE OF ALEXANDRA TOLSTOY   Illus. with photographs. Putnam, 1982. (grade 7 and up)

Biography combined with history introduces reader to the period before, during, and after the Russian Revolution. Well-researched, the biography moves quickly and vividly, informally drawing a picture of Alexandra Tolstoy's life that is richly conversational in tone.

<hr>

FLORA TRISTAN
1803–1844

French feminist, socialist, social advocate

Flora Tristan's father was an aristocrat, her mother a poor country-woman. Her father died when she was only five, and she, her mother, and her little brother were penniless. Her mother became depressed and erratic in behavior, and filled Flora's childhood with tales of imagined splendors. At eighteen, she married a man who ultimately was imprisioned for trying to kill her, but the restrictions placed on women and children, then supported by the law, made her a fugitive when she took her children and left him.

Noting the social injustices that surrounded her, she chose to fight them, and published several works which reflected her beliefs that workers are a class and need to unite. Her book *Workers Union*, which called upon this need, was published five years before Karl Marx's *Communist Manifesto* with the same plea.

The concept of solidarity was most precious to her, and she idealistically saw workers' and women's emancipation as the same fight, without violence.

Her daughter married a militant writer and their son Paul Gauguin become of the most famous artists and rebels of his time.

A woman clearly ahead of her time, her feminist and socialistic convinctions were the result of her brilliant mind and the injustices she saw and experienced.

Schneider, Joyce Anne FLORA TRISTAN Morrow, 1980. (grade 7 and up)
Excellent biography brings to its reader's attention a remarkable woman who despite personal hardships became an important force in world thinking. Well-researched and documented, it is an absorbing portrait.

~~~~~~

SOJOURNER TRUTH
c.1797–1883

Abolitionist, reformer, feminist, preacher

Sojourner Truth, as Isabella Baumfree was known, was born a slave in New York, survived the cruelties of several owners, saw all her brothers and sisters and children sold and separated, but won a legal case against her son being sold south.

After obtaining her freedom she worked as a domestic. Mystical visions told her to become a preacher. Though illiterate, she knew the Bible well, and her powerful stirring voice and manner attracted listeners in churches, highways, and streets. In her travels she crossed paths with abolitionist and women's rights leaders, and in embracing these causes became the first black woman to give antislave and feminist lectures in America.

During the Civil War Sojourner Truth raised funds for black volunteer regiments, was received in the White House by President Lincoln, and after emancipation worked with freed blacks and in hospitals. At her urging many blacks migrated west.

Her speech at a women's rights convention has been recorded as one of the most stirring polemics for equal rights and she is remembered today as the symbol against the oppression of black women.

Lindstrom, Aletha Jane SOJOURNER TRUTH: SLAVE, ABOLITIONIST, FIGHTER FOR WOMEN'S RIGHTS Illus. Messner, 1980. (grades 5–9)
This biography vividly depicts Sojourner Truth's harsh life as child-slave, and her separation from loving parents and later from her own son. She became a self-assured woman who was a strong advocate for abolition and women's rights. Despite fictionalization it is historically and biographically accurate.

Ortiz, Victoria SOJOURNER TRUTH: A SELF-MADE WOMAN Illus. with old prints and photographs. Lippincott, 1974. (grade 6 and up)
Well-researched and based on facts as far as they are presently known, this very fine, warm, and human biography combines a carefully drawn portrait of Sojourner Truth with a good description of the feminist and abolitionist movements. The split that often existed between the two groups is discussed here, and Sojourner Truth's role in both is clearly established.

Pauli, Hertha HER NAME WAS SOJOURNER TRUTH Avon, 1971. (grade 7 and up)
Unusually fine, thoroughly researched, stirring account of the life of Sojourner Truth also gives a good picture of the times. Author draws parallels between her life and the current civil rights movement, adding to the interest and value of the book.

Peterson, Helen SOJOURNER TRUTH: FEARLESS CRUSADER Illus. Garrard, 1972. (grades 3–6)
Brief, simple but nonetheless superb and dramatic account of Sojourner Truth explains the principles by which she lived, and clearly shows the unusual determination and courage she demonstrated, as well as the inherent evils of slavery.

HARRIET TUBMAN
1820–1913

Fugitive slave, rescuer of slaves, Civil War spy and nurse

Known as the Moses of her people, fugitive slave Harriet Tubman, in the ten years preceding the Civil War, courageously and cleverly delivered three hundred southern slaves to freedom in the North. She herself was born a slave, worked as a field hand while still a child, and at thirteen was struck over the head by an overseer with a two-pound weight, the effects from which she never fully recovered.

Harriet Tubman worked closely with the Underground Railroad and spoke at many abolitionist meetings. After escaping from Maryland to Philadelphia she returned to guide safely all the members of her family to freedom, and then became so successful a "conductor" that she boasted that in her nineteen trips she "never lost a passenger." At one time rewards for her capture were as high as $40,000.

During the Civil War she was a cook and nurse and the only black woman to serve as a Union scout and spy. After emancipation she worked at a freedmen's hospital, established a home for poor aged blacks, and, though illiterate herself, worked to establish southern black schools. Harriet Tubman was a firm supporter of the suffrage movement, and also helped to establish the African Methodist Episcopal Church in New York State.

Bains, Rae HARRIET TUBMAN: THE ROAD TO FREEDOM Illus. Troll, 1982. (grades 4–8)

Excellent biography focusses on Tubman's early years, depicting the courage of Harriet Tubman as well as other blacks and slaves. The author draws a good picture of slave family life and of southern life in general.

Conrad, Earl HARRIET TUBMAN: NEGRO SOLDIER AND ABOLITIONIST International Publishers, 1942. (grade 9 and up)

Brief, extremely good, straightforward account is well researched, accurate, and informative. Nonfictionalized, it is moving and dramatic.

Epstein, Sam, and Epstein, Beryl HARRIET TUBMAN: GUIDE TO FREEDOM Illus. Garrard, 1968. (grades 3–6)

Simple early reader, or read-aloud book, is a stirring account of the rescuer of Tubman's people. Vivid and colorful, this is a story of the times as well as of the life of Harriet Tubman.

Grant, Matthew G. HARRIET TUBMAN Illus. Creative Educ. Soc., 1974. (grades 3–5)
Graphically illustrated, this simple biography lacks the fire and spirit displayed by Tubman. Older reluctant readers will find it attractive and easygoing, without being too immature in approach.

Heidish, Marcy A WOMAN CALLED MOSES Houghton Mifflin, 1976. (grades 5–9)
Like the author's book on Anne Hutchinson (page 114) this book is described by publisher as fiction, but it is packed with accurate information presented in a readable, lively fashion. Written in the first person, it is useful as an adjunct to biographical information. A historical afterword and author's note following text are also worthwhile.

Humphreville, Frances HARRIET TUBMAN: FLAME OF FREEDOM Houghton Mifflin, 1966. (grades 4–6)
Satisfactory biography lacks literary distinction but gives a good, highly fictionalized account of Harriet Tubman's life. Author focusses on Tubman's childhood, but also gives a good summary of her adult activities.

Lawrence, Jacob HARRIET AND THE PROMISED LAND Illus. Simon & Schuster, 1968. (preschool and up)
Beautifully written and illustrated picture book offers an unsentimental but immensely dramatic picture of Harriet Tubman and her successful efforts on behalf of other slaves.

McGovern, Ann WANTED DEAD OR ALIVE: THE STORY OF HARRIET TUBMAN (original title: RUNAWAY SLAVE) Scholastic, 1977. (grades K–3)
Excellent biography of Harriet Tubman gives an intimate, colorful, and compelling picture of her goals, activities, and accomplishments.

Petry, Ann HARRIET TUBMAN: CONDUCTOR ON THE UNDERGROUND RAILWAY Crowell, 1955. (grade 7 and up)
Truly superb study is an outstanding example of biography. Written with realism and warmth, it gives a dramatic picture of a remarkable woman.

Sterling, Dorothy FREEDOM TRAIN Illus. Doubleday, 1954. (grade 6 and up)
Exciting, fast-moving account of Harriet Tubman's activities is competently told. Perceptive and intimate, it offers a warm picture of her life.

247

Winders, Gertrude HARRIET TUBMAN: FREEDOM GIRL Bobbs-Merrill, 1969. (grades 3–7)

Despite concentration on her childhood and youth, a good biography of Harriet Tubman. The author vividly describes family slave life, and Tubman's personality from childhood emerges consistently independent and resourceful. A small part of the book describes her adult life competently and dramatically.

~~~~~~

TASHA TUDOR
1915–

Author and illustrator of children's books

Tasha Tudor was born in Boston. Her mother was a portrait painter, and she was exposed early to art. She was educated unconventionally, primarily at home, and went on to marry and raise four children on a New Hampshire farm without the benefit of electricity or running water.

As in her life, she created a world of old-fashioned delicate charm in her work, with watercolors and ink. Her illustrations are noteworthy for their pastoral simplicity. She is well-known for her illustrations for *Mother Goose, Wind in the Willows, My Secret Garden, The Night before Christmas* as well as for special holiday volumes, animal and folk tales, and calendars. She has twice been a Caldecott medal runner-up and a winner of the Child Study Association's Children's Book of the Year. Her work has been likened to that of Beatrix Potter. Most of the approximately fifty books she has illustrated were also written by her.

She still lives in a farmhouse in Vermont, where she makes candles, spins yarn, weaves cloth, and raises all her own food.

Tudor, Bethany DRAWN FROM NEW ENGLAND: TASHA TUDOR, A PORTRAIT IN WORDS AND PICTURES Illus. with photographs. Collier, 1979. (grades 4–8)

This biography, written by Tasha Tudor's daughter, is a loving portrait which captures the spirit and flavor of the author-artist and her work. Beautiful and well-organized, it is enhanced by many family photographs and reproductions of her work.

ELIZABETH VAN LEW
1818–1900

Southern spy for the Union

Socially prominent Elizabeth Van Lew was known in Richmond, Virginia, to be an abolitionist even before the Civil War. She and her wealthy mother had freed not only their own slaves, but purchased other slaves and freed them too. She openly supported the Union during the Civil War, bringing supplies to federal officers who were imprisoned in the South. She helped many escape, and obtained vital military information for transmission to the North.

Because of her high social position, Van Lew was able to engage in her espionage activities with little interference, and when the Union Army reached Richmond she maintained five relay stations between the city and their headquarters. So as not to arouse suspicion, she affected a peculiar dress and behavior, earning the name "Crazy Bet."

After the war Elizabeth Van Lew, who had spent her fortune on war activities, was appointed postmistress of Richmond by President Grant. Despite the hostility of her neighbors and the scorn of Richmond society, she carried on her duties admirably. During her last years she fought for women's rights, protesting against taxation without representation.

Nolan, Jeannette YANKEE SPY: ELIZABETH VAN LEW   Messner, 1970. (grade 7 and up)

Very good, convincingly fictionalized account of the espionage activities of Elizabeth Van Lew shows her as a woman unwilling to compromise her beliefs for the sake of society's acceptance. Fast-moving and dramatic, it also offers a good picture of the Civil War period and life in the South.

PABLITA VELARDE
1918–

Artist

In an Indian school near Santa Fe, New Mexico, Pablita Velarde was first introduced to various art forms and was encouraged to express herself within the traditions and culture of her native Pueblo Indians. Somewhat defiant of society, Pablita Velarde decided to become a painter even though, in her pueblo, painting was considered men's work. Instead of marrying like her sisters when she completed school, she took various jobs, many of which consisted of routine decorative painting. She did, however, sell many of her paintings which, like her life, are a mixture of Indian and non-Indian culture. In her desire to portray Indian life she reproduced many scenes and subjects and also wrote down many of the old Indian tales with which she had become familiar as a child, illustrated them, and published them in book form.

Velarde has won many awards and is now a very successful painter, as is her daughter, Helen Hardin.

Nelson, Mary Carroll Pablita Velarde Illus. Dillon, 1971. (grade 5 and up)
Extremely fine account of the life of the Indian artist discusses in depth the culture from which she came, as well as her private and professional life. Immensely readable, this book is very appropriate for older reluctant readers as well as elementary and junior high readers.

~~~~~~

QUEEN VICTORIA
1819–1901

Queen of England

Victoria, who was to become queen of England during one of its most glorious periods, spent a most unhappy and lonely childhood. Her father died before she was one year old and she and her mother lived in seclusion and relative poverty. She succeeded to the British throne shortly after her eighteenth birthday and was delighted to gain quickly the love of her subjects. Her happiness grew during her courtship and marriage to her intelligent and handsome cousin, Prince Albert.

The queen relied heavily on Albert's recommendations concerning Parliamentary affairs, and although she personally opposed many reform proposals, she followed Albert's advice and publicly supported the government in most of its endeavors. Victoria took her position as head of the army seriously; during the Crimean War she established England's highest war decoration, the Victoria Cross, and later the Regiment of the Royal Irish Guards.

After her beloved Albert's death in 1861, Victoria stepped out of public life. Finally, as her popularity declined, she became a more active ruler and regained the public's esteem. In 1874 Parliament bestowed the title Empress of India upon Victoria in recognition of her strong support of the imperialist policy. In 1887 her fiftieth year as queen was celebrated by an elegant jubilee. The pageantry was repeated ten years later when delegates from throughout the world came to London to honor Queen Victoria.

When Victoria died in 1901 after reigning sixty-four years (the longest reign in English history), she left thirty-one grandchildren and thirty-seven great grandchildren, many of whom were crowned rulers in Europe.

Glendinning, Sally QUEEN VICTORIA: ENGLISH EMPRESS Illus. Garrard, 1970. (grades 4–8)

Well-done, interesting, though brief and simple biography of Queen Victoria offers a good picture of her life and times. Vivid and colorful writing brings the subject to life with warmth and style.

Grant, Neil VICTORIA: QUEEN AND EMPRESS Illus. Watts, 1970. (grade 7 and up)

Good, though somewhat textbookish portrait of Queen Victoria is especially useful as an aid to social studies, for it describes her life against the historical period in which she lived. Depicting her strengths and weaknesses, it offers a well-rounded study of her as an individual, too.

Haycraft, Molly Costain QUEEN VICTORIA Messner, 1956. (grades 6–10)

Author paints a vivid picture of Queen Victoria, showing her as a real living woman in this warm, personal biography. Emphasis is on her as an individual, rather than on the period in which she reigned.

Yglesias, J. R. C. QUEEN VICTORIA Illus. Ladybird, 1976. (grades 5–8)

A comprehensive, though fairly brief biography of the queen gives a reasonably well-balanced account of her life and times.

LILLIAN WALD
1867–1940

Public health nurse, social worker, and reformer

After graduating from the New York Hospital training school for nurses, Lillian Wald went to medical school, but while teaching health and nursing care to tenement dwellers in New York's Lower East Side decided to give up medicine in order to devote her energies to public health nursing. She obtained financial backing from wealthy Jewish philanthropists to set up a program which she later developed into the Visiting Nurse Service and the Henry Street Settlement House, a neighborhood center for civic, education, and social work.

Lillian Wald was instrumental in creating the first public school nursing program in the nation, worked for legislation to end child labor, was active in the peace movement, mobilized nurses for emergencies during World War I, worked for political candidates, supported women's suffrage, wrote two autobiographies, and was an enormously successful fundraiser. Her importance in the field of social work was great, but it is for her contributions to the profession of public health nursing that she is best remembered.

Block, Irvin NEIGHBOR TO THE WORLD: THE STORY OF LILLIAN WALD
Crowell, 1969. (grades 5–9)
  Outstanding straightforward account of the life of Lillian Wald depicts her as a woman who devoted her life to helping the poor of New York's Lower East Side and had a profound effect on many other social issues of her day. Warm, dramatic, and stirringly told.

Rogon, Sally LILLIAN WALD: THE NURSE IN BLUE   Illus. Jewish Public Society of New York, 1977. (grade 6 and up)
  Excellent biography depicts Lillian Wald as a woman born to privilege but with a determination to help others. Her professional life as a nurse and crusader for social reform is dramatically told.

Siegel, Beatrice LILLIAN WALD OF HENRY STREET   Macmillan, 1983. (grade 7 and up)
  Very fine biography of Lillian Wald gives equal emphasis to her work as a nurse, social worker, and social reformer. She emerges as a strong,

committed person who was able to recruit others to her causes and won the respect and affection of those with whom she worked and served.

Williams, Beryl, and Epstein, Samuel   LILLIAN WALD: ANGEL OF HENRY STREET   Messner, 1948. (grade 6 and up)
Very fine, convincingly fictionalized biography of Lillian Wald moves along at a dramatic pace and offers insights into the woman whose entire life was one of service to others, and whose abilities were used to obtain many needed reforms.

~~~~~~

BARBARA WALTERS
1931–

Television correspondent

Whenever polls are taken to select the most respected, admired, or influential women in America, the name Barbara Walters is certain to appear. As one of the most successful television newscasters and interviewers in the world, she also commands one of the largest salaries ever paid to anyone in her field.

Barbara Walters' father, a nightclub owner, travelled a great deal, and the family often entertained show business stars; meeting famous people has been a part of her life since childhood.

After graduating from college she went to work in television. As she increased her skills and proved her talent for writing and producing she advanced in positions. Eventually she became a writer and producer on NBC's "Today" show, and then gained the opportunity to appear on camera. Gradually she took on additional on-camera responsibilities and became co-host. In the earlier days of television, women usually handled only so-called women's or family news. Her position as co-host on a national show with such high ratings was unprecedented.

Barbara Walters travelled all over the world, including to China with President Nixon, for special reports for "Today," and also made appearances on other radio and television shows.

When she decided to leave "Today" in 1976, she signed a five-million-dollar, five-year contract with ABC. She now is a special correspondent who covers stories worldwide.

She has interviewed world leaders, big stars and ordinary people, and because she can put anyone at ease, her interviews are significant for their honesty and completeness. She has proved to herself and the world that a woman can be effective as a newscaster, and has paved the way for other women to gain equal opportunities in television reporting and as news anchors.

Barbara Walters makes her home in New York with her teenaged daughter, Jacqueline.

Fox, Mary Virginia, and Westman, Paul BARBARA WALTERS: THE NEWS HER WAY Illus. with photographs. Dillon, 1980. (grades 3–8)

Despite its simplicity, this excellent, objective biographical narrative clearly demonstrates Barbara Walters' seriousness of purpose. Factual and interesting, it will be of interest to older, reluctant readers as well as younger ones.

~~~~~~

NANCY WARD
1738–1822

Cherokee leader, peace advocate

Nancy Ward long held the most honored office in the Cherokee nation, that of "Beloved Woman." She first earned it as a teenager when she replaced her husband as war chief, after he was killed in battle. She retained her influential role with her people until the end of her long life.

During the Revolutionary War, Nancy Ward worked for peace by discouraging Cherokee involvement with either side. By warning Americans of impending raids she often saved lives on both sides. She helped negotiate treaties between Cherokees and Americans, but found they were often later broken.

As owner of one of the first cattle herds in the Cherokee Nation, she introduced dairying and taught her people to make butter and cheese. She also fought hard against American attempts to seize Cherokee lands. As a result of all her efforts on their behalf, and not because of her inherited position, the Cherokee people sought Nancy Ward's advice on all matters. She is sometimes called the

"Pocahontas of the West"; her wisdom and leadership were acknowledged not only by the Cherokee nation, but also by surrounding white settlers and traders.

Felton, Harold NANCY WARD, CHEROKEE Illus. Dodd, 1975. (grades 4–8)

Highly fictionalized, historically accurate, beautifully written text embodies the spirit of the woman, her culture, and her work in behalf of her people. The author does not spare America guilt in the treatment of the Cherokees and shows that although the subject's influence on her people was great, she was unable to halt many of their mistakes and others' injustices. By refraining from eulogizing her, the author brings Nancy Ward to life as a warm human being.

~~~~~~

ANNIE DODGE WAUNEKA
1912–

Navajo Indian leader,
winner of Medal of Freedom award

Annie Dodge Wauneka's father, a highly respected traditional Navajo Indian leader, encouraged her and other young Indians to become educated. He often depended on her for assistance in serving their people. She was particularly helpful as an interpreter and later followed in his footsteps to become a member of the Tribal Council, the first woman to hold such a position.

Her particular interest was better health and sanitation, and as head of the Health Commission she worked to eradicate tuberculosis among the Navajos, to improve maternal and child health services, and to encourage education.

In 1963 Wauneka was awarded the Medal of Freedom Award for her long crusade to improve health services. She has served as an advisor to the United States surgeon general and is active in the Girl Scouts of America and the Head Start program. Two of her daughters have also become public health workers, following their mother and grandfather in their dedication to the Navajo nation.

Nelson, Mary Carroll ANNIE WAUNEKA Dillon, 1972. (grade 5 and up)
   Highly inspirational, dramatic portrait of Annie Dodge Wauneka is also a vivid picture of the Navajo culture. Good, readable text is suitable for older less-able readers as well as elementary and junior high students.

~~~~~~

IDA WELLS-BARNETT
1862–1931

Journalist, lecturer, and reformer

Ida Wells-Barnett's parents were slaves, and she too was born to slavery. She was educated at a freedmen's school and at fourteen became the head of her family when her parents and three of their eight children died of yellow fever. To support them she became a teacher, continued her own education, and occasionally wrote articles for a local newspaper. Eventually she became half-owner of the *Memphis Free Speech.*

In 1892 three black male friends were lynched. She used her paper to attack the crime, and began investigating and publishing the facts about other lynchings. The paper was mobbed and destroyed and Wells subsequently became totally committed to a zealous crusade against lynching. She wrote, lectured, organized antilynching societies and black women's clubs, founded the first black women's suffrage society, and tirelessly worked for other civil rights. She continued this work after her marriage to a prominent black attorney and the birth of their four children.

Although Ida Wells-Barnett worked closely with white women in the feminist movement, and with Jane Addams in a successful struggle to prevent segregated schools in Chicago, she was philosophically a black militant. She did not want or trust the help of whites in black causes, and after she helped organize the National Association for the Advancement of Colored People was disappointed to find it committed to accommodation and compromise.

Wells, Ida B. CRUSADE FOR JUSTICE: THE AUTOBIOGRAPHY OF IDA B. WELLS ed. Alfreda M. Duster. Illus. Univ. of Chicago Pr., 1970. (grade 9 and up)

Autobiography of Ida B. Wells-Barnett, edited and introduced by her daughter, is a moving dramatic story of her life and the causes she espoused. Written clearly, in a straightforward manner, it is vivid and inspiring.

~~~~~~

EDITH WHARTON
1862–1937

Author

Edith Wharton's father taught her to read as a youngster and encouraged her love for books. At sixteen she wrote and published a volume of poetry, and much later sold some verses and stories to magazines. Her first major work, coauthored with an architect, was *The Decoration of Houses*, a defense of the classical style in interior decoration. Collections of short stories followed, and when she was forty she published her first novel, *The Valley of Decision*. Her 1905 novel *The House of Mirth* dealt with the contemporary New York social scene and received critical and popular acclaim. Other "novels of manners" included the famed *Ethan Frome* and her Pulitzer Prize–winning *The Age of Innocence*.

Wharton lived most of her life in Europe, where she travelled, enjoyed gardening, continued to write, and moved in literary circles. She received awards from France and Belgium for her work with refugees and the wounded during World War I. She returned to the United States in 1923 to receive an honorary degree from Yale University, and later was made a member of the National Institute of Arts and Letters and the American Academy of Arts and Letters.

Coolidge, Olivia EDITH WHARTON Scribner, 1964. (grade 9 and up)

Well-written biography of the life of Edith Wharton discusses her work, the society in which she lived, and her personal relationships with other literary figures. Her life is treated somewhat superficially, but for those familiar or interested in her writing, this is a good nonfictionalized account.

~~~~~~

PHILLIS WHEATLEY
c.1753–1784

Poet

African-born Phillis Wheatley was only seven or eight when she landed in America. The wealthy Bostonians who purchased her were so impressed with her intelligence that they taught her to speak and read English. Within a little more than a year, she had achieved the literacy level of an adult.

Young Phillis's poetry brought her to the attention of many prominent Boston citizens who invited her to their homes and requested her to write poems for specific people and occasions. When a poem she wrote to George Washington was published, the general invited her to visit his military headquarters. During a visit to England, Phillis Wheatley was entertained by nobility, and plans were made to publish a book of her poetry.

Phillis Wheatley's accomplishments helped dispel the beliefs that blacks could not benefit from education and that intelligence and talent were restricted to whites. Years after she and her young children had died in poverty, the abolitionists brought her work to the attention of the public, and today it is included in many anthologies.

Fuller, Miriam PHILLIS WHEATLEY: AMERICA'S FIRST BLACK POET-ESS Illus. Garrard, 1971. (grades 3–6)
Despite its brevity and simplicity, this is a very fine, tender, sympathetic biography of the young poet. She emerges as a gentle, bright, and talented young woman.

Graham, Shirley STORY OF PHILLIS WHEATLEY Illus. Messner, 1949 (grades 6–10)
Convincingly fictionalized, apparently well-researched biography of Phillis Wheatley is a sad story, for despite her talent and early opportunities, her life ended in poverty and early death.

258

~~~~~~

NARCISSA PRENTISS WHITMAN
1808–1847

Missionary

New York–born Narcissa Whitman was a religious child who dreamed of a missionary career even before she met and married physician and missionary Dr. Marcus Whitman. They accepted a commission in Oregon, and made the long and rugged trip there. She and the other woman in their party became the first white women to cross the Continental Divide.

Once in the Northwest the Whitmans established their mission among the Cayuse Indians. Narcissa Whitman taught in the school, and, when Marcus Whitman had to go east, managed the mission. She helped administer medical services to the Indians and settlers who came through the area, and attempted to establish peaceful relations with the Cayuse. Her only child was accidentally drowned, but over the years she cared for eleven foster children, for seven of whom she and her husband became the legal guardians.

In 1847 a measles epidemic carried by settlers from the East hit the community. Because the Indians had no immunity to the disease it had a devastating effect on them. While white children responded to medical care, the Indians did not, and great numbers of the children died. The Indians attributed this to witchcraft and retaliated in a raid, killing Marcus and Narcissa Whitman and fourteen others.

Cranston, Paul To HEAVEN ON HORSEBACK: THE ROMANTIC STORY OF NARCISSA WHITMAN   Messner, 1952. (grade 7 and up)
   A beautiful love story which depicts Narcissa Whitman as a woman who went west more from duty and love for her husband than from any inner drive or motivation of her own.

Eaton, Jeannette NARCISSA WHITMAN: PIONEER OF OREGON   Illus. Harcourt, 1941. (grade 7 and up)
   Very fine, fictionalized account of the life of Narcissa Whitman shows her as a true pioneer, a woman of remarkable intelligence, courage, and warmth. Absorbing and dramatic, it is history as well as biography.

Place, Martin T. MARCUS AND NARCISSA WHITMAN, OREGON PIO-
NEERS Illus. Garrard, 1967. (grades 2–5)
Very good, well-told account of the lives of the Whitmans is more his
story, for her role is somewhat minimized. Exciting and dramatic, this is a
touching and vivid story which depicts them both as dedicated,
perseverant human beings.

Sabin, Louis NARCISSA WHITMAN: BRAVE PIONEER Illus. Troll, 1982.
(grades 4–8)
This book succeeds as a description of life in rural America in the early
nineteenth century. As a biography, however, it offers very little of Narcissa Whitman's adult life.

Warner, Ann S. NARCISSA WHITMAN: PIONEER GIRL Illus. Bobbs-
Merrill, 1953. (grades 3–7)
Overly fictionalized account of the childhood of Narcissa Whitman is
nevertheless fairly accurate, gives a good picture of the times, and demonstrates her early purposefulness and intelligence. Her later life is summarized in the final portion of the book.

KATHY WHITWORTH
1939–

Professional golfer

When professional golfer Kathy Whitworth was named woman
athlete of the year in 1965 and 1966, it was hard to believe that this
tall, well-built athlete had weighed two hundred pounds when she
was only thirteen years old.

Young Kathy discovered golf when she was fourteen and
promptly fell in love with the game. She entered her first big
tournament after graduating from high school and won it. In 1959
she turned professional and after one year was ranked number
twenty-six. At this time she began steadily to lose weight.

Her marvelous long drive was beginning to be matched by increased skill in her putting and chip shots. By 1962 she was winning tournament after tournament, and finished second among
professional women golfers in earnings. In 1965, Whitworth won
the first of six awards which are given to the woman who wins the
most tournaments in a year.

Kathy Whitworth has served as president of the Ladies Professional Golf Association (LPGA), has been named LPGA Player of the Year many times, and is one of the all-time big money winners of LPGA.

Eldred, Patricia Mulrooney KATHY WHITWORTH Illus. Creative Educ. Soc., 1975. (grades 4–8)
Good, colorfully illustrated biography of the golfer discusses her athletic career in detail and describes her role in fostering new interest in woman's golf which has purposefully coincided with the increase in prize money given to women players. Lacking somewhat in drama and excitement, it is nonetheless a more than adequate protrayal of Whitworth.

KATE DOUGLAS WIGGIN
1856–1923

Author and kindergarten educator

Kate Douglas Wiggin's family fostered her love for reading and books. Despite an erratic early education, she turned to writing and had some stories accepted for publication. When a school for training kindergarten teachers opened in California, she was one of the first students, and her warmth and talent with children and in the arts flourished. She headed the first free kindergarten in California and later opened a school for training other teachers.

A natural writer, Wiggin wrote a book based on her own experiences, collections of short stories, and explanations of kindergarten principles. Among her most popular books for young people were *The Birds' Christmas Carol* and *Mother Carey's Chickens*, and the classic *Rebecca of Sunnybrook Farm* which has been made into a play and a movie, and is still enjoyed by children:

Mason, Miriam E. KATE DOUGLAS WIGGIN: THE LITTLE SCHOOLTEACHER Illus. Bobbs-Merrill, 1957. (grades 3–7)
Good though highly fictionalized account of the life of Kate Wiggin emphasizes her childhood, but shows the personality, determinism, and assertiveness that eventually culminated in outstanding achievements.

————. Yours with Love, Kate Illus. Houghton Mifflin, 1952. (grade 7 and up)

Very well-written faithful account of the author and educator shows her as an active, assertive little girl grown into an active, accomplished, and very personable woman.

~~~~~~

LAURA INGALLS WILDER
1867–1957

Author of children's books

Laura Wilder's career as author of the beloved Little House series of children's books began in 1932 when she was sixty-five. She had published several farming articles before beginning the semiauto-biographical series on American pioneer life. The books were enormously popular with young readers and literary critics alike. Included in the series, which was written to be on a progressively more advanced reading level, are *Little House in the Big Woods*, *Little House on the Prairie*, *On the Banks of Plum Creek*, *By the Shores of Silver Lake*, *Little Town on the Prairie*, *The Long Winter*, *These Happy Golden Years*, and *Farmer Boy*.

Laural Wilder won many awards and honors, her books were translated into twenty-six languages, a library was named after her, and the Children's Library Association established an award in her name to be given once every five years for a lasting contribution to literature for children. She was the award's first recipient.

The popular, highly acclaimed television series "Little House on the Prairie" is based on her books.

Blair, Gwenda Laura Ingalls Wilder Illus. Putnam, 1981. (grades 1–4)

Lovely book for early readers that, despite brevity, captures the essence of her life. Will be of special interest to young readers who watch the television series, and also serves as an introduction to the Little House books.

Wilder, Laura On the Way Home ed. Rose Lane. Harper, 1962. (grade 7 and up)

Interesting journal of Laura Ingalls Wilder covers the period of her journey from South Dakota to Mississippi in 1894. Her daughter Rose Wilder Lane, then seven years old, accompanied her parents and has edited this journal and added a "setting" of her own. Although not truly biography, it is a personal narrative of interest to adults working with children's literature, and those readers young and old who have never really outgrown Laura Wilder's Little House books.

————. WEST FROM HOME: LETTERS OF LAURA INGALLS WILDER, SAN FRANCISCO   ed. Roger L. MacBride. Harper 1950. (grade 6 and up)
    This collection of letters which Laura wrote to her husband describes her trip from Mansfield, Missouri, to San Francisco during the 1915 Panama Pacific Exposition. Interesting and lively, the letters form an account and memoir of the trip which may loosely be termed biography. For those Wilder devotees who wish to know more about her life following her early Little House books, this is a welcome addition.

Zochert, Donald LAURA: THE LIFE OF LAURA INGALLS WILDER   Illus. with photographs. Contemporary Books, 1976. (grade 9 and up)
    Worthwhile, comprehensive biography of interest to older readers and to those professionally engaged in the world of children's literature.

NOTE: Although the Little House books are essentially biographical, libraries do not shelve them with biographies, and so they have not been evaluated as such here. They do, however, offer fine pictures of young Wilder from childhood to maturity, as well as vivid portraits of pioneer life.

∿∿∿

FRANCES WILLARD
1839–1893

Temperance leader, feminist

New York State–born, Wisconsin-reared Frances Willard enjoyed the same interests and outdoor games as her brothers and also wanted to share their opportunities. Her father objected to her desires for an education, but she did manage to get some schooling and a degree from a Methodist institution. It was enough to enable her to become a teacher, and she soon became a well-recognized educator and dean of women at Northwestern University.

In 1873 a group of church women who were organizing a temperance crusade asked Frances Willard to become their leader. She accepted, and thus began her life-long struggle as a leader of the movement. A founder of the national Woman's Christian Temperance Union (WCTU), she became its president and also a promoter of other causes which would advance and aid the status of women. Among these were labor, health, prison reform, peace, and women's suffrage. She set up groups abroad to fight alcohol and narcotic abuse and tried to pressure politicians. Mainly because she stressed themes of home and family, her huge following was composed mostly of basically conservative women whose only real concern was temperance. Frances Willard, however, widened their interests and was able to involve many of them in other major social issues.

Mason, Miriam E. FRANCES WILLARD: GIRL CRUSADER Illus. Bobbs-Merrill, 1961. (grades 3–7)

Despite the emphasis and focus on her childhood, this is a very fine biography of the temperance leader and reformer which gives more than satisfactory attention to her adult accomplishments, as well as a good portrait of her childhood. Willard emerges as a strong, purposeful leader in this readable and fast-moving account.

~~~~~~

SARAH WINNEMUCCA
c. 1844–1891

Piute leader

Sarah Winnemucca, the daughter of a Piute chief, spent part of her childhood on a ranch. She later lived with an army family where she learned Spanish and English and accepted Christianity, combining it with her Indian beliefs.

As the influx of white settlers into Nevada increased, a Piute reservation was established and her people were exploited, physically and economically. For a time she served as an interpreter at an army camp, a role for which she was well suited because of her facility with languages. She taught school for a while, and left her first husband, an army officer, because of his drunkenness. She later married an Indian man whom she also left because of his abuse. Her third husband, an army officer, died after they were married five years.

Sarah Winnemucca is remembered for her strong advocacy for the understanding and equitable treatment of her people. In 1880 she went to Washington at government expense to plead the Indians' cause, and later lectured throughout the East and wrote a book, *Life among the Piutes*.

In her later years she opened a school for Piute children, and despite her poor health, successfully helped to bring education to her people. A tireless worker for the rights of the Piutes, she was referred to by those who knew her as the most famous Indian woman of the Pacific Coast.

Kloss, Doris SARAH WINNEMUCCA Illus. with photographs. Dillon, 1981. (grades 5–9)
  Intelligent, well-written, absorbing book gives the reader a background of the history and culture of the Piutes. Winnemucca emerges as a devoted and dynamic leader of her people.

Morrison, Dorothy Nafus CHIEF SARAH Illus. Atheneum, 1980. (grades 5–9)
  A fine biography which captures the mood and spirit of Indian life as it depicts Sarah Winnemucca as a strong advocate for her people.

~~~~~~

MAIA WOJCIECHOWSKA
1927–

Children's author

Maia Wojciechowska's family escaped from Poland at the start of the German invasion. They lived in various parts of France during World War II, and moved first to London and then to the United States. She and her older brother, loyal to their beloved Poland and scornful of the French who collaborated with the Nazis, spent most of their time in France committing acts of sabotage against the Nazis. Maia vowed never to speak to the Germans or the French for the duration of the war, a vow which created great difficulties in and out of school.

Today Wojciechowska is a very successful author of many books for young readers. *Shadow of a Bull* won the 1965 Newbery Medal; *Odyssey of Courage* is the biography of Cabeza da Vaca, the Spanish explorer.

Wojciechowska, Maia   TILL THE BREAK OF DAY   Harcourt, 1972. (grade 6 and up)

Very moving, dramatic autobiography shows Wojciechowska's rejection of values of her elders and of her attempt to reconcile her own conflicts and ambivalences. Of interest to adults as well as young readers because of its psychological insights and fine writing.

~~~~~~

JACQUELINE GLICENSTEIN WOLF
1928–

World War II survivor

When the Nazis occupied France during World War II, Jacqueline Glicenstein Wolf's parents were seized by the Gestapo, and their parting words to young Jacqueline were, "Take care of Josette," her four-year-old sister.

Until the war, they had lived a comfortable middle-class life, where the family, non-observant Jews, perceived themselves as primarily French. The war brought forth the realization that since they were Jews they would be persecuted as such.

Jacqueline, although only a youngster, struggled to take care of herself and Josette, and found help, sympathy, and generous assistance from many non-Jews. They were also disappointed by many, both Jews and non-Jews, who had promised to help.

After World War II they emigrated to the United States, where they were again disappointed when the promised assistance from American relatives never materialized. The two young women struggled to make new lives for themselves, which, as American citizens they have done. They still remain devoted to each other. Jacqueline Wolf is married and has two children.

Wolf, Josette TAKE CARE OF JOSETTE: A MEMOIR IN DEFENSE OF OCCUPIED FRANCE   Watts, 1981. (grade 7 and up)
Beautiful, moving memoir is a remarkable portrayal of a young woman, only fourteen, who made her own way during World War II as she cared for her little sister and herself, and tried to contact her parents in the concentration camp.

~~~~~~

MARY WOLLSTONECRAFT
1759–1797
Feminist, critic, author

Mary Wollstonecraft, the author of *A Vindication of the Rights of Women*, is the earliest feminist writer. The book, like many of her other writings, is a persuasive argument for education, job opportunities, and legal rights for women. She was a journalist and critic of note and was the only woman in a London circle of intellectuals that included Thomas Paine and William Blake.

She argued that women's wasted lives were a result of men's tyranny and though *a Vindication of the Rights of Women* brought her fame, it was widely attacked by contemporary critics. Feminists a century later were greatly influenced by it and the work has long been considered a classic in the women's rights movement.

Wollstonecraft's childhood was filled with the misery of poverty and violence and an unhappy love affair when she was thirty resulted in the birth of a daughter. She later fell in love with the famed freethinker William Godwin, whom she married. At thirty-eight, Mary Wollstonecraft gave birth to another daughter and died four days later. The child grew up to become Mary Shelley (page 217), the author of *Frankenstein*, and wife of the poet Percy Bysshe Shelley.

Flexner, Eleanor MARY WOLLSTONECRAFT   Coward, 1972. (grade 9 and up)
Outstanding, scholarly, completely feminist adult biography is highly suitable for mature teenagers. Despite being scholarly, it is immensely readable, interesting, fast-moving, and touching account. Psychologically

oriented, the author attempts successfully to explain much of the thought and behavior of Wollstonecraft, evoking much sympathy for the remarkably intelligent woman who suffered so enormously and died so tragically.

〰〰〰〰〰〰〰〰〰〰〰〰〰〰〰〰〰〰〰〰〰〰〰〰〰〰〰

VICTORIA CLAFLIN WOODHULL
1838–1927

Entrepreneur, feminist

During her long life, Victoria Claflin Woodhull espoused many theories, philosophies, and causes, some compatible with each other, some in distinct conflict.

From a large, essentially rootless family which was devoted to spiritualism, the production of a medicine show, and psychic remedies, Victoria and her sister Tennessee emerged as beautiful, clever, and highly unconventional. In 1868 they came from the Midwest to New York where they met the railroad magnate, Cornelius Vanderbilt, who had recently been widowed. He was enthusiastic about mysticism and their charms, and helped to launch their business careers.

Initially they invested successfully in real estate, and then opened a brokerage firm on Wall Street. This too was successful. Then Victoria Woodhull became interested in politics, and in 1870 she announced her candidacy for president, the first women ever to do so. She launched a newspaper in which unconventional political and social reforms were advocated. Free love, legalized prostitution, and communism were among the topics discussed in the paper and during her lectures. Although she had no prior interest in the women's suffrage movement, she became actively involved in the cause.

Here too, her own unconventional beliefs caused conflicts. She was arrested for some of the published accusations she cast at various public figures, and although she was acquitted, her reputation was severely damaged.

She and her sister then went to England, determined to gain respectability and financial security. Victoria Woodhull married a wealthy banker and her sister a wealthy merchant; both women lived out their lives in affluence.

Victoria Woodhull, the better known of the two sisters, and Tennessee Claflin were fascinating women who came from humble, chaotic beginnings and with intelligence, charisma, and cleverness demonstrated that women could, even in those days, chart their own futures.

Meade, Marion FREE WOMAN: THE LIFE AND TIMES OF VICTORIA WOODHULL   Knopf, 1976. (grade 7 and up)
A very fine, well-rounded biography represents a stimulating, sympathetic look at the highly unconventional businesswoman.

~~~~~~

DOROTHY WORDSWORTH
1771–1855

Diarist, writer of descriptive prose, critic, and poet

Although Dorothy Wordsworth was not the gifted or prolific poet her brother William Wordsworth was, she had an unsurpassed talent for describing ordinary things in a most extraordinary way. Her brother frequently relied on these descriptions to provide material for his poems.

William and Dorothy Wordsworth shared a love of nature, and she served as both his inspiration and critic. They had a life-long friendship with Samuel Taylor Coleridge, and he too made use of her phrases and descriptions in such major works as "The Rime of the Ancient Mariner" and "Christabel."

Dorothy Wordsworth did not write for the public, but kept diaries and journals which were published after her death. This work provides a guide to the dates when Wordsworth's poems were written and reveals the extent of her genius for description.

Manley, Seon   DOROTHY AND WILLIAM WORDSWORTH: THE HEART OF A CIRCLE OF FRIENDS.   Illus. Vanguard, 1974. (grade 8 and up)
Beautifully written book captures the spirit and mood of the Wordsworths and their surroundings. Mostly a biography of the poet William Wordworth, it is also the story of Dorothy's life, and a portrait of their dear

269

friend, poet Samuel Taylor Coleridge. Dorothy Wordsworth is depicted as far more than her brother's inspiration but as a writer, critic, and poet herself. Some of William's poetry is appropriately woven into the text, and the book is greatly enhanced by the inclusion (in an appendix) of excerpts from Dorothy Wordsworth's journal, a few of her poems, and a selection of William's poetry.

~~~~~~

FRANCES WRIGHT
1795–1852

Author, reformer, feminist

Frances Wright was a wealthy, brilliant, well-educated young Scotswoman who wrote a popular, enthusiastic travel memoir of her American visit. Attracted to many radical causes, she later moved to the United States where she established a commune which was intended to give slaves a chance to work, eventually earning their freedom. The experiment proved a failure and cost Wright half of her fortune as well as her popularity.

She became one of the first women to advocate publicly such social issues as birth control; free public education for all; equal rights for women; liberal divorce laws; and an end to organized religion, segregated schools, and capital punishment. She was sharply criticized for her own lifestyle, that of her close associates, and for the causes she pleaded in her lectures and in the newspaper that she published. Only her belief in free education received wide support.

Frances Wright was a freethinker and reformer who opposed marriage but eventually married. She financially supported her husband for the fifteen years of their marriage, but after their divorce, he was awarded all her property.

Stiller, Richard COMMUNE ON THE FRONTIER: STORY OF FRANCES WRIGHT Illus. Crowell, 1972 (grades 6–10)
Very well-written, stirring account is well balanced, showing Wright's weaknesses as well as strengths, her failures as well as achievements, and depicting her also as an inspirational, exciting, sympathetic human being.

ELIZABETH YATES
1905–

Children's author

Best known for her award-winning book AMOS FORTUNE: FREE MAN, Elizabeth Yates has written more than twenty-five books, as well as contributing to many magazines and journals.

Some of her biographies, such as PRUDENCE CRANDALL: WOMAN OF COURAGE (see page 58) and LADY FROM VERMONT: DOROTHY CANFIELD FISHER'S LIFE AND WORLD (see page 75), have the dual distinction of being popular with young readers and recommended by teachers and librarians for further reading on various academic topics.

The second of seven children in a loving, affluent family, she grew up in Buffalo, New York, with opportunities to enjoy the outdoors, nature, and animals and to develop her talent for writing.

Her family agreed to her education, but believed she should then return home to take her place in society. Determined to become a professional writer, she finally convinced her parents that such a career was not inconsistent with devotion to her family, and they then offered their encouragement and support.

In 1982 she received an award from the state of New Hampshire, where she makes her home, in recognition of her many years of civic work on behalf of libraries and the handicapped. She is the recipient of seven honorary doctoral degrees.

Yates, Elizabeth MY DIARY—MY WORLD Illus. with photographs. Westminster, 1981. (grades 5–9)

Excellent book makes liberal use of diaries and journals the author saved from her growing up years, 1917–1925. The book gives a good picture of life in the first part of the twentieth century and an appreciation of Yates's determination and the difficulties she faced in becoming a writer over of her family's objection.

Yates, Elizabeth MY WIDENING WORLD: THE CONTINUING DIARY OF ELIZABETH YATES Westminster, 1983. (grade 6 and up)

A continuation of *My Diary—My World*, this book, also based on Yates's journals, begins with her career in New York City in the 1920s and continues to her marriage to a young engineer and the beginning of a new life in England in 1929. A very readable, interesting account of her growing maturity.

~~~~~~

MILDRED "BABE" DIDRIKSON ZAHARIAS
1913–1956

Athlete

"Babe" Didrikson's athletic accomplishments seem not to have been exceeded by anyone, male or female. She won almost every honor and award given to athletes, including ninety-two medals for sports feats. As a teenager, she set national records in basketball and became known as a one-woman track team by setting records in several different events. She won two Olympic gold medals, and every title in amateur and professional golf.

Babe excelled in every sport she tried, including javelin throwing, the hurdle race, high jump, shot put, discus throw, tennis, billiards, diving, skating, and lacrosse. She also sewed many of her own clothes, cooked, and was an expert typist.

Even after cancer surgery, Babe Didrikson continued to win golf tournaments. When illness finally forced her to stop competing, she made personal appearances to aid cancer fund-raising and dictated her autobiography. She and her husband, wrestler George Zaharias, established a fund in her name to support cancer clinics, and also established a trophy to be awarded annually to the leading amateur woman athlete in the United States.

De Grummond, Lena Y., and Delaune, Lynn D. BABE DIDRIKSON: GIRL ATHLETE Bobbs-Merrill, 1963. (grades 3–7)
Excellent biography of Babe Didrikson emphasizes her childhood and youth, but gives a good capsule view of her adult achievements. From her earliest years she was an unusual athlete and a remarkable individual, and the authors have skillfully conveyed this, her personality, and her achievements.

Hahn, James, and Hahn, Lynn ZAHARIAS! Illus. with photographs. Crestwood, 1981. (grades 3–8)

Warm, nonfictionalized biography reveals Babe Zaharias as a courageous woman in sports and in her fight against cancer. Easy to read, but of interest to older, less able readers.

Johnson, William Oscar, and Williams, Nancy P. "WHATA-GAL:" THE BABE DIDRIKSON STORY Illus. with photographs. Little-Brown, 1977. (grades 5–10)

Absorbing, excellent, fast-moving biography tugs emotionally at readers. Journalistic style is anecdotal, but not fictionalized, giving a balanced picture of Babe and others in her life.

Schoor, Gene BABE DIDRIKSON: THE WORLD'S GREATEST WOMAN ATHLETE Illus. with photographs. Doubleday, 1978. (grade 7 and up)

Excellent biography traces Babe Didrikson's life from childhood to her death from cancer. Dialogue is used judiciously, and she emerges as a determined, courageous woman.

Smith, Beatrice S. THE BABE: MILDRED DIDRIKSON ZAHARIAS Illus. with photographs. Raintree, 1976. (grades 4–8)

Excellent biography captures Babe's spirit and deals openly and frankly with her cancer surgery and the recurrence that finally killed her. Although there is some use of dialogue, the book is not highly fictionalized.

Zaharias, Babe Didrikson THIS LIFE I'VE LED: AN AUTOBIOGRAPHY, as told to Harry Paxton. Illus. with photographs. Barnes, 1955. (grade 7 and up)

Very fine personal narrative by the subject while she was in the terminal stages of her illness is unusually warm, colorful, and never morbid. Written for adults, it is immensely readable, and is further enlivened by numerous photographs.

MARGOT ZEMACH
1931–

Children's book illustrator and author

Margot Zemach has lived in many places in the United States and Europe and has been interested in art since she was quite young. She has illustrated more than thirty books for children, and received, among her many awards, two Caldecott Honor awards and the Caldecott Medal. Some of her most popular books are *The Judge, It Could Be Worse,* and *Duffy and the Devil.*

She has sometimes painted herself, her children, and the family dog into her work. Many of her books were written with her late husband. Margot Zemach says she loves her work, and "I am working on books because it is my job. It not only buys us shoes and toothpaste but is a real privilege and a pleasure."

Zemach, Margot SELF-PORTRAIT: MARGOT ZEMACH Illus. Addison-Wesley, 1978. (grades 4–7)
A charming, beautiful self-portrait in words and pictures by the artist. Many anecdotes help to bring the artist alive, and the book will be especially enjoyed by those youngsters who are familiar with her work.

~~~~~~

SARA PLAGER ZYSKIND
1928–

World War II survivor

Sara Plager was only a eleven years old when the Nazis marched into Lodz, Poland, where she had been a happy, healthy, much-loved only child. Her happy childhood ended then, when the deprivations began.

She and her parents, along with all the other Jews, were placed in a ghetto. Deprived of proper diet and medical care, her mother died. Later her father died, and still Sara clung to life, surrounded by loving relatives. The miserable conditions of the ghetto were followed by the horrors and atrocities of Auschwitz. Sara survived, and emigrated to Israel where she married another Holocaust survivor. They have three children.

Zyskind, Sara STOLEN YEARS Lerner, 1981. (grade 8 and up)
An important document, translated from Hebrew, that pays tribute to the indominatable spirit of millions of Holocaust victims and survivors, but remains in addition a significant biography of one young girl whose adolescence was stolen. The reader gains an understanding of the brutal-

ity of the Nazi regime and shares Sara's anger with the Nazis and those who chose not to believe the brutality really happened. Despite her shock and disappointment to learn that the survivors were not welcomed throughout the world, she was determined to put her life together. An absorbing book.

Collective Biographies

Abdul, Raoul FAMOUS BLACK ENTERTAINERS OF TODAY Illus. with photographs. Dodd, 1974. (grades 6–9)

Profiles of Aretha Franklin, soul singer; Martina Arroyo, opera singer; Micki Grant, composer, lyricist, and performer; Diana Ross, singer-actress; and Cicely Tyson, actress, are, for the most part, interesting and readable. Some are written as interviews; others are narratives. Stylistically uneven, the biographies are somewhat lacking in the vitality displayed by the subjects themselves.

Adams, Russell L. GREAT NEGROES, PAST AND PRESENT Illus. Afro-American, 1969. (grade 6 and up)

Attractively designed collection gives brief, informal studies of blacks in sciences, business, religion, education, literature, theater, music, and art. Arranged by historical periods and by subject, these nonfictionalized profiles are readable and informal. Useful for reference but also suitable for browsing, they have appeal to junior high and high school students, and adults. Half-page illustrations by Eugene Winslow contribute greatly to the text. Included are singers Marian Anderson and Leontyne Price; educators Mary McLeod Bethune and Mary Church Terrell; dancer Katherine Dunham; journalist-reformer Ida Wells-Barnett; sculptor Edmonia Lewis; abolitionists Sojourner Truth and Harriet Tubman; banker Maggie Lena Walker; cosmetician and businesswoman Sarah Breedlove Walker (known as Madame C. J. Walker); actress and singer Ethel Waters; slave poet Phillis Wheatley; and Pulitzer Prize–winning poet Gwendolyn Brooks.

Aesang, Nathan COMEBACK: STARS OF PRO SPORTS Illus with photographs. Lerner, 1983. (grade 4 and up)

Included in these lively, short profiles of sports figures is Virginia Wade, English tennis player. She won the U.S. Open in 1968, but only after her sixteenth try in 1977 did she win at Wimbledon.

————. TRACK'S MAGNIFICENT MILERS Illus. with photographs. Lerner, 1981. (grade 5 and up)

Brisk, easy-to-read profile of Mary Decker Tabb, the world record-breaking track star gives a good overview of both her personal and professional life.

————. WINNERS NEVER QUIT Lerner, 1980. (grade 4 and up)

Kitty O'Neill, a stunt performer who lost her hearing at two years of age, is one of those profiled in this collection of athletes who achieved despite handicaps or obstacles. Older, less able readers will find this book inspiring as it vividly recreates their lives.

————. WINNING WOMEN OF TENNIS Illus. with photographs. Lerner, 1981. (grade 4 and up)

Profiles of Helen Wills, Althea Gibson, Margaret Smith Court, Billie Jean King, Chris Evert, Evonne Goolagong, Martina Navratilova, and Tracy Austin move along at a fast clip without sacrificing information or style, and will be especially appealing to older, less competent readers.

————. WORLD-CLASS MARATHONERS Illus. with photographs. Lerner, 1982. (grade 4 and up)

Short, but very good profile of Norwegian-born long distance runner Grete Waitz will interest all followers of the sport. Easy to read, the profiles are appropriate for all ages, especially older readers who are not reading at grade level.

Alexander, Rae Pace YOUNG AND BLACK IN AMERICA Illus. Random, 1970. (grade 6 and up)

Eight black individuals describe their youth in this book. A brief overview precedes long, well-chosen excerpts from Anne Moody's *Coming of Age in Mississippi* and Daisy Bates's *Long Shadow of Little Rock*. Both selections are good representations of young black womanhood and, although the extracts stand well by themselves, they should also act as a spur to reading the complete autobiographies.

Anticaglia, Elizabeth TWELVE AMERICAN WOMEN Nelson-Hall, 1975. (grade 9 and up)

Substantial profiles of Anne Hutchinson, religious dissenter and leader; Mercy Otis Warren, American Revolution writer, patriot, historian; Emma Hart Willard, educator; Margaret Fuller, feminist author; Susan B. Anthony, feminist, suffragist, abolitionist; Dorothea Dix, reformer; Jane Addams, social reformer, Nobel Peace Prize-winner; Ruth St. Denis, dancer and choreographer; Margaret Sanger, birth control advocate; Eleanor Roosevelt, humanitarian, first lady; Rachel Carson, scientist, ecologist; and Margaret Mead, anthropologist, present each women as innovative and willing to go against the mainstream. The early life of each is traced, but the focus is on adult achievements. The vivid presentations bring to life these women who will serve as excellent role models for young readers.

Archer, Jules FAMOUS YOUNG REBELS Messner, 1973. (grade 8 and up)

Outstanding, nonfictionalized, and brisk in-depth narratives of the lives of twelve people who rebelled against society. Objective, well-balanced, and thoroughly researched accounts of birth control advocate Margaret Sanger; feminist and suffragist Elizabeth Cady Stanton; and socialist labor reformer Elizabeth Gurley Flynn highlight the women's accomplishments at the same time depicting them as unique human beings.

Atkinson, Margaret F., and Hillman, May DANCERS OF THE BALLET   Illus. with photographs. Knopf, 1962. (grades 7–9)

Attractively arranged profiles of ballet dancers are preceded by an overview of the ballet field. The training of dancers, traditions and techniques of ballet, as well as the work of those who are not seen onstage are told clearly and precisely, and terms used in the ballet are explained. The profiles of the dancers give career highlights as well as information about personal lives. Though not a current book, much of it is still of interest, particularly to would-be dancers.

Included are Diana Adams, Alicia Alonso, Ruthanna Boris, Leslie Caron, Yvette Chauviré, Yvonne Chouteau, Alexandra Danilova, Elaine Fifield, Margot Fonteyn, Beryl Grey, Rosella Hightower, Renée Jeanmarie, Nora Kaye, Tanaquil LeClerq, Colette Marchand, Alicia Markova, Mary Ellen Moylan, Nina Novak, Janet Reed, Tatiana Riabouchinska, Moira Shearer, Mia Slavenska, Maria Tallchief, Marjorie Tallchief, Tamara Toumanova, and Jocelyn Vollmar.

Balliett, Whitney IMPROVISING   Oxford University Pr., 1977. (grade 8 and up)

In this book, which describes sixteen jazz musicians and their art, a profile of Mary Lou Williams is well written and will be of interest to older readers with a special interest in and knowledge of music.

Barrett, Thomas, and Morrisey, Robert, Jr. MARATHON RUNNER   Illus. with photographs. Messner, 1981. (grade 7 and up)

Well-written, intelligent profile of Grete Waitz, Norwegian-born long distance runner gives a picture of the sport as well as the woman, and serves as a good introduction to marathon running.

Barton, Peter STAYING POWER   Dial, 1980. (grade 7 and up)

Brief biographical sketches precede first-person interviews with performers, all of whom are dedicated to their professions and work hard to achieve and maintain success. None are stars, but all emerge as human, warm individuals with their own strengths and weaknesses. An especially good book for career-minded readers. Included are Elizabeth Johnstone, a free-lance French horn player; Jean Bonard, singer; Hilda Morales, Puerto Rican ballet dancer; Robin Silver, modern dancer; Tisa Chang, Chinese-American actress, director of the Pan-Asian Repertory Theatre; Rebecca Rice, actress of the Living Stage Improvisation Company.

Bearden, Romare, and Henderson, Harry SIX BLACK MASTERS OF AMERICAN ART   Illus. Doubleday, 1972. (grade 7 and up)

281

Outstanding profile of Augusta Savage is distinguished for its simple but stirring narrative which gives a vivid picture of the life of the black sculptor. Savage's work was exhibited widely, but she made her most enduring mark in the art world as the teacher and mentor of many younger artists. This profile details her early personal and later professional life, clearly stating the prejudices and the obstacles she faced because she was a black woman. Photographs of her and of her work enhance the material.

Benet, Laura FAMOUS NEW ENGLAND AUTHORS Illus. Dodd, 1970. (grade 7 and up)

Intelligent profiles of Harriet Beecher Stowe, Emily Dickinson, Mary Eleanor Wilkins Freeman, Amy Lowell, Edna St. Vincent Millay, Louisa May Alcott, and Sarah Orne Jewett have a textbook quality but are clearly written and most informative. For those readers who want their facts without any garnishment, this is a welcome volume.

————. FAMOUS POETS FOR YOUNG PEOPLE Illus. with photographs. Dodd, 1964. (grades 7–9)

Author has interwoven their poetry into these brief, lively, and thoughtful profiles of Rosemary Carr Benet, Emily Dickinson, Rachel Field, Eleanor Farjeon, Jane Taylor, Ann Taylor, Christina Rossetti, and Laura E. Richards.

————. FAMOUS STORY TELLERS FOR YOUNG PEOPLE Illus. with photographs. Dodd, 1968. (grades 7–9)

Objective, utilitarian, clear if sometimes dry profiles of Frances Hodgson Burnett, Mary Mapes Dodge, Lucretia Peabody Hale, Margaret Sidney, Kate Wiggin, Edith Nesbit, Juliana Horatia Ewing, Charlotte Mary Yonge, Dinah Maria Murlock Craik, and Mary L. S. Molesworth provide good accounts of their lives.

Bennett, Lerone, Jr. PIONEERS IN PROTEST Johnson, 1968. (grade 9 and up)

Outstanding profiles of Sojourner Truth and Harriet Tubman are included in a collective of those who pioneered in the black protest and civil rights movements. These colorful and elucidating accounts offer warm, human, and intimate views of the lives of two early fighters for black freedom.

Biddle, Marcia M. CONTRIBUTIONS OF WOMEN: LABOR Illus. with photographs. Dillon, 1979. (grade 6 and up)

In clear, lucid biographies of Mary Harris "Mother" Jones, union organizer; Mary Heaton Vorse, reporter; Frances Perkins, secretary of labor; Addie Wyatt, union leader, and Dolores Huerta, Mexican-American labor organizer are described within the context of their times, places and work. Good background reading for history or career consideration.

Bliven, Bruce A MIRROR FOR GREATNESS: SIX AMERICANS McGraw, 1975. (grade 7 and up)
Vivid, compelling narrative includes a substantial portrait of abolitionist and feminist Sojourner Truth which will interest competent readers in elementary school as well as young adults.

Bloom, Naomi CONTRIBUTIONS OF WOMEN: RELIGION Illus. with photographs. Dillon, 1978. (grade 6 and up)
Older readers as well as junior high school students will find the profiles of Anne Hutchinson, religious dissenter and leader; Ann Lee, founder of the Shakers; Mary Baker Eddy, founder of the Christian Science church; Henrietta Szold, founder of Hadassah; and Dorothy Day, founder of the *Catholic Worker* to be absorbing and dramatic. The book also serves as a fine introduction to a number of religious groups.

Blumberg, Rhoda FIRST LADIES: A FIRST BOOK Watts, 1981. (grades 4–9)
Lively, short profiles of each first lady are nonadulatory, and wherever possible reveal each woman as a person in her own right, with her own accomplishments.

Bolton, Sarah K. FAMOUS AMERICAN AUTHORS Crowell, 1954. (grade 7 and up)
Rather ordinary collection is reprinted and partly revised from the original book written in 1905. The writing style appears uneven, the flowery phrases are unappealing to young readers, and material is too superficial for older readers. Undocumented, it nevertheless offers accurate information on the lives of Louisa May Alcott, Harriet Beecher Stowe, Edith Wharton, and Willa Cather.

————. LIVES OF GIRLS WHO BECAME FAMOUS Illus. Crowell, 1949. (grades 7–10)
This is a revision of a 1914 publication, which explains why the literary style and treatment are outdated. However, the readable profiles are still interesting and valuable. Included are social reformer Jane Addams; authors Louisa May Alcott, Julia Ward Howe, Harriet Beecher Stowe, and Margaret Fuller; singer Marian Anderson; feminist Susan B. Anthony; American Red Cross founder Clara Barton; actresses Ethel Barrymore and Katharine Cornell; scientist Marie Curie; aviator Amelia Earhart; educator Mary Lyon; painter Rosa Bonheur; poet Elizabeth Barrett Browning; handicapped humanitarian Helen Keller; nurse Elizabeth Kenny; singer

Jenny Lind; cabinet member Frances Perkins; humanitarian Eleanor Roosevelt; pioneer nurse Florence Nightingale; and French author Madame de Staël.

Bontemps, Arna   FAMOUS NEGRO ATHLETES   Dodd, 1964. (grades 7–9)
Fast-moving, enthusiastic profile catches the spirit of champion tennis player Althea Gibson. Substantial in length, this is an appealing, warm study of the only woman included.

————.   WE HAVE TOMORROW   Houghton Mifflin, 1945. (grades 7–10)
Somewhat laudatory and old-fashioned in tone, the profiles of Mildred Blount, hat designer; Hazel Scott, pianist; and Beatrice Johnson Trammell, nurse, are satisfactory. Only the very early career of Scott is discussed; the profile of Blount is highly fictionalized, but satisfactory; and the sketch of Trammell is quite interesting.

Borstein, Larry   AFTER OLYMPIC GLORY: THE LIVES OF TEN OUTSTANDING MEDALISTS   Illus. Warner, 1978. (grades 6–9)
Brisk, readable profiles highlight the sports achievements and activities *after* their Olympic days. Included are Tenley Albright, ice-skater, now surgeon; Donna De Varona, swimmer, now television sportscaster; Micki King, diver, now in the Air Force; Nell Jackson, track and field champion, now a director of women's athletics and the holder of a doctorate in physical education with the handicapped. This book is a fine answer to the question "What ever happened to . . . ?" A book that will be of interest to young sports enthusiasts, and which points out that sports competition is only one facet of a well-rounded, fulfilling adult life.

Bowe, Frank   COMEBACK   Harper, 1981. (grade 7 and up)
The author, himself deaf since age three, skillfully presents colorful profiles of individuals who have interesting careers. Only after each person is thoroughly introduced to the reader is the disability revealed. This approach presents the disability as just another dimension of the total person. Included are Eunice Fiorto, leader in rights for the disabled, who is blind; Susan Daniels, head of the department of rehabilitative counseling at Louisiana State University's Medical Center, who had polio as a youngster; and Nansie Sharpless, biochemist who is deaf as the result of meningitis when she was in high school.

Bowman, Kathleen   NEW WOMEN IN ART AND DANCE   Illus. with photographs. Creative Ed., 1976. (grades 5–10)
Absorbing portrayals of Martha Graham, dancer; Louise Nevelson, sculptor; Barbara Morgan, photographer; Charlene Burningham, weaver; Marie Burton, mural artist; and Judith Jamison and Cynthia Gregory,

dancers, demonstrate the dedication and intense preparation required of these talented artists. Profiles provides insight into personal as well as professional lives.

———. New Women in Entertainment   Illus. with photographs. Creative Ed., 1976. (grades 5–10)
Well-written profiles of seven women who have been successful reveals them to be multidimensional people dedicated to their crafts and, in many instances, eager to make an impact on society. Included are comedian Lily Tomlin; Native-American singer and political activist Buffy Sainte-Marie; singer Judy Collins; actress Cicely Tyson; actress Valerie Harper; singer Diana Ross; and singer and songwriter Malvina Reynolds.

———. New Women in Media   Illus. with photographs. Creative Ed., 1976. (grades 4–9)
Profiles of Barbara Walters, television journalist; Katherine Graham, newspaper publisher; Judith Viorst, adult and juvenile author; Annie Leibowitz, photojournalist; Connie Goldman, radio journalist; Ann Chevalier, television camera operator; and Loretta Long, television actress and educator, provide an inside view of the work life of women in communications. Written in an easy style, these accounts will be of special interest to readers who may wish to consider careers in the media. The very easy-to-read profiles are suitble for older, less capable readers.

———. New Women in Medicine   Illus. with photographs. Creative Ed., 1976. (grades 5–9)
Very fine collective focusses on women of varying specialties and highlights their contribution to medicine and to the people who are the beneficiaries of their work, and also makes note of their personal lives. It will be useful to high school students as well as to the younger readers for whom it is intended. Included here are Mary Calderone, director of SEICUS (Sex Information and Educational Council of the United States); Kathryn Nichol, pediatrician; Anna Elington, neurologist; Mary Louise Robbins, researcher; Estelle Ramey, endocrinologist; Margaret Hewitt, nurse-midwife; Elisabeth Kubler-Ross, psychiatrist known for her work with the terminally ill.

———. New Women in Politics   Illus. with photographs. Creative Ed., 1976. (grades 5–8)
In these colorful, perceptive profiles the impressive achievements of Bess Myerson, former Miss America who later became New York City's commissioner of consumer affairs and has remained active in politics; Elizabeth Holtzman, congresswoman from New York; Dolores Huerta, Mexican-American labor organizer; Patsy Mink, congresswoman from

Hawaii, Barbara Jordan, congresswoman from Texas; Yvonne Burke, congresswoman from California; and Ella Grasso, governor of Connecticut, are clearly cited. Each woman emerges with a strong commitment to her work and to women's rights.

————. NEW WOMEN IN SOCIAL SCIENCES Illus with photographs. Creative Ed., 1975. (grades 4–9)
Profiles of various lengths focus on the accomplishments of Joyce Brothers, psychologist; Margaret Mead, anthropologist; Jane Goodall, animal behaviorist; Sylvia Porter, financial writer; Barbara Tuchman, historian; Cynthia Cone, anthropologist; and Alice Rivlin, economist. Each profile is presented in a clear, readable manner which will interest older, reluctant readers as well as the younger ones. A brief look at each woman's personal life is also included.

Boynick, David King WOMEN WHO LED THE WAY: EIGHT PIONEERS FOR EQUAL RIGHTS Crowell, 1972. (grade 7 and up)
Originally entitled *Pioneers in Petticoats*, this edition consists of the same thoroughly researched, lively profiles of educator Mary Lyon; feminist Susan B. Anthony; attorney Belva Ann Lockwood; feminist and minister Antoinette Brown; physician Alice Hamilton; industrial engineer Lillian Gilbreth; aviator Amelia Earhart; and department store executive Dorothy Shaver. Each woman emerges as a persistent, determined, and highly individualistic person who has made important contributions to society.

Brimberg, Stanlee BLACK STARS Illus. with photographs. Dodd, 1974. (grades 4–7)
Very fine, anecdotal, but not overly fictionalized accounts of the lives of Harriet Tubman and singer Billie Holiday bring the women to life in a realistic and very readable style.

Brin, Ruth F. CONTRIBUTIONS OF WOMEN: SOCIAL REFORM Illus. with photographs. Dillon, 1977. (grade 6 and up)
Believable portraits of Harriet Tubman, abolitionist, slave, and spy; Frances Willard, temperance leader, feminist; Jane Addams, Nobel Peace Prize winner; Florence Kelley, social worker; Margaret Sanger, birth control advocate; and Eleanor Roosevelt, humanitarian and first lady, document and examine their lives in a straightforward, interesting manner. Their contributions to society are evident in each profile.

Bruner, Richard W. BLACK POLITICIANS McKay, 1971. (grades 6–8)
Outstanding profile of congresswoman Shirley Chisholm is simply but perceptively written, making good use of quotations from her autobiography and other published material.

Buckmaster, Henrietta WOMEN WHO SHAPED HISTORY Illus. with photographs. Macmillan, 1966. (grade 7 and up)

Interestingly detailed profiles of women whose lives were characterized by a dedication to an idea or principle and who have influenced history are included in this collection. Nonfictionalized, interesting, and accurate, the portraits are long enough to capture the personalities of the subjects, but short enough for those merely wishing reference material. A commendable selection of women, many of whom worked for equal rights for women and blacks. Included are mental health reformer Dorothea Lynde Dix; educator and abolitionist Prudence Crandall; feminist Elizabeth Cady Stanton; physician Elizabeth Blackwell; abolitionist Harriet Tubman; and founder of the Christian Science church, Mary Baker Eddy.

Burgess, Mary W. CONTRIBUTIONS OF WOMEN: EDUCATION Dillon, 1975. (grades 6–10)

Fictionalized (but not overly so), comprehensive profiles cover all salient details of the lives of six prominent educators in an informal, interesting manner. The author gives a strong impression of personality as well as the accomplishments of each woman in a style that will have appeal to older reluctant readers as well as to younger competent ones. Included are profiles of Emma Hart Willard, a pioneer in secondary education for girls; Mary Lyon, the founder of Mount Holyoke College; Martha Berry, founder of schools in the Appalachians; Patty Smith Hill, a pioneer of modern kindergartens; Florence Sabin, physician, scientist, researcher, and teacher; and Mary McLeod Bethune, black educator and founder of a college.

Burnett, Constance B. FIVE FOR FREEDOM Greenwood Pr., 1968 (repr. of 1953 ed.) (grade 9 and up)

A truly distinguished and competently researched work which traces the individual lives of Lucretia Mott, Elizabeth Cady Stanton, Susan B. Anthony, and Lucy Stone, pioneers in the women's rights movement; and Carrie Chapman Catt, whose strong leadership led to the final passage of the Nineteenth Amendment. An adult, but readable and stirring account of their lives is told against the background of the fight for women's rights, and the transitions from one profile to the next are adroitly handled to show that the five women's lives were interwoven. Stylistically smooth, this book combines fine literary prose and good character insights with clearly stated facts, providing fascinating and inspiring reading for high school students.

Burt, Olive W. BLACK WOMEN OF VALOR Illus. Messner, 1974. (grades 4–8)

Fictionalized profiles of social worker and humanitarian Juliette Derricotte, banker Maggie Walker, journalist Ida Wells-Barnett, and educator Septima Poinsette Clark are good, but lack drama, warmth, and vitality. Somewhat self-consciously nonsexist and nonracist, a certain spontaneity and spark appear to be missing. However, the author throws interesting light on the accomplishments of the women, and stresses the roles they played in working towards helping others and achieving success themselves.

Busman, Gene THE SUPERSTARS OF ROCK: THEIR LIVES AND THEIR MUSIC Illus. with photographs. Messner, 1980. (grade 7 and up)

Forthright, honest nonadulatory profiles of singers Aretha Franklin, Janis Joplin, and Donna Summers highlight their personal lives as well as their musical careers.

Butler, Hal SPORTS HEROES WHO WOULDN'T QUIT Messner, 1973. (grade 6 and up)

Lively, warm, informal profile clearly depicts swimmer Gertrude Ederle to be a sports personality "who wouldn't quit" when the nineteen-year-old woman became the first woman and the sixth person to swim the English Channel.

Butwin, Miriam, and Chaffin, Lillie AMERICA'S FIRST LADIES 1789–1865; AMERICA'S FIRST LADIES 1865—PRESENT Illus. Lerner, 1969; rev., 1981. (reading level, grades 4–6; interest level through high school)

This two-volume set focuses more on the presidents' achievements than on the personalities and accomplishments of the first ladies. Directed to slow or reluctant readers, the profiles offer brief, undistinguished summaries of the lives of the women. Photographs and paintings of the first ladies and their families somewhat perk up this only adequate book. Volume 1 includes Martha Washington through Mary Todd Lincoln. Volume 2 includes Eliza Johnson through Pat Nixon. The 1981 edition includes the first ladies through Nancy Reagan. The more recent profiles place an emphasis on the women themselves.

Cavanah, Frances WE CAME TO AMERICA Macrae, 1954. (grades 7-11)

Mostly personal accounts, these profiles include Anna Howard Shaw, a minister and feminist from England; Princess Ileana of Rumania; Mary Antin, author from Russia; Lily Daché, hat designer from France; and Phillis Wheatley, young black poet from Africa. Other firsthand accounts by women immigrants from Ireland, Mexico, Holland, Poland, Sweden, and Switzerland are of women who are not prominent. Their stories are moving and recreate their era well. Each chapter in this fine book is excerpted from other works; complete citations are included. A brief but good introduction precedes the accounts, and suggested readings further enhance the value of the book.

————. WE WANTED TO BE FREE   Macrae, 1971. (grade 7 and up)

Warm, human, and moving stories by twentieth-century refugees are richly varied by national origin and by mood and tempo. Some describe conditions in their native country; others tell of the earliest experiences as refugees. Maria von Trapp, Austrian singer, relates an amusing story; Helen Vlachos, Greek newspaper publisher, tells a suspenseful one. Others are touching or anecdotal, all are good. Also included are memoirs by Mary Antin, Russian-born author; Laura Fermi, Italian-born author; and Sigrid Undset, Norwegian winner of the Nobel Prize in literature.

Chamberlin, Hope   A MINORITY OF MEMBERS: WOMEN IN THE U.S. CONGRESS   Illus. Praeger, 1973. (grade 9 and up)

Very fine adult book which will be of interest and use to high school students for reading and research. Profiles of varying lengths focus on the political and professional careers of the women who have served in the United States Congress in an interesting, polished journalistic style that is forthright, perceptive, and lively. Included are Jeanette Rankin, Rebecca Latimer Felton, Alice M. Robertson, Winifred Mason Huck, Mae Ella Nolan, Florence P. Kahn, Mary T. Norton, Edith Nourse Rogers, Katherine Langley, Pearl Peden Oldfield, Ruth Hanna McCormick, Ruth Bryan Owen, Ruth Baker Pratt, Effiegene L. Wingo, Willa B. Eslick, Hattie W. Caraway, Virginia Ellis Jenckes, Kathryn O'Loughlin McCarthy, Marian Williams Clarke, Isabella Greenway, Caroline O'Day, Nan Wood Honeyman, Elizabeth Hawley Gasque, Rose McConnell Long, Dixie Bibb Graves, Gladys Pyle, Frances P. Bolton, Margaret Chase Smith, Jessie Sumner, Clara G. McMillan, Florence Reville Gibbs, Katherine Edgar Byron, Veronica B. Boland, Winifred C. Stanley, Willa L. Fulmer, Clare Boothe Luce, Emily Taft Douglas, Helen Gahagan Douglas, Chase Going Woodhouse, Helen Douglas Mankin, (Eliza) Jane Pratt, Vera C. Bushfield, Georgia L. Lusk, Katherine St. George, Reva Beck Bosone, Cecil M. Harden, Edna F. Kelly, Marguerite Stitt Church, Ruth Thompson, Elizabeth Kee, Vera D. Buchanan, Gracie Pfost, Leonor K. Sullivan, Eva Bowring, Hazel H. Abel, Iris F. Blitch, Edith Green, Martha W. Griffiths, Coya Knutson, Kathryn E. Granahan, Florence P. Dwyer, Catherine May, Edna Simpson, Jessica McCullough Weis, Julia Butler Hansen, Catherine D. Norrell, Louise Goff Reece, Corinne Boyd Riley, Maurine B. Neuberger, Charlotte T. Reid, Irene Bailey Baker, Patsy T. Mink, Lera M. Thomas, Margaret M. Heckler, Shirley Chisholm, Bella S. Abzug, Ella T. Grasso, Louise Day Hicks, Elizabeth B. Andrews, Elaine S. Edwards, Yvonne

Brathwaite Burke, Marjorie Holt, Elizabeth Holtzman, Barbara Jordan, Patricia Schroeder.

Chapin, Victor GIANTS OF THE KEYBOARD Illus. Lippincott, 1967. (grade 8 and up)
  Good straightforward discussions of the lives of German pianist Clara Schumann and Venezuelian pianist Teresa Carreño are factual but somewhat dry. Of interest chiefly to readers with a knowledge of music, the biographies emphasize the subjects' professional lives, with some attention given to their contemporaries.

Chittenden, Elizabeth PROFILES IN BLACK AND WHITE: MEN AND WOMEN WHO FOUGHT AGAINST SLAVERY Illus. with photographs and engravings. Scribner, 1973. (grade 6 and up)
  Anecdotal profiles are interestingly written, appealing to younger or unenthusiastic readers as well as mature, eager ones. Graphically attractive collection includes profiles of Prudence Crandall, white educator of blacks; Ann Wood, teenage slave who led others to freedom; Ellen Craft, fugitive slave and educator; Charlotte Forten, free black educator; Sarah Dickey, white educator of blacks.

Chu, Daniel AMERICA'S HALL OF FAME Four Winds, 1972. (grade 7 and up)
  Concise biographies of Mary Lyon and Emma Hart Willard, pioneers in education for women, are accurate and interesting and should be a spur to further reading.

Christopher, Maurine BLACK AMERICANS IN CONGRESS Crowell, 1976. (grade 9 and up)
  Serious, nonfictionalized profiles focus on each woman's work in Congress, but also give a well-rounded picture of earlier years, motivations, and future plans. Included are Shirley Chisholm of New York, Yvonne Brathwaite Burke of California, Cardiss Collins of Illinois, and Barbara Jordan of Texas.

Clyne, Patricia Edwards PATRIOTS IN PETTICOATS Illus. Dodd, 1976. (grade 5 and up)
  Fresh, appealing profiles of a number of women, the result of thorough research, clearly demonstrates each woman's impact on the fight for America's independence. Included are "Mad Anne" Bailey, Penelope Barker, Mary Lindley Murray, Margaret Corbin, Sybil Ludington, Lydia Darragh, Nancy Hart, Mary Hays, Sally Townsend, Hannah Hendee, Tempe Wick, Elizabeth Champe, Deborah Sampson, Phoebe Reynolds, Betty Zane, Rebecca and Abigail Bates and Mary Pickersgill. Historical sites pertaining to the women that can be visited are also listed. A final

chapter briefly tells about several other women who served the cause, and the appropriate sites for visiting are also included. An excellent book for youngsters studying the American Revolution.

Coates, Ruth Allison GREAT AMERICAN NATURALISTS Illus. Lerner, 1974. (reading level, grades 4–6; interest level, grade 7 and up)

Somewhat pedestrian, but adequate profile of Rachel Carson, marine biologist and conservationist, lacks drama and warmth and tries to credit Carson with all environmental reforms, rather than just the ones for which she is responsible. However, her accomplishments are clearly stated, and the biography is fairly interesting, although the style is hampered by the demands of writing for reluctant readers.

Cohen, Daniel MASTERS OF THE OCCULT Illus. Dodd, 1971. (grades 7 and up)

Satisfactory, but not especially exciting profiles give a well-rounded picture of each woman. Included are Elena (or Helena) Petrovna Blavatsky, Russian theosophist, and Eileen Garrett, medium. Both women are described as psychics.

Collins, Jean SHE WAS THERE: STORIES OF PIONEERING WOMEN JOURNALISTS Illus. with photographs. Messner, 1980. (grade 7 and up)

Excellent collection of contemporary (from 1920s to present) women journalists written in a lively, fast-moving first person style. The author gives a brief overview of each subject's life, followed by episodes well developed to reveal important facets of their professional life. An introduction gives an overview of women in journalism, and points out some common threads that run through their lives. Particularly meaningful to those readers considering a career in journalism or media. Included are Emma Bugbee, Kathleen McLaughlin, Mildred Gilman, Norma Abrams, Sonia Tomara, Irene Corbally Kuhn, Carolyn Anspacher, Hazel Garland, Mary Morris, Mary Garber, Judith Crist, Celestine Sibley, Marie Torre, and Helen Thomas.

Conta, Marcia WOMEN FOR HUMAN RIGHTS Illus. with photographs. Raintree, 1979. (grades 4–8)

Very fine book clearly places each woman within the context of time and place. The authors wisely relate situations to contemporary events so that even young readers with no historical background can appreciate the women's accomplishments. This collection should serve as a spur to further reading, an especially good feature since the book is written at a high interest but low reading level. Included are congresswoman Shirley Chisholm; journalist Dorothy Day; advocate for the rights of the elderly Maggie Kuhn; civil rights leader, Rosa Parks; humanitarian and first lady,

Eleanor Roosevelt; and 1976 Nobel Peace Prize–winners for their efforts to restore peace in Northern Ireland, Mairead Corrigan and Betty Williams.

Cook, Fred J. THE MUCKRAKERS: CRUSADING JOURNALISTS WHO CHANGED AMERICA Doubleday, 1972. (grade 9 and up)
Overall picture of early crusading journalists includes an outstanding chapter on Ida Tarbell, the woman who exposed the Standard Oil trust, which is extensive in coverage. The author painstakingly explains muckraking and gives a substantial portrait of Tarbell's pioneering contributions.

Coolidge, Olivia WOMEN'S RIGHTS: THE SUFFRAGE MOVEMENT IN AMERICA 1848–1920 Illus. with photographs and old prints. Dutton, 1966. (grade 6 and up)
Excellent feminist history of the women's suffrage movement highlights the major events in the lives of individual feminists, and clearly depicts their contributions. Included are early suffragists and feminists Susan B. Anthony, Elizabeth Cady Stanton, Lucy Stone, Lucretia Mott, and later-day suffragists Alice Paul and Carrie Chapman Catt.

Cooper, Alice C., and Palmer, Charles TWENTY MODERN AMERICANS Illus. Harcourt, 1942. (grades 6–9)
Lively, informal biographies of aviator Amelia Earhart, sculptor Malvina Hoffman, tennis champion Helen Wills, author Pearl Buck, and social worker Jane Addams are written in polished prose style. Appropriately anecdotal, yet straightforward, they are flawed only by a somewhat parochial attitude towards other nationalities, a rather widespread attitude at the time this collection was written. For example, Indians and Africans are called primitives in the profile of Malvina Hoffman; dialects are unnecessarily used in the profile of Jane Addams. However, these are minor points.

Crawford, Deborah FOUR WOMEN IN A VIOLENT TIME Crown, 1970. (grade 7 and up)
Fast-moving narrative tells the stories of four women who went to America to escape religious persecution but found they still had to fight for freedom of worship. The women are Anne Hutchinson, Mary Dyer, Lady Deborah Moody, and Penelope Stout. Their lives are not told in individual profiles but are intertwined in this very readable book.

Crawley, Kitty FIRST WOMEN OF THE SKIES Illus. with photographs. Contemporary Perspectives, 1978. (grades 2–5)
Highlights of the careers of Harriet Quimby, the first American woman pilot to become certified; Mathilda Moisant, the second American woman pilot to become certified; Bessie Coleman, pilot; Valentina Tereshkova, Russian cosmonaut; and Emily Warner, who in 1973 became the first

American woman to fly for an American airline, provide a good overview and introduction to flying and the women who were among the pioneers.

Darling, Edward WHEN SPARKS FLY UPWARD Washburn, 1970. (grades 6–10)

In a fine introduction to this excellent collection the author states he has written profiles of people who "set out to do their own thing." Chatty profiles of Eleanor Roosevelt and Susan B. Anthony are informal but respectful, and anecdotes are used to draw parallels to other more current events which may be more familiar to young readers.

Dash, Joan A LIFE OF ONE'S OWN: THREE GIFTED WOMEN AND THE MEN THEY MARRIED Harper, 1973. (grade 9 and up)

Thoroughly researched and documented substantial biographies of Margaret Sanger, birth control advocate; Edna St. Vincent Millay, poet; and Maria Goeppert-Mayer, first woman to win a Nobel Prize in physics since Marie Curie, capture the essence of their professional lives as well as perceptively reveal their personal lives and the motivating characteristics that led them to their success. Adult readers and young competent readers will find this book of great interest.

Daugherty, Sonia TEN BRAVE WOMEN Illus. Lippincott, 1953. (grades 7–9)

Excellent profiles are written from the perspective of one important date in the life of each woman. The author employs the use of flashbacks to give the reader a complete picture of each of these women: religious liberal Anne Hutchinson; feminist and first lady Abigail Adams; first lady Dolley Madison; pioneer and missionary Narcissa Whitman; educator Mary Lyon; mental health reformer Dorothea Dix; feminist and author Julia Ward Howe; feminist Susan B. Anthony; historian, journalist, and muck-raker Ida Tarbell; humanitarian and first lady Eleanor Roosevelt.

David, Jay, ed. BLACK DEFIANCE: BLACK PROFILES IN COURAGE Morrow, 1972. (grade 7 and up)

Very fine profiles of Sojourner Truth, black abolitionist and feminist; Harriet Tubman, black abolitionist; and Fannie B. Williams, an organizer of women's clubs and author, are preceded by a very brief, succinct summary of their lives. The profiles themselves focus on the role of the subject in defying society and are well selected for their content and style. The treatments of Sojourner Truth and Harriet Tubman are excerpted from longer biographies; the material on Fannie B. Williams is autobiographical.

———. GROWING UP BLACK Morrow, 1968. (grade 7 and up)

An outstanding, thought-provoking collection of personal narratives offers insights into various experiences of "growing up black." Selections by civil rights worker Daisy Bates, author Elizabeth Adams, and entertainer Ethel Waters are well chosen for their impact and clear picture of the psychological and physical difficulties of being a black child in America. The editor's brief introduction to each selection offers enough background to make the excerpt from the longer work understandable and more meaningful. The selections themselves are emotional and shocking, and serve as a spur to reading the complete biography.

————. GROWING UP JEWISH Morrow, 1969. (grade 7 and up)
Twenty-five Jewish writers recollect incidents from their youth in a well-organized, well-chosen collection. The editor briefly introduces each selection, giving some background of the subject. The biographical narratives of Glueckel of Hamelin; Rebekah Kohut, educator and social worker; Edna Ferber, novelist; Edna Sheklow, playwright; Gertrude Berg, writer, actress, and producer; and Elsa Rosenberg, Canadian author, are all written from the perspective of the adult looking back at her Jewish childhood. The long excerpt from Anne Frank's diary was written by her when she was only fourteen and hiding from the Nazis. The general introduction and the briefer ones to each selection are informative and tie the collection together. The selections themselves are admirable and diversified, yet show some of the common links that exist among Jewish people of all nations and times.

David, Jay, and Crane, Elaine LIVING BLACK IN WHITE AMERICA Morrow, 1971. (grade 8 and up)
A variety of profiles about individual blacks and their experiences in society. Interesting selections from their own adult recollections by Elizabeth Keckley, who served as confidante and dressmaker to Mary Lincoln; Mary Church Terrell, feminist, educator, and author; and Billie Holiday, singer, are included. A longer, particularly dramatic and moving excerpt from author Ellen Tarry's own autobiography, *The Third Door*, is included as well as portions of the autobiographical books by Anne Moody (*Coming of Age in Mississippi*) and Daisy Bates (*Long Shadow of Little Rock*). [Note: These last two are not the same selections included above in *Growing Up Black* by Jay David.] Each selection in this collection is preceded by a very brief, well-written capsule summary of the subject's life, particularly in relation to the profile that is included in the book.

Davis, Mac ONE HUNDRED GREATEST SPORTS FEATS Illus. Grosset, 1964. (grades 6–9)
Excellent, fast-moving accounts of the lives and sports accomplishments of Gertrude Ederle, swimmer; Marion Laedwig, bowler; Sonja Henie, ice skater; Patricia McCormick, diver; "Babe" Didrikson Zaharias,

all-around athlete; Fanny Blankers-Koen, track star; Wilma Rudolph, track and field star; Althea Gibson, tennis champion; Nancy Vanderheide, archer; and Stella Walsh, track star.

————. ONE HUNDRED GREATEST SPORTS HEROES Illus. Grosset, 1958. (grades 6–9)
Brief profiles of swimmers Gertrude Ederle and Florence Chadwick; tennis champions Suzanne Lenglen, Maureen Connolly, and Helen Wills; all-around athlete "Babe" Didrikson Zaharias; ice skater Sonja Henie; markswoman Annie Oakley; and track star Stella Walsh are written in crisp journalistic style and arranged in an attractive, appealing format. The illustrations are worthwhile additions to this attractive volume.

Davis, Mary L. WOMEN WHO CHANGED HISTORY: FIVE FAMOUS QUEENS OF EUROPE Illus. Lerner, 1975. (grade 7 and up)
Informal, objective biographies of Eleanor of Aquitaine, queen of France and England; Queen Isabella of Spain; Queen Elizabeth I of England; Marie Antoinette of France; and Catherine the Great of Russia portray the queens as independent, intelligent women. Although not outstanding in literary style, the material is interesting and readable.

Dekle, Bernard PROFILES OF MODERN AMERICAN AUTHORS Tuttle, 1969. (grade 9 and up)
Pearl Buck is succinctly portrayed in a precise, well-written profile in this collection of twenty-nine modern American authors. Not a critical essay, but a good summary of Buck's personal life and her works, this enjoyable as well as utilitarian short profile is a good introduction to her writing.

Delderfield, Eric R. KINGS AND QUEENS OF ENGLAND Illus. Stein & Day, 1972. rev. ed.
Fine reference book is enhanced by reprints of portraits, genealogical trees, and illustrations of coats and arms. Good clear profiles provide utilitarian accounts in readable form. This is a revised but similar edition to a 1966 book (Taplinger) which may still be available in libraries.

Deur, Lynne DOERS AND DREAMERS: SOCIAL REFORMERS OF THE 19TH CENTURY Illus. Lerner, 1972. (grade 4 and up)
Unusually fine profiles are informative and accurate yet simple enough to be understood by less able readers. Included are feminists Susan B. Anthony, Elizabeth Cady Stanton, and Lucy Stone; mental health reformer Dorothea Dix; feminist and journalist Amelia Jenks Bloomer; author and feminist Julia Ward Howe; and social reformer Jane Addams. The lively text is greatly enhanced by the inclusion of many photographs, some quite rare.

Devaney, John GREAT OLYMPIC CHAMPIONS   Illus. with photographs. Putnam, 1967. (grades 5–9)

Top-notch profiles of "Babe" Didrikson Zaharias and Carol Heiss convey their championship qualities. Adding to the value of this informative, lively book is an appendix which, arranged by events, lists in chronological order all the Olympic champions, their records, and their nationalities.

Dillon, Ann, and Bix, Cynthia CONTRIBUTIONS OF WOMEN: THEATRE Illus. with photographs. Dillon, 1978. (grade 6 and up)

Each subject emerges as a multifaceted woman with a rich professional life in these absorbing, substantial portrayals. Included are profiles of actresses Minnie Maddern Fiske, Ethel Barrymore, Julie Harris, Helen Hayes, and playwright Lillian Hellman which fully explore their careers and also focus on their personal lives. Also included are very brief profiles of Anne Bancroft, Fanny Brice, Katharine Cornell, Colleen Dewhurst, Ruth Gordon, Mary Martin, Ethel Merman, Rita Moreno, Maureen Stapleton, and Ethel Waters.

Dobler, Lavinia, and Toppin, Edgar A. PIONEERS AND PATRIOTS: THE LIVES OF SIX NEGROES OF THE REVOLUTIONARY ERA   Doubleday, 1965. (grades 4–8)

Good illustrations and reproductions of a page from a handwritten manuscript enhance the profile of Phillis Wheatley. The informally drawn portrait of the poet is sympathetic and appealing.

Dobrin, Arnold VOICES OF JOY, VOICES OF FREEDOM   Illus. Coward, 1972. (grade 5 and up)

Good profiles of black singers Ethel Waters, Marian Anderson, and Lena Horne are written from the perspective of how they met racial prejudice. These fairly accurate accounts are somewhat pedestrian and lack the spark that the subjects themselves displayed.

Dolan, Edward F., Jr. GREAT MOMENTS IN THE INDY 500   Illus. with photographs. Watts, 1982. (grade 5 and up)

Collective includes a candid, readable biography of Janet Guthrie which reflects the excitement of the sport.

Drotning, Phillip T., and Smith, Wesley W. UP FROM THE GHETTO Cowles, 1971. (grade 7 and up)

Very fine profiles of Anna Langford, attorney; Shirley Chisholm, congresswoman from New York; and Gwendolyn Brooks, prize-winning poet, are included here. All black women, they came from humble roots and moved to the top of their professions. The authors dramatically and inspirationally make clear the routes the women took to achieving success.

Duckett, Alfred CHANGING OF THE GUARD: THE NEW BREED OF BLACK POLITICIANS Illus. Coward, 1972. (grade 7 and up)

Interesting profiles of congresswoman Shirley Chisholm; civil rights leader Fannie Lou Hamer; attorney Anna Langford; jurist and spokesperson for the NAACP Constance Baker Motley; and Myrlie Evers, widow of Medgar Evers, relate their accomplishments and contributions to society.

Eiseman, Alberta REBELS AND REFORMERS: THE LIVES OF FOUR JEWISH AMERICANS Illus. Doubleday, 1976. (grades 5–8)

Excellent, believable portraits of Ernestine Rose, Polish-born feminist, author, and reformer; and Lillian Wald, social worker, public health nurse, and reformer capture the many dimensions of these complex women.

Emberlin, Diane D. CONTRIBUTIONS OF WOMEN: SCIENCE Illus. with photographs. Dillon, 1977. (grade 6 and up)

Very good, easy-to-read profiles of Annie Cannon, astronomer; Lillian Gilbreth, engineer; Margaret Mead, anthropologist; Rachel Carson, environmentalist; Ruth Patrick, ecologist; and Eugenie Clark, ichthyologist and oceanographer afford youngsters an informative look at these women who have achieved success in the sciences.

Epstein, Perle INDIVIDUALS ALL Macmillan, 1972. (grade 8 and up)

Excellent accounts of the lives of Americans who defied established customs and laws. The profile of poet Emily Dickinson offers some good insights and incorporates her poetry into the text. The treatment of modern dancer Isadora Duncan is objective and gives an excellent, well-balanced portrait. A chapter about the Brook Farm commune, a nineteenth-century attempt to create an ideal, completely self-sufficient community, discusses Sophia Ripley and Margaret Fuller.

Eunson, Roby THE SOONG SISTERS Illus. with photographs. Watts, 1975. (grade 7 and up)

An unusually fine biography of three Chinese women who have helped to shape their country's history. All three women were educated in the United States and after returning to their native land married three of the most prominent men of China.

The oldest sister, Ch'ing-ling, married Dr. Sun Yat-sen, the revolutionary leader. Although she has been widowed for more than fifty years, she has remained consistently active in the revolutionary and Communist movements. Today she resides in Peking and serves as the vice premier of the People's Republic of China.

Ai-ling, the middle sister, married H. H. Kung, one of the most successful businessmen of China. She herself was a shrewd businesswoman and acquired much property in her own name. She taught at the college her husband founded and her philanthropic and war work during World War II was noteworthy.

The youngest sister, Mei-ling, became the most famous and most controversial of the three sisters. Married to President Chiang Kai-shek, she was not only a first lady, but also an extremely important Chinese leader. Among her most important achievements during World War II were her efforts to interpret for the Western world China's position and needs. A frequent visitor to the United States, she was largely responsible for that country's strong endorsement of her husband's government, during and after World War II.

This biography moves along at a brisk pace, interestingly tracing the lives of the women, and also giving a good picture of the political history of modern China. Objective in style and tone, the author depicts both the personal and political strengths and weaknesses of each woman and her husband. The political and ideological rift between Mei-ling Chiang and Ch'ing-ling Sun is clear, and yet the reader learns of the personal loyalties that long existed among the Soong family.

Faber, Doris PETTICOAT POLITICS: HOW AMERICAN WOMEN WON THE RIGHT TO VOTE Illus. with photographs, old prints, and cartoons. Lothrop, 1967. (grades 7–10)
Despite a flippant title, this is a serious, thoughtful narrative of the struggle for women's rights. Profiles of Susan B. Anthony, Lucy Stone, Elizabeth Cady Stanton, Lucretia Mott, Alice Paul, Carrie Chapman Catt, and the Pankhursts are given within the context of the feminist and suffragist movement. Good bibliography and appendix consisting of the text of the Declaration of Sentiments issued at the 1848 Women's Rights Convention at Seneca Falls add immeasureably to the value of this fine text.

Faber, Harold, and Faber, Doris AMERICAN HEROES OF THE 20TH CENTURY Illus. Random, 1967. (grades 5–9)
Especially attractive, readable collection of profiles is enhanced by numerous photographs. Lively, vivid profiles of singer Marian Anderson; handicapped humanitarian Helen Keller; photographer Margaret Bourke-White; aviator Amelia Earhart; and suffragist and peace worker Carrie Chapman Catt are included.

Facklam, Margery WILD ANIMALS, GENTLE WOMEN Illus. with drawings and photographs. Harcourt, 1979. (grade 6 and up)
Very fine profiles introduce readers to women who work in many capacities with wild animals. The book is of particular value to youngsters considering a career in this field, as each biography discusses how the

subject initially gained interest in pursuing a career, and a final chapter discusses career planning for the reader. Included are Belle Benchley, zoo director; Ruth Harkness, expedition leader; Jane Goodall, animal behaviorist; Kay McKeever, owl researcher; Hope Buyukmihci, beaver protector; Karen Pryor, researcher; Eugenie Clark, icthyologist; Diane Fossey, who works with gorillas; Biruté Galdikas, who works with red apes; and Leone Pippard and Heather Malcolm, who study whales.

Farmer, Lydia H. BOOK OF FAMOUS QUEENS Crowell, 1964. (grade 7 and up)

Profiles of Nefertiti, Cleopatra, Zenobia, Isabella of Spain, Catherine de Medici, Elizabeth I, Mary Queen of Scots, Maria Theresa, Catherine II of Russia, Marie Antoinette, Josephine, Victoria, Tzu Hsi, Wilhelmina, Juliana, and Elizabeth II are well-balanced, readable accounts. Useful for reference or reading, they highlight important events in the life of each woman.

Fax, Elton C. CONTEMPORARY BLACK LEADERS Illus. with photographs. Dodd, 1970. (grade 7 and up)

Outstanding, fast-moving narratives pay tribute to the courageous efforts of black civil rights workers Coretta Scott King, Fannie Lou Hamer, and Ruby Dee. The book offers insights into the character of each woman, and the superficiality often common to collections is artfully avoided.

————. SEVENTEEN BLACK ARTISTS Illus. with photographs. Dodd, 1971. (grade 9 and up)

Excellent, well-rounded portraits of black artists discussing their black experiences as well as their artistic ones in a warm, informal manner, without resorting to chattiness or fictionalization. Women included are Elizabeth Catlett, Faith Ringgold, Norma Morgan, and Charlotte Amévor.

Feurlicht, Roberta IN SEARCH OF PEACE: THE STORY OF FOUR AMERICANS WHO WON THE NOBEL PEACE PRIZE Illus. Messner, 1970. (grade 6 and up)

Excellent profile of Jane Addams is enhanced by many photographs which complement the text and help make her seem alive to contemporary readers. The text focuses equally on Addams's efforts for peace and her settlement work.

Fink, Greta GREAT JEWISH WOMEN: PROFILES OF COURAGEOUS WOMEN FROM THE MACCABEAN PERIOD TO THE PRESENT Bloch, 1978. (grade 5 and up)

Outstanding profiles present women as multifaceted. Achievements, personal life, and Jewish heritage is fully explored and the interrelations of each aspect of her life is discussed. Included are Beruriah, an ancient scholar; Doña Garcia, fifteenth-century business woman and philanthropist; Glueckel of Hamelin, writer; Rebecca Gratz, philanthropist and educator; Ernestine Rose, author and reformer; Rachel, actress; Hannah G. Solomon, founder of the Council of Jewish Women; Henrietta Szold, founder of Hadassah; Lillian Wald, social worker; Emma Goldman, feminist and reformer; Helena Rubenstein, cosmetics executive; Gertrude Stein, writer; Nelly Sachs, Nobel Prize winner for literature; Ana Pauker, sociologist; Louise Nevelson, sculptor; Dorothy Schiff, publisher; Rosalind Franklin, scientist; and Golda Meir, prime minister of Israel.

Fleming, Alice PIONEERS IN PRINT: ADVENTURES IN COURAGE Reilly & Lee, 1971. (grade 6 and up)

Dramatic, moving profile of Lorraine Hansberry, the black playwright and author of *Raisin in the Sun*, discusses her early life, professional career, marriage, and early death from cancer.

————. REPORTERS AT WAR Illus. Regnery, 1970. (grades 5–9)

Marguerite Higgins, World War II and Korean War correspondent, is profiled in a brisk, candid narrative. Told with sympathy and dignity, the account reflects the courage and determination displayed by Higgins.

Flynn, James NEGROES OF ACHIEVEMENT IN MODERN AMERICA Dodd, 1970. (grade 7 and up)

Straightforward narratives are interesting, informative portrayals of children's librarian Augusta Baker, Congresswoman Shirley Chisholm, educator Mary McLeod Bethune, singer Marian Anderson, and jurist Constance Baker Motley.

Foster, G. Allen VOTES FOR WOMEN Illus. Criterion, 1966. (grade 8 and up)

An outstanding overview of the struggle for women's rights as well as of the right to vote. Well-researched, documented, and dramatically interesting, this book is written from a feminist perspective. Included is much biographical material on feminists and suffragists Lucy Stone, Lucretia Mott, Susan B. Anthony, Elizabeth Cady Stanton, Carrie Chapman Catt, Victoria Woodhull (first woman candidate for president), and Anna Ella Carroll (Civil War military strategist). A fine book, which can be considered a collective biography, will serve as a spur to further reading of individual biographies.

Fowler, Carol CONTRIBUTIONS OF WOMEN: ART Illus. with photographs. Dillon, 1976. (grades 5–8)

Substantial profiles depict each woman as an accomplished artist. The focus is on their work including the important personal and professional influences in their lives. Of special interest to readers who have some knowledge of art, but not so technical or specialized as to limit its appropriateness for any reader who enjoys art. Included are Mary Cassatt, Grandma Moses, Georgia O'Keeffe, Louise Nevelson, Helen Frankenthaler, and Suzanne Jackson.

————. CONTRIBUTIONS OF WOMEN: DANCE   Illus. with photographs. Dillon, 1979. (grade 6 and up)
Profiles of Isadora Duncan, Martha Graham, Agnes De Mille, Twyla Tharp, and Gelsey Kirkland are richly detailed accounts of their professional and personal lives and also provide information about dance. Dance fans or those considering a career in the field will find the book of special interest.

Freedman, Russell TEENAGERS WHO MADE HISTORY   Illus. Holiday, 1961. (grade 8 and up)
Very fine, energetic biographies of athlete "Babe" Didrikson Zaharias and poet Edna St. Vincent Millay focus on the years before they were twenty, but also briefly discuss later events. Intimate and vivid accounts provide good inspiration for young readers. Selections from Millay's poetry as well as suggested readings contribute to the value of this collection.

French, Laura WOMEN IN BUSINESS   Illus. with photographs. Raintree, 1979. (grades 4–8)
In an easy-to-read format, profiles clearly show the motivating factors, interests, and accomplishments of the women. Older readers will find the book interesting; although the reading level is low, the interest level is high. Included are Mercedes Bates, Gabrielle "Coco" Chanel, Barbara Gardner Proctor, Dorothy Shaver, and Irma Wyman.

Fry, John WINNERS ON THE SKI SLOPES   Illus. with photographs. Watts, 1979. (grades 2–5)
Extremely brief but lively profiles of seven skiers include Suzy Chaffee, Barbara Ann Cochran, and Nancy Greene.

Gardner, Sandra SIX WHO DARED   Illus. with photographs. Messner, 1981. (grade 4 and up)
Easy-to-read, colorful, brisk profiles of Kitty O'Neill, stunt performer, and Diana Nyad, swimmer, will be of interest to older, less able readers.

Garfinkel, Bernard THEY CHANGED THE WORLD: THE LIVES OF 44 GREAT MEN AND WOMEN   Illus. Platt & Munk, 1973. (grades 4–9)
Exceptionally attractive collection contains full-page color portraits and small black-and-white photographs, enhancing the excellent, succinct profiles of the following women: Queen Elizabeth I of England, scientist Marie Curie, founder of the nursing profession Florence Nightingale,

handicapped humanitarian Helen Keller, and scientist-author Rachel Carson. Despite the brevity, each profile captures something of the subject's personality and discusses her most salient characteristics and important accomplishments.

Gelfand, Ravina, and Patterson, Letha THEY WOULDN'T QUIT: STORIES OF HANDICAPPED PEOPLE Illus. Lerner, 1962. (reading level, grades 4–6; interest level, grades 4–12)

Inspiring profiles of track and field star Wilma Rudolph, who was lame as a child; medical scientist Dr. Florence Seibert, who was a polio victim; and singer Kate Smith, who faced a serious weight problem. Intended for all readers but will have a special meaning to those who have limitations or handicaps of their own.

Gelman, Steve YOUNG OLYMPIC CHAMPIONS Illus. with photographs. Grosset, rev. 1973. (grades 6–10)

Good informative profiles employ very informal journalistic style but give good accounts of the lives of all-around athlete "Babe" Didrikson Zaharias, track star Wilma Rudolph, ice skater Sonja Henie, and swimmer Chris Von Saltza. A long appendix lists Olympic winners in individual and team events, adding considerable value to this readable volume.

Genett, Ann CONTRIBUTIONS OF WOMEN: AVIATION Illus. with photographs. Dillon, 1975. (grades 5–8)

Absorbing, well-organized, nonfictionalized profiles offer substantial, well-rounded views of six women in aviation. Written in a lively style and employing appropriate anecdotes, the profiles are immensely readable and are suitable for older, less capable readers as well as elementary school youngsters. Included here are Amelia Earhart and Jacqueline Cochran, pioneer award-winning aviators; Anne Morrow Lindberg, navigator and pilot; Jerrie Mock, first woman to fly solo around the world; Geraldyn Cobb, first woman to pass the astronaut testing program; and Emily Howell, the first woman pilot for a United States scheduled airline. A final chapter contains very brief profiles on other women in aviation.

Gilbert, Lynn, and Moore, Gaylen PARTICULAR PASSIONS Illus. with photographs. Potter, 1981. (grade 8 and up)

An excellent book which explores the successful achievements as well as the earlier lives of forty-six contemporary women is greatly enhanced by perceptive photographs. Some of those included are Rosalyn Yallow, scientist and winner of the Nobel Prize in 1977; Helen B. Taussig, pediatric cardiologist; Chien-Shiung Wu, Chinese-born physicist; Louise Nevelson, sculptor; Mary Lou Williams, jazz musician; Lillian Hellman, playwright; Agnes De Mille, choreographer; Margaret Kuhn, advocate for the elderly; Justine Wise Polier, jurist; Elizabeth Duncan Koontz, educator and civil rights activist; Constance Baker Motley, jurist; Eleanor Holmes Norton, head of New York City Commission on Human Rights; Gloria Steinem, co-founder of *Ms.* magazine; Addie Wyatt, labor leader; Bella Abzug, congresswoman; Ada Louise Huxtable, architect; Julia Child, culinary expert; Sylvia Porter, financial expert; Sarah Caldwell, conductor; Alberta Hunter, jazz singer; Mary Steichen Calderone, physician-founder of Sex Information and Education Council of the U.S. (SEICUS); Joan Ganz Cooney, head of the Children's Television Workshop; Barbara Walters, television reporter; and Betty Friedan, feminist writer.

Gilfond, Henry HEROINES OF AMERICA   Illus. with photographs. Fleet, 1970. (grades 8–10)
Excellent, easy-to-read profiles give enough details to draw well-balanced, sympathetic portrayals of these women: social reformer Jane Addams; founder of Visiting Nurses Service, Lillian Wald; pioneer physician Elizabeth Blackwell; athlete "Babe" Didrikson Zaharias; United States senator Margaret Chase Smith; congresswoman Shirley Chisholm; handicapped humanitarian Helen Keller; humanitarian and first lady Eleanor Roosevelt; singer Marian Anderson; painter Georgia O'Keeffe; photographer Margaret Bourke-White; astronomer Maria Mitchell; civil rights leader Coretta Scott King; colonial journalist Anna Zenger; young slave poet Phillis Wheatley; author Harriet Beecher Stowe; poet Edna St. Vincent Millay; author Pearl Buck; author and scientist Rachel Carson; actresses Maude Adams, Ethel Barrymore, Helen Hayes, Katherine Cornell, and Minnie Maddern Fiske.

Gleasner, Diana BREAKTHROUGH: WOMEN IN SCIENCE   Illus. with photographs. Walker, 1983. (grade 6 and up)
A fine introductory chapter reviews women's role in science, and the profiles of each woman clearly delineate her work and motivation and tells something of her personal life. Well-written, interesting, and fast-moving, this book will be of special interest to those considering a career in the sciences. Included are marine biologist Sylvia Earle Mead; Nobel Prize winner for physics Rosalyn Yallow; physicist Betty Ancker-Johnson; astronomer Zera Rubin; economist Muriel Siebert; and structural engineer Billie Campbell.

———. BREAKTHROUGH: WOMEN IN WRITING   Illus. with photographs. Walker, 1980. (grades 5–10)
Excellent, well-written collection has a fine introduction, followed by biographical sketches of Judy Blume, best-selling author of children's books; Erma Bombeck, syndicated columnist; Erica Jong, poet and author

of *Fear of Flying*; Jessamyn West, novelist; and Phyllis A. Whitney, novelist. Each profile focusses on the writer's beginnings, motivations, and attitudes toward work. The book will be particularly memorable to those considering writing as a career, but all competent young readers and older less competent readers will find the book of interest.

————. WOMEN IN SPORTS: SWIMMING   Illus. with photographs. Harvey House, 1975. (grade 5 and up)

Fast-moving, extremely easy-to-read profiles of diver Christine Loock, speed swimmer Kathy Heddy, synchronized swimmer Gail Johnson Buzonas, marathon swimmer Diana Nyad, and speed swimmer Shirley Babashoff will interest older less capable readers as well as younger competent ones. The author focusses on both the careers and the personal lives of the swimmers from a feminist perspective.

————. WOMEN IN SPORTS: TRACK AND FIELD   Illus. with photographs. Harvey House, 1977. (grades 5–9)

Lively tales offer vivid portraits of track and field stars Thelma Wright, Joni Huntley, Robin Campbell, Kathy Schmidt, Jane Frederick, and Patty Van Wolvelaeré.

Glickman, William G.   WINNERS ON THE TENNIS COURTS   Illus. with photographs. Watts, 1978. (grades 4–7)

Vivid, easy-to-read examinations of the lives and careers of Chris Evert, Evonne Goolagong, and Billie Jean King on their achievements in the field of professional tennis that was dominated by men.

Goffstein, M. B.   LIVES OF THE ARTISTS   Illus. with photographs. Farrar, 1981. (grade 7 and up)

Very brief biographies of five artists include Louise Nevelson, sculptor. Despite brevity, each profile captures the spirit of the woman and serves as an incentive for the reader to learn more about the artist and her work. Includes a full-color and a black-and-white reproduction of her work.

Golden, Flora   WOMEN IN SPORTS: HORSEBACK RIDING   Illus. with photographs. Harvey House, 1978. (grade 5 and up)

A very fine introduction presents an insightful overview of many aspects of riding. The profiles of the women reveal the training, dedicated hard work, and rewards of the sport. Included are Denise Boudrot, jockey; Michele McEnroy, horseshow competitor; Hilda Gurney, Olympic competitor; Sue Sally Jones, polo player; and Helen Crabtree, horsetrainer and coach.

Gould, Jean   AMERICAN WOMEN POETS: PIONEERS OF MODERN POETRY   Dodd, 1980. (grade 7 and up)

Very well-written, substantial biographies are geared to reader with a serious interest in poetry. The profiles discuss each woman's work and personal life, helping to bring to life their work. Extensive bibliography included. Poets included are Emily Dickinson, Amy Lowell, Gertrude Stein, Sara Teasdale, Elinor Wylie, Marianne Moore, Edna St. Vincent Millay, Louise Bogen, Babette Deutsch, and Hilda Doolittle.

Gray, Dorothy WOMEN OF THE WEST Les Femmes, 1976. (grade 7 and up)

Excellent book has biographies of varying length, some of which are also substantial in depth. All offer a good picture of America's West and the role of women in its development, as well as the effects of the harsh life on women and families. Included are Sacajawea, Indian guide; Narcissa Whitman, missionary; Juliet Brier, pioneer who crossed Death Valley in 1849; Dame Shirley, western writer; Juanita, Latin American woman who was lynched; Donaldina Cameron, Chinese slave trade reformer; Esther Morris, Wyoming suffragist; Carrie Chapman Catt, suffragist; Ann Eliza Young, nineteenth wife of the Mormon leader Brigham Young, who not only defected but led a successful campaign against polygamy; Susette La Flesche, Omaha Indian, reformer; Anna Howard Shaw, feminist, religious leader; Bethenia Owens-Adair, physician; Miriam Davis Colt, pioneer; Mary Elizabeth Lease, Populist party speaker; Willa Cather, author; and several women ranchers.

Greenebaum, Louise G. CONTRIBUTIONS OF WOMEN: POLITICS AND GOVERNMENT Illus. with photographs. Dillon, 1977. (grade 6 and up)

A very fine book that provides an inside view of the lives of some multifaceted women who have made an impact upon America's political life and government. Included are Jeanette Rankin, congresswoman; Margaret Chase Smith, United States senator; Clare Boothe Luce, author, congresswoman; Martha W. Griffiths, sponsor of Equal Rights Amendment, congresswoman; Ella Grasso, governor of Connecticut; and Barbara Jordan, congresswoman.

Greenfield, Eloise, and Little, Lessie Jones (with material by Patti Ridley Jones) CHILDTIMES: A THREE-GENERATION MEMOIR Illus. with photographs from family albums. Crowell, 1979 (grade 5 and up)

A beautiful recounting of a black family from the 1880s to the 1950s. The authors, a mother and daughter, capture their own lives and that of the younger author's grandmother. A richly detailed account, filled with nostalgia and mood-evoking experiences.

Gridley, Marion E. AMERICAN INDIAN WOMEN Illus. Hawthorn, 1974. (grades 7–10)

Inspiring, extremely well-told profiles of Native American women are competently researched and give much information on the history and culture of each tribe, as well as telling of the individual lives and careers of the women. Writing with candor, the author provides an objective view of several issues and disputes. Included are Wetamoo, Pocasset leader; Pocahontas, Indian princess; Mary Musgrove Bosomworth, Creek leader; Nancy Ward, Cherokee leader; Sacajawea, interpreter and guide to Lewis and Clark; Winema, Modoc princess amd peacemaker; E. Pauline Johnson, Canadian Mohawk poet; Susan La Flesche Picotte, Omaha physician; Gertrude Simmons Bonnin, Sioux educator; Roberta C. Lawson, community leader; Pablita Velarde, Pueblo painter; Maria Martínez, Pueblo potter; Anne Dodge Wauneka, Navajo leader; Esther Burnette Horne, educator; Maria and Marjorie Tallchief, Osage prima ballerinas; Wilma L. Victor, Choctaw educator and government official; Elaine Abraham Ramos, Tlingit college educator; Milly Hadjo Francis, Creek Indian; and Sarah Winnemucca, Piute Indian teacher and interpreter.

————. CONTEMPORARY AMERICAN LEADERS   Illus. with photographs. Dodd, 1972, (grades 5–8)
Accurate portrayals of several Native-American leaders are somewhat dry as they attempt to crowd too many details into easy-to-read, simplistic profiles for young readers. the author clearly stands in admiration of the individual subjects as well as the of Indian tribes, and although the profiles are not as lively as readers might desire, they offer useful information about the leaders and about the customs and history of Indians. Women included are educator LaDonna Harris, potter Maria Martínez, and advisors to the government Annie Dodge Wauneka and Helen L. Peterson.

Grimsley, Will, and Associated Press eds. THE SPORTS IMMORTALS   Illus. with photographs. Prentice-Hall, 1972. (grade 7 and up)
First-rate, journalistically informal biographies not only let the records speak for themselves, but also provide engaging realistic glimpses of the private lives of each sports figure. Adults as well as young readers will enjoy the profiles of all-around athlete "Babe" Didrikson Zaharias, skater Sonja Henie, and tennis champion Helen Wills.

Gross, David PRIDE OF OUR PEOPLE: THE STORIES OF ONE HUNDRED OUTSTANDING JEWISH MEN AND WOMEN   Illus. Doubleday, 1979. (grade 5 and up)
A very fine, intelligently written collection is interesting and inspiring. Despite its brevity and straightforwardness, it has depth and captures the essence of each person. Included here are Golda Meir, prime minister of Israel; Anne Frank, World War II figure; Rebecca Gratz, founder of the first Jewish Sunday school system in the United States; Lena Kuchler,

World War II survivor and child psychologist who helped in the settling of children in Israel; Emma Lazarus, poet; Roslyn Yallow, first American woman to win the Nobel Prize for science; Haviva Reik, World War II heroine; Miriam Ben-Porat, Israeli Supreme Court judge; Bess Myerson, former Miss America, now consumer advocate, writer, and television personality; Henrietta Szold, founder of Hadassah, Zionist leader, educator; Tzivia Lubetkin, World War II heroine; Recha Freier, World War II heroine; Lillian Wald, nurse, social worker, and founder of the visiting nurse service.

Gurko, Miriam THE LADIES OF SENECA FALLS: THE BIRTH OF THE WOMEN'S RIGHTS MOVEMENT Illus. Macmillan, 1974; Shocken, 1976. (grade 9 and up)

This extraordinarily well-written and interesting book is not technically biography. It is, rather, a well-researched, vigorous history of the early feminist movement in the United States. The sympathetic author has integrated substantial unvarnished portraits of those women whose involvement with the movement really *was* the movement. Included here are Elizabeth Cady Stanton, Mary Wollstonecraft (although not an American, her influence was considerable), Frances Wright, Sarah and Angeline Grimké, Lucretia Mott, Margaret Fuller, Susan B. Anthony, and Lucy Stone. The text of the Declaration of Sentiments and Resolutions, as issued at Seneca Falls in 1848, is included as well as many old prints and photographs, all of which enhance this particularly valuable book.

Gutman, Bill MODERN WOMEN SUPERSTARS Illus. with photographs. Dodd, 1977. (grade 6 and up)

Slow or reluctant older readers will like these lively, readable tales of superstars of the sports world. Included are gymnast Nadia Comaneci, tennis player Chris Evert, skater Dorothy Hamill, equestrian Kathy Kusner, skier Cindy Nelson, and golfer Judy Rankin.

————. MORE MODERN WOMEN SUPERSTARS Illus. with photographs. Dodd, 1979. (grade 4 and up)

An outstanding collection of very easy-to-read biographies of women athletes are equally suitable for older, less competent readers and younger ones. Each profile captures the personality of the woman and the uniqueness of her sport. Included are Nancy Lopez, golfer; Janet Guthrie, car racer; Tracy Austin, tennis player; Diana Nyad, swimmer; Joan Joyce, softball pitcher; and Carol Blazejowski, basketball player.

————. SUPERSTARS OF THE SPORTS WORLD Illus. with photographs. Messner, 1980. (grades 5–8)

Included is an excellent, well-balanced profile of Chris Evert, which gives a good personal portrait as well as a fast-moving description of tennis.

Haber, Louis WOMEN PIONEERS OF SCIENCE Rev. ed. Illus. with photographs. Harcourt, 1979. (grades 5–9)

An introduction to this extremely fine volume gives an overview of some women in science not profiled in this book. Each individual biography is a thorough, well-written, factual account of the person's contribution to science. Included are Alice Hamilton, pathologist; Florence Sabin, physician, scientist, and researcher; Lise Meitner, nuclear physicist; Leta S. Hollingworth, educational psychologist; Rachel Fuller Brown, biochemist; Gladys Anderson Emerson, biochemist and nutritionist; Maria Goeppart Mayter, nuclear physicist and winner of Nobel Prize for physics in 1963; Dorothy Crowfoot Hodgin, crystallographer, winner of Nobel Prize for chemistry in 1964; Jane C. Wright, oncologist; Rosalyn Yallow, nuclear physicist, winner of Nobel Prize for medicine and physiology in 1977; Sylvia Earle Mead, marine biologist; and Myra Adele Logan, physician and surgeon.

Halacy, Daniel S. MASTER SPY Illus. McGraw, 1968. (grades 5–8)

Readable, crisp profiles of Rose O'Neal Greenhow, American Confederate spy; Mary Louvestre, former slave and Union spy; and Mata Hari, World War I spy for the Germans, are fast-moving and appealing.

Harris, Stacy COMEDIANS OF COUNTRY MUSIC Illus. with photographs. Lerner, 1978. (grades 5–8)

In this collective biography there is a very lively, believable profile of Minnie Pearl, the comic star of Grand Ole Opry.

Hayden, Robert C., and Harris, Jacqueline NINE BLACK-AMERICAN DOCTORS Illus. with photographs. Addison-Wesley, 1976. (grade 6 and up)

Profiles of Jane C. Wright, medical oncologist, and Angella D. Ferguson, sickle-cell anemia researcher, focus on their careers and accomplishments. Interesting and lucid, these profiles can provide inspiration for young readers.

Hayman, Leroy ACES: HEROES AND DAREDEVILS OF THE AIR Illus. with photographs. Messner, 1981. (grade 7 and up)

One chapter, "Dauntless Women of the Air," brightly discusses pioneer aviators Amelia Earhart, Jacqueline Cochran and German-born Hanna Reitsch, who was the first pilot, man or woman, to fly a glider over the Alps. Fast-moving, it provides good accounts of their activities.

Hays, H. R. EXPLORERS OF MAN: FIVE PIONEERS IN ANTHROPOLOGY Illus. Macmillan, 1971. (grade 9 and up)

An outstanding profile of anthropologist Margaret Mead focuses on her early career and the professional aspects of her life. Not a personal sketch, it gives a good interpretation of her work, explaining it and serving to act as a spur to reading some of her own books. Good bibliography is included.

Heiderstadt, Dorothy MORE INDIAN FRIENDS AND FOES Illus. McKay, 1963. (grades 3–7)
Good profiles of Kateri Terakwitha, a Canadian Indian who became a nun, and Pasquala, an Indian who warned a mission of an impending attack, are well told but lack distinction and excitement.

Henry, Sondra, and Taitz, Emily WRITTEN OUT OF HISTORY Block, 1978. (grade 9 and up)
A well-researched, documented book which successfully attempts to rectify the omissions of women in most of Jewish history. This volume includes the matriarchs of the Bible; Glueckel of Hamelin; and modern women such as Rebecca Gratz, educator and philanthropist; Penina Morse, poet; Grace Aguilar, author; and Emma Lazarus and Nina Salaman Davis, poets, as well as many other unknown or little-known women.

Higdon, Hal CHAMPIONS OF THE TENNIS COURT Illus. Prentice-Hall, 1972. (grades 5–9)
Very good, brief, but somewhat superficial profiles of Suzanne Lenglen, Helen Wills, Maureen Connolly, and Billie Jean King tell a bit about their personal lives as well as about their tennis careers. Simply written, the profiles do not really capture the personalities of the women too well, but are interesting and will appeal to young elementary school tennis enthusiasts as well as older, less able readers.

Hirsch, Carl S. GUARDIANS OF TOMORROW: PIONEERS IN ECOLOGY Illus. Viking, 1971. (grade 6 and up)
In an extremely well-written, thoughtfully organized book, one chapter ("Something in the Wind") discusses Rachel Carson's contributions to ecology. This is not a personal biography; the entire focus is on her work and writing. It clearly reveals the extent of Carson's foresight, brilliance, and concerns for the environment.

Hoff, Rhoda FOUR AMERICAN POETS: WHY THEY WROTE Walck, 1969. (grade 7 and up)
Thoughtful, but somewhat prosaic profile of Emily Dickinson is followed by a good selection of her poetry. Atttractively designed book is appealing, and though the subject moves with some reality and warmth, the profile lacks distinction.

Hollander, Phyllis AMERICAN WOMEN IN SPORTS Illus. Grosset, 1972. (grade 5 and up)

309

Fascinating survey of women who have achieved fame and distinction in the sports world. Well-organized by sport, chapters cover horseback riders, swimmers, runners, tennis players, ice skaters, golfers, skiers, and bowlers as well as chapter devoted exclusively to all-around athlete "Babe" Didrikson Zaharias.

A fine introduction briefly summarizes the role women have played as spectators and as participants, and an epilogue reflects on the progress women have made and are continuing to make in the male-dominated field of sports. The profiles themselves are written in a breezy style.

Included are horseback riders Eleanor Sears, Kathy Kusner; swimmers Gertrude Ederle, Florence Chadwick, Patricia McCormick, Chris Von Saltza; track and field athletes Stella Walsh, Olga Connolly, Wilma Rudolph, Wyomia Tyus Simburg; tennis players Helen Wills, Helen Hull Jacobs, Alice Marble, Maureen Connolly, Althea Gibson, Billie Jean King; ice skaters Theresa Weld, Tenley Albright, Carol Heiss, Laurence Owen, Peggy Fleming; golfers Glenna Collett, Patty Berg, Mickey Wright, Kathy Whitworth; skiers Gretchen Fraser, Andrea Mead Lawrence, Penny Pitou, Marilyn Cochran; bowlers Floretta McCutheon, Marion Laedwig, Sylvia Wene Martin.

————, and Hollander, Zander It's the Final Score That Counts Illus. Grosset, 1973. (grade 6 and up)

In this collective biography of people who have achieved success in life after first becoming prominent as athletes, there is a chapter, written in a brisk, narrative style, on Tenley Albright, Olympic gold medal figure skating champion, who is now a surgeon practicing in Boston. We are introduced to the subject as a young girl who, although dedicated to skating, is equally devoted to her studies and graduates from Radcliffe College and Harvard Medical School; becomes a surgeon; marries; and raises a family.

————, ed. They Dared to Lead: america's black athletes Illus. Grosset, 1972. (grade 5 and up)

A vividly written profile of Althea Gibson, championship tennis player, is exciting and offers much inspiration.

————. Winners under 21: america's spectacular young sports champions. Random, 1982. (grade 5 and up)

Written in a lively, journalistic style, the profiles of Tracy Austin, tennis player, and Beth Heiden, ice skater, capture their spirit as well as providing ample biographical material.

Hood, Robert E. Twelve at War: great photographers under fire Illus. with photographs. Putnam, 1966. (grades 6–10)

310

Outstanding, nonfictional profile of Margaret Bourke-White traces her professional career, briefly touching on her personal life. Her courage, single-mindedness, and personality are skillfully captured without the book being sentimental.

Hopkins, Lee B. BOOKS ARE BY PEOPLE: INTERVIEWS WITH 104 AUTHORS AND ILLUSTRATORS OF BOOKS FOR YOUNG PEOPLE Illus. with photographs. Citation, 1969. (grade 6 and up)

These short, extremely lively, and well-written profiles are suitable for both young readers and adults. Each profile is about three pages, and in anecdotal fashion tells something of the personal and professional life of the author or illustrator. Included are authors Pura Belpré, Claire Huchet Bishop, Sonia Bleeker, Sara W. Brewton, Beatrice Schenk de Regniers, Aileen Fisher, Lou Ann Gaeddart, May Garelick, Virginia Kahl, Ruth Krauss, Joan Lexau, Myra Cohn Livingston, Phyllis McGinley, Ann McGovern, May McNeer, Eve Merriam, Elsa Holmelund Minarik, Lillian Moore, Lillian Morrison, Tillie S. Pine, Mariana Prieto, Ann Herbert Scott, Millicent E. Selsam, Ruth A. Sonnerborn, Ellen Tarry, Blanche Jennings Thompson, Janice May Udry, Sandol Stoddard Warburg, Julia Wilson, Rose Wyler, Margaret B. Young, Charlotte Zolotow; illustrators Adrienne Adams, Ann Grifalconi, Nonny Hogrogian; author-illustrators Jeanne Bendick, Marcia Brown, Barbara Cooney, Ingri D'Aulaire, Barbara Emberley, Marie Hall Ets, Louise Fatio, Berta Hader, Dahlov Ipcar, Dorothy Lathrop, Lois Lenski, Anita Lobel, Winifred Lubell, Katherine Milhous, Evaline Ness, Maud Petersham, Ellen Raskin, Margret Rey.

————. MORE BOOKS BY MORE PEOPLE: INTERVIEWS WITH 65 AUTHORS OF BOOKS FOR CHILDREN Illus. with photographs. Citation, 1974. (grade 6 and up)

Similar to the above books by Hopkins, these profiles of authors and illustrators for older children are equally informal and informative and will appeal both to young readers, and adults.

Included are authors Natalie Babbitt (who also illustrates books), Carol Ryrie Brink, Betsy Byars, Natalie Savage Carlson, Ann Nolan Clark, Beverly Cleary, Elizabeth Coatsworth, Hila Colman, Julia Cunningham, Marguerite Lofft De Angeli (who also illustrates her books), Elizabeth Borton de Treviño, Lavinia Dobler, Julie Edwards (known also as actress-singer Julie Andrews), Eleanor Estes, Jean Fritz, Genevieve Foster, Jean Craighead George, Shirley Glubok, Virginia Hamilton, Esther Hautzig, Carolyn Haywood, Irene Hunt, Elaine L. Konigsburg, Nancy Larrick, Jean Lee Latham, Madeleine L'Engle, Jean Merrill, Emily Cheney Neville, Barbara Rinkoff, Charlemae Hill Rollins, Louisa Shotwell, Zilpha Keatley Snyder, Virginia Sorensen, Elizabeth George Speare, Dorothy Sterling, Mary

Stolz, Sydney Taylor, Pamela (P. L.) Travers, Mary Hays Weik, Sister Noemi Weygant (who is also a photographer), Maia Wojciechowska, and Elizabeth Yates.

Horwitz, Elinor Lander CONTEMPORARY AMERICAN FOLK ARTISTS Illus. Lippincott, 1975. (grades 7–9)
Very fine sketches of Sister Gertrude Morgan, preacher and painter; Clementine Hunter, southern painter; Hattie Brunner, Pennsylvania Dutch painter; and Inez Nathaniel, painter, are preceded by an excellent introduction which explains folk art. A source of interesting material to both those already familiar with folk art, and those who are not yet acquainted with it.

Hughes, Langston FAMOUS AMERICAN NEGROES Illus. Dodd, 1954. (grade 7 and up)
Truly outstanding, beautifully written profiles of poet Phillis Wheatley, abolitionist and slave Harriet Tubman, and singer Marian Anderson are accurate, sensitive, and touching accounts.

————. FAMOUS NEGRO HEROES OF AMERICA Illus. Dodd. 1958. (grade 7 and up)
Brief profiles of abolitionist Harriet Tubman and journalist Ida Wells-Barnett are dramatic and stirring accounts, clearly revealing the subjects' contributions to history.

————. FAMOUS NEGRO MUSIC MAKERS Illus. with photographs. Dodd, 1955. (grade 5 and up)
Stirring profiles of singers Bessie Smith, Ethel Waters, Marian Anderson, Mahalia Jackson, and Lena Horne make liberal use of quotations and anecdotes. The dignified informality contributes to the flow the text and helps dramatize the lives of the women.

Hume, Ruth GREAT WOMEN OF MEDICINE Illus. Random, 1964. (grades 7–11)
Excellent, informal biographies are lively, readable, and accurate and are further enhanced by photographs and old prints. Included are inspirational profiles of women who pioneered in the health fields: Florence Nightingale, nurse; Elizabeth Blackwell and Mary Putnam Jacobi, American physicians; Elizabeth Garrett-Anderson and Sophia Jex-Blake, British physicians; and Marie Curie, Nobel Prize-winning French scientist. There is also a chapter on more contemporary women.

Hunter, Thomas C. BEGINNINGS Illus. with photographs. Crowell, 1978. (grade 6 and up)
A thoroughly motivating and inspirational collection for all young read-

ers exploring career possibilities. Included are twenty-four successful people, eight of whom are these women: Erma Bombeck, syndicated columnist; Yvonne Brathwaite Burke, congresswoman; Mary S. Calderone, physician and health educator; Judith Crist, film critic; Roberta Flack, vocalist; Louise Fletcher, actress; Patricia McBride, ballerina; and Bari Wood, novelist. A brief profile of each women is included, and then each woman discusses her early life and career. Their inner drives, hard work, and the people who offered emotional support to them are described, and the readers can draw analogies to their own lives. Success is seen as the result of many contributory factors, as well as talent.

Johnston, Johanna THE INDIANS AND THE STRANGERS Illus. Dodd, 1972. (grades 2–5)
Twelve beautifully written short stories in blank verse about Indians include an excellent profile of Sacajawea, the Indian interpreter to Lewis and Clark. Based on the known facts of her life, the compelling narrative is dignified without being sentimental. Excellent woodcuts by Rocco Negri are effective and contribute greatly to the book.

————. A SPECIAL BRAVERY Illus. Dodd, 1967. (grades 2–5)
Unusually fine book is designed for young readers or for reading aloud. Literary style is somewhat like free verse, warmly and dramatically highlighting and conveying the ideas and deeds of singer Marian Anderson, educator Mary McLeod Bethune, and abolitionist Harriet Tubman. Important details and facts are included in a brief appendix, rather than allowing them to interfere with the flow of the text. Illustrations by Ann Grifalconi are beautiful, and they share equal importance with the text in this rather unique book.

————. WOMEN THEMSELVES Illus. Dodd, 1973. (grades 3–6)
Extraordinarily fine book richly combines the best in literature, biography, and feminism. The author introduces the book with an overview of women and how they have been limited in their opportunities, and she ends with a fine discussion on where women are presently and what the future holds. In between are superb, though brief, blank verse profiles of fifteen women. Each portrait gives a general overview of the woman, but focusses on the salient point of her career and shows clearly the uniqueness of her accomplishments, particularly so in the context of the way women were viewed during the subject's lifetime. Strongly feminist, the author is never self-consciously or militantly so, instead gently but firmly reminding the reader either of the discrimination the subject faced, or what her deeds meant to other women. Included are Anne Hutchinson, colonial religious leaders and dissenter; Anne Bradstreet, colonial poet;

313

Deborah Moody, landowner and builder; Phillis Wheatley, black colonial poet; Abigail Adams, colonial feminist; Emma Willard, pioneer educator; Ernestine Rose, feminist and reformer; Elizabeth Blackwell, pioneer woman physician; Elizabeth Cady Stanton, feminist and abolitionist; Harriet Beecher Stowe, abolitionist author; Clara Barton, founder of the American Red Cross; Victoria Woodhull, feminist and presidential candidate; Nellie Bly, pioneer woman reporter; Carrier Chapman Catt, feminist and suffragist.

Jones, Betty Millsaps WONDER WOMEN OF SPORTS Illus. with photographs. Random, 1981. (grade 3 and up)
   Extremely easy-to-read profiles are nonetheless accurate and lively. A very fine book for beginning readers or older, slow readers. Included are Diana Nyad, swimmer; Billie Jean King, tennis player; Annie Peck, mountain climber; Nadia Comaneci, gymnast; Mickey Wright, golfer; Wilma Rudolph, track athlete; Joan Joyce, softball pitcher; Kitty O'Neill, stunt performer; and Roberta Bingay, marathon runner.

Jones, Hettie BIG STAR FALLIN' MAMA: FIVE WOMEN IN BLACK MUSIC Illus. with photographs and old prints. Viking, 1974. (grade 7 and up)
   Outstanding collection is distinguished by its insightful views of the subject as well as by a literary style that captures the mood of the women and their lives. The interesting, informative first chapter deals with the origins of the "blues," and is followed by substantial, in-depth chapters on each of the five women. Included are blues singers Ma Rainey, Bessie Smith, Billie Holiday, and Aretha Franklin, and gospel singer Mahalia Jackson. Candid in the appraisal of each woman, never eulogistic in tone, the author also conveys a good picture of the racial discrimination that the women faced in both their careers and personal lives.

Katz, Jane B. THIS SONG REMEMBERS Houghton, 1980. (grade 7 and up)
   A very fine book that gives a thoughtful overview of the creative contributions of Native Americans to various art forms. The individuals are introduced with a description of their work and culture, followed by their personal recollections and perceptions told in their own words. Included are Pitseolak, Eskimo graphic artist; Pearl Sunrise, Navajo weaver and basket maker; Mary Mouz, Navajo painter; Grace Medicine Flower, Tewa potter; Helen Hardin, Tewa painter; Cecelia White, Tlingit dancer; and Leslie Silko, Laguna poet and novelist.

Keese, Parton THE MEASURE OF GREATNESS Prentice-Hall, 1981. (grade 6 and up)

In this profile of Billie Jean King, the author explores attitudes, feelings, and uniqueness other than talent. The author's inquiry into "the measure of greatness" that sets some people apart from their contemporaries provides for an unusual book.

Kelen, Emery Fifty Voices of the Twentieth Century   Lothrop, 1970. (grade 7 and up)

Very brief profiles provide only a summary of each life, but are followed by a good selection of quoted statements made by each subject. Despite excessive brevity, the biographical information is well presented, and the format and content of the book provide a good reference source. The women included are singer Marian Anderson; anthropologist Margaret Mead; former prime minister of Israel, Golda Meir; poet Marianne Moore; and Indian diplomat Vijaya Pandit.

Kittlekamp, Larry Investigating Psychics   Morrow, 1977. (grade 6 and up)

In this interesting and unusual book, the introductory chapter describes theories, some experiments, and findings where science and the occult overlap. Profiles of English medium Rosemary Brown, and American healer Olga Ripich describe their personal lives and abilities and how their psychic abilities were recognized when they were children and then again as adults.

Kostman, Samuel Twentieth Century Women of Achievement   Richards Rosen Pr., 1976. (grade 7 and up)

Very fine absorbing portrayals are well balanced, anecdotal, straightforward accounts. Included are Mary Baker Eddy, founder of the Christian Science Church; Mary McLeod Bethune, educator; Margaret Sanger, birth control advocate; Pearl Buck, author; Marie Curie, Nobel Prize–winning scientist; Golda Meir, Israel's prime minister; Margaret Mead, anthropologist; Marian Anderson, singer; Gloria Steinem, feminist writer; and Billie Jean King, tennis player.

Krishef, Robert K. More New Breed Stars   Illus. with photographs. Lerner, 1980. (grade 4 and up)

Appealing to youngsters who like fan magazines, these profiles are well written and portray the country and pop singers as hard working, talented and ambitious performers. Included are Crystal Gayle, Anne Murray, Olivia Newton-John, and Linda Ronstadt.

———. The New Breed   Illus. with photographs. Lerner, 1978. (grade 5 and up).

Good, nonfictionalized profiles combine a picture of the world of country music with those who live and work within it. An introduction gives an overview of the recent changes in country music, and the individual biographies of Emmylou Harris, who blends country and hard rock, and Dolly Parton, one of the first country music singers to ever have a hit record, are interesting and well paced.

————, *and Lake, Bonnie* WESTERN STARS OF COUNTRY MUSIC Illus. with photographs. Lerner, 1978. (grade 5 and up)
This easy-to-read book will be especially appealing to youngsters who are interested in country and western music and performers, and may serve to encourage them to further reading. Included are Patsy Montana, the first of the women country stars to sell a million records, and Judy Lynn, successful country and western singer.

Kufrin, Joan UNCOMMON WOMEN Illus. with photographs. New Century, 1981 (grade 7 and up)
Clearly based on in-depth interviews, these very fine profiles present a fascinating picture of the artists' personal and professional lives. The women share the motivations and tasks which brought them to the peaks of their art fields. Included are poet Gwendolyn Brooks, conductor Sarah Caldwell, actress Julie Harris, novelist Mary McCarthy, painter Alice Neel, opera singer Roberta Peters, dancer Maria Tallchief, composer Mary Lou Williams, and musician Eugenia Zuckerman.

Laklan, Carli GOLDEN GIRLS: TRUE STORIES OF OLYMPIC WOMAN STARS Illus. McGraw-Hill, 1980. (grade 6 and up)
An outstanding book which flows smoothly. Instead of separate individual biographies, the author relates the women to each other and to their sport. All the golden girls were Olympic contenders or winners. Included are Babe Didrikson, all-around athlete; Donna De Varona, swimmer; Helen Wills, tennis player; Gertrude Ederle, swimmer; Sonja Henie, Tenley Albright, Carol Heiss, Peggy Fleming, Dorothy Hamill, and Sheila Young, skaters; Tatiana Averina, Soviet javelin and shotput champion; Wilma Rudolph and Wyomia Tyus, track stars; Dawn Fraser, Australian speed swimmer; Fanny Blankers-Koen, Dutch track star; Olga Korbut, Nadia Comaneci, and Cathy Rigby, gymnasts; and Jill Kinmont, skier.

Lamson, Peggy IN THE VANGUARD Houghton, 1979.(grade 9 and up)
Very fine, in-depth profiles of six women in public life review their earliest days, but focus on their current work and impact on American life. Included are Millicent Fenwick, New Jersey congresswoman; Juanita Kreps, secretary of commerce; Elizabeth Holtzman, New York congresswoman; Elaine Noble, former member of the Massachussetts House of Representatives; Eleanor Holmes Norton, chairperson of the Equal Employment Opportunity Commission; and Rose Bird, chief justice of the California Supreme Court.

Lavine, Sigmund FAMOUS MERCHANTS Illus. Dodd, 1965. (grade 7 and up)

Excellent profiles focus on the professional rather than on the personal lives of Elizabeth Arden, cosmetician and founder of a huge beauty business, and Margaret Fogharty Rudkin, founder of Pepperidge Farm bread. Interesting, fast-moving accounts comprehensively cover the women's achievements.

Lawrence, Andrew TENNIS: GREAT STARS, GREAT MOMENTS, Putnam, 1976. (grades 5–7)

Fast-moving profiles focus on specific events in tennis careers of Suzanne Lenglen, Helen Wills Moody, Billie Jean King, Chris Evert, and Evonne Goolagong and should serve as a spur to reading other biographies of these women and more about tennis in general.

Lawson, Don TEN FIGHTERS FOR PEACE: AN ANTHOLOGY Lothrop, 1971. (grade 7 and up)

A very fine anthology of articles written by those who have worked for peace includes an article by Jeanette Rankin—who has worked all her long life for peace and who was the first woman elected to the United States House of Representatives—and a selection from *Daybreak*, the autobiography of Joan Baez, folk singer and peace worker.

Lee, Essie E. WOMEN IN CONGRESS Illus. Messner, 1979. (grade 7 and up).

An excellent collection of profiles of women who served in Congress currently or in the recent past. The focus is on their work and preparation for their career. This book will have special meaning to any reader considering a career in public service. Included are Bella Abzug, New York; Lindy Hale Boggs, Louisianna; Yvonne Braithwaite Burke, California; Shirley Chisholm, New York; Cardiss Collins, Illinois; Millicent Fenwick, New Jersey; Marjorie Holt, Maryland; Margaret M. Heckler, Massachusetts; Elizabeth Holtzman, New York; Barbara Jordan, Texas; Martha Keys, Kansas; Marilyn Loyd, Tennessee; Helen Stevenson Meyner, New Jersey; Barbara A. Mikulski, Maryland; Patsy Mink, Hawaii; Mary Rose Oakar, Ohio; Shirley N. Pettis, California; Patricia S. Schroeder, Colorado; Virginia Smith, Nebraska; Gladys Noon Spellman, Maryland; and Leonor K. Sullivan, Missouri.

Lefkowitz, William FIGHT FOR FREEDOM: EXCITING STORIES OF REAL PEOPLE Xerox, 1976. (grades 3–5)

Easy-to-read, fictionalized biographies of Sybil Ludington, Deborah Sampson, and Phillis Wheatley, American Revolution figures, are based on facts, and although somewhat superficial, the book will encourage younger readers to read more about the subjects and early American history.

Lerner, Gerda THE WOMAN IN AMERICAN HISTORY Addison-Wesley, 1971. (grade 9 and up)

This unusually superb book for adults is an ambitious, objective survey of the roles and contributions of individual women and groups of women in the history of the United States. Some women are identified by a sentence or two; others are discussed in detail—therefore, the book cannot be considered true biography. The author, a noted scholar and historian, writes in a clear, readable, well-paced style and this book could be used as a text, as an introduction to further study, or as simply background information.

Levinger, Elma E. GREAT JEWISH WOMEN Behrman, 1940. (grades 3–7)

Extremely well-written profiles are short on facts, but provide very worthwhile views of biblical women and ten modern women. The essence of each woman is captured, and though not useful for reference purposes, these are thought-provoking accounts which will inspire young readers to delve further. Included are many biblical women as well as these women of more recent times: actress Elisa-Rachel Felix (known as Rachel); writer Grace Aguilar; philanthropists Judith Montefiore, Clara de Hirsch, Sophie Irene Loeb, and Lina Strauss; educator Rebecca Gratz; poets Penina Moise and Emma Lazarus; and heroine Sarah Chizick.

Levinson, Nancy CONTRIBUTIONS OF WOMEN: BUSINESS Illus. with photographs. Dillon, 1980. (grade 6 and up)

This very fine book skillfully combines information about each woman's early career, interests, and personal life as they contributed to her total personality and achievements. Included are Tillie Lewis, who founded a successful food-packing company; Mary G. Roebling, first woman president of a major bank in the United States; Jane Trahey, owner of a large advertising agency; Jane "Casey" Cousins, owners of a top real estate company; and Joan Ganz Cooney, television producer and creator of the Children's Television Workshop.

Levy, Elizabeth DOCTORS FOR THE PEOPLE Knopf, 1977. (grade 6 and up)

Profiles of Dorothy Brown, first black woman to practice surgery in the South, and Marcia Storch, New York gynecologist, are liberally laced with direct quotations and are anecdotal in style. Well-written and admiring but not adulatory, the book may inspire a reader toward a health career.

318

————. LAWYERS FOR THE PEOPLE: A NEW BREED OF DEFENDERS AND THEIR WORK Knopf, 1974. (grade 8 and up)

Though not a biography in the true sense, each of these profiles discusses a lawyer and her work, giving a good picture of the focus of her practice, her clients, and something about her own background. Informally written in a facile, lively, journalistic style, it is also a good introduction to the profession of law. Included among those attorneys who have worked for various causes are Linda Huber, a public defender who defends juveniles and has worked to establish children's rights in courts; Fay Stender, an expert on prison reform; Carol Libow, a member of an all-women law firm; and Eleanor Holmes Norton, a black civil liberties lawyer and New York City's commissioner of human rights.

————, and Miller, Mara POLITICIANS FOR THE PEOPLE Knopf, 1979. (grade 6 and up)

Profiles of Nancy Stevenson, lieutenant governor of South Carolina and Polly Baca-Barragan, a Mexican-American who is a state senator in Colorado, are written with a simple, natural conversational flow as they focus on the reasons why the women entered politics and how they juggle the various aspects of their lives.

Lieberman, Mark THE PACIFISTS: SOLDIERS WITHOUT GUNS Praeger, 1972. (grades 7–10)

In an excellent and thoughtful profile of Jane Addams, social worker and Nobel Peace Prize–winner, her life and social work activities are summarized, but the focus is on her pacifist beliefs and her efforts to avert war and to insure peace after World War I. The author also discusses the harsh treaty of World War I (which Jane Addams had opposed) as a factor contributing to the onset of World War II.

Lieser, Julia F. OUTSTANDING AMERICAN WOMEN Illus. Youth Publications/The Saturday Evening Post, 1977. (available from National Women's Hall of Fame, P.O. Box 335, Seneca Falls, N.Y. 13148) (grades 4–8)

Brief, lively profiles of twenty-two women provide colorful, and factual overviews of their lives. Included are Louisa May Alcott, author; Elizabeth Blackwell, physician; Ethel Barrymore, actress; Emily Dickinson, poet; Amelia Earhart, pilot; Mary Lyon, educator; Fannie Merritt Farmer, cooking expert and author; Margaret Fuller, feminist author; Lillian Gilbreth, engineer; Helen Keller, author and humanitarian; Elizabeth Cady Stanton, feminist and author; Belva Lockwood, attorney; Dolley Madison, first lady; Eleanor Roosevelt, first lady and humanitarian; Julia Ward Howe, author and feminist; Harriet Tubman, abolitionist and slave; Ellen Swallow Richards, chemist and educator; Lillian Russell, entertainer; Florence Sabin, physican; Harriet Beecher Stowe, abolitionist and author; C. J. Walker, business entrepreneur; and Babe Didrikson Zaharias, all-around athlete.

Litsky, Frank WINNERS IN GYMNASTICS Illus. with photographs. Watts, 1978. (grades 4–7)
    Lively, attractive profiles of Nadia Comaneci, Olga Korbut, Nelli Kim, and Cathy Rigby bring gymnastics to life.

————. WINNERS ON ICE Illus. with photographs. Watts, 1979. (grades K–3)
    Extremely easy-to-read, brief profiles of Dorothy Hamill, Peggy Fleming, Irina Rodina, and Sheila Young are enhanced with photographs. Ice-skating enthusiasts will find the book of special interest.

Lorimer, Lawrence, ed. BREAKING IN: NINE FIRST-PERSON ACCOUNTS ABOUT BECOMING AN ATHLETE Random, 1974. (grade 7 and up)
    One very well selected chapter is adapted and abridged from Althea Gibson's book *I Always Wanted to Be Somebody.* This excerpt tells of her beginning tennis career at fourteen. A brief but good introduction and afterword by the editor bring Gibson's own words into context and remind readers of her inspiration to women and blacks.

Lund, Candida MOMENTS TO REMEMBER Thomas More Pr., 1980. (grade 7 and up)
    Excellent collection has brief biographies followed by meaningful excerpts from each woman's own writings. Although each woman's remembrance can be read and enjoyed independently of her more substantial work, the reader should be inspired to further investigate the life of each. Included are actress Helen Hayes; columnist Ann Landers; nurse Edith Cavell; performer Frances Farmer; social reformer Jane Addams; writer Zelda Fitzgerald; suffragist Emmeline Pankhurst; first lady Dolley Madison; singer Marian Anderson; author Anne Morrow Lindbergh; writer Virginia Woolf; actress Ellen Terry; columnist Jory Graham; Queen Victoria; writer Harriet Beecher Stowe; social reformer Rosa Luxemburg; writer Sylvia Plath; educator Mary McLeod Bethune; playwright Lillian Hellman; social reformer Emma Goldman; columnist Erma Bombeck; actress Fanny Kemble; performer Beatrice Lillie; Saint Thérèse of Lisieux; actress Liv Ullman; writer Pearl Buck; writer Caitlan Thomas; humanitarian Eleanor Roosevelt; prime minister of Israel Golda Meir; writer Charlotte Brontë, writer Mary McCarthy; author Helen Keller; scientist Marie Curie; writer Louisa May Alcott; aviator Amelia Earhart;

writer George Sand; nurse Florence Nightingale, actress Sarah Siddons; consort of Henry VIII, Anne Boleyn; and writer and actress Cornelia Otis Skinner.

Lutzker, Edythe   WOMEN GAIN A PLACE IN MEDICINE   Illus. McGraw, 1969. (grade 8 and up)

An excellent, factual, and inspirational discussion of the first British women doctors, with a focus on the careers of pioneers Sophia Jex-Blake, Edith Pechey, Isabel Thorne, Matilda Chaplin, and Helen Evans. Elizabeth Blackwell and Elizabeth Garrett-Anderson, whose careers preceded the aforementioned, are also discussed, as well as the men and women who encouraged, discouraged, and strongly opposed them. The author has done her research well, and she combines the history of medical treatment for women with biography, doing both competently. Throughout the book, the discrimination women doctors faced is stressed, and the final chapter reminds readers that women still face discrimination in medicine as well as in other fields.

McKown, Robin   HEROIC NURSES   Illus. Putnam, 1966. (grades 5–9)

Unusually fine collection of profiles of nurses is not directed only to the career-minded reader. Well-documented, the book serves as a reference as well as a source of inspiration for any young reader. Included is a chapter on the earliest nurses followed by profiles of Jeanne Mance, a seventeenth-century French-Canadian nurse; Florence Nightingale, pioneer nurse; Mary Bickerdyke, Civil War nurse; Clara Barton, founder of the American Red Cross; Rose Hawthorne Lathrop, nurse for the incurably ill; Edith Cavell, nurse and spy; Mary Breckinridge, frontier nurse; Sister Elizabeth Kenny, polio nurse; and Princess Tsahai Haile Selassie.

McLenighan, Valjean   WOMEN AND SCIENCE   Illus. with photographs. Raintree, 1979. (grade 4 and up)

Easy-to-read, nonfictionalized profiles capture the essence of each woman's work and, at the same time, give a good picture of the surrounding culture. Especially good for youngsters whose reading level is not up to grade level. Included are Annie Jump Cannon, astronomer who identified and classified more stars than anyone else; Rachel Carson, marine biologist; Alice Hamilton, physician; Margaret Mead, anthropologist; Florence Sabin, research physician; and Chien Shiung Wu, Chinese-born nuclear physicist.

————.   WOMEN WHO DARED   Illus. with photographs. Raintree. 1979. (grade 4 and up)

Good, fast-moving profiles are easy to read and give more than a glimpse of the lives of Margaret Bourke-White, photojournalist; Mrs. E. J. Guerin, who lived as Mountain Charley and for thirteen years dressed as a man and led a life of adventure; Janet Guthrie, race car driver; Diana Nyad, swimmer; Kitty O'Neill, stunt performer; and Annie Smith Peck, the first woman to climb the Matterhorn. All of these women have risked their lives to prove obstacles can be overcome. Useful for slow readers.

McNeer, May ARMED WITH COURAGE Illus. Abingdon, 1957. (grades 4–9)
Handsome, extremely readable profiles of Florence Nightingale, pioneer in nursing, and Jane Addams, social reformer and winner of Nobel Peace Prize, stress their roles as crusaders. Partially fictionalized text is enhanced by Lynd Ward's outstanding illustrations. These biographies are as suitable for reading aloud as they are for older, independent readers.

————. GIVE ME FREEDOM Illus. Abingdon, 1964. (grades 4–9)
Simply written, beautifully told and illustrated biographies of black singer Marian Anderson and feminist Elizabeth Cady Stanton emphasize their courage and determination in the face of opposition. The illustrations by Lynd Ward add immeasurably to the semifictionalized text. Although directed to older elementary and junior high students, these biographies are also recommended for reading aloud to younger children.

McReynolds, Ginny WOMEN IN POWER Illus. with photographs. Raintree, 1979. (grade 4 and up)
A good book that gives young readers a sense of public service and the possibility of careers in government for women. Each woman is profiled in a straightforward manner and despite brevity, a true picture of the individual emerges. Included are Ella Grasso, who was governor of Connecticut; Elizabeth Holtzman, congresswomen from New York; Barbara Jordan, congresswoman from Texas, now an educator; Juanita Kreps, cabinet member; Golda Meir, prime minister of Israel; and Jeanette Rankin, first woman elected to Congress.

Madison, Arnold POLISH GREATS McKay, 1980. (grade 6 and up)
Satisfactory, thoughtful profiles of Queen Jadwiga, known as the Polish Joan of Arc; Helena Modjeska, actress; and Nobel Prize–winning scientist, Marie Curie.

Malvern, Gladys THE SIX WIVES OF HENRY VIII Illus. Vanguard, 1972. (grade 7 and up)
Extremely well-written, absorbing, balanced account of the lives of the women who married King Henry VIII of England. The queens—Catherine of Aragon, Anne Boleyn, Jane Seymour, Anne of Cleves, Catherine Howard, and Catherine Parr—emerge as distinct personalities. Although each profile can stand by itself, the book is best read as a continuing saga.

Other important people of the period are discussed and the society in which they lived is clearly explained so that readers with little or no knowledge of the history will find the book completely understandable.

Manchel, Frank TALKING CLOWNS: FROM LAUREL AND HARDY TO THE MARX BROTHERS Illus. with photographs. Watts, 1976. (grade 6 and up)
Well-balanced account of the world-famous performer Mae West is written with admiration but is nonadulatory.

Marks, Geoffrey, and Beatty, William K. WOMEN IN WHITE Illus. Scribner, 1972. (grade 9 and up)
Outstanding history of women in medicine thoroughly researches and documents their contribution since antiquity. The role of women in the science of midwifery is reviewed and the struggle to win a place in modern medicine is fully discussed with the focus on pioneer physicians Elizabeth Blackwell, Elizabeth Garrett-Anderson, Sophia Jex-Blake, Mary Putnam Jacobi, Emily Dunning Barringer, and Alice Hamilton. Women in related fields are considered too, and there are good portraits of Florence Nightingale, founder of the profession of nursing; Dorothea Lynde Dix, crusader for humane treatment of the mentally ill; Jane Addams, in whose settlement house preventive medicine was practiced; and Marie Curie, the discover of radium. A final chapter summarizes the outstanding work of contemporary women. Crisp, clear, readable text is geared to the serious high school reader.

May, Antoinette DIFFERENT DRUMMER: THEY DID WHAT THEY WANTED Les Femmes, 1976. (grade 7 and up)
Very fine, substantial profiles of women who, going against the mainstream, carved out meaningful careers. The women emerge as strong, single purpose individuals who defy all obstacles. Included are Victoria Woodhull, feminist; Amelia Earhart, pioneer aviator; Isadora Duncan, dancer; Helena Blavatsky, Russian mystic; Ernestine Schuman-Heink, Austrian-born opera singer; and Sarah Bernhardt, French actress.

Maynard, Olga AMERICAN MODERN DANCERS: THE PIONEERS Illus. Little, 1965. (grade 7 and up)
Good introduction to modern dance told through the biographies of Mary Wigman, Isadora Duncan, Ruth St. Denis, Martha Graham, Hanya Holm, and Tamaris. The emphasis on the professional lives of the women is sometimes technical but not difficult to understand, and is of particular interest to youngsters attracted to the art of dance.

Meade, Marion WOMEN IN SPORTS: TENNIS Illus. with photographs. Harvey House, 1975. (grade 5 and up)
Highly readable profiles of tennis stars Billie Jean King, Rosemary

Casals, Chris Evert, Evonne Goolagong, and Margaret Court give equal emphasis to their careers and their personal lives. Clearly feminist in perspective, the biographies will be of interest to older reluctant readers as well as to younger enthusiastic ones.

Melick, Arden Davis WIVES OF THE PRESIDENTS   Illus. Hammond, 1972. (grade 6 and up)

Attractive collection of profiles is a readable, thoughtful examination of the lives of the first ladies of the United States. Of historical as well as biographical interest, the book may serve best for reference, for it chronicles details of the lives of the women that are often omitted from such collections. At all times, the focus is on the woman, not on her husband. Pages are added to the book to include each new first lady.

Merriam, Eve GROWING UP FEMALE IN AMERICA   Illus. Doubleday, 1971. (grade 9 and up)

Really superb, feminist book includes a brief biographical sketch of ten women, followed by stories told in their own words taken from letters, diaries, or other writings. The editor has chosen her subjects well, and has constructed an interesting, moving picture of what it has been like for these and other similar women to grow up in America. Included are Eliza Southgate, an eighteenth-century New England schoolgirl; Elizabeth Cady Stanton, feminist; Maria Mitchell, astronomer; Mary Ann Webster Loughborough, wife of a Confederate officer; Arvazine Angeline Cooper, pioneer; Dr. Anna Howard Shaw, minister; Susie King Taylor, black Civil War nurse; Mary Harris "Mother" Jones, labor reformer and organizer; Elizabeth Gertrude Stern, social worker and writer; Mountain Wolf Woman, a Winnebago Indian.

————. INDEPENDENT VOICES.   Illus. Atheneum, 1968. (grades 4–6)

Outstanding biographies in verse of Elizabeth Blackwell, pioneer American physician; Ida Wells-Barnett, black journalist; and Lucretia Mott, feminist and abolitionist. Good for reading aloud, these are recommended by the author for school assemblies, and indeed they serve many purposes. The profiles capture the personalities and accomplishments of the women, without being too factual in approach.

Mersand, Joseph, ed. GREAT AMERICAN SHORT BIOGRAPHIES   Dell, 1966. (grade 7 and up)

Reprinted in this well-edited collection are profiles of poet Emily Dickinson, dancer-choreographer Agnes de Mille, and singer Marian Anderson. The profiles are reprinted from other sources. Louis Untermeyer's short biography of Emily Dickinson is an exquisitely written, perceptive picture, which discusses her life within the context of her work. The fast-moving, exciting profile of Agnes De Mille by Eleanor Clymer and Lillian Erlich gives an intimate view of the woman who contributed so much to the world of ballet and show business. Ruth Woodbury Sedwick's beautifully written profile of Marian Anderson first appeared in 1940 and, as stated in a brief afterword by the editor, represents her career up to that time; the reader is brought up to date by the editor but the profile is timeless because it so warmly captures the essence of the woman.

Meyer, Edith Patterson CHAMPIONS OF FOUR FREEDOMS Little, 1966. (grade 7 and up)

Clearly written, well-researched profiles of Julia Lathrop, a pioneer in establishing juvenile courts and who later became first chief of the United States Children's Bureau; and Eleanor Roosevelt, first lady, humanitarian, and United Nations delegate, are included among a series of biographies of people and institutions who worked to establish and continue freedom of speech and of religion and freedom from want and from fear. Appendixes containing President Roosevelt's 1941 speech which outlined the four freedoms and the preamble to the Charter of the United Nations add to the value of this fine book.

————. IN SEARCH OF PEACE: THE WINNERS OF THE NOBEL PEACE PRIZE 1901–1975 Illus. Abingdon, 1978. (grades 6–9)

A fine, well-written, researched book spans the history of the Nobel Peace Prize, its establishment, and the people and organizations who have been the recipients. The book not only reviews the life of the winners, it also gives a good picture of the times. Profiles of Bertha von Suttner, Austrian author who won the award in 1901, Emily Balch, economist and winner in 1946, and Jane Addams, social reformer who was the 1931 winner, are good, though not substantial in length or depth.

Nathan, Dorothy WOMEN OF COURAGE Random, 1964. (grade 6 and up)

Top-notch biographies of Susan B. Anthony, Mary McLeod Bethune, Amelia Earhart, and Margaret Mead move quickly and dramatically. Immensely readable, these lively biographies give full portraits of the subjects, allowing the reader to see the women as warm and accomplished individuals.

Neilson, Frances, and Neilson, Winthrop SEVEN WOMEN: GREAT PAINTERS Illus. Chilton, 1968. (grade 7 and up)

Splendid personal and critical profiles of seven women artists are distinguished by insights into their lives and work, with careful mention of the special problems they encountered because of their gender. Each profile is accompanied by several black-and-white and at least one color reproduction of the artist's work. The vivid portrayals of each painter are further enhanced by careful, well-organized documentation, and an appendix offers a partial but substantial listing of museums and galleries with representative works by the artists. The readable narration makes the book suitable for young readers, but it is of equal interest and use to adults. The seven painters included are Swiss-born Angelica Kauffman; Elizabeth Louise Vigee-Librun, Berthe Morisot, and Marie Laurencin of France; and Americans Cecilia Beaux, Mary Cassatt, and Georgia O'Keeffe.

Newlon, Clarke FAMOUS PUERTO RICANS Illus. with photographs. Dodd, 1975. (grade 7 and up)
A fine introduction to Puerto Rican history and culture is followed by profiles of varying lengths. Included in this collection are excellent biographies of Carmen Maymi, director of the Women's Bureau of the United States Department of Labor; Miriam Colón, actress-founder of the Puerto Rican National Theatre; Cóncha Meléndez, writer and critic; Lupe Anguiano, educator; and Vikki Carr, singer. The profiles focus equally on the women's careers and their Puerto Rican identity.

Nies, Judith SEVEN WOMEN: PORTRAITS FROM THE AMERICAN RADICAL TRADITION Viking, 1977. (grade 9 and up)
History and biography are combined to produce a very fine book that shows the women's rare vision to recognize needed social changes, and their courage to work towards their implementation. Very well-written substantial narrative moves smoothly and is suitable for serious readers. Included are Sarah Grimke, abolitionist; Harriet Tubman, abolitionist and slave; Elizabeth Cady Stanton, feminist; Mary Harris "Mother" Jones, labor leader; Charlotte Perkins Gilman, feminist author; Dorothy Day, journalist, founder of *The Catholic Worker*; and Anne Louise Strong, writer, specialist in social issues.

Noble, Iris CONTEMPORARY WOMEN SCIENTISTS OF AMERICA Illus. with photographs. Messner, 1979. (grade 7 and up)
Well-written, colorful profiles of eight women clearly demonstrate the early influences of parents, teachers, and others who believed in them, as well as their own feelings that they would achieve their goals. An introduction gives a good overview of earlier women pioneers in science. Included are anthropologist Margaret Mead; meteorologist Joanne Simpson; physiologist and endocrinologist Estelle Ramey; medical microbiologist Charlotte Friend; nuclear physicist Chien Shiung Wu; marine biologist Dixy Lee Ray; crystallographer Isabelle Karle; geneticist Elizabeth Shull Rus-

sell; and electrical engineer Mildred Dresselhaus. An especially fine book for readers who enjoy science.

NOTABLE AMERICAN WOMEN, 1607–1950: A BIOGRAPHICAL DICTIONARY Belknap/Harvard, 1971. (grade 9 and up)
Superb encyclopaedia-length profiles of over a thousand women are good for browsing as well as serious research. This three-volume collection is an important edition to libraries.

NOTABLE AMERICAN WOMEN, THE MODERN PERIOD: A BIOGRAPHICAL DICTIONARY. Belknap/Harvard, 1980. (grade 9 and up)
Matching the earlier volumes in quality, this one-volume book contains biographical essays of more than four hundred American women, all of whom died between 1951 and 1975. Belongs in all libraries.

Olivar, Carl PLANE TALK: AVIATORS AND ASTRONAUTS OWN STORIES Illus. with photographs. Houghton, 1980. (grade 6 and up)
A lively history of aviation in the United States is followed by first-person narratives. Included here are excerpts from Amelia Earhart's discussion of her two Atlantic crossings in *The Fun of It*, written in 1932, and Jacqueline Cochran's description of setting flying records in *The Stars at Noon*, written in 1954.

O'Neill, Lois Decker, ed. THE WOMAN'S BOOK OF WORLD RECORDS AND ACHIEVEMENTS Doubleday, 1979. (grade 7 and up)
A superb encyclopaedia-like collection for reference or delightful browsing. Included are over five thousand women who have achieved recognition in the late nineteenth or twentieth century.

Osen, Lynn M. WOMEN IN MATHEMATICS MIT Pr., 1974. (grade 7 and up)
Straightforward biographies lack spark but give a good picture of each woman's contribution to math, and it should be of special interest to readers interested in mathematics. Included are Hypatia, Emile de Breteuil, Marquise du Châtelet, Caroline Herschel, Sophie Germain, and Mary Fairfax Somerville.

Peavy, Linda, and Smith, Ursula WOMEN WHO CHANGED THINGS Scribner, 1983. (grade 7 and up)
Very fine volume includes serious, well-documented substantial biographies of nine American women whose lives spanned the years from 1880 to 1930. The straightforward, highly readable studies portray each woman within the context of her time, indicating too the constraints of the year in which they lived. Competent junior high school readers and high school and adult readers will find the book of great interest. Included are Sara

Josephine Baker, physician who was a New York public health administrator and a pioneer in child health advocacy; Kate Barnard, Oklahoma social and political reformer; Williamina Fleming, astronomer; Orie Latham Hatcher, pioneer in vocational guidance; Leta Stetter Hollingworth, educational psychologist and author of important studies on the gifted; Mary McDowell, settlement house director and social reformer; Annie Smith Peck, mountain climber; Candace Thurber Wheeler, pioneer in American textile design and interior decoration; and Ida Wells-Barnett, journalist and reformer.

Perl, Teri MATH EQUALS Addison, 1978. (grade 7 and up)
A very attractive volume includes biographies of mathematicians Hypatia, Emilie du Châtelet, Maria Gaetena Agnesia, Sophie Germain, Mary Fairfax Somerville, Ada Byron Lovelace, Sonya Kovalevskaya, Grace Chisholm Young, and Emmy Noether. Related mathematical activities are also included. The biographies are lively, and the book will be of interest not only to mathematics buffs but to general readers. Most of the women struggled to become educated and to become mathematicians; their determination is clearly demonstrated.

Peters, Margaret THE EBONY BOOK OF BLACK ACHIEVEMENT Illus. Johnson, 1970; revised ed., 1976. (grade 6 and up)
Good, brief, factual but informal profiles of journalist Ida Wells-Barnett and educator Mary McLeod Bethune. Although no attempt is made to capture their personalities or to give an intimate view of their lives, the book serves well for reference purposes. The revised edition also includes poet Phillis Wheatley.

Petry, Ann LEGENDS OF THE SAINTS Illus. Crowell, 1970. (grades 1–4)
Outstanding book includes beautiful color illustrations by Anne Rockwell and contains the stories of Saint Catherine of Alexandria and Joan of Arc. The literary style is exceptionally fine, and is touching and dignified without being morbid or overly sentimental.

Phillips, Julien STARS OF THE ZIEGFELD FOLLIES Illus. Lerner, 1972. (grade 9 and up)
Exceedingly superficial, easy-to-read profiles of Fanny Brice, Marilyn Miller, and Anna Held are written in fan-magazine style and are directed towards reluctant or less able readers. Although the book may capture the interest of such readers, the lack of depth and warmth means the profiles offer little of value in inspiration or information

Pizer, Vernon GLORIOUS TRIUMPHS: ATHLETES WHO CONQUERED ADVERSITY Illus. with photographs. Dodd, 1980. (grade 7 and up)

Excellent book focuses only on the women's athletic careers, and the difficulties they faced in achieving triumphant careers. Included are Babe Didrikson, all-around athlete; Althea Gibson, tennis player; and Tenley Albright and Carol Heiss, ice skaters.

————. SHORTCHANGED BY HISTORY: AMERICA'S NEGLECTED INNOVATORS Illus. Putnam, 1979. (grades 6–8)
Very fine profile of Sara Josephine Baker, physician and director of the Bureau of Child Hygiene in New York serves well as an inspiration to all young readers to learn more about other important but not always well-known achievers, and to consider a career option.

Polsky, Milton TODAY'S YOUNG STARS OF STAGE AND SCREEN Illus. with photographs. Watts, 1979. (grades 5–8)
Very easy-to-read, lively profiles are somewhat adulatory but will appeal to fan magazine enthusiasts. Included are actresses Danielle Brisebois, Quinn Cummings, Melissa Gilbert, Andrea McArdle, Brooke Shields, and Danielle Spencer.

Poole, Lynn, and Poole, Gray SCIENTISTS WHO WORK OUTDOORS Illus. Dodd, 1963. (grade 8 and up)
Very fine biographies focus on the professional careers of marine biologist Dixy Lee Ray and anthropologists Margaret Mead and Betty Jane Meggers, discussing their education and early training as well as some of their accomplishments. Highly readable, these biographies are of particular value to those wishing to know more about the professions of the subjects.

Ranahan, Demerris CONTRIBUTIONS OF WOMEN: MEDICINE Illus. with photographs. Dillon, 1981. (grade 6 and up)
Excellent, absorbing collective book contains profiles of a well-balanced selection of women physicians. Each woman is shown to be a multi-dimensional individual. Substantial profiles of Helen Taussig, pediatric cardiologist; Virginia Apgar, who devised an evaluatory scale for newborn babies; Savitri Ramcharan, Indian-American researcher; Adele Hofman, adolescence physician; and Olga Jonasson, transplant surgeon. Very brief profiles of Elizabeth Blackwell, first American physician; Anna Fisher, emergency medicine specialist; Alice Hamilton, industrial physician; Karen Horney, psychiatrist; Mary Putnam Jacobi, feminist and physician; Susan La Flesche Picotte, Native American physician; Jane C. Wright, oncologist; and Marie Zakrzewska, pioneer physician. A book which should appeal to general readers as well as those with a special interest in medicine.

Raskin, Joseph, and Raskin, Edith Spies and Traitors Lothrop, 1976. (grades 3–7)

Included in this collection of lively, fictionalized accounts are Lydia Darragh, Quaker who spied on the British for the American patriots; and Belle Boyd and Elizabeth Van Lew, Civil War spies. Very easy to read, and somewhat superficial, the book has appeal for younger or less competent readers.

Raven, Susan, and Weir, Alison Women of Achievement Illus. with photographs. Harmony, 1981. (grade 7 and up)

Excellent, very brief profiles of 476 outstanding women, organized by category, make this a useful book for reference or for casual browsing. An important acquisition for libraries.

Reeder, Red Bold Leaders of the Revolutionary War Little, 1973. (grades 7–10)

Short biographies of Margaret Corbin, a woman who filled her husband's place in battle when he was killed, and Deborah Gannett Sampson, who, disguised as a man, enlisted and fought in the Revolutionary War, are well researched and documented and provide absorbing and lively reading. The emphasis is on their role in the Revolutionary War, but other material about their lives is also included.

Reidman, Sarah R. Men and Women behind the Atom Abelard-Schuman, 1958. (grade 7 and up)

Very good though rather technical biographies of Marie Curie, Nobel Prize–winning scientist; her daughter Irene Joliot-Curie, also a Nobel Prize–winning scientist; and information on Lise Meitner, a pioneer in work on the splitting of the atom. The book provides good background information for further study and for reading of individual biographies by the science student or enthusiast.

Rice, Tamara Talbot Czars and Czarinas of Russia Illus. Lothrop, 1968. (grade 7 and up)

Good profiles are straightforward, interesting narratives of Elizabeth Petrovna and Catherine the Great. Provides useful background for further reading or studying, and captures the personalities of the women.

Richardson, Ben Great American Negroes Illus. Crowell, 1956. (grade 7 and up)

Very fine, warm, and informative biographies trace the entire lives of singer Marian Anderson, educator Mary McLeod Bethune, dancer and anthropologist Katherine Dunham, and author Ann Petry.

————, *and Fashey, William A.* Great Black Americans Illus. with photographs. Rev. ed. Crowell, 1976. (grade 7 and up)

The revised edition of the above 1956 book includes a profile of author Ann Petry; Althea Gibson, tennis champion; Marian Anderson, singer; Katherine Dunham, anthropologist, choreographer, and dancer; and Mary McLeod Bethune, educator. As in the earlier edition, which included all of the preceding except Althea Gibson, the biographies are fine, warm and informative and trace the entire lives of the subjects.

Rittenhouse, Mignon SEVEN WOMEN EXPLORERS Lippincott, 1964. (grades 7–9)
Clearly written, factual biographies of seven women who had an urge to learn of new lands and who were willing to travel hazardous roads. The seven women, some of whom were single and others who were married to explorers, all made individual contributions to knowledge and these profiles give good, unemotional accounts of this and also discuss some aspects of their private lives. The women are Alexine Tinnè, Florence von Sass Baker, and Delia J. Denning Akeley, explorers of Africa; Fanny Bullock Workman, explorer of the Himalayas in India; Kathleen M. Kenyon, who worked in the Near East; Louise Arner Boyd, an Arctic explorer; and Isabella Lucy Bird Bishop, who explored Asia.

Rollins, Charlamae FAMOUS AMERICAN NEGRO POETS Illus. Dodd, 1965. (grades 6–9)
Especially good, brief, readable, and dramatic profiles of poets Frances Harper, Effie Lee Newsome, Margaret Walker, Phillis Wheatley, and Gwendolyn Brooks. The author skillfully has interwoven examples of their poetry into the biographies, which are suitable for reference and background material as well as for casual reading.

————. THEY SHOWED THE WAY: FORTY AMERICAN NEGRO LEADERS Crowell, 1964. (grade 4 and up)
Brief but very fine biographies of Ida Wells-Barnett, reformer and journalist; Mary McLeod Bethune, educator; Frances Ellen Watkins Harper, abolitionist and poet; Edmonia Lewis, sculptor; Harriet Tubman, abolitionist; Phillis Wheatley, poet; and Maggie Lena Walker, banker. Also included is a profile of Deborah Gannet (also known as Deborah Gannet Sampson) which lacks proper documentation. (According to most authoritative sources, Sampson is descended from Governor William Bradford, Miles Standish, and John Alden and there is no indication that she was not white.)

Rosenblum, Morris HEROES OF ISRAEL Illus. Fleet, 1972. (grades 7–10)
Very well-written narratives, despite their brevity, are broad in scope as they trace the lives of Israeli heroines Hannah Senesh and former Prime

Minister Golda Meir. The emphasis is on their contributions to Israel, and their stories are told with dignity and drama.

Ross, Nancy   HEROINES OF THE EARLY WEST   Random, 1960. (grades 7–11)

Remarkably good book deals with many underlying feminist issues. Profiles of Abigail Scott Duniway, feminist and pioneer of the West; Sacajawea, interpreter to Lewis and Clark; Narcissa Whitman, missionary; Mary Richardson Walker and Sister Mary Loyola, missionaries, are vivid, exciting, and dramatic. An introductory chapter discusses pioneer women in general, illuminating the impact they had on the recorded history of this nation.

Ross, Pat, comp.   YOUNG AND FEMALE: TURNING POINTS IN THE LIVES OF EIGHT AMERICAN WOMEN   Random, 1972. (grade 7 and up)

Well-chosen selections from the autobiographies of eight American women are compiled in this brief collection. The editor has chosen women whose backgrounds and areas of achievement vary, but she has neatly coordinated the material to show that each woman, at some point in her youth, made a decision that helped her find direction. An excellent feminist foreword discusses the pressure to conform to stereotypic sex roles that faced these young women, and the determination and intelligence which enabled them to become successful, well-rounded human beings. Each selection is introduced with a brief overview of the subject's life, emphasizing her spirit and uniqueness. Included are actress, feminist, and political worker Shirley MacLaine; black congresswoman Shirley Chisholm; feminist, reformer, and journalist Dorothy Day; engineer and author Emily Hahn; birth control advocate Margaret Sanger; black tennis champion Althea Gibson; reporter and author Edna Ferber; and photojournalist Margaret Bourke-White.

Rubinstein, Charlotte Streifer   AMERICAN WOMEN ARTISTS FROM EARLY INDIAN TIMES TO THE PRESENT   Illus. Avon, 1982. (grade 9 and up)

A thoroughly researched and documented volume combines art history and biography, resulting in a highly readable, informative book that acknowledges the quality and quantity of art produced by American women. Useful for reference, but equally suitable for casual reading.

Ryan, Joan   CONTRIBUTIONS OF WOMEN: SPORTS   Illus. Dillon, 1975. (grade 6 and up)

Very fine, lively profiles of all-around athlete Babe Didrikson Zaharias, Olympic equestrienne and jockey Kathy Kusner, track athlete Wilma Rudolph, tennis player Billie Jean King, ice skater Peggy Fleming, and swimmer Melissa Belote are told from a feminist perspective, showing the women's unique contributions to sports and focusing on the increasing recognition given to women in sports. Each chapter highlights the woman's athletic career, but attention is also given to her personal life.

Sabin, Francene WOMEN WHO WIN   Illus. with photographs. Random, 1975. (grades 5–8)

A very fine feminist introduction discusses the obstacles that have stood in the way of women entering and rising to the top of the sports world. The informal, narrative profiles themselves are also written from a feminist perspective, giving well-balanced accounts of the personal and professional life of each woman. The author explains many important points about each sport, enhancing the profiles, but also making them more comprehensible to those who are not sports-oriented. Included are tennis champion Billie Jean King; figure skater Janet Lynn; Olympic track star Cheryl Toussaint; swimmers Jenny Bartz, Lynn Genesko, Nina MacInnis, and Sharon Berg; bowler Paula Sperber; gymnast Cathy Rigby; skiers Marilyn, Barbara, and Lindy Cochran; diver Micki King; and golfer Kathy Whitworth.

Sabin, Louis   100 GREAT MOMENTS IN SPORTS   Putnam, 1978. (grade 5 and up)

Arranged alphabetically, each brief vignette, written in good journalistic style, describes a memorable event in the careers of sports stars, but gives a good overview of the stars' lives. This book will be of special interest to youthful sports fans. Included are tennis players Tracy Austin, Chris Evert, Althea Gibson, and Billie Jean King; basketball player Carol Blazejowski; skier Barbara Cochran; gymnasts Nadia Comaneci and Cathy Rigby; skaters Dorothy Hamill and Janet Lynn; swimmer Gertrude Ederle; diver Micki King; horseback rider Kathy Kusner; bowler Paula Sperber; Olympic runner Cheryl Toussaint; golfer Kathy Whitworth; and all-around athlete Babe Didrikson.

Schacher, Susan, ed.   HYPATIA'S SISTERS: BIOGRAPHIES OF WOMEN SCIENTISTS, PAST AND PRESENT   Illus. Feminist Northwest, 1976. (grade 7 and up)

Brief but very good profiles of seventeen women will be inspiring to young junior high, high school, and college women and of interest to all readers. Additional readings are listed following each profile, adding substance to this little volume. Included are Agnodice and Aspasia, physicians; Hypatia, mathematician; Trotula, eleventh-century physician; Hildegard of Bingen, healer; Jacoba Felicie, thirteenth-century physician; Emilie du Châtelet, mathematician; Mary Somerville, physicist; Maria Mitchell, astronomer; Florence Nightingale, nurse; Ellen Swallow, chemist; Beatrix Potter, botanist, author; Marie Curie, physicist; Margaret Sanger, birth control advocate; Rachel Carson, ecologist; Chien Shiung Wu, physicist; and Jane Goodall, animal behaviorist.

Schwartz, Bert GREAT BLACK ATHLETES Pendulum Pr., 1971. (grade 8 and up)

Outstanding profile of Althea Gibson focuses on her tennis career from its beginnings until her championships at Wimbledon and Forest Hills in 1957. There is little discussion of her personal life: the emphasis is on her tennis game and on her status as the first black tennis player to compete at Forest Hills.

Sheafer, Silvia WOMEN OF THE WEST Illus. with photographs. Addison-Wesley, 1980. (grade 7 and up)

A good picture of the West emerges in this fine book which incorporates profiles of some unknown and some famous women. Each woman emerges as an individual in these lively accounts. Included are Lotta Crabtree, actress; Charlie Parkhurst, stagecoach driver, a woman in man's disguise; Elanor Dumont, who ran a gambling parlor; Lola Montez, actress; Emma Wixon, opera singer; Cassie Hill, one of the first women telegraphers; and Donaldina Cameron, superintendant of the Presbyterian Mission in San Francisco, who rescued hundreds of Chinese women from slavery.

Smaridge, Norah FAMOUS AUTHOR-ILLUSTRATORS FOR YOUNG PEOPLE Dodd, 1973. (grade 7 and up)

Informative short biographies of author-illustrators Kate Greenaway, Beatrix Potter, Wanda Gág, Lois Lenski, Marie Hall Ets, Marcia Brown, and Joan Walsh Anglund are extremely well written and interesting. Nonanecdotal, straightforward narratives discuss the achievements, literary and artistic style, and personal lives of each subject. Valuable to adults interested in children's literature as well as to young readers.

————. FAMOUS BRITISH WOMEN NOVELISTS Illus. Dodd, 1967. (grades 7–10)

Short, interesting, and sometimes anecdotal profiles of British novelists Jane Austen; Anne, Charlotte, and Emily Brontë; Fanny Burney; Agatha Christie; George Eliot; Rumer Godden; Sheila Kaye-Smith; Victoria Sackville-West; Dorothy Sayers; Mary Stewart; Mary Webb; and Virginia Woolf provide good background for further study or the reading of their works.

————. FAMOUS LITERARY TEAMS FOR YOUNG PEOPLE Illus. with photographs. Dodd, 1977. (grade 7 and up)

Profiles of a number of literary teams who write for young people are polished studies laced with anecdotes as well as facts. Included are Ingri and Edgar D'Aulaire, Berta and Elmer Hader, Mary and Conrad Buff, Maud and Miska Petersham, Dorothy and Marguerite Bryan, Carroll Lane and Mildred Adams Fenton, Lynd Ward and May McNeer, Adrienne Adams and Lonzo Anderson, Taio and Mitsu Yashima, Adele and Cateau DeLieuw, Erik and Lenore Blegvad, Ed and Barbara Emberley, Tom and Muriel Feelings, and Wende and Harry Devlin.

———. FAMOUS MODERN STORYTELLERS FOR YOUNG PEOPLE Illus. Dodd, 1969. (grades 7–9)
Excellent profiles of Laura Wilder, Eleanor Farjeon, Mary Norton, Claire Huchet Bishop, Elizabeth Enright, Marguerite De Angeli, Carol Ryrie Brink, Elizabeth Coatsworth, Rumer Godden, P. L. Travers, Astrid Lindgren, and Marguerite Henry offer good insights into the personalities of these writers who are familiar to young readers. The style is lively and readable, without resorting to fictionalization.

Smith, Betsy Covington BREAKTHROUGH: WOMEN IN RELIGION Illus. with photographs. Walker, 1978. (grade 6 and up)
A good introduction discusses some of the barriers that women have faced in assuming leadership roles in religion, preceding the biographies of Jeanette Picard and Daphne Hawkes, Episcopalian priests; Sandy Sasso, Conservative Jewish Rabbi; Patricia Green, African Methodist Episcopal Zion minister; and Sister Jogues Egan, reformer, pacifist. Each woman emerges in this very fine collective as an outstanding example of an individual determined to achieve her goals.

———. BREAKTHROUGH: WOMEN IN TELEVISION Illus. with photographs. Walker, 1981. (grade 6 and up)
An excellent collection of profiles of women who have varied and interesting careers in television. The obstacles they encountered and overcame are all made clear. Included are Renée Poussaint, anchorwoman; Ann ("Andy") Austin, sketch artist; Pamela Hill, executive producer and vice president of ABC; Carmen Culver, writer; Betty Rollins, national news correspondent and writer; Risa Korris, camera operator; Judy Wormington, promotion manager; and Chloe Aaron, producer.

Smith, Elizabeth Simpson BREAKTHROUGH: WOMEN IN AVIATION Illus. with photographs. Walker, 1981. (grade 6 and up)
Brisk, interesting profiles of contemporary women whose careers span many years in aviation. Included here are Tina Marie Skrzypiec, boom operator; Jill Elaine Brown, cargo pilot; Linda Elaine Barber, aviation inspector; Sandra Williams Case, corporation pilot; Joyce Carpenter

Myers, aeronautical engineer; Ann Orlitzki Smethurst, Captain, USAF; Margaret Rhea Seddon, astronaut; and Judy Ann Lee, flight engineer.

————. BREAKTHROUGH: WOMEN IN LAW ENFORCEMENT Illus. with photographs. Walker, 1982. (grade 6 and up)

An excellent collective biography which explores both the personal and professional life of women in a variety of law enforcement agencies. There are substantial profiles of Donna Marie Perice, undercover agent; Jean Garmen Spiecher, Florida marine patrol; Priscilla Pepper Karansky, mounted police; Elizabeth Aytes Kandler, corrections superintendent; and shorter profiles of five other women—border patrol agent, jailer, airport security agent, police detective, and state director of prisons. Two excellent appendixes on criminal justice educational opportunities and jobs within the criminal justice system make this a fine book for those interested in pursuing a career in law enforcement.

General readers who are interested in biographies of women who have made careers in this nontraditional field will also find this book worthwhile.

Smith, Margaret Chase, and Jeffers, Paul H. GALLANT WOMEN McGraw-Hill, 1968. (grades 4–8)

Senator Margaret Chase Smith has written fine introductions to short, partially fictionalized biographies of ten courageous and determined American women who overcame obstacles to reach a goal. The collection includes a good cross-section of American women, and each biography offers insights into why the subject has chosen her particular route to self-fulfillment and achievement, clearly outlining her contributions to society. Despite the informality and simplicity of style, the biographies focus on important aspects of the women's lives and reflect sound research. The biography of Dolley Madison places too much emphasis on her role as an adjunct though it clearly reports her heroism in saving important documents; but the other biographies are extremely well-balanced treatments. They include colonial religious leader Anne Hutchinson; black abolitionist Harriet Tubman; author Harriet Beecher Stowe; founder of the American Red Cross, Clara Barton; pioneer physician Elizabeth Blackwell; feminist Susan B. Anthony; teacher of Helen Keller, Annie Sullivan (Macy); aviator Amelia Earhart; black tennis champion Althea Gibson; cabinet member Francis Perkins; humanitarian, first lady, and United Nations delegate, Eleanor Roosevelt.

Squire, C. B. HEROES OF CONSERVATION Illus. Fleet, 1974. (grades 7–10)

Outstanding, short, but reasonably thorough summary of the adult and professional life of Rachel Carson clearly shows her sense of responsibility, her foresight, and the criticism to which she was subjected. Woven into the narrative are quotations from her writings which may act as a spur to reading her own works.

Squire, Elizabeth D. Heroes of Journalism   Fleet, 1974. (grades 7–10)
Straightforward narrative focusses on the journalistic career of pioneer newspaper reporter Nellie Bly and photojournalist Margaret Bourke-White. Although fairly brief, the profiles are somewhat comprehensive and the crisp, clear, nonfictionalized text introduces subjects vigorously and succinctly.

Stambler, Irwin   Women in Sports   Illus. with photographs. Double-day, 1975. (grade 7 and up)
A very fine introduction discusses the role of women in sports. With a strongly feminist focus, it points out that women have not had equal opportunities but are now approaching more equity in both status and money. Substantial profiles emphasize the athletic careers but also give unvarnished, objective views of the personal lives of twelve women in different sports. These colorful and elucidating accounts should appeal even to those who are not especially knowledgeable or enthusiastic about sports. Included are profiles of "Babe" Didrikson Zaharias, all-around athlete; Cathy Rigby, gymnast; Billie Jean King, tennis champion; Anne Henning, speed skater; Robyn Smith, jockey; Mary Decker and Wyomia Tyus Simburg, track champions; Shirley Muldowney, drag racer; Barbara Ann Cochran, skier; Micki King, diver; and Theresa Shank, basketball player.

Sterling, Dorothy   Black Foremothers   Feminist Pr., McGraw-Hill, 1979. (grade 9 and up)
Absorbing, fine portrayals of Ellen Craft, fugitive slave and abolitionist; Ida B. Wells, journalist and reformer; and Mary Church Terrell, feminist and educator are almost full-length individual biographies of each woman. Well documented, they show evidence of scholarly research, but can be read with facility by young competent readers.

———, *and Quarles, Benjamin*   Lift Every Voice   Doubleday, 1965. (grades 5–9)
Very fine profile of Mary Church Terrell, black educator, is a substantial, straightforward account. Informal in style, it nevertheless recreates in detail the accomplishments of Terrell, who was the first black woman to serve on a school board in the United States.

Sterling, Philip, and Logan, Rayford   Four Took Freedom   Double-day, 1967. (grades 7–10)

Harriet Tubman is one of the four blacks profiled in this excellent collective volume. This accurate and thoughtful portrayal of the remarkable abolitionist who escaped from slavery and helped others to do likewise is movingly told.

Sterne, Emma Gelders   I HAVE A DREAM   Illus. Knopf, 1965. (grade 5 and up)
Skillfully written account of the black struggle in America includes brief portraits of Daisy Bates, leader in school integration; Marian Anderson, singer and civil rights worker; and Rosa Parks, who led the way to the end of bus segregation. Very readable, the information imparted is considerable and suggested readings contribute to the value of the book.

————.   THEY TOOK THEIR STAND   Illus. Macmillan, 1968. (grades 7–12)
Informative account of the abolition and civil rights movements as told through the lives of southern white people includes sensitive, appealing portraits of Sophia Auld, first teacher of slave and abolitionist Frederick Douglas; Angelina Grimké, abolitionist and feminist; and Anne Braden, daughter of a contemporary segregationist family who became active as a civil rights worker. History and biography are interwoven to provide an immensely readable and thoughtful book.

Stevenson, Janet   WOMEN'S RIGHTS   Illus. Watts, 1972. (grade 5 and up)
Included in this superb feminist history of women's rights are brief profiles and photographs of Lucretia Mott, Elizabeth Cady Stanton, Lucy Stone, Susan B. Anthony, and Anna Howard Shaw, all early feminists, as well as Stanton's daughter Harriet Stanton Blatch and Carrie Chapman Catt, latter-day suffragists. Discussed also, but in less detail, are Angelina and Sarah Grimké, abolitionists and feminists, and Alice Paul, feminist and suffragist. A graphically attractive and immensely readable volume, this book provides a colorful and elucidating account of the important events and themes in the struggle for women's rights. Suitable for browsing, reading, or reference, this volume is a fine accompaniment to other more detailed biographies.

Stirling, Nora   WHO WROTE THE CLASSICS?   vol. 1. Day, 1965. (grade 8 and up)
Very fine profiles of Jane Austen and the Brontës are included here. The chapter on the Brontës treats them as individuals and is perceptive and interesting; the one on Jane Austen give a personal as well as critical view of her work. These nonfictional narratives are warm and appealing.

————. WHO WROTE THE CLASSICS? vol. 2. Day, 1969. (grade 8 and up)
An excellent profile of Edith Wharton is brief but animated, and describes the effects of the author's personality on her writing.

————. WHO WROTE THE MODERN CLASSICS? Illus. Day, 1970. (grade 9 and up)
Beautifully written, informative biography of Willa Cather is substantial in length and depth. Her life, personality, and works are discussed, and this book provides good background for the reading of Cather's works.

Stoddard, Hope FAMOUS AMERICAN WOMEN Illus. Crowell, 1970. (grade 7 and up)
These superb collective biographies of modern women who have been successful in their endeavors are extremely valuable. Accurate and informative, the biographies offer engrossing, intimate views of each woman and provide considerable information about their personal lives and achievements. The author highlights experiences of childhood, youth, and adulthood to show the complete personalities and characters of each subject. Informal and extremely readable, the biographies provide good reading as well as useful reference material. Included are social reformers Jane Addams, Dorothea Dix, Margaret Sanger; photographer Dorothea Lange; dancers Agnes De Mille, Isadora Duncan, Martha Graham; philosopher Susanne Langer; singers Rosa Ponselle, Marian Anderson; authors Louisa May Alcott, Willa Cather, Gertrude Stein, Harriet Beecher Stowe, Edith Hamilton; feminists Susan B. Anthony, Margaret Fuller, Lucretia Mott; actress Ethel Barrymore; artist Mary Cassatt; educators Mary McLeod Bethune, Mary Lyon; aviator Amelia Earhart; humanitarian and first lady Eleanor Roosevelt; poets Emily Dickinson, Edna St. Vincent Millay, Harriet Monroe; cabinet member Oveta Culp Hobby; sculptor Malvina Hoffman; anthropologist Margaret Mead; astronomer Maria Mitchell; jurist Constance Baker Motley; scientist Florence Sabin; senator Margaret Chase Smith; abolitionist and slave Harriet Tubman; athlete "Babe" Didrikson Zaharias; industrial engineer Lillian Gilbreth; founder of Christian Science church, Mary Baker Eddy; religious leader Sister Frances Xavier Cabrini; and handicapped humanitarian Helen Keller.

Sullivan, George MODERN OLYMPIC SUPERSTARS Illus. Dodd, 1979. (grades 3–6)
Easy-to-read biographies are intelligently written, capture the personalities of the individuals, and give good overviews of their sports and the great effort and preparation needed to become a champion. Included are Sheila Young, Olympic gold medal winner for speed skating; Nelli Kim, Russian gymnast; and Kornelia Ender, swimmer.

————. QUEENS OF THE COURT   Illus. with photographs. Dodd, 1974. (grades 5–9)

Substantial, lively portraits of tennis champions Margaret Court, Billie Jean King, Chris Evert, Evonne Goolagong, Rosemary Casals, and Virginia Wade focus on their professional lives. The author also incorporates explanations of the game which will aid those who do not know much about tennis to enjoy the profiles more, but will not bore those who are already knowledgeable about tennis. An introduction discusses some of the advances and changes made in women's tennis today, and a concluding chapter discusses some of the outstanding women of the past. A glossary of tennis terms and many good action photographs further enhance the text.

————. SUPERSTARS OF WOMEN'S TRACK   Dodd, 1981. (grades 3–6)

Easy-to-read, lively profiles will be enjoyed by older, less competent readers who enjoy watching or participating in track. Included are Mary Decker, Grete Waitz, Evelyn Ashford, Madeline Manning, Julie Shea, and Candy Young.

Surge, Frank   FAMOUS SPIES   Illus. Lerner, 1969. (grades 4–6)

Mediocre, sketchy views of spies Delilah, Mata Hari, Belle Boyd, Emma Edmonds, Rose O'Neal Greenhow, and Elizabeth Van Lew are somewhat enlivened by good photographs. In an obvious attempt to entice reluctant readers, the author treats a subject with wide appeal oversimplistically and not too sucessfully.

————. SINGERS OF THE BLUES   Illus. Lerner, 1969. (grades 4–6)

Despite some literary flaws, these are fairly good profiles of Billie Holiday and Bessie Smith. A profile of Ma Rainey is too brief to be of much value.

Terkel, Studs   GIANTS OF JAZZ   Illus. Crowell, 1957; revised, 1975. (grade 7 and up)

Warm, informal profiles of Bessie Smith and Billie Holiday are brief, but cover the important events of their professional lives in a lively, dramatic style.

Tharp, Edgar   GIANTS OF SPACE   Illus. Grosset, 1970. (grades 5–9)

Accurate, brief profile of the Russian cosmonaut Valentina Tereshkova gives equal emphasis to her personal life as well as to her contributions to space exploration. Somewhat superficial, it is nevertheless a good introduction to her accomplishments.

Thomas, Arthur E.   LIKE IT IS,   ed., Emily Roetch. Dutton, 1981 (grade 7 and up)

Excellent, perceptive, and insightful collection consists of interviews conducted for television program "Like It Is." Each essay is preceded by a short biographical sketch of the subject. Included are author Maya Angelou, civil rights activist Rosa Parks, poet Nikki Giovanni, and author Michele Wallace.

Thurman, Judith I BECAME ALONE: FIVE WOMAN POETS Illus. Atheneum, 1975. (grade 7 and up)
Good intelligent profiles of poets followed by substantial examples of their work. Included are Sappho, Louise Labé, Ann Bradstreet, Juana Inés de la Cruz, and Emily Dickinson. The work of Labè and la Cruz are translated by author. Will be of particular interest to serious students of poetry, but can also serve as an introduction to those unfamiliar with poetry.

Trease, Geoffrey SEVEN SOVEREIGN QUEENS Illus. Vanguard, 1971. (grade 7 and up)
Well-written, interesting biographies of Cleopatra, Boudicca, Galla Placida, Isabella, Christina, Maria Theresa, and Catherine the Great combine history and biography, doing justice to both.

————. SEVEN QUEENS OF ENGLAND Vanguard, 1953. (grade 6 and up)
Warm, informal portraits of Maud, Mary, Elizabeth I, Mary II, Anne, Victoria, and Elizabeth II are interesting and well written, suitable for reading as well as for reference.

————. SEVEN STAGES Vanguard, 1965. (grades 7–10)
Very fine profiles of actress Sarah Siddons, singer Jenny Lind, and dancer Anna Pavlova are included in this collection of people prominent in the theatrical fields. Good straightforward narratives reveal the motivations and the accomplishments of the three women, and comprehensively cover the highlights of their lives and careers.

Truman, Margaret WOMEN OF COURAGE Morrow, 1976. (grade 9 and up)
Outstanding book offers individual, highly readable, informal profiles of Susan Livingston, who defended her home against the British soldiers during the American Revolution; Dolley Madison, first lady; Sarah Winnemucca, Native-American teacher and interpreter; Prudence Crandall, abolitionist, educator; Ida Wells-Barnett, journalist; Mary Harris "Mother" Jones, labor leader; Elizabeth Blackwell, pioneer physician; Susan B. Anthony, feminist, suffrage leader; Marian Anderson, singer and civil rights leader; Kate Barnard, advocate for Native-American orphans; Margaret Chase Smith, senator; and Frances Oldham Kelsey, medical officer with the Food and Drug Administration who refused to aprove

Thalidomide until proof of its safety was demonstrated. Each woman is presented within the context of her time and is seen developing real courage in the face of obstacles. A very fine introduction precedes the biographies.

Van Steenwyck, Elizabeth STARS ON ICE Illus. with photographs. Dodd, 1980. (grade 5 and up)

Skating enthusiasts will enjoy the believable portraits of Linda Fratiane, Tai Babilonia, Lisa-Marie Allen, and Stacy Smith and the thumbnail sketches of other skating stars, past and present.

————. WOMEN IN SPORTS: FIGURE SKATING Illus. with photographs. Harvey House, 1976. (grade 5 and up)

The figure-skating careers of Peggy Fleming, Janet Lynn, Karen Magnussen, Diane deLeeuw and Dorothy Hamill are traced, along with an excellent overview of skating and the important maneuvers needed for competition. The collective moves along briskly, in a highly readable manner, and will have apeal to all those interested in skating.

Walker, Greta WOMEN TODAY: TEN PROFILES Hawthorn, 1975. (grade 7 and up)

An outstanding, briskly written collection includes many women of whom little or nothing has been published for young readers. A very fine feminist introduction precedes portraits of women who have carved out successful careers for themselves, and who have shown evidence of struggling to get what they want out of life. However, the emphasis is not so much on career guidance or modelling, but on seeing the women as people who have set forth goals, and followed the appropriate routes to getting there. Included in these journalistically informal, highly readable profiles are Betty Friedan, feminist writer and lecturer; Dorothy Pitman Hughes, day care center advocate; Marketa Kimbrell, actress and street theater organizer; Eleanor Holmes Norton, attorney and New York City commissioner of Human Rights; Eve Queler, pianist and conductor; Lola Redford, cofounder of Consumer Action Now; Marlene Sanders, television producer; Gertrude Schimmel, police inspector; Gloria Steinem, feminist, writer, publisher; and Marcia Storch, physician. Young adult and adult readers will also find this book interesting and worthwhile; junior high readers will not find it too difficult.

Wayne, Bennett, ed. BLACK CRUSADERS FOR FREEDOM Illus. Garrard, 1974. (grades 3–4)

The outstanding biographies of Harriet Tubman, the rescuer of other slaves, and Sojourner Truth, abolitionist and feminist, originally written for early elementary school readers, have been combined with other biographies in this one volume and reset with smaller print and with photographs and old prints rather than line drawings, making them more appealing to older readers. The result is an outstanding book for older reluctant readers, easy to read, but nonetheless dramatic and stirring.

————. FOUR WOMEN OF COURAGE Illus. Garrard, 1975. (grades 3–4)
    Four books for early elementary school readers have been combined in this one volume, reset with smaller print and with photographs rather than line drawings, thus making it more suitable in format for older readers. The biographies of aviator Jacqueline Cochran, pioneer nurse Linda Richards, and humanitarian Helen Keller are fast-moving, warm, and interesting and should be of great interest to older readers despite the limited vocabulary and shorter-than-usual sentences. The biography of Dorothea Dix is also good, but is somewhat dry and not quite as good as the others. Generally, though, this is an outstanding book for reluctant readers.

————. THEY LOVED THE LAND Illus. Garrard, 1974. (grades 3–4)
    This excellent biography of Rachel Carson, marine biologist, writer, and conservationist is combined here with other biographies. Minor editing and changes in format result in a very fine book for older, reluctant readers who will find the subject and presentation appealing.

————. WOMEN IN THE WHITE HOUSE: FOUR FIRST LADIES Illus. Garrard, 1976. (grades 3–4)
    Biographies of Martha Washington, Abigail Adams, Dolley Madison, and Mary Todd Lincoln, originally written for younger children, are reset in smaller print, with photographs and prints rather than line drawings. This makes these biographies more suitable for older, reluctant readers. A satisfactory but not distinguished book.

————. WOMEN WHO DARED TO BE DIFFERENT Illus. with photographs. Garrard, 1973. (grades 3–4)
    The editor has chosen four women who achieved success in fields which excluded women, and reprinted individual biographies of them which Garrard published in an easy-to-read format for younger children. Incorporating the theme of women who dared to be different, highlighted by photographs, the book is further enhanced by the inclusion of brief notes and photographs of contemporary women who have been successful in related fields. The women whose lives are told in simple, but detailed narrative are Annie Oakley, markswoman; Maria Mitchell, astronomer; Nellie Bly, reporter; and Amelia Earhart, aviator. Extremely well organized, neither the text nor the format is so juvenile as to "embarrass" the older reader. Both the content and format have interest and appeal to older

readers, and because it is career-oriented as well as being good biography, this is a collection of unusual merit and one of the very few for reluctant readers.

————. WOMEN WITH A CAUSE   Illus. Garrard, 1975. (grades 3–4)

Four individual biographies of Anne Hutchinson, colonial religious dissenter; Lucretia Mott and Susan B. Anthony, feminists and abolitionists; and Eleanor Roosevelt, humanitarian, are combined in a format more suitable for older reluctant readers. Reset in smaller type, and old prints and photographs substituted for line drawings, they are warm and inspiring and although easy to read are not too childish for older readers. The biography of Susan B. Anthony is slightly stilted, but nonetheless good, and the ones of the other women are truly excellent.

Weinberg, Arthur, and Weinberg, Lila SOME DISSENTING VOICES World, 1970. (grade 7 and up)

A very fine profile of Jane Addams is included in this collective of six American dissenters. Equal emphasis is given to her activities and work among the poor surrounding Hull House and her efforts in behalf of peace. The authors show both crusades as reflective of Addams's great interest in humanity and her willingness to go against the main stream of prevailing beliefs. Her achievements as well as her unfulfilled dreams are described vividly in this well-balanced account of her life.

Werner, Vivian SCIENTIST VERSUS SOCIETY   Hawthorn, 1975. (grade 9 and up)

The author has included well-written accounts of the lives of seven scientists who were surrounded by controversy during their lifetime because their work opposed prevailing societal beliefs. Included in this collection is a profile of Ada Augusta, the countess of Lovelace. The daughter of the poet Lord Byron, she was a mathematical genius who was prevented from developing and making use of her abilities because of her sex. There is more emphasis on her personal life than on her actual mathematical prowess, but this is a warm, interesting profile that clearly shows the limitations imposed on women in the nineteenth century.

Wheelock, Warren HISPANIC HEROES OF THE U.S.A.   Book 1 Illus. EMC, 1976. (grade 4 and up)

Easy-to-read profile of Vikki Carr stresses her professional life but also discusses her other activities such as fundraising for Hispanic causes.

————. HISPANIC HEROES OF THE U.S.A.   Book 3 Illus. EMC, 1976. (grade 4 and up)

Highly readable biography focuses on Puerto Rican–born Carmen Rosa

Magmi, social worker who became director of the United States Woman's Bureau.

Wilcox, Desmond TEN WHO DARED Little, 1977. (grade 7 and up)
Based on the television series of the same name. The profile of Mary Kingsley is an intelligent commentary and account of the African explorer's life and accomplishment. Readers of all ages will find it of interest.

Williams, Barbara BREAKTHROUGH: WOMEN IN ARCHEOLOGY Illus. with photographs. Walker, 1981. (grade 6 and up)
Very fine book which focuses on the personal and professional lives of six contemporary women archeologists. Their early lives, varied backgrounds, education, and motivations, and the prejudices they encountered as women are all described. Young people considering archeology as a career will find the book of substantial interest and assistance; in addition to the biographies, there is specific information on schools and museum departments which can furnish information on education.

————. BREAKTHROUGH: WOMEN IN POLITICS Illus. with photographs. Walker, 1979. (grade 6 and up)
Excellent, highly readable book tells of each woman's early life and struggles to obtain positions in American government. Their personal lives are discussed, but emphasis is on achievement and motivation. Included are Genevieve Atwood, Utah state legislator; Janet Gray Hayes, mayor of San Jose, California; Dixy Lee Ray, governor of Washington; Millicent Fenwick, congresswoman from New Jersey; Nancy Landon Kassebaum, United States senator from Kansas; Esther Peterson, presidential appointee to several administrations; and Yvonne Brathwaite Burke, congresswoman from California.

Williams, Eric, ed. THE WILL TO BE FREE: GREAT ESCAPE STORIES Nelson, 1970. (grade 6 and up)
Dramatic escape stories tell, in individual chapters, the experiences of Anne Brusselman, a Belgium woman who hid and passed on to safety Allied soldiers during World War II, and Christine Arnothy, a teenage girl who escaped from Hungary when the Russians took over the country. Told in the words of the subjects, the book is exciting and well organized.

Wilson, Beth P. GIANTS FOR JUSTICE: BETHUNE, RANDOLPH AND KING Illus. Harcourt, 1978. (grades 5–8)
A chapter on Mary McLeod Bethune provides an excellent, easy-to-read portrait of the educator's early life and later achievements. Older reluctant readers as well as elementary school students will find the book moving.

Wintterle, John, and Cramer, Richard S. PORTRAITS OF NOBEL LAUREATES IN PEACE   Abelard-Schuman, 1971. (grade 7 and up)

Very fine, vivid studies of Bertha von Suttner, Jane Addams, and Emily Greene Balch are included here. Von Suttner, the author who worked for peace and helped to inspire Alfred Nobel to create the award, received it herself in 1905. Jane Addams, social reformer and peace advocate, was awarded her prize in 1931. Balch, economist and sociologist and international secretary and honorary president of the Women's International League for Peace, received the award in 1946. Well-researched, straightforward narratives bring each woman to life clearly, but place the emphasis on her work rather than on her personal life.

Wohl, Gary, and Ruibal, Carmen Cadilla   HISPANIC PERSONALITIES: CELEBRITIES OF THE SPANISH SPEAKING WORLD   Illus. Regents, 1978. (grade 7 and up)

Good, short profiles highlight Hispanic culture. The book is described by publisher as a textbook for students of Hispanic descent in an English-as-a-second-language class. However, this collective is also of interest to general readers. Included are Cuban dancer Alicia Alonso, Chilean poet Gabriela Mistral (Nobel Prize–winner for literature in 1945), Puerto Rican–born actress Rita Moreno, and Puerto Rican poets Lola Rodriguez De Tio and Julia de Burgos.

Wright, Helen, and Rapport, Samuel   GREAT ADVENTURES IN NURSING   Harper, 1960. (grade 7 and up)

Excellent book directed to the career-oriented young woman gives a dramatic, vivid picture of nursing. Composed of reprints of articles and biographical sketches, this volume gives a general approach to nursing and also presents the personal and professional life stories of individual nurses. Included are Sister Elizabeth Kenny, polio nurse; Princess Ileana of Rumania; Mary Breckinridge, frontier nurse; Lillian Wald, founder of the Visiting Nurses Service; Florence Nightingale, pioneer nurse; Mother Bickerdyke, Civil War nurse; and Edith Cavell, World War I nurse and spy.

Young, Margaret   BLACK AMERICAN LEADERS   Illus. Watts, 1969. (grade 7 and up)

Despite their brevity, these profiles are useful for reference and as a spur to further reading. Thirty-six different black leaders are grouped into four categories: civil rights, government, international, and political leaders. Included are abolitionist Harriet Tubman; educator Mary McLeod Bethune; jurist Constance Baker Motley; state official Ersa Hines Poston; attorney Patricia Roberts Harris; congresswomen Shirley Chisholm and Barbara Jordan (at the time of publication, a state senator from Texas); and city official Vel Phillips. The book is attractively designed with vital statistics preceding the brief capsule summaries of the life of each subject, and the photographs contribute to the book's value.

Zanderbergen, George   LAUGH IT UP   Illus. with photographs. Crestwood, 1976. (grade 4 and up)

Very good, easy-to-read biogaphies of comic actresses Carol Burnett and Mary Tyler Moore will capture the interest of older reluctant readers or younger enthusiastic ones, particularly those television fans who admire these performers.

————.   NASHVILLE MUSIC   Illus. with photographs. Crestwood, 1976. (grade 4 and up)

Profile of country and western singer Loretta Lynn is included.

————.   SINGING SWEETLY   Illus. with photographs. Crestwood, 1976. (grade 4 and up)

Profiles of singers Cher, Roberta Flack, and Olivia Newton-John are included.

————.   STAY TUNED   Illus. with photographs. Crestwood, 1976. (grade 4 and up)

Profile of actress Valerie Harper is included.

These three, easy-to-read books are very good, and are expressly designed to appeal to reluctant readers. Despite the simplicity of writing style they are neither oversimplistic nor superficial.

I WISH MA COULD VOTE

Appendixes

A

British (con't.)

Browning, Elizabeth Barrett
Burney, Fanny
Catherine of Aragon
Christie, Agatha
Craik, Dinah Murlock
Edwards, Julie
Eleanor of Aquitane
Eliot, George
Elizabeth I
Elizabeth II
Evans, Helen
Ewing, Juliana
Farjeon, Eleanor
Fonteyn, Margot
Franklin, Rosalind
Fry, Elizabeth
Garrett-Anderson, Elizabeth
Godden, Rumer
Goodall, Jane
Greenaway, Kate
Grey, Beryl
Grey, Lady Jane
Jex-Blake, Sophia
Johnson, Amy
Kaye-Smith, Sheila
Kemble, Frances "Fanny"
Kenyon, Kathleen
Lovelace, Ada Byron
Markova, Alicia
Mary I
Mary II

Maud
Nesbit, Edith
Nightingale, Florence
Norton, Mary
Pankhurst, Adele
Pankhurst, Christabel
Pankhurst, Emmeline
Pankhurst, Sylvia
Parr, Catherine
Pechey, Edith
Potter, Beatrix
Rossetti, Christina
Sackville-West, Victoria
Sayers, Dorothy
Seymour, Jane
Shelley, Mary Wollstonecraft
  Godwin
Siddons, Sarah Kemble
Stewart, Mary
Taylor, Ann
Taylor, Jane
Terry, Ellen
Thorne, Isabel
Travers, P. L.
Victoria
Wade, Virginia
Webb, Mary
Wollstonecraft, Mary
Woolf, Virginia
Wordsworth, Dorothy
Yonge, Charlotte Mary
Young, Grace Chisholm

Canadian

Johnson, Pauline
Mance, Jeanne

Rosenberg, Elsa
Takashima, Shizuye

Chilean

Mistral, Gabriela

Chinese

Chiang, Mei-ling Soong
Kung, Ai-ling Soong

Sun, Ch'ing-ling Soong
Tzu Hsi

Cuban

Alonso, Alicia

Czechoslovak

Connolly, Olga Fikotoua

Navratilova, Martina

Dutch

Blankers-Koen, Fanny
Frank, Anne
Hari, Mata
Juliana

Reiss, Johanna
Tinné, Alexine
Wilhelmina

Egyptian

Cleopatra

Nefertiti

Ethiopian

Haile Selassie, Tsahai

French

Auriol, Jacqueline
Bernhardt, Sarah
Bishop, Claire Huchet
Bonheur, Rosa
Breteuil, Emile de
Catherine de Medici
Chanel, Gabrielle "Coco"
Chauviré, Yvette
Daché, Lily
Eleanor of Aquitaine

Felicie, Jacoba
Germain, Sophie
Jeanmarie, Renée
Joan of Arc
Johnstone, Elizabeth
Joliot-Curie, Irene
Josephine
LeClerq, Tanquil
Lenglen, Suzanne
Marchard, Colette

French (con't.)
Marie Antoinette
Morisot, Berthe
Rachel

Sand, George
Tristan, Flora
Vigee-Librun, Elizabeth Louise
Wolf, Jacqueline

German

Glueckel of Hamlin
Goeppert-Mayer, Marie
Herschel, Caroline
Holm, Hanya

Kollwitz, Käthe
Noether, Emmy
Reitsch, Hanna
Schumann, Clara Wieck
Zakrzewska, Marie Elizabeth

Greek

Agnodice
Hypatia

Vlachos, Helen

Hungarian

Arnothy, Christine

Siegal, Aranka

Indian

Gandhi, Indira
Pandit, Vijaya Lakshmi

Ramcharan, Savitri

Irish

Corrigan, Mairead
De Markievich, Constance

Garrett, Eileen
Williams, Betty

Israeli

Ben-Porat, Miriam
Chizick, Sarah
Meir, Golda

Senesh, Hannah
Szold, Henrietta
Zyskind, Sara

Italian

Agnesia, Maria Gaetena
Aspasia
Deledda, Grazia

Fermi, Laura
Montessori, Maria
Trotula

Japanese

Sasaki, Sadako

Mexican

Cruz, Juana Inés de la

Norwegian

D'Aulaire, Ingri   Undset, Sigrid
Henie, Sonja   Waitz, Grete

Polish

Curie, Marie   Novak, Nina
Hautzig, Esther   Rose, Ernestine
Jadwiga   Rubinstein, Helena
Modjeska, Helena   Wojciechowska, Maia

Rumanian

Comaneci, Nadia   Ileana

Russian

Abramson, Manya Polevoi   Korbut, Olga
Antin, Mary   Kovalevskaya, Sonya
Averina, Tatiana   Loeb, Sophie
Blavatsky, Helena   Pavlova, Anna
Catherine the Great   Riabouchinska, Tatiana
Danilova, Alexandra   Tereshkova, Valentina
Elizabeth Petrovna   Tolstoy, Alexandra
Goldman, Emma   Toumanova, Tamara
Kim, Nelli

Scottish

Grant, Anne MacVicar   Shearer, Moira
Mary, Queen of Scots   Slessor, Mary
Molesworth, Mary   Somerville, Mary Fairfax

355

Spanish

Isabella

Swedish

Christina   Lindgren, Astrid
Lind, Jenny

Swiss

Kauffman, Angelica

Syrian

Zenobia

Yugoslav

Slavenska, Mia   Mother Teresa

B

Americans Classified by Ethnic Group

Asian-American

Chang, Tisa   Wu, Chien-Shiung
Mink, Patsy

Black American

Amévor, Charlotte   Craft, Ellen
Anderson, Marian   Davis, Francis Reed Elliot
Angelou, Maya   Dee, Ruby
Arroyo, Martina   Dunham, Katherine
Bailey, Pearl   Elington, Anna
Baker, Augusta   Evers, Myrlie
Bates, Daisy   Ferguson, Angella D.
Bethune, Mary McLeod   Flack, Roberta
Blount, Mildred E.   Franklin, Aretha
Bonard, Jean   Freeman, Elizabeth "Mumbet"
Brooks, Gwendolyn   Gibson, Althea
Brown, Dorothy   Grant, Micki
Brunner, Hattie   Green, Patricia
Burke, Yvonne Braithwaite   Hamer, Fannie Lou
Catlett, Elizabeth   Hansberry, Lorraine
Chisholm, Shirley   Harper, Frances Ellen Watkins
Clark, Septima Poinsette   Holiday, Billie
Cole, Natalie   Horne, Lena
Coleman, Bessie   Hughes, Dorothy Pitman
Collins, Cardiss   Hunter, Alberta

357

Black American (con't.)
Hunter, Clementine
Jackson, Mahalia
Jackson, Nell
Jackson, Suzanne
Jamison, Judith
Jordan, Barbara
Keckley, Elizabeth
King, Coretta Scott
Langford, Anna Riggs
Lewis, Edmonia
Louvestre, Mary
Mebane, Mary E.
Morgan, Norma
Morgan, Sister Gertrude
Motley, Constance Baker
Nathaniel, Inez
Newsome, Effie Lee
Norton, Eleanor Holmes
Parks, Rosa
Petry, Ann
Phillips, Vel
Poston, Ersa Hines
Price, Leontyne
Proctor, Barbara Gardner
Rainey, Ma
Rice, Rebecca

Ringgold, Faith
Ross, Diana
Rudolph, Wilma
Savage, Augusta
Scott, Hazel
Smith, Bessie
Summer, Donna
Taylor, Susie King
Terrell, Mary Church
Terry, Ellen
Tituba
Toussaint, Cheryl
Trammell, Beatrice Johnson
Truth, Sojourner
Tubman, Harriet
Tyson, Cicely
Walker, Maggie Lena
Walker, Margaret
Walker, Sarah Breedlove
Waters, Ethel
Wells-Barnett, Ida
Wheatley, Phillis
Williams, Fannie B.
Williams, Mary Lou
Wood, Ann
Wright, Jane C.
Wyatt, Addie

Mexican-American

Anguiano, Lupe
Baca-Barragan, Polly

Carr, Vikki
Huerta, Dolores
Lopez, Nancy

Native Americans

Bonnin, Gertrude Simmons
Bosomsworth, Mary Musgrove
Chouteau, Yvonne
Francis, Milly Hadjo
Harris, LaDonna
Hardin, Helen
Hightower, Rosella
Horne, Esther Burnette
Johnson, E. Pauline
La Flesche, Susan
La Flesche, Susette
Lawson, Roberta C.
Lewis, Edmonia
Martínez, Maria
Medicine Flower, Grace
Mountain Wolf Woman
Mouz, Mary
Pasquala

Peterson, Helen L.
Pitseolak
Pocahontas
Ramos, Elaine Abraham
Sacajawea
Silko, Leslie
Sunrise, Pearl
Tallchief, Maria
Tallchief, Marjorie
Terakwitha, Kateri
Velarde, Pablita
Victor, Wilma L.
Ward, Nancy
Wauneka, Annie Dodge
Wetamoo
White, Cecelia
Winema
Winnemucca, Sarah

Puerto Rican

Burgos, Julia de
Colón, Miriam
Maymi, Carmen
Meléndez, Cóncha

Morales, Hilda
Moreno, Rita
Rincón, Felisa
Rodriguez De Tio, Lola

359

C

Vocations and Avocations

Abolitionists

Anthony, Susan Brownell
Auld, Sophia
Bethune, Mary McLeod
Child, Lydia Maria
Craft, Ellen
Crandall, Prudence
Forten, Charlotte
Foster, Abigail Kelley
Grimké, Angelina
Grimké, Sarah

Harper, Frances Ellen Watkins
Kemble, Frances "Fanny"
Mott, Lucretia
Stanton, Elizabeth Cady
Stone, Lucy
Stowe, Harriet Beecher
Terrell, Mary Church
Truth, Sojourner
Tubman, Harriet

Actresses

Adams, Maude
Andrews, Julie
Angelou, Maya
Bailey, Pearl
Bancroft, Anne
Barrymore, Ethel
Berg, Gertude
Bernhardt, Sarah
Brice, Fanny
Burnett, Carol
Chang, Tisa
Colón, Miriam

Cornell, Katharine
Crabtree, Lotta
Dee, Ruby
Dewhurst, Colleen
Farmer, Frances
Fiske, Minnie Maddern
Fletcher, Louise
Fonda, Jane
Gordon, Ruth
Harper, Valerie
Harris, Julie
Hayes, Helen

Held, Anna
Henie, Sonja
Kemble, Frances "Fanny"
Kimbrell, Marketa
Lillie, Beatrice
Long, Loretta
Luce, Clare Boothe
MacLaine, Shirley
Martin, Mary
Merman, Ethel
Miller, Marilyn
Modjeska, Helena
Montez, Lola
Moreno, Rita

Mowatt, Anna Cora
Rachel
Rice, Rebecca
Ross, Diana
Siddons, Sarah Kemble
Skinner, Cornelia Otis
Stapleton, Maureen
Terry, Ellen
Tomlin, Lily
Tyson, Cicely
Ullman, Liv
Waters, Ethel
West, Mae

Advocates for Social Reform

Abzug, Bella
Addams, Jane
Anderson, Marian
Anguiano, Lupe
Baker, Sara Josephine
Balch, Emily Greene
Barton, Clara
Bates, Daisy
Blackwell, Elizabeth
Bloomer, Amelia Jenks
Bly, Nellie
Booth, Evangeline
Braden, Anne
Buck, Pearl
Cameron, Donaldina
Carter, Rosalynn
Chisholm, Shirley
Corrigan, Mairead
Daniels, Susan
Day, Dorothy

Dee, Ruby
Derricotte, Juliette
Dickey, Sarah
Egan, Sister Jogues
Evers, Myrlie
Fiorto, Eunice
Flynn, Elizabeth Gurley
Fonda, Jane
Ford, Betty
Friedan, Betty
Fry, Elizabeth
Fuller, Margaret
Goldman, Emma
Gratz, Rebecca
Hamer, Fannie Lou
Huerta, Dolores
Hughes, Dorothy Pitman
Jones, Mary Harris "Mother"
Kelley, Florence
King, Coretta Scott

Advocates (con't.)
Kohut, Rebekah
Koontz, Elizabeth Duncan
Kuhn, Maggie
La Flesche, Susette
Lathrop, Julia
Lathrop, Rose Hawthorne
Lease, Mary Elizabeth
Lifton, Betty Jane
Lockwood, Belva Ann
Loeb, Sophie
Lovejoy, Esther Pohl
Low, Juliette Gordon Low
MacLaine, Shirley
Marillac, Saint Louise de
Maymi, Carmen
McDowell, Mary
Nation, Carry
Nightingale, Florence
Parks, Rosa
Paul, Alice
Perkins, Frances
Rankin, Jeanette
Redford, Lola
Ripley, Sophia
Roosevelt, Eleanor

Rose, Ernestine
Sanger, Margaret
Solomon, Hannah G.
Steinem, Gloria
Stout, Penelope
Strong, Anne Louise
Suttner, Bertha von
Szold, Henrietta
Tarbell, Ida
Teresa, Mother
Tolstoy, Alexandra
Trahey, Jane
Tristan, Flora
Truth, Sojourner
Wald, Lillian
Walker, Mary
Wauneka, Annie Dodge
Wells-Barnett, Ida
Willard, Frances
Williams, Betty
Williams, Fannie B.
Wollstonecraft, Mary
Wright, Frances "Fanny"
Wyatt, Addie
Young, Ann Eliza

American Civil War Figures

Barton, Clara
Bickerdyke, Mary Ann
Boyd, Belle
Carroll, Anna Ella
Edmonds, Sarah Emma
Forten, Charlotte
Greenhow, Rose O'Neal

Loughborough, Mary Ann
  Webster
Truth, Sojourner
Tubman, Harriet
Van Lew, Elizabeth
Walker, Mary

362

American Colonial Figures

Bradstreet, Anne Dudley	Pinckney, Eliza Lucas
Hutchinson, Anne	Zenger, Anna

American Revolutionary Figures

Adams, Abigail Smith	Ludington, Sybil
Bailey, "Mad Anne"	Murray, Mary Lindley
Barker, Penelope	Pickersgill, Mary
Bates, Abigail	Reynolds, Phoebe
Bates, Rebecca	Ross, Betsy
Champe, Elizabeth	Sampson, Deborah
Corbin, Margaret	Townsend, Sally
Darragh, Lydia	Warren, Mercy Otis
Hart, Nancy	Wick, Tempe
Hays, Mary	Zane, Betty
Hendee, Hannah	

Ancient World Figures

Agnodice	Galla Placida
Aspasia	Hypatia
Beruriah	Nefertiti
Cleopatra	

Artists and Illustrators

Adams, Adrienne	Cassatt, Mary
Amévor, Charlotte	Catlett, Elizabeth
Anglund, Joan Walsh	Cooney, Barbara
Austin, Ann "Andy"	D'Aulaire, Ingri
Babbitt, Natalie	De Angeli, Marguerite Lofft
Beaux, Cecilia	Emberley, Barbara
Bendick, Jeanne	Ets, Marie Hall
Bonheur, Rosa	Fatio, Louise
Brown, Marcia	Frankenthaler, Helen
Brunner, Hattie	Gág, Wanda
Burningham, Charlene	Greenaway, Kate
Burton, Marie	Grifalconi, Ann

Artists (con't.)
Hader, Berta
Hardin, Helen
Hawthorne, Sophie Peabody
Hoffman, Malvina
Hogrogian, Nonny
Hunter, Clementine
Hyman, Trina Schart
Ipcar, Dahlov
Jackson, Suzanne
Kauffman, Angelica
Kollwitz, Käthe
Lathrop, Dorothy
Laurencin, Marie
Lenski, Lois
Lewis, Edmonia
Lobel, Anita
Lubell, Winifred
Martínez, Maria
Medicine Flower, Grace
Milhous, Katherine
Morgan, Norma
Morgan, Sister Gertrude
Moses, Anna Mary Robertson
  "Grandma"

Mouz, Mary
Nathaniel, Inez
Neel, Alice
Ness, Evaline
Nevelson, Louise
O'Keeffe, Georgia
Petersham, Maud
Pitseolak
Potter, Beatrix
Raskin, Ellen
Ream, Vinnie
Rey, Margret
Ringgold, Faith
Savage, Augusta
Sharon, Mary Bruce
Sunrise, Pearl
Takashima, Shizuye
Tudor, Tasha
Velarde, Pablita
Vigee-Librun, Elizabeth Louise
Wheeler, Candace Thurber
Zemach, Margot

Athletes
ALL-AROUND ATHLETES
O'Neill, Kitty   Zaharias, "Babe" Didrikson
ARCHER
Vanderheide, Nancy
BASKETBALL PLAYERS
Blazejowski, Carol   Shank, Theresa
Lieberman, Nancy

BOWLERS

Laedwig, Marion
Martin, Sylvia Wene

McCutcheon, Floretta
Sperber, Paula

GOLFERS

Berg, Patty
Collett, Glenna
Lopez, Nancy

Rankin, Judy
Whitworth, Kathy
Wright, Mickey

GYMNASTS

Comaneci, Nadia
Kim, Nelli
Korbut, Olga

Rice, Joan Moore
Rigby, Cathy

ICE SKATERS

Albright, Tenley
Fleming, Peggy
Hamill, Dorothy
Heiden, Beth
Heiss, Carol
Henie, Sonja

Henning, Anne
Lynn, Janet
Owen, Laurence
Rodina, Irina
Weld, Theresa
Young, Sheila

JOCKEYS, HORSEBACK RIDERS, AND TRAINERS

Boudrot, Denise
Crabtree, Helen
Gurney, Hilda
Jones, Sue Sally

Kusner, Kathy
McEnroy, Michele
Sears, Eleanor
Smith, Robyn

RACE CAR DRIVERS

Guthrie, Janet

Muldowney, Shirley

ROLLER SKATER

Dunn, Natalie

SOFTBALL PITCHER

Joyce, Joan

SKIERS

Chaffee, Suzy
Cochran, Barbara Ann

Cochran, Lindy
Cochran, Marilyn

Athletes (con't.)
Fraser, Gretchen K.
Greene, Nancy
Kinmont, Jill

Lawrence, Andrea Mead
Nelson, Cindy
Pitou, Penny
Proell, Annemarie

STUNT PERFORMER

O'Neill, Kitty

SWIMMERS

Babashoff, Shirley
Bartz, Jenny
Belote, Melissa
Berg, Sharon
Buzonas, Gail Johnson
Chadwick, Florence
DeVarona, Donna
Ederle, Gertrude
Fraser, Dawn

Genesho, Lynn
Heddy, Kathy
King, Micki
Loock, Christine
MacInnis, Nina
McCormick, Patricia
Nyad, Diana
Von Saltza, Chris

TENNIS PLAYERS

Austin, Tracy
Casals, Rosemary
Connolly, Maureen
Court, Margaret
Evert, Chris
Jacobs, Helen Hull
Jaeger, Andrea

King, Billie Jean
Lenglen, Suzanne
Marble, Alice
Navratilova, Martina
Wade, Virginia
Wills, Helen

TRACK AND FIELD

Averina, Tatiana
Bingay, Roberta
Blankers-Koen, Fanny
Campbell, Robin
Connolly, Olga Fikotova
Decker, Mary
Frederick, Jane
Huntley, Joni
Jackson, Madeline Manning
Jackson, Nell

Rudolph, Wilma
Schmidt, Kathy
Simburg, Wyomia
Toussaint, Cheryl
Van Wolvelaere, Patty
Waitz, Grete
Walsh, Stella
Wright, Thelma
Zaharias, "Babe" Didrikson

Attorneys
(not including Congresswomen and Senators)

Bird, Rose
Huber, Linda
Langford, Anna Riggs
Libow, Carol

Lockwood, Belva Ann
Norton, Eleanor Holmes
Poston, Ersa Hines
Stender, Fay

Authors

Adams, Elizabeth
Aguilar, Grace
Alcott, Louisa May
Angelou, Maya
Anglund, Joan Walsh
Antin, Mary
Arnothy, Christine
Austen, Jane
Babbitt, Natalie
Bendick, Jeanne
Berg, Gertrude
Bishop, Claire Huchet
Bleeker, Sonia
Blegvad, Lenore
Blume, Judy
Bombeck, Erma
Brewton, Sara W.
Brink, Carol Ryrie
Brontë, Anne
Brontë, Charlotte
Brontë, Emily
Brothers, Joyce
Brown, Marcia
Bryan, Dorothy
Bryan, Marguerite
Buck, Pearl
Buff, Mary
Burnett, Frances Hodgson
Burney, Fanny

Byars, Betsy
Carlson, Natalie Savage
Carson, Rachel
Cather, Willa
Child, Julia
Child, Lydia Maria
Christie, Agatha
Clark, Ann Nolan
Cleary, Beverly
Coatsworth, Elizabeth
Colman, Hila
Cooney, Barbara
Craik, Dinah Murlock
Cruz, Juana Inés de la
Cunningham, Julia
D'Aulaire, Ingri
De Angeli, Marguerite Lofft
Deledda, Grazia
De Lieuw, Adele
De Lieuw, Cateau
De Regniers, Beatrice Schenk
Devlin, Wende
Dobler, Lavinia
Dodge, Mary Mapes
Edwards, Julie
Eliot, George
Emberley, Barbara
Enright, Elizabeth
Estes, Eleanor

Authors (con't.)

Ets, Marie Hall
Ewing, Juliana
Farjeon, Eleanor
Fatio, Louise
Feelings, Muriel
Fenton, Mildred Adams
Ferber, Edna
Fermi, Laura
Fisher, Aileen
Fisher, Dorothy Canfield
Fitzgerald, Zelda
Foster, Genevieve
Freeman, Mary Eleanor
  Wilkins
Friedan, Betty
Fritz, Jean
Fuller, Margaret
Gaeddart, Lou Ann
Gág, Wanda
Garelick, May
George, Jean Craighead
Gilman, Charlotte Perkins
Glubok, Shirley
Glueckel of Hamlin
Godden, Rumer
Graham, Jory
Grant, Anne MacVicar
Greenaway, Kate
Hader, Berta
Hahn, Emily
Hale, Lucretia Peabody
Hale, Sarah
Hamilton, Edith
Hamilton, Virginia
Hansberry, Lorraine

Hautzig, Esther
Hawthorne, Sophie Peabody
Haywood, Carolyn
Hellman, Lillian
Henry, Marguerite
Howe, Julia Ward
Hunt, Irene
Ipcar, Dahlov
Jewett, Sarah Orne
Jong, Erica
Kahl, Virginia
Kaye-Smith, Sheila
Keller, Helen
Kemble, Frances "Fanny"
Konigsburg, Elaine L.
Krauss, Ruth
Kubler-Ross, Elisabeth
Landers, Ann
Larrick, Nancy
Latham, Jean Lee
Lathrop, Dorothy
L'Engle, Madelene
Lenski, Lois
Lexau, Joan
Lifton, Betty Jean
Lindbergh, Anne Morrow
Lindgren, Astrid
Livingston, Myra Cohn
Lobel, Anita
Lubell, Winifred
Luce, Clare Boothe
McCarthy, Mary
McGinley, Phyllis
McGovern, Ann
McNeer, May
Mead, Margaret

Mebane, Mary E.
Meléndez, Cóncha
Merriam, Eve
Merrill, Jean
Milhous, Katherine
Minarik, Elsa Holmelund
Molesworth, Mary
Moore, Lillian
Morrison, Lillian
Nesbit, Edith
Ness, Evaline
Neville, Emily Cheney
Norton, Mary
Petersham, Maud
Petry, Ann
Pine, Tillie S.
Plath, Sylvia
Porter, Sylvia
Potter, Beatrix
Prieto, Mariana
Raskin, Ellen
Reiss, Johanna de Leeuw
Rey, Margret
Rinkoff, Barbara
Rollins, Betty
Rollins, Charlemae Hill
Roosevelt, Eleanor
Rose, Ernestine
Rosenberg, Elsa
Sachs, Nelly
Sackville-West, Victoria
Sand, George
Sayers, Dorothy
Scott, Ann Herbert
Selsam, Millicent E.
Sheklow, Edna

Shelley, Mary Wollstonecraft
   Godwin
Shirley, Dame
Shotwell, Louisa
Sidney, Margaret
Silko, Leslie
Skinner, Cornelia Otis
Smedley, Agnes
Snyder, Zilpha Keatley
Sone, Monica
Sonnerborn, Ruth
Sorensen, Virginia
Speare, Elizabeth George
Stanton, Elizabeth Cady
Stein, Gertrude
Sterling, Dorothy
Stern, Elizabeth G.
Stewart, Mary
Stolz, Mary
Stowe, Harriet Beecher
Strong, Anne Louise
Suttner, Bertha von
Takashima, Shizuye
Tarbell, Ida
Taylor, Sydney
Terry, Ellen
Thomas, Caitlan
Thompson, Blanche Jennings
Trahey, Jane
Travers, P. L.
Treviño, Elizabeth Borton de
Tuchman, Barbara
Tudor, Tasha
Udry, Janice May
Undset, Sigrid
Viorst, Judith

Authors (con't.)

Warburg, Sandol Stoddard
Warren, Mercy Otis
Webb, Mary
Weik, Mary Hays
West, Jessamyn
Weygant, Sister Noemi
Wharton, Edith
Whitney, Phyllis A.
Wiggin, Kate Douglas
Wilder, Laura Ingalls
Wilson, Julia

Wojciechowska, Maia
Wollstonecraft, Mary
Wood, Bari
Woolf, Virginia
Wordsworth, Dorothy
Wright, Frances
Wyler, Rose
Yashima, Mitsu
Yates, Elizabeth
Yonge, Charlotte Mary
Young, Margaret B.
Zolotow, Charlotte

Aviators and Astronauts

Auriol, Jacqueline
Brown, Jill Elaine
Case, Sandra Williams
Cleaves, Mary
Cobb, Geraldyn
Cochran, Jacqueline
Coleman, Bessie
Dunbar, Bonnie
Earhart, Amelia
Fisher, Anna
Howell, Emily
Johnson, Amy

Lindbergh, Anne Morrow
Lucid, Shannon
Mock, Jerrie
Moisant, Mathilda
Quimby, Harriet
Reitsch, Hanna
Resnik, Judith
Ride, Sally
Seddon, Rhea
Sullivan, Kathryn
Tereshkova, Valentina
Warner, Emily

Business Women and Entrepreneurs

Arden, Elizabeth
Bates, Mercedes
Blount, Mildred E.
Chanel, Gabrielle "Coco"
Cochran, Jacqueline
Cooney, Joan Ganz
Cousins, Jane "Casey"
Daché, Lily

Dumont, Eleanor
Garcia, Doña
Graham, Katherine
Kung, Ai-ling Soong
Laurencin, Marie
Lewis, Tillie
Proctor, Barbara Gardner
Roebling, Mary G.

Rubinstein, Helena
Rudkin, Margaret Fogharty
Schiff, Dorothy
Shaver, Dorothy
Trahey, Jane

Walker, Maggie Lena
Walker, Sarah Breedlove
Wheeler, Candace Thurber
Woodhull, Victoria Claflin
Wyman, Irma

Dancers

Adams, Diana
Alonso, Alicia
Boris, Ruthanna
Chauviré, Yvette
Chouteau, Yvonne
Danilova, Alexandra
De Mille, Agnes
Duncan, Isadora
Dunham, Katherine
Fifield, Elaine
Fonteyn, Margot
Graham, Martha
Gregory, Cynthia
Grey, Beryl
Hari, Mata
Hightower, Rosella
Holm, Hanya
Jamison, Judith
Jeanmarie, Renée
Kaye, Nora
Kirkland, Gelsey
LeClerq, Tanquil

MacLaine, Shirley
Marchard, Colette
Markova, Alicia
McBride, Patricia
Morales, Hilda
Moylan, Mary Ellen
Novak, Nina
Pavlova, Anna
Reed, Janet
Riabouchinska, Tatiana
Shearer, Moira
Silver, Robin
Slavenska, Mia
St. Denis, Ruth
Tallchief, Maria
Tallchief, Marjorie
Tamaris
Tharp, Twyla
Toumanova, Tamara
Vollmar, Jocelyn
White, Cecelia
Wigman, Mary

Educators

Berry, Martha
Bethune, Mary McLeod
Bonnin, Gertrude Simmons
Clark, Septima Poinsette
Crandall, Prudence

Dickey, Sarah
Forten, Charlotte
Gratz, Rebecca
Hamilton, Edith
Harris, LaDonna

Educators (con't.)
Hatcher, Orie Latham
Hill, Patty Smith
Hollingworth, Leta S.
Horne, Esther Burnette
Kinmont, Jill
Kohut, Rebekah
Koontz, Elizabeth Duncan
Long, Loretta
Lyon, Mary
Macy, Anne Sullivan
Mead, Margaret
Mebane, Mary E.
Moise, Penina
Montessori, Maria
Moore, Anne Carroll
Palmer, Alice Freeman
Ramos, Elaine Abraham
Richards, Ellen Swallow
Sabin, Florence
Sanford, Maria
Terrell, Mary Church
Victor, Wilma L.
Willard, Emma Hart

Explorers

Akeley, Delia J. Denning
Baker, Florence von Sass
Bishop, Isabella Lucy Bird
Boyd, Louise Arner
Kenyon, Kathleen
Peck, Annie Smith
Tinné, Alexine
Workman, Fanny Bullock

Feminists and Suffrage Leaders
(historical)

Adams, Abigail Smith
Anthony, Susan Brownell
Blatch, Harriet Stanton
Bloomer, Amelia Jenks
Catt, Carrie Chapman
Child, Lydia Maria
Duniway, Abigail Scott
Foster, Abigail Kelley
Fuller, Margaret
Gilman, Charlotte Perkins
Goldman, Emma
Grimké, Angelina
Grimké, Sarah
Howe, Julia Ward
Jacobi, Mary Putnam
Lease, Mary Elizabeth
Lockwood, Belva Ann
Luxemburg, Rosa
Mott, Lucretia
Pankhurst, Adele
Pankhurst, Christabel
Pankhurst, Emmeline
Pankhurst, Sylvia
Paul, Alice
Rankin, Jeanette
Rose, Ernestine
Shaw, Anna Howard
Stanton, Elizabeth Cady

Stone, Lucy
Terrell, Mary Church
Tristan, Flora
Truth, Sojourner
Walker, Mary

Willard, Frances
Wollstonecraft, Mary
Woodhull, Victoria Claflin
Wright, Frances

Government and Political Figures
(American and international)

Abel, Hazel
Abzug, Bella
Andrews, Elizabeth
Baca-Barragan, Polly
Baker, Irene Bailey
Ben-Porat, Miriam
Bird, Rose
Blitch, Iris
Boggs, Lindy Hale
Boland, Veronica
Bolton, Frances
Bosone, Reva Beck
Bowring, Eva
Buchanan, Vera
Burke, Yvonne Braithwaite
Bushfield, Vera
Byron, Katherine Edgar
Caraway, Hattie W.
Chiang, Mei-ling Soong
Church, Marguerite Stitt
Collins, Cardiss
Douglas, Emily Taft
Douglas, Helen Gahagan
Dwyer, Florence P.
Edwards, Elaine
Eslick, Willa B.
Felton, Rebecca Latimer
Fenwick, Millicent

Fulmer, Willa L.
Gandhi, Indira
Gasque, Elizabeth Hawley
Gibbs, Florence R.
Granahan, Kathryn E.
Grasso, Ella T.
Graves, Dixie Bibb
Green, Edith
Greenway, Isabella
Griffiths, Martha
Hansen, Julia Butler
Harden, Cecil M.
Heckler, Margaret M.
Hicks, Louise Day
Hobby, Oveta Culp
Holt, Marjorie
Holtzman, Elizabeth
Honeyman, Nan Wood
Huck, Winifred Mason
Jenckes, Virginia Ellis
Jordan, Barbara
Kahn, Florence P.
Kee, Elizabeth
Kelly, Edna F.
Keys, Martha
Knutson, Coya
Kreps, Juanita
Langley, Katherine

Gov't. Figures (con't.)
Lathrop, Julia
Loyd, Marilyn
Long, Rose McConnell
Luce, Clare Boothe
Lusk, Georgia L.
Mankin, Helen Douglas
May, Catherine
McCarthy, Kathryn
  O'Loughlin
McCormick, Ruth Hanna
McMillan, Clara G.
Meir, Golda
Meyner, Helen Stevenson
Mikulski, Barbara A.
Mink, Patsy T.
Motley, Constance Baker
Myerson, Bess
Neuberger, Maurine B.
Noble, Elaine
Nolan, Mae Ella
Norrell, Catherine D.
Norton, Eleanor Holmes
Norton, Mary T.
Oakar, Mary Rose
O'Connor, Sandra Day
O'Day, Caroline
Oldfield, Pearl
Owen, Ruth Bryan
Pandit, Vijaya Lakshmi
Perkins, Frances
Pettis, Shirley N.
Pfost, Gracie

Phillips, Vel
Polier, Justine Wise
Poston, Ersa Hines
Pratt, (Eliza) Jane
Pratt, Ruth Baker
Pyle, Gladys
Rankin, Jeanette
Ray, Dixy Lee
Reece, Louise Goff
Reid, Charlotte
Riley, Corinne Boyd
Rincon, Felisa
Robertson, Alice M.
Rogers, Edith Nourse
Schroeder, Patricia
Simpson, Edna
Smith, Margaret Chase
Smith, Virginia
Spellman, Gladys Noon
St. George, Katherine
Stanley, Winifred C.
Stevenson, Nancy
Sullivan, Leonor K.
Sumner, Jessie
Sun, Ch'ing-ling Soong
Thomas, Lera M.
Thompson, Ruth
Victor, Wilma L.
Wauneka, Annie Dodge
Weis, Jessica McCullough
Wingo, Effiegene
Woodhouse, Chase Going

Handicapped Women

Bridgman, Laura
Daniels, Susan
Fiorto, Eunice
Keller, Helen
Kinmont, Jill

O'Neill, Kitty
Rudolph, Wilma
Seibert, Florence
Sharpless, Nansie

Journalists and Newscasters

Abrams, Norma
Anspacher, Carolyn
Bombeck, Erma
Bourke-White, Margaret
Crist, Judith
Day, Dorothy
Garber, Mary
Garland, Hazel
Gilman, Mildred
Goldman, Connie
Graham, Jory
Graham, Katherine
Higgins, Marguerite
Kuhn, Irene Corbally
Landers, Ann
Leibowitz, Annie

McLaughlin, Kathleen
Morris, Mary
Pauley, Jane
Porter, Sylvia
Poussaint, Renée
Schiff, Dorothy
Sibley, Celestine
Smedley, Agnes
Steinem, Gloria
Thomas, Helen
Tomara, Sonia
Torre, Marie
Vlachos, Helen
Vorse, Mary Heaton
Walters, Barbara
Wells-Barnett, Ida
Zenger, Anna

Law Enforcement Officers

Kandler, Elizabeth Aytes
Karanksy, Priscilla Pepper
Perice, Donna Marie

Schimmel, Gertrude
Spiecher, Jean Garmen

Legendary Heroines and Figures

Joan of Arc
Pocahontas

Ross, Betsy
Sacajawea

Mathematicians

Agnesia, Maria Gaetena
Breteuil, Emile de
Germain, Sophie
Herschel, Caroline
Hypatia

Kovalevskaya, Sonya
Lovelace, Ada Byron
Noether, Emmy
Somerville, Mary Fairfax
Young, Grace Chisholm

Missionaries

Mary Loyola, Sister
Slessor, Mary

Walker, Mary Richardson
Whitman, Narcissa Prentiss

Musicians, Including Singers and Composers

Anderson, Marian
Arroyo, Martina
Bailey, Pearl
Bonard, Jean
Boone, Debby
Brice, Fanny
Caldwell, Sarah
Carr, Vikki
Cole, Natalie
Collins, Judy
Crabtree, Lotta
Flack, Roberta
Franklin, Aretha
Gayle, Crystal
Grant, Micki
Harris, Emmylou
Holiday, Billie
Horne, Lena
Hunter, Alberta
Jackson, Mahalia
Johnstone, Elizabeth
Joplin, Janis
Lind, Jenny

Lynn, Judy
Lynn, Loretta
Martin, Mary
Merman, Ethel
Miller, Marilyn
Montana, Patsy
Murray, Anne
Newton-John, Olivia
Parton, Dolly
Pearl, Minnie
Peters, Roberta
Ponselle, Rosa
Price, Leontyne
Queler, Eve
Rainey, Ma
Ronstadt, Linda
Ross, Diana
Schuman-Heink, Ernestine
Schumann, Clara Wieck
Scott, Hazel
Sills, Beverly
Simon, Carly
Smith, Bessie

376

Smith, Kate
Summer, Donna
Trapp, Maria von
Waters, Ethel

West, Mae
Williams, Mary Lou
Wixon, Emma
Zuckerman, Eugenia

Nobel Prize–winners

Addams, Jane
Balch, Emily Green
Corrigan, Mairead
Curie, Marie
Deledda, Grazia
Goeppert-Mayer, Maria
Hodgin, Dorothy Crowfoot

Joliot-Curie, Irene
Sachs, Nelly
Suttner, Bertha von
Teresa, Mother
Williams, Betty
Yallow, Rosalyn

Nurses

Barton, Clara
Bickerdyke, Mary Ann
Breckinridge, Mary
Cavell, Edith
Davis, Francis Reed Elliot
Edmonds, Sarah Emma
Fitzgerald, Alice
Haile Selassie, Tsahai
Hewitt, Margaret
Ileana

Kenny, Sister Elizabeth
Lathrop, Rose Hawthorne
Mance, Jeanne
Nightingale, Florence
Richards, Linda
Sanger, Margaret
Taylor, Susie King
Trammell, Beatrice Johnson
Wald, Lillian

Philanthropists

Garcia, Doña
Gratz, Rebecca
Hirsch, Clara de
Kung, Ai-ling Soong

Lathrop, Rose Hawthorne
Loeb, Sophie
Montefiore, Judith
Strauss, Lina

Photographers

Bourke-White, Margaret
Lange, Dorothea
Leibowitz, Annie

Morgan, Barbara
Weygant, Sister Noemi

Physicians

Agnodice
Albright, Tenley
Apgar, Virginia
Aspasia
Baker, Sara Josephine
Barringer, Emily Dunning
Blackwell, Elizabeth
Brown, Dorothy
Calderone, Mary
Elington, Anna
Evans, Helen
Ferguson, Angella D.
Fisher, Anna
Garrett-Anderson, Elizabeth
Goeppert-Mayer, Maria
Guion, Connie
Hamilton, Alice
Hofman, Adele
Jacobi, Mary Putnam
Jex-Blake, Sophia

Jonasson, Olga
Kelsey, Frances
Kubler-Ross, Elisabeth
La Flesche, Susan
Lovejoy, Esther Pohl
Montessori, Maria
Nichol, Kathryn
Owens-Adair, Bethenia
Pechey, Edith
Ramcharan, Savitri
Ramey, Estelle
Sabin, Florence
Storch, Marcia
Taussig, Helen
Thorne, Isabel
Trotula
Walker, Mary
Wright, Jane C.
Zakrzewska, Marie Elizabeth

Physicist

Meitner, Lise

Wu, Chien-Shiung

Pioneers

Brier, Juliet
Colt, Miriam Davis
Cooper, Arvazine Angeline
Duniway, Abigail Scott

Walker, Mary Richardson
Whitman, Narcissa Prentiss
Wilder, Laura Ingalls

Poets

Bates, Katherine Lee
Benet, Rosemary Carr
Bogen, Louise
Bradstreet, Anne Dudley

Brooks, Gwendolyn
Browning, Elizabeth Barrett
Burgos, Julia de
Davis, Nina Salaman

Deutsch, Babette
Dickinson, Emily
Doolittle, Hilda (H.D.)
Field, Rachel
Harper, Frances Ellen Watkins
Johnson, Pauline
Jong, Erica
Lazarus, Emma
Lowell, Amy
McGinley, Phyllis
Merriam, Eve
Millay, Edna St. Vincent
Mistral, Gabriela
Monroe, Harriet

Moore, Marianne
Morse, Penina
Newsome, Effie Lee
Petry, Ann
Plath, Sylvia
Rodriguez De Tio, Lola
Rossetti, Christina
Silko, Leslie
Taylor, Ann
Taylor, Jane
Teasdale, Sara
Walker, Margaret
Wheatley, Phillis
Wylie, Elinor

Psychics

Blavatsky, Helena
Brown, Rosemary

Garrett, Eileen
Ripich, Olga

Religious Leaders and Saints

Brown, Antoinette
Cabrini, Sister Frances Xavier
Catherine of Alexandria
Day, Dorothy
Dyer, Mary
Eddy, Mary Baker
Egan, Sister Jogues
Green, Patricia
Hawkes, Daphne
Hildegard of Bingen
Hutchinson, Anne
Joan of Arc
Lathrop, Rose Hawthorne
Lee, Ann

Mary Loyola, Sister
Moise, Penina
Moody, Deborah
Picard, Jeanette
Sasso, Sandy
Shaw, Anna Howard
Slessor, Mary
Stout, Penelope
Terakwitha, Kateri
Teresa, Mother
Theresa of Lisieux
Walker, Mary Richardson
Whitman, Narcissa Prentiss
Young, Ann Eliza

Royalty

Angouleme, Marie Therese
Anne
Anne of Cleves
Boleyn, Anne
Boudicca
Catherine de Medici
Catherine of Alexandria
Catherine of Aragon
Catherine the Great
Christina
Cleopatra
Dyer, Mary
Eleanor of Aquitaine
Elizabeth I
Elizabeth II
Elizabeth Petrovna
Galla Placida
Grey, Lady Jane
Haile Selassie, Tsahai
Howard, Catherine

Ileana
Isabella
Jadwiga
Josephine
Juliana
Maria Theresa
Marie Antoinette
Mary I
Mary II
Mary, Queen of Scots
Maud
Nefertiti
Parr, Catherine
Seymour, Jane
Tzu Hsi
Victoria
Wilhelmina
Zenobia

Scientists

Ancker-Johnson, Betty
Anning, Mary
Brown, Rachel Fuller
Campbell, Billie
Cannon, Annie Jump
Carson, Rachel
Clark, Eugenie
Cleaves, Mary
Curie, Marie
Dresselhaus, Mildred
Dunbar, Bonnie
Emerson, Gladys Anderson
Fisher, Anna

Fleming, Williamina
Franklin, Rosalind
Friend, Charlotte
Gilbreth, Lillian
Hodgin, Dorothy Crowfoot
Joliot-Curie, Irene
Karle, Isabelle
Logan, Myra Adele
Lucid, Shannon
Mead, Sylvia Earle
Meitner, Lise
Mitchell, Maria
Patrick, Ruth

Ray, Dixy Lee
Resnik, Judith
Richards, Ellen Swallow
Ride, Sally
Robbins, Mary Louise
Rubin, Zera
Russell, Elizabeth Shull
Sabin, Florence

Seddon, Rhea
Seibert, Florence
Sharpless, Nansie
Siebert, Muriel
Simpson, Joanne
Slye, Maude
Sullivan, Kathryn
Yallow, Rosalyn

Slaves

Craft, Ellen
Freeman, Elizabeth "Mumbet"
Louvestre, Mary
Tituba

Truth, Sojourner
Tubman, Harriet
Wheatley, Phillis
Wood, Ann

Social Scientists

Balch, Emily Green
Benchley, Belle
Brothers, Joyce
Buyukmihci, Hope
Cone, Cynthia
Fossey, Diane
Galdikas, Birute
Goodall, Jane
Harkness, Ruth
Hollingworth, Leta S.

Kenyon, Kathleen
Malcolm, Heather
McKeever, Kay
Mead, Margaret
Meggers, Betty Jane
Pauker, Ana
Pippard, Leone
Pryor, Karen
Rivlin, Alice

Spies

Boyd, Belle
Cavell, Edith
Edmonds, Sarah Emma
Greenhow, Rose O'Neal

Hari, Mata
Tubman, Harriet
Van Lew, Elizabeth

Television and Theater Production Personnel

Aaron, Chloe
Austin, Ann "Andy"

Chevalier, Ann
Cornell, Katharine

Television (con't.)
Culver, Carmen
Hill, Pamela
Korris, Risa

Long, Loretta
Oakley, Annie
O'Neill, Kitty
Wormington, Judy

World War II and Holocaust Figures

Arnothy, Christine
Brusselman, Anne
Frank, Anne
Freier, Recha
Hautzig, Esther
Koehn, Ilse
Leitner, Isabella
Lubetkin, Tzivia

Reiss, Johanna de Leeuw
Sasaki, Sadako
Senesh, Hannah
Siegal, Aranka
Wojciechowska, Maia
Wolf, Jacqueline
Zyskind, Sara

Indexes

Author-Title Index

compiled by Schroeder Editorial Services

396

399

Subject Index

compiled by Schroeder Editorial Services

413

415

Mary-Ellen Kulkin Siegel is a Senior Teaching Associate with the Department of Community Medicine (Social Work) at the Mount Sinai School of Medicine (City University of New York). She has written on a variety of topics and has hosted a New York radio program where she interviewed people who changed the direction of their personal or working lives.